*The
Conciliar-Evangelical
Debate:
The Crucial Documents,
1964-1976*

The Conciliar-Evangelical Debate: The Crucial Documents, 1964-1976

Donald McGavran
Editor

Expanded Edition of *Eye of the Storm: The Great Debate in Mission,* Including Documents on Bangkok and Nairobi

533 HERMOSA STREET • SOUTH PASADENA, CALIF. 91030

Copyright © 1972 by Word, Inc.
Copyright © 1977 by Donald A. McGavran

All rights reserved. No part of this book may be used or reproduced in any manner whatsoever without written permission, except in the case of brief quotations embodied in critical articles or reviews.

First edition published in 1972 by Word, Inc. under the title *Eye of the Storm: The Great Debate in Mission*. Second edition, enlarged, published in 1977 by the William Carey Library by arrangement with Word, Inc.

Library of Congress catalog number: 77-1705
International Standard Book Number: 0-87808-733-8

Published by the William Carey Library
533 Hermosa St., South Pasadena, California 91030

PRINTED IN THE
UNITED STATES OF AMERICA

Scripture quotations from the Revised Standard Version of the Bible (RSV), copyright © 1946 and 1952 by the Division of Christian Education of the National Council of the Churches of Christ in the United States of America, are used by permission.

Quotations from *The New English Bible, New Testament* (NEB), copyright © 1961, 1970 by The Delegates of the Oxford University Press and The Syndics of the Cambridge University Press, are reprinted by permission.

CONTENTS

PREFACE TO THE 1977 EDITION 9
                Donald McGavran
INTRODUCTION TO THE 1972 EDITION 11
                Donald McGavran

Part I. 1964: What Is Evangelism?

A. THE CALL TO EVANGELISM 41
                J.C. Hoekendijk
B. ESSENTIAL EVANGELISM 56
                Donald McGavran

Part II. 1967: Are Conversion Missions Outmoded?

A. YES! CONVERSION AND THE MISSION OF THE CHURCH 69
                Ronan Hoffman
B. NO! THE CHANGING NATURE OF MISSION 87
                Avery Dulles

Part III. 1965-1968: Church Growth and Mission Strategy

A. WRONG STRATEGY—THE REAL CRISIS IN MISSION 97
                Donald McGavran
B. ANSWERS FROM THE WHOLE WORLD
    1. *Church Growth: A Faulty American Strategy* 108
                Walter J. Hollenweger
    2. *Evangelism and the Growth of the Church* 115
                Mathew P. John
    3. *Numerical Growth–An Adequate Criterion of Mission?* 121
                Jordan Bishop, O.P.
    4. *Church Growth: A Critique* 128
                J.G. Davies
    5. *Hindrances to Church Growth* 136
                J.B.A. Kessler

    6. *A Pentecostal's View of Mission Strategy* 142
                    Melvin L. Hodges
    7. *Does the World Need Fantastically Growing Churches?* 150
                    Marie-Louise Martin
    8. *Counterpoint* 158
                    Mme. C. Gouzée
    9. *Christian Presence and One of Its Critics* 166
                    Herbert Neve
C. THE GROWTH OF THE CHURCH—*The Iberville Statement* 171
                  WCC Department of Missionary Studies
D. CHURCH GROWTH STRATEGY CONTINUED 177
                  Donald McGavran

Part IV. 1968: Presence and Proclamation as Forms of Mission

A. PRESENCE AND PROCLAMATION 189
                  Max Warren
B. PRESENCE AND PROCLAMATION IN CHRISTIAN MISSION 205
                  Donald McGavran
C. PRESENCE AND PROCLAMATION 219
                  Hans J. Margull

Part V. 1968: The Uppsala Controversy on Mission

A. CRITICISM OF THE WCC WORKING DRAFT ON MISSION
    1. *Will Uppsala Betray the Two Billion?* 233
                  Donald McGavran
    2. *Further Comment on "Drafts for Sections"* 242
                  Ralph D. Winter
    3. *For Uppsala to Consider* 246
                  Alan R. Tippett
B. RENEWAL IN MISSION 249
C. DEFENSE AND FURTHER DEBATE
    1. *"Renewal in Mission"* 259
                  Eugene L. Smith
    2. *"Renewal in Mission"* 262
                  Philip Potter

3. Does Section Two Provide Sufficient Emphasis on
   World Evangelism? 266
      John R.W. Stott
4. The Theology of Section Two 269
      David Allan Hubbard
5. Uppsala's "Program for Mission" and Church Growth 273
      Donald McGavran

Part VI. 1970: The Frankfurt Declaration on Mission

A. BACKGROUND OF THE DECLARATION 283
      Donald McGavran
B. TEXT OF THE DECLARATION 287
      Frankfurt Theological Convention

Part VII. 1972: Bangkok, Salvation Today, What Is It?

BANGKOK: AN EVANGELICAL EVALUATION 297
      Arthur Glasser

Part VIII. 1975: Nairobi—Liberation and Justice (And a Little Evangelism?)

A. LOOKING TOWARD THE FIFTH ASSEMBLY
   1. Will Nairobi Champion the Whole Man? 309
         Peter Wagner and Donald McGavran
   2. The Nature of Salvation 315
         Stephen Neill
B. REPORTS OF THE NAIROBI ASSEMBLY
   1. The Fifth Assembly and Evangelization 324
         Harvey Hoekstra
   2. Nairobi '75–Crisis of Faith 334
         Bruce Nicholls
C. THEOLOGICAL ASSESSMENTS OF THE ECUMENICAL/EVANGELICAL SCHISM
   1. Pre-Suppositions in Contemporary Theological Debate 350
         Klaus Bockmuhl

2. Two Theologies of Mission Battle for Control 360
   Donald McGavran
3. Berlin Vs. Geneva: Our Relationship with the Evangelicals 366
   Hendrikus Berkhof
4. Nairobi: No Turning Point 373
   German Evangelical Alliance

Epilogue

EPILOGUE 381
   Donald McGavran

PREFACE TO THE 1977 EDITION

Donald McGavran

This book is a documentary history of a critically important debate on mission affecting the whole future of the Church.
The last thirteen years have seen radical changes proposed in the nature of Christian missions, and their gradual adoption by many denominations and conciliar organizations. These years have also seen a growing awareness of the questionable nature of the changes and a mounting alarm at their size and sub-biblical character.
The year 1977 sees the two positions hardening. Each is being openly espoused by Christians, congregations and denominations. This volume allows the reader to see what is involved in each position as it develops in debate and interaction with the other. I, the editor, am an Evangelical; but have handled the Conciliar position fairly, letting its eminent spokesmen present and defend their positions.
The first edition of this book, published in 1972 under the title *Eye of the Storm: The Great Debate in Mission,* carried the reader through the first years, 1964-1970, when the new position was emerging and capturing the Secretariat at Geneva and many mainline churches. At the Fourth Assembly of the World Council of Churches, Uppsala 1968, the new position was given official expression. The storm of responses makes good reading.
This 1977 edition of the book, now named *The Conciliar-Evangelical Debate: The Crucial Documents,* 1964-1976, adds ten documents. One deals with the 1972 meeting of the Commission on World Mission and Evangelism at Bangkok, and asks "Salvation Today — What Is It?" Nine deal with the tremendously significant issues and policies discussed and determined upon at the Fifth Assembly of the World Council of Churches at Nairobi, Kenya, in November-December 1975. The ten writers come, not from some narrow segment of the Church, but from ten great churches and four countries. They are scholars, theologians, missiologists, and international leaders of the Church.
All concerned with the evangelization of the world and the carrying out of the Great Commission should awake to the huge changes which have been

proposed and are being put into effect in most countries of the world. They ought to read carefully the considered disagreements which Evangelical leaders have penned and published and are here gathered together and republished.

Conciliar leaders have determined on far-reaching policies regarding world mission, affecting how tens of thousands of ministers and missionaries and millions of dollars in funds are to be employed, year after year for the foreseeable future. Evangelical leaders focus attention upon these doctrines and policies and propose more effective, rational, and biblical ways of mission.

February, 1977

Donald McGavran, Editor
Fuller Theological Seminary
School of World Mission
Pasadena, California

INTRODUCTION TO THE 1972 EDITION

Donald McGavran

Among the multitudinous questions which surround mission, one stands out clearly. *What part does the propagation of the gospel properly play in the mission of God today?*

In this book twenty eminent leaders of mission speak to this question. In here we are concerned neither with everything God is doing and wants done nor with controversies about the numberless problems confronting Christians. *Eye of the Storm* discusses, pro and con, effective communication of the gospel, increase of Christ's Church, and the resulting well-being of mankind. We do not deny the importance of other questions of the day, about some of which we hold deep convictions; but in this book we focus attention on the Church's responsibility to bring the nations to faith in and obedience to Jesus Christ. *That* is what *Eye of the Storm* is about. How important is that task? Is it the only task of missions? Or only one of many? Or a chief and irreplaceable task? In our time should the establishment of justice and the perfecting of existing Christians take precedence over the extension of the gospel? Some speak on one side and some on the other of these questions.

Sharply differing opinions as to ends and means mark this volume. This is no mild, one-sided, sentimental presentation. Here in the rough and tumble of vigorous disagreement, men answer questions of life and death. Here convictions of major mission thinkers are examined, weighed in the balances of reason and revelation, and when found adequate embraced, and when found wanting rejected. In these writings men venture their reputations, and vested interests clash. But this is no mere brawl, for each writer is convinced that he is speaking for God. He sets forth his best thought in a holy cause.

Not everyone can be right. If some correctly voice God's desires in this revolutionary and suffering world, then others are mistaken. They have misread the signs of the times. No matter how good their intentions, they have not rightly understood the task. Who is right and who is wrong? The fascination of *Eye of the Storm* lies in the following fact. Most of the data is well-known to the readers. As they read, they themselves will be weighing the evidence and pondering the positions advanced, the conclusions advocated, and rendering judgment.

THE DOCTRINAL BACKGROUND OF THE DEBATE

The thirty-one essays which comprise this book appear against two aspects of the general confusion which mark contemporary mission, and help us see the communication of the gospel in its true setting. Knowledge of this general background is essential if we are to comprehend the depth and significance of what the writers say.

The first aspect is doctrinal. Controversy rages as to what in this modern world Christians ought to believe—indeed, what they can believe. Eight illustrations illuminate this doctrinal dimension.

1. The nature of the Church is in dispute all around the world. The old issues—as to whether only that is the true Church which is ruled over by bishops in the apostolic succession or only that made up of penitent believers living in conscious obedience to the living Lord—now share the center of the stage with shadowy "new forms of the Church" and the question as to whether the Church has value *in itself* or as an instrument toward making this a better world.

Disillusionment with the Church as an organization of baptized believers is widespread. The Church is being vaguely talked about, if not defined, as the community of those of any religion who, discerning God's presence in every activity directed toward the creation of a better world, labor with Him "for others." Some Protestants feel that the institutional Church of today will vanish and in its place will come some form of Church yet to be defined—possibly an association of all those of any system of belief, or of none, who labor in love for their fellow men. Such people see Gandhi on the one hand and Che Guevera on the other, as evidences of God working in human history creating a people for himself, and hence see them as forerunners of some new kind of Church.

Richard McBrien, of the Pope John XXIII National Seminary of Weston, Massachusetts, in his recent book *Do We Need the Church?* distinguishes sharply between the pre-Einsteinian and post-Einsteinian Church. The old Church, he says,

> is entering a period when her theology, liturgy, and her structures are going into the melting pot. This is not simply changing the

husk or shell. Something entirely new will come out of the cauldron, and the only similarity it must bear with the primitive Church of the New Testament is that it must be a community which explicitly acknowledges that Jesus of Nazareth is the meaning of all life and history and which dedicates itself, without qualification, to the task of building and sustaining the human community.[1]

He concludes his book with these words:

Do we need the Church? . . . "No" if by the Church we mean the pre-Einsteinian Church [which holds that "the Church is the ordinary means of salvation and that the Church's primary . . . task is to grow and multiply"—p. 15]. Even traditional theology admits that men can be saved apart from explicit membership in the Christian community. The one norm of salvation is living acceptance of the will of God (if only implicitly), and his will is that we should have love one for another. Salvation comes through participation in the Kingdom of God rather than through affiliation with the Christian Church.

But the answer is clearly "Yes" if, by the Church, we mean the post-Einsteinian Church. Christians need this Church because it is the place where, by the choice of God, they have been called into the fellowship of his Son, Jesus Christ our Lord (I Cor. 1:9) who through them "spreads the fragrance of the knowledge of him everywhere" (II Cor. 2:14). . . .

If the thesis of this book is wrong and if the Church is, in fact, primarily in the salvation business as understood by traditional theology, then I foresee little future for the Church as a vital instrument of God's Kingdom. If the Church continues to believe that it is the divinely appointed ordinary means of salvation . . . it will always be preoccupied with itself.[2]

McBrien would avoid these questions: is a person who "explicitly acknowledges that Jesus of Nazareth is the meaning of all life and history," and only he, a new creature in Christ? Is becoming a new creature in this sense a step of *eternal* significance? Apparently he prefers to remain agnostic on such matters, insisting that whatever the unseen dimension of such explicit acknowledgment may be, the visible dimension is all that counts. If a man does not "stand in the forefront of the struggle for peace, racial justice, and the alleviation of poverty, illiteracy, sickness, and all the evils of slumism" (p. 218), he is scarcely a Christian at all. McBrien says without qualification that "the Church exists for the Kingdom and for no other reason" (p. 219). Not, we ask, to praise God? Not to bring men into redemptive relationship to Jesus Christ? Not thus to save men? Not even thus to transform men so they *can* struggle for a just society? We wonder if Father McBrien has not fallen prey to the sharp dichotomy of his own argument?

However that may be, his argument exhibits well the debate in regard to the nature of the Church. Is it a society of the redeemed obeying the Redeemer? Or a society of loving men devoted to the ethical improvement of mankind? While none of the essays in this book sets forth a specific doctrine of the Church, most of them have such, and these vary greatly one from the other. Each doctrine affects the part which propagation of the gospel should play in mission.

2. Similarly controversy continues as to *the nature of conversion*. In the last hundred and fifty years and indeed, since the days of the apostles, it has been assumed that conversion meant turning from sin and from other gods or none, to Jesus Christ the Savior, following Him obediently into the waters of baptism and walking in the Way (including the fellowship of the saints) so clearly taught in the New Testament. John R. Mott, for example, in Edinburgh in 1910 said,

> The preaching or teaching of the revealed gospel . . . cannot be regarded as otherwise than indispensable. The chief aim must ever be to persuade human hearts everywhere that Jesus Christ is their Saviour, standing ready in an attitude of love, compassion and power, to realize to them, upon conditions of repentance and faith, all that the gospel promises to do for a soul that receives it.

But today, on all kinds of counts, one influential party in the Church is proclaiming (and, ironically, *vigorously persuading men*) that, since the goal is to cooperate with God in the creation of a more humane world, conversion to the Christian faith is not required, and consequently persuading "human hearts everywhere" that Jesus is the Savior is unnecessary, if not illegitimate. As Eric Sharpe says,

> If, as is increasingly the case, it is genuinely believed that this type of community—virtually the sole sign of which is service—can exist even among people who expressly repudiate the name of Christian, there can be no conceivable reason to press for conversion at all.[3]

The World Council of Churches' discussion of conversion, guided and summarized by Paul Löffler on the basis of word studies in the Old and New Testaments, states, "conversion belongs to the essential characteristic of the Church's life and mission." True conversion, biblical conversion, he goes on to say, is something which occurs in accordance with a particular view of the theology, eschatology, and teaching of the Bible. The motive of mission must *not* be, "I have been converted to Christ and want you, dear friend, to have this same glorious experience." It must *not* be to save men from wicked lives. Conversion must *not* aim at numerical church extension which brings the blessings of Christ to multitudes. In conversion, "the key question is not how churches can grow numerically, but how they can grow in grace and become God's representative number." Conversion is "a turning around in order to participate by faith in a new reality which is the true future of the whole creation."

Loffler's discussion of conversion reveals a profound suspicion that church growth is motivated, not by obedience to the command of Christ, but by desire for denominational aggrandizement, i.e., that church growth in reality always means my church growing at the expense of your church. The hesitations concerning church growth voiced by authors on one side of the great debate often are born in this suspicion.

Bishop Lesslie Newbigin in *The Finality of Christ* devotes a chapter to conversion and writes:

> One of the most hotly debated of the issues [is this:] does fidelity to Christ require us also to try to draw men into the fellowship of the visible Church. Is not God also active—and savingly active—in the world outside the Church? [4]

Newbigin is right. The issue is hotly debated. Part of the coolness toward church growth, which some documents in this book voice, arises in the minds of those who believe that it is wrong to "try to draw men into the fellowship of the visible Church." On the contrary, part of the theological conviction which demands church growth is that an essential part of the duty of the Christian is precisely to persuade and encourage men to believe in Jesus Christ as Lord and Savior, and, holding that genuine conversion does lead men to become members of the Body of Christ, to draw them into the Church.

3. These discussions as to the Church and conversion carry with them *questions as to culture and Christianity*. As the Protestant missionary movement spread the gospel across Oceania, Asia, Africa, and Latin America, for the first hundred years after 1800, it propagated chiefly the kind of Christianity the missionaries knew—which was inevitably a mixture of New Testament Christianity and Western culture. The Bible, followed as the rule of faith and practice, was a Bible seen through Eurican* eyes. Western civilization and the Christian faith seemed bonded together.

---

* An adjective derived from a combination of "European" and "American." The noun is "Eurica."

For example, though there is no biblical command to deny baptism to polygamists who believe in Jesus Christ as Savior and Lord, or to make breaking of caste a prerequisite of baptism, both were universally done. But today, partly as a result of the rise of independent Africasian‡ nations and partly through a better understanding of the myriad cultures of mankind, Christians are seeing that valid forms of Christianity can arise which abandon the trappings of Eurican civilization and array themselves in Africasian cultures. Rigorous debate continues as to what are "Eurican trappings," and what is the enduring core of biblical faith in Jesus Christ.

For example, in India recently Dr. Kaj Baago has been advocating that becoming a follower of Christ should involve neither baptism nor becoming a Christian. He does this because he is profoundly convinced that *to Hindus* (a) baptism is the rite by which one breaks caste, renounces his culture, and joins another people; and (b) the Christian religion is the beef-eating religion of Western imperialists. In an extreme way, Baago is raising the question as to whether men cannot become Christians within their culture and without taking on the ephemeral trappings of Eurica. However, when these "ephemeral trappings" are considered to include conversion, baptism in the Name, membership in a church of Christ, acceptance of the Bible as the rule of faith and practice, and faith in Jesus Christ as God and Savior according to the Scriptures, one must ask: if these are ephemeral, what is the eternal core of the Christian religion?

4. Similarly, controversy resounds as to *who Christ is:* the Second Person of the Trinity once incarnated in Jesus of Nazareth, *or* the cosmic Christ who manifests himself in many ages, many ways, many men, and speaks with many voices uttering different truths. Some maintain that Jesus Christ is of one substance with the Father; others that the concept of "one substance" is too Greek for other cultures and the divinity of Jesus Christ consists in this, that His personality truly mirrored God and has for us the value of God.

In India, many Hindus accord a place of honor to the Lord Jesus as God-Incarnate, but accord the same honor to the Lords Gautama, Krishna, and Rama, to mention only three. That the Word became flesh and dwelt among the men of Judea and Galilee and that Jesus of Nazareth was crucified, dead and buried, and rose again on the third day, is accepted by most Christians. But

---

‡ Derived from a combination of "African," (Latin) "American," and "Asian." The noun is "Africasia."

some reject the Lord's word in John 14:6: "no man cometh unto the Father but by me." They will not confine the cosmic Christ (God-as-He-shows-himself-to-men) to the One who walked the Galilean hills. Thus Floyd Ross says:

> The early Christians did put forth the claim that "There is no other name given under heaven for the salvation of men." That the early Christians may have been overzealous in stating it this way is a possibility the Christian must live with.[5]

William Ernest Hocking has written: "The Only Way ... is ... already present in all [religions], either explicitly or *in ovo*. The several universal religions are already fused together, so to speak, at the top." [6]

It seems clear that during the next decades, Christians again, as in the first two centuries, will fight the long battle against syncretism and religious relativism. And for the same reason— namely, that they are again in intimate contact with multitudes of non-Christian *peers* who believe that many paths lead to the top of the mountain. The concept of the cosmic Christ, some maintain, is a way out of "the arrogance which stains the Christian when he proclaims Jesus Christ as the only Way to the Father." Other Christians believe that the concept of a "cosmic Christ operating through many religions" sacrifices truth, for if there are, in fact, many revelations, then each voices an approximation of the truth. Indeed, since they often voice contradictions, truth itself disappears.

Be that as it may, the question *who Jesus Christ is* is certain to be heard with increasing frequency during the coming confrontation between Christianity and the non-Christian ideologies and religions—from Marxism and Judaism to Hinduism and animism. As hundreds of Christian and semi-Christian denominations spring into being across Africa, Asia, and other lands of earth, some will inevitably hold biblical and others syncretistic views of the Person of Christ.

5. A gritty controversy has frequently arisen and will arise again in regard to *the function of the Holy Spirit*. Is God the Holy Spirit at work in all the good movements of our day? The ancient creedal statement that the Holy Spirit proceeds ever from the Father and the Son is one clear answer to the question. The *filioque* clause ("and the Son") is no mere quibble of hair-splitting theologians. The problem the Church fathers faced was that non-Christians all about them spoke of spirits—from the spirits of fields and hearth to the philosophical configurations of the educated elite. "Our

spirits," these non-Christians said, "are of God. They are, indeed, God at work."

In the terse *filioque* clause, the Church replied: "God is, indeed, at work outside the Church, has of old spoken in diverse manners (Heb. 1:1), and is continually making himself known to the eye of reason (Rom. 1:19–20). Furthermore, the Logos is certainly the light which enlightens every man (John 1:9). Nevertheless, the Triune God making himself known to men (the Holy Spirit) is also the Second Person of the Trinity, and therefore always acts in harmony with the revelation of himself in *Jesus of Nazareth as recorded in the Scriptures*. The Holy Spirit ever proceeds from the Father *and the Son*."

All spirits, all inspiration, all claims that God is at work in current history, in the forces of nature, or in the spirits of the air, must be tested by the simple question: do they harmonize with God's Spirit, manifested in Jesus of Nazareth? If they do not, either they are not of the Holy Spirit and hence not of God, or they are God's action colored and distorted by His human agents. The Master Measure remains Jesus Christ.

The debate about the Holy Spirit can be seen today in many areas. I give two illustrations. Many independent churches (new denominations, nativistic movements) believe that the Spirit is at work in them. The Shakers on the Yakima Indian reservation in the state of Washington (no connection with the Shakers of Pennsylvania) for many years have maintained that they have the Spirit far more than white churches and that He has for them an authority exceeding that of the Bible. In plain English, this means that when they do what they feel is right, what Indian custom, upbringing, economic condition, state of education, and religious excitement moves them to do, then they are being led of the Spirit. They submit to His leading whether this accords with the teaching of the Bible or not. At the other end of the spectrum, some avant-garde and sophisticated Christians maintain that God is at work in the revolutions of the day. Among His servants are Mao and Lenin. He who sent Cyrus of old and used the Assyrians for His purposes is at work today outside the Church in the men and events of our time, destroying the injustices and oppressions under which His people groan, and building a better social order.

If the Holy Spirit is at work in all good movements and salvation is proceeding perhaps even more outside the Church than within it, then the need for any kind of witness to Christ or proclamation of the Cross and the Resurrection is materially diminished. The writers in this volume are arrayed on both sides of this doctrinal issue; but they never write specifically to it.

6. *The doctrine of universalism*, defined as the belief that all men will eventually be saved, has recently come to be a storm center. At stake is the correct understanding of the atonement, salvation, the future life, and specially other religions. To some leaders of the Church, the enemy is religious relativism, the belief that all religions are paths to God. To others, who view this situation from the reverse side, the enemy is a narrow bigotry which, holding that all men are lost forever unless they believe on Jesus Christ, ardently persuades men to become His disciples. Clearly the attitude of mission leaders toward church growth is vitally affected pro or con by the view they hold as to the doctrine of universalism.

7. The doctrine which most closely underlies this book, or to change the metaphor, forms the largest part of the background, is that which concerns *the discipling of the nations* (Matt. 28:19), making the gospel known "to all nations to bring them to the obedience of the faith" (Rom. 16:26), and extending "grace to more and more people" (2 Cor. 4:15, RSV), to the end that "at the name of Jesus every knee should bow . . . and . . . every tongue confess that Jesus Christ is Lord, to the glory of God the Father" (Phil. 2:10, 11, RSV). The thirty-one essays herein, one way or another, bear upon this doctrine. They are either for it or against it. They accept it literally or interpret it away. Some apparently deny that there is any such doctrine. Others believe it sums up the purpose of Christ's being. Among these who accept the great commission as binding on the Church, there is much difference of opinion as to the part it should play in Christian mission. Some, in lands where a majority are baptized Christians, appear to believe that God intends for other countries to get along with one-tenth of one percent of the people confessed Christians. Others appear to believe that only when there is a living church in every hamlet, ward, and high-rise apartment in the world, will the entire creation have had the gospel preached to it.

8. The eighth doctrine, about *practicing the faith*, though absent from the ancient creeds, is vividly present in contemporary thought. This doctrine rests on the clear biblical teaching that God is a God of righteousness, truth, and mercy, and directs His household to manifest these virtues. Christians are new creatures, are granted the righteousness of God, must not continue on in sin, and must do good to all men. The Christian is salt which preserves the whole loaf. He is light and should so shine that men may glorify God. This doctrine is taken for granted in the current

orthodoxy that the Church must alleviate suffering and influence the environment for good. The ministry to the physical suffering of the world, the dedicated drive to build a righteous and merciful framework of society, and the enormous labor of the Church to educate and enlighten both Christians and mankind in general, stem from a belief that all these activities are pleasing to God. They are clearly the outcome of the ethical life graciously given to Christians by the indwelling Holy Spirit.

These eight doctrines (concerning the Church, conversion, culture, Christ, the Holy Spirit, universalism, discipling of the nations, and practice of the faith) are intertwined with each other. Many other doctrines also, such as the authority of the Bible, the nature of revelation, the nature of God and man, sin and salvation, free will and election, are inevitably involved. The opinions of any man concerning what church growth *is*, the part it ought to play in mission policy, and the share of attention—and budget—it should receive, depend on his convictions concerning these doctrines.

All these doctrines flit in and out of this book, on and off the stage. Some play a greater and some a lesser part. In the last two centuries, the center of the stage has always been held by the great commission. Today, however, many Christians have guilty feelings about sub-Christian aspects of the present scene in "Christian lands," and believe that the center ought really to be held by practicing the Christian faith, "being for others," serving humanity and re-forming society. The doctrinal aspect of the debate on mission and church growth concerns, so to speak, who the hero of the play is—discipling the nations or having love for one another. Does action center on soteriology or ethics?

THE ORGANIZATIONAL BACKGROUND

The second dimension of the background of the debate on mission to some Christians dwarfs matters of doctrine. It concerns organizational matters such as centralization of power, the unity of the Church, the establishment of large merged denominations, the intricacies of church-mission relationships, and the arrangements of convenience between Eurican and Africasian churches. To some, these housekeeping considerations are all that really matter. Many missions have spent decades working out schemes for promoting harmonious relationships between missionaries and nationals. Years go into the writing and rewriting of constitutions; and no sooner written than further years go into

INTRODUCTION—*McGavran* 21

amending them. Cumbersome and tedious procedures fill untold man hours.

National churches, too, become absorbed in these labors. Several large churches in India, for example, since the end of World War II, have been consumed by protracted conversations about church union. Though other matters are discussed, nothing else really matters. Whether churches minister to the remarkable openness of the Shudras in Andhra Province to the gospel or not, they must work at church union. In India, among the larger churches at any rate, the debate on church growth is a minor matter. Organizational concerns, church union, and struggles for power within the national churches themselves get prime time and prime space.

Part of the organizational background consists of the large, philanthropic institutions of Asia, Africa, and Latin America built up by the missions and the churches. These receive an overwhelming share of mission resources and constantly need more. Some of them are defended on grounds that they are evangelistically potent, others that they are good for the younger churches, and still others that they are what Christians ought to do in the face of human need.

Controversy is common about organizational matters. All of the topics mentioned in this section have been storm centers. Strong opinions are held about each of them pro and con. To a limited degree, each has a bearing upon the communication of the gospel. Indeed, there is no stronger evidence that the propagation of the Christian faith is central to the life of the Church than that those in favor of church union plead it desirable because a united Church will be a more credible and effective advocate of the faith. They quote our Lord's high priestly prayer, "that they may all be one . . . *that the world may believe."* Occasionally a united church does grow better than separated churches; but often merged denominations grow less and care less about growing. Church union has only a limited bearing on credibility. Similarly those advocating transfer of authority to nationals (a very necessary step) commonly appeal to the dubious argument that nationals make the church grow better than missionaries can. Occasionally they do, but usually where churches were growing before transfer, they have continued to grow. Where they were static before transfer, they have remained static.

Even struggles for power within a denomination or congregation may result in more effective communication of the gospel—a denomination splits and both sections grow! This is no argument for splitting, but it does show that everything the Church does affects its ability to communicate Christ.

Eye of the Storm, however, will not feature discussions about the housekeeping matters of Church and mission. These, too, though more or less involved in the extension of the faith and the salvation of men, do not in this volume hold the center of the stage.

THE MAIN ARENA—POLICIES AND PROPOSALS FOR ACTION

Against the doctrinal and organizational background just described, the authors of this book carry on a debate *as to the policies* of the Church as regards sending missionaries, preaching the gospel, reconciling men to God in Christ and communicating the faith. Policies have inescapable theological bearings and this is doubly true of policies about the propagation of the gospel.

Despite this fact, the thirty-one documents of this book are not treatises in systematic theology. They might be considered essays in applied theology; but it is probably better to think of them as *proposals for action* which bring with them certain theological nuances. To varying degrees their authors are aware of the theological assumptions of their proposals, but they do not vigorously and consistently harmonize the latter with the former.

What has happened is that our authors have decided—on various grounds—that such and such courses of action are desirable and have defended their choice with theological and biblical reasons. Readers should judge to what extent each policy advocated, in fact, accords with the main thrust of Scripture and common sense. Proof texts should be tested to see if they are correctly exegeted and in the mainstream of God's revelation. Policies should be inspected to see what they are supposed to deliver —and what the actual outcome *is*.

These authors, then, propose policies in missions. They set forth modes of action which the Church ought to use to carry forward the mission of God or to disciple the nations. Conversely, they maintain that modes of action someone else proposes are wrong, will not achieve God's purposes, do not suit the present situation, or cannot be God's will for our generation.

Of particular importance in this regard are subsections two and three of "Renewal in Mission," under Part V. These subsections set forth the practical emphases in mission which the Fourth Assembly of the World Council of Churches, at Uppsala, believed should mark the seventies, the mission policies, strategies, and modes of action which "are most relevant to the contemporary situation." With the exception of one sentence readily distinguished, subsections two and three advocate a consistent view of mission governed by one set of theological presuppositions. The critique of these subsections is governed by other presuppositions. Readers should observe carefully the foundations on which each edifice stands.

Eye of the Storm is a source book and displays many different policies advocated by many different leaders of mission. It prints documents which are parts of the surging sea of opinion in which the Church sails. Readers are invited to press on from these opinions concerning *policies* to the underlying *theological and biblical issues*. Each reader should try to frame a policy for *his* sphere of responsibility which secures the gain promised by any proposed mode of action and avoids the loss, which embraces the truth and rejects the error. Readers will cheat themselves if they do not penetrate the strategies which *Eye of the Storm* discusses to the doctrines which lie beneath.

CARRIED ON IN THE REAL WORLD

Conversations as to policies and modes of action in mission are being carried on in the revolutionary world of the closing decades of the twentieth century. Enormous advances of technology; unimaginable amounts of new power; a bewildering array of new substances, processes, and tools; fiercely sovereign nations each defending its autonomy; the irreversible flow of secularism; the rush to the cities; horrible injustices involving huge numbers of God's children; strident demands by the masses for their share of the good things of life; potential tyranny and potential servanthood of the mass media; population explosions not yet contained; grim races between national decadence and inner control; tremendous spread of the Christian faith in some countries together with growing indifference to it in others; the unheralded but colossal formation of conviction and character in millions of churches and homes, as Christians submit themselves to the control of the Word—all these are parts of the real world.

As one turns from this composite, he finds that the average Eurican Christian—and even the average intelligent Christian—is acutely aware of some parts of the picture only. These are called to his attention by his newspapers and television screens. Wars, tumults, city burnings, racial friction, loss of colonial possessions, maulings of the Church, exclusion of missionaries from a few countries, famines, the plight of refugees in Jordan and orphans in Biafra—all these have been burned into his consciousness by the secular mass media. He often believes that these are the only needs! That these constitute the real world!

The average intelligent Christian is remarkably uninformed about the spiritual needs of mankind. These receive no coverage by the mass media which know nothing of the divine dimension, and would not talk about it if they did. The spiritual destitution of the two billion without any experience or knowledge of the Lord Jesus, the devastating hunger of those who never receive the bread and the wine, and the ethical emptiness of over a billion who never read a word of any Scripture, is only vaguely sensed by most Christians. They do hear about them from the pulpit, but are inclined to consider them "Sunday talk" and give them minor attention.

Furthermore, the average Christian, whose mind is so largely formed and controlled by the secular mass media, is colossally ignorant about the triumphs of the Christian faith. He never suspects, for example, that the racial revolution in the United States was born in and nurtured by three extended and fervent Christian movements involving millions of Christians.

(1) Fifty years of ardent Christian abolitionism (1810–1960) stoked fires of conviction and steeled resolves to abolish slavery. The heat thus generated alone made possible the Emancipation Proclamation and assured victory in the war to preserve the Union. (2) Seventy-five years of patient education of thousands of the liberated slaves in academies, schools, and colleges was paid for and manned by committed Christians. (3) Enormous denominations of self-respecting, orthodox, Bible-believing Negro Christians, through an extremely trying time, lifted the recently liberated but greatly oppressed blacks to a genuine inner commitment to Christ. Martin Luther King and a hundred thousand other Christian leaders would have been impossible had the Negro community not been ardently Christian.

Similarly, the intelligent Eurican Christian never imagines that the Africasian surge to independence (1947–1970), through which at least one billion people became self-governing, is itself a triumph of the Christian faith. The sweeping movement cannot be imagined in a Hitlerian or Marxist society, nor in the Rome of the Caesars. At the very time of their greatest military might, pressured in large part by their Christian convictions, Eurican nations made their colonies over to nationals rather than engage in protracted and bloody repression. That the colonies pressed them to do this—sometimes by violent and sometimes by nonviolent means—in no way diminishes the force of the statement.

Feeding the movements to independence were, of course, other factors; nevertheless it is beyond question that Christian missions helped. During a hundred and fifty years, in the churches of every Eurican nation, thousands of missionaries each year were speaking about the nationals of other countries as fellow Christians, men and women of ability. The friendly image of Asia and Africa which missionaries projected in Eurican nations, plus the tremendous numbers of Asians and Africans educated in Christian schools and given a passion for equality and worthfulness, has helped in no small measure to bring about the self-determination of Afericasian nations and the juster world we see.

Another triumph of the gospel is visible in the remarkable receptivity to Christ now being manifested in many populations. For example, Africa south of the Sahara is in process of turning to the Christian faith. Churches in that huge subcontinent are multiplying fantastically. Twenty years ago, Christians there numbered only twenty million. Now there are at least fifty million, and Dr. David Barrett, the Anglican, estimates that by the year 2000 there will be 357 million. If his careful calculation (see the May 1969 issue of *Church Growth Bulletin*) is only half right and, in A.D. 2000, Africa contains only 178 million Christians, it will still have been a most notable discipling. Tremendous growth of some churches in Chile and Brazil, Taiwan and Korea, Indonesia and Congo, adds to the growing receptivity. Even the resistance of India is showing signs of giving way to receptivity in some of the middle castes.

IN LIGHT OF ALL THE FACTS

The debate on the growth of Christ's Church must proceed in the light of all the facts—including the triumphs of the gospel. It must not be carried on solely in the distorted flicker of the television tube or the faint glow of the Church's limited growth in—let us say—Egypt, Israel, or some land recently conquered by totalitarian Marxists. What the Church ought to do must be decided neither in the quivering parochial beams of postwar Europe shuddering from its catastrophic losses nor in the transient glare of present injustices gradually being rectified. Policies pleasing to God should be formed in the full light of all the facts as well as His promises and commands. Global Christian thinking is required.

The demands for justice and humanitarian action are an unquestioned part of the picture, as will be seen again and again in the documents herein. No one is defending injustice. All are demanding its removal. The crucial question is: what part of the present labors of missions around the world are properly spent in church multiplying and what in humanitarian labors and battles for justice? Furthermore, what are the right proportions in each of the thousands of pieces of the mosaic which is mankind? What proportions *please God? That* is the question. Or, to put it precisely, *what proportions in each piece of the mosaic at a particular time please God in view of His revelation in His Son our Savior and His Word?*

OTHER WRITINGS AND ADDRESSES ON THE DEBATE

Many books have been written to set forth some aspect of the world mission. Thus articles and books on the race question, economic justice, evangelism, approach to non-Christian religions, Christian presence, church growth, dialogue, church union, stewardship, the indigenous church, responsible mission, and and many others pour from the presses. Each sets forth its own position with zeal. Contrary positions are seldom mentioned. When they are, they are usually neither understood nor treated fairly. The literature abounds with caricatures of the positions of "the other side."

A few men have attempted to get both sides to state their positions. Under Norman Horner's editorship a valuable volume has come out called *Protestant Crosscurrents in Mission.*[7] Three men from one side and three from the other set forth their views. Unfortunately, each article goes its own way, stating its convictions, neither mentioning nor controverting those of the other side. Thus there is no meeting of minds.

The debate splits Protestant and Roman Catholic alike. It runs through most of the major denominations of Protestantism and the great orders of the Church of Rome. As modern Christians observe the world and the Church in the midst of the tremendous revolution which marks our day, some are sure that the expansion of the Church is at an end. They are against church growth. They argue that the Church is irrelevant and will be replaced entirely, as the synagogue replaced Hezekiah's temple worship and the Christian church replaced the synagogue. Others are sure that we stand in the sunrise of missions, not the sunset, and that the Church, in recognizably the same form, will go from strength to strength, bringing its blessings to population after population. Cardinal Agaganian of Propaganda Fide a few years ago wrote that all missions to the present are but prologue, the major discipling of the nations is yet to come, and the great days of the liberation of mankind lie ahead.

THIS BOOK

As a small contribution to understanding what both sides are saying in regard to great commission mission, this book is produced. Its focus is frankly, but not narrowly, on church growth, because that is the meaning of both classical and biblical mission. Reconciling men to God in Christ and the discipling of the nations (church growth) is the one unifying element in the existing bewildering diversity of good mission activities. If one were to define mission as "everything which God wants done" and reproduce the debates which that gargantuan concept and its infinite facets generate, his writing would be so wide as to be paper thin.

THE MEANING OF MISSION

Part of the confusion in mission today lies at exactly this point. During the last fifteen years, for a variety of reasons, several branches of the Church Universal have defined mission in the broadest possible terms. The mission is God's, they say, and hence everything God wants done is "mission." Thus, in their writings the word has become largely meaningless and is equivalent to what our fathers called "doing one's Christian duty." While some of our authors have fallen prey to this usage, this book as a whole refuses to walk down that ambiguous road. Granted that churches ought to do many things, this book is not talking about everything the churches ought to do. It is debating those activities of the Church, those biblical doctrines, those theories of mission which have to do with making Jesus Christ known, loved, and obeyed throughout the whole earth. The following articles are, in one way or another, about *that*. Either they favor it or are against it. Either they give it high priority or low.

TRUTH ISSUES OUT OF CLASH

The merit of this book is that issues are defined. They can be seen. Proposals, put forward by some, are attacked by others. The theory back of the book is that truth is advanced when propositions are not merely stated but attacked in the light of proved errors. Clash is sedulously avoided by some moderns. They prefer to seize the machines of publication and pour forth a barrage of *their* ideas, hoping thus to capture the constituency. We believe that, on the contrary, nothing furthers truth more than open discussion. And nothing is more interesting!

Debate should be honest. On occasion it ought to be ruthless, but never rude or mean. The Church is well served by those who examine the pronouncements of the day in the light of well-established criteria and declare them true or false, beneficial or harmful, pleasing to God or hateful to God. Such critics will not always be right but they perform an invaluable service.

The debate proceeds before the Church and the verdict will be rendered by its members. At stake is the whole future course of Christian mission. Since the annual treasury of mission, out of North America alone, is well in excess of two hundred million dollars ($200,000,000) per year, supporters of mission owe it to their Lord to study carefully the major trends, listen to the arguments on both sides, and vote with their dollars.

Let me assure readers that the issues discussed in these thirty-one documents are both real and "hot." All the denominations and missionary societies affiliated with the World Council of Churches, and many which are not, are constantly irradiated by the beam of convictions, the theory of missions, the theological convictions abundantly illustrated by some of the authors of *Eye of the Storm*. This is the prestigious view of missions today. This style of missions is "in." One has simply to dip at random into contemporary writings on mission to see how popular it is. A second widely popular view of missions is held by many denominations, congregations, and individuals, by many missionaries, ministers, and missions, including many formally affiliated with the World Council of Churches. This second view is also represented in the chapters which follow.

In this Introduction, I am neither commending nor criticizing either point of view, though mine is clearly the second and any claim to impartiality would be dishonest. I am trying, without weighting the argument in either direction, to call attention to the significance of these documents and the issues they present. It is perhaps too much to hope that either side will be satisfied that its position has been fairly introduced. I myself chafe at the necessity to introduce both right and wrong positions with a neutral phrase. I intend in other writings to argue the case for what seems to me so clearly right. Those who hold other views, too, are likely to feel I have been less than successful in my efforts to introduce their arguments. They will, I trust, forgive me and state and argue their position further before the Church.

THE PARTS OF THIS BOOK

I present then six cases where the debate in missions has erupted in a visible clash of opinion. The difference of conviction thus exposed to view will illuminate the real situation facing Christians today in regard to the evangelization of the world.

Since permission from the authors to reprint their articles has been secured on the assurance that what they wrote would appear *as they wrote it*, editing which tightened the writing and sharpened the issues could not be done. The fact, also, that the editor was on one side of the debate made it necessary for him to avoid making editorial changes in the essays. If he sharpened the issues, he might, unintentionally, distort them in favor of his position. Thus the essays are printed exactly as they were written and published (with only spelling changed to make the book consistent). The six parts of *Eye of the Storm* are as follows:

1. *What Is Evangelism?*

Dr. Hoekendijk's ideas on evangelism are sharply challenged in an Open Letter by Dr. McGavran addressed to him and printed in the *Occasional Papers* of the Division of Study of the World Council of Churches. Readers will note the welcome extended by the World Council of Churches to expression of contrary opinion. Indeed, though the WCC first printed Hoekendijk, it cannot be said that his convictions are those of the World Council of Churches. They have given him a platform; but they gave McGavran a platform, too!

2. *Are Conversion Missions Outdated?*

In the year 1967, at a Roman Catholic Conference in Washington, D.C., a revealing exchange of opinion concerning mission—quite similar to much Protestant discussion—took place between Drs. Hoffman and Dulles. Ronan Hoffman, Associate Professor of Missiology and Modern Church History in the School of Theology, Catholic University of America, Washington, D.C., affirmed that conversion mission is, or should be, ended.[8] His article appeared in the *Journal of Ecumenical Studies*. He was answered by Avery Dulles, S.J., Professor of Systematic Theology at Woodstock College in New Jersey.

3. Church Growth and Mission Strategy

In the October 1965 *International Review of Missions*, Dr. McGavran advocated church growth as a controlling consideration in the formation of mission strategy. Three years later, church growth as a controlling consideration in the formation of mission policy and, indeed, as a goal of mission was vigorously attacked by a carefully assembled battery of writers in the July 1968 *International Review of Missions*. Dr. McGavran was invited to respond to the attack and his second article on mission strategy therefore appeared in that number.

Of particular importance in this section on Church Growth and Mission Strategy is *The Iberville Statement*. This appears as item C under the heading, "The Growth of the Church." This pronouncement, drawn up by a Consultation on Church Growth convened by the World Council of Churches Division of Missionary Studies at Iberville, Quebec, in 1963, is a most forthright endorsement of church growth. It reads like something out of an evangelical gathering. Though it was adopted at a worldwide consultation called by an agency of the World Council, and drafted by Victor E. W. Hayward, head of the Division of Missionary Studies at Geneva, it has played little or no part in the church growth debate. It is heavy with implication for the theory and theology of mission, but to my knowledge has never been quoted by spokesmen for the Division of World Mission and Evangelism. I have reprinted it a number of times, enclose it in my letters, and give it to career missionaries taking advanced courses here at the School of Missions of Fuller Theological Seminary. Since its inclusion had not been planned, I asked that it be printed in the July 1968 issue of the *International Review*. Its significance lies in part in the competency of the document and in part in the oblivion to which the Division of World Mission and Evangelism has apparently consigned it. On both counts it deserves a careful reading.

4. Presence and Proclamation as Forms of Mission

In April 1968, the European Consultation on Mission Studies was held at Selly Oak Colleges, Birmingham, England. It was attended by professors of missions from universities and colleges all over Europe and America. The papers read there on "Presence and Proclamation" are reproduced here. In them, Canon Max Warren, General Secretary Emeritus of the Church Missionary Society, an eminent leader of missions for many years, and Dr. Hans Margull, then of the World Council staff at Geneva, develop and advocate Christian Presence as an acceptable missionary mode for today. Dr. Donald McGavran examines the concepts of

INTRODUCTION—*McGavran* 31

Presence and Proclamation critically, pointing out the circumstances under which, from the point of view of evangelical Christianity, they are beneficial and those under which they are harmful.

5. *The Uppsala Pronouncement on Mission in the Seventies*

Section Two of the Uppsala Pronouncement, titled "Renewal in Mission," provides unusual opportunity to see major issues in the contemporary debate. Three key documents bearing on that pronouncement form the fifth part of this volume:

(a) A trenchant criticism of the Preliminary Draft of Section 2 was framed by the faculty of the School of Missions at Fuller Theological Seminary and printed in the May 1968 issue of the *Church Growth Bulletin*.

(b) The Final Draft of Section Two (Uppsala's official pronouncement on mission) was printed in the *Church Growth Bulletin* for September 1968, and in the *Ecumenical Review*, October 1969, in the form in which it appears here.

(c) The November 1968 *Bulletin* carried articles pro and con. Philip Potter, Executive Secretary of the Division of World Mission and Evangelism, and Eugene Smith of the World Council of Churches, New York Office, spiritedly defend the preliminary draft and rebut the criticism in the May issue. John Stott, minister of All Souls Church in London, David Hubbard, President of Fuller Theological Seminary, and Donald McGavran comment further on the Final Draft, its patchwork nature and its inadequate understanding of mission.

6. *The Frankfurt Declaration on Mission*

The great debate on missions has only recently become fully visible. Leaders knew, of course, that in this rapidly changing world new problems demanded new solutions. The old formulas no longer applied. New goals and new methods were clearly indicated. In the resulting ferment of thought, differences of opinion inevitably arose and seemed a natural part of the picture.

But that many of these differences were forming a coherent body of opinion, departing in a major way from classical mission and becoming "the approved line" in one wing of the Church was not immediately apparent. On both sides of the Atlantic, Christians were loath to believe the extent and seriousness of the deviation. As the movement of thought portrayed in the preceding five sections was, however, more and more clearly seen, hundreds of the leaders of churches and missions looked in dismay at the spate of increasingly dubious proposals. The biblical base of mission was being chipped away. Different ends were being substituted.

Yet, since the proposals and principles were put forward by reputable organizations and respected leaders, men sincerely trying to adjust mission to the revolutionary world of today, leaders on both sides of the Atlantic hesitated to voice their disagreements. They did not like what Hoekendijk, Hoffman, Hollenweger, and above all Uppsala were saying, but after all these were intelligent leaders and Uppsala was the Fourth Assembly of the World Council of Churches!

Finally, a group of eminent German missiologists and theologians felt they had to speak. Differences of opinion were one thing; distortion of biblical priorities and objectives were quite another. Facing this situation, they were led to state the enduring biblical base of Christian mission. They had to be *for* the truth, as God gave them to see the truth, and to be *against* those policies and doctrines which betrayed the gospel and led the churches astray. They drew up the Frankfurt Declaration which in a remarkable way crystallizes the situation.

It focuses the debate. It sets forth the issues clearly. It calls certain trends "insidious falsification of the motives and goals" of the missionary movement. It maintains that "inner decay" is riddling modern missions. It calls missions and churches forward to biblical positions. This courageous document is enormously germane to mission in the 1970s.

The Frankfurt Declaration helps redress the balance of this debate. It assures the readers that the eight authors arrayed against great commission mission and the growth of the Church in Part Three were not representative of European Christian opinion. It is proof that the convictions of the Fuller School of World Mission are shared by many missiologists and theologians around the world. As such, it is welcome to us in Pasadena. We were beginning to feel a bit lonely.

Furthermore, arising as it did in Germany, entirely independent of the American conservative evangelical movement, it is a welcome assurance that the side of the debate we have espoused is widely shared by sensible Christians in many lands. The Frankfurt Declaration was drawn up by confession-minded Lutheran theologians, whose connection with the American missionary movement and American theology was minimal. We had nothing to do with the framing of their statement and have not yet seen it in its original German form. Yet, these men have defended the position we have been upholding—more effectively, perhaps, than we.

Part Six of this book, consisting of an introductory essay and the text of the Frankfurt Declaration forms a fitting climax and conclusion to *Eye of the Storm*.

MUCH MORE DEBATE YET TO COME

The extended debate as to mission theory and theology, going on in most churches, missionary societies, and denominations is by no means exhausted in these thirty-one documents. Much more has been and will be written. Kindred ideas—such as the meaning of conversion and salvation—are being and will be explored. Areas of agreement and disagreement will be demarcated. This book lays no claim to being a comprehensive presentation. The Rev. Philip Potter, Executive Secretary of the WCC's Division of World Mission and Evangelism, raised just this point as we were discussing publishing the book. He wrote,

> I am not at all sure whether the group of articles that you suggest really brings out the many sidedness of this debate. For example, the *Ecumenical Review* of . . . April 1969 on Evangelism had many constructive things to say on the subject. Other things have been written. You confine your choice to certain types of articles. . . .

If this volume claimed to be a comprehensive exposition of the great debate, I would share Mr. Potter's hesitation. All that the book attempts to do, however, is to present some of the important and contrasting articles about Christian mission—defined in the classical sense of proclaiming Christ as God and only Savior and persuading men to become His disciples and responsible members of His Church.

It is particularly necessary to say that "the church growth school of thought" is very much larger than my few essays reproduced in this volume. It has been expounded in *Understanding Church Growth* and other books by me, *Church Growth and the Word of God* and other books by Dr. Alan Tippett, the notable writings of Dr. George Peters, the continent-wide, authoritative survey *Latin American Church Growth* by William R. Read, and his associates, and a multitude of serious articles by noted leaders of mission published in the *Church Growth Bulletin* over many years. Church growth theory and theology is further developed by missionary and national scholars in at least a hundred ethno-histories of churches in many lands. Over forty of these have now been published. The corpus of church growth materials is rapidly expanding. This volume, showing how church growth thinking deals with a few specific issues, in no sense sets forth a comprehensive statement of the position. If one wants that, he should do extensive reading in the books mentioned in the Church Growth Bibliography at the end of this book.*

This cluster of writings opens the subject. It is a sample of current essays. It brings between two covers something of what

---

*This section is omitted in the 1977 edition.

is being said. My purpose has been to expose the clash of opinion as clearly as possible and in *the words of the debaters*. Because the world changes, the authors, were they to write today, might say something different. Solutions and positions which seemed effective when they wrote might appear outdated in 1972. But this is what they *did* say.

After this book is read, I hope we shall see considered articles from advocates of both kinds of mission which speak directly to the issues raised, make clear their position, answer objections, attack errors, and build up what they consider more reasonable, correct, or biblical positions. It is in this fashion that theory in any field of knowledge is constructed, refined, and made more effective.

SERIOUS WEIGHTY VIEWS PRESENTED

Granting the partial nature of these thirty-one essays, they are not chance remarks. They state mature positions of men thinking seriously on Christian mission. They have been prepared in responsible fashion and printed in learned journals. For example, Dr. Hoekendijk's article on evangelism was first printed in the April 1950 issue of the *International Review of Missions*. It was later published in the book *The Church Inside Out,* and again in 1963, in Series II, Number 7, of *Occasional Papers,* edited by Victor Hayward of Geneva. The article "Wrong Strategy: The Real Crisis in Mission" appeared in the October 1965 *International Review of Missions* and was a considered statement of my position. The articles attacking it were in preparation for a long time. Finally published in July 1968, they can fairly be held to be both their authors' serious views *and* sufficiently careful statements on church growth to merit (in the eyes of the Division of World Mission and Evangelism of the World Council of Churches) a place in the prestigious *International Review of Missions*.

The betrayal felt by many Christian leaders in the Uppsala '68 preliminary draft on mission—a meticulously prepared document —found expression in the May 1968 issue of *Church Growth Bulletin*—another meticulously prepared document. As the May issue circulated, encouraging some and angering others, Mr. Potter and Dr. Smith asked for space in *Church Growth Bulletin* to defend the DWME Statement. Space was cheerfully granted. To insure that further debate took place on the final draft prepared at Uppsala, Mr. Potter kindly sent me the official copy of Section Two as passed by the World Council, and I printed it in the September

INTRODUCTION—McGavran

1968 *Bulletin*. Mr. Potter's and Dr. Smith's articles defending the final draft and Mr. Stott's, Dr. Hubbard's, and mine pointing out some of its weaknesses, formed the November issue of the *Church Growth Bulletin*. Such a considered exchange over a major pronouncement of the World Council of Churches on Mission must be judged significant in understanding the debate on church growth and is therefore reproduced in this volume.

EMINENT CHRISTIAN AUTHORS

Eye of the Storm consists of the writings of eminent leaders of Christian mission. This is part of its importance. The table of contents is a roster of leaders carrying heavy responsibilities in mission, men in the forefront of mission thinking. What these men say is worth the close attention of all interested in the mission of the Church. It is doubly weighty when they are writing about the propagation of "the gospel" which, Scripture tells us, was "by eternal God's command made known to all nations, to bring them to faith and obedience" (Rom. 16:26, NEB).

Not only are these authors eminent, but they are deeply Christian. The exchange goes on between Christians who disagree as to the best way to carry on mission. *Eye of the Storm* is Christians thinking out loud and differing as to what the Master has commanded. Mission is always to specific populations. The question is not what does the Lord command, but what does the Lord command in specific populations at specific times, bearing in mind that the Church is given specific resources. No wonder eminent Christians differ as to what should be done.

WHAT IS RIGHT AND TRUE?

But from the complexity of the situation and the eminence of the authors, no one should conclude that all policies proposed are therefore equally right and equally effective in carrying out God's will. On the contrary, the very complexity of the problem demands utmost care in determining what is God's will. The longer and more intricate the journey, the more essential it becomes to know the goal, follow right directions, and possess a true compass. The debate arises from the fact that what one side believes is correct strategy and policy, exactly *that* the other side believes to be substantially wrong. In every section of the book, questions of right and wrong demand answer.

Is it *true*, as Hoekendijk avers, that "it is impossible to think of the *plantatio ecclesiae* (church planting) as the end of evangelism"? Is Father Hoffman *right* in regard to conversion or is Father Dulles? Both cannot be. Is a chief and irreplaceable end of the Christian mission that Christ be proclaimed and men be persuaded to become His disciples and responsible members of His Church, as I have affirmed? Or is such church growth an outgrown, erroneous concept from which the churches must withdraw, substituting for it an emphasis on serving humanity and establishing solidarity with mankind whatever its ideologies and religions, as subsections two and three of the Uppsala pronouncement on mission affirm?

TOWARD RECONCILIATION

Part of the confusion is doctrinal—on which no compromise is possible—but part of it is caused by our sudden immersion in "one world." Differences in the second part are negotiable. For example, the phrase "mission in all six continents"—though not occurring in the Bible—has suddenly become a new orthodoxy. It seeks to define mission so that it is the same in every country. The pressure to formulate this definition arose from Africasian churchmen who resented their countries being so often the object of mission. It was as if the "righteous West" was always evangelizing the "sinful East"! Or rich Eurica was always giving largesse to poor Africasia! This one worldwide definition of mission has obvious advantages; but its fatal weakness is that mission cannot be the same everywhere, even in one continent. What mission *is* depends partly on God's will and partly on the population to which He sends His emissaries. When He sends them in Berlin to wealthy, baptized youth, now alienated from the state church, the program He ordains will be radically different from that in Sumatra, where He sends them to pagan Karo Batak peasants longing for the gospel and eagerly accepting baptism and incorporation into Christian congregations. In short, mission in the six continents is bewilderingly different, not the same.

Possibly therefore, part of the tension which *Eye of the Storm* exhibits on every page would be resolved if those who are thinking out of the background of Europe's state churches or North America's wealthy institutionalized denominations would recognize that the solutions they set forth apply chiefly to the problems of Europe and America. They might fit there. Perhaps those thinking out of the background of evangelism on new ground should recognize that the policies they propose suit churches arising on new ground—not nations discipled a thousand years ago.

Obviously what is the right proportion of the various ingredients of mission in Europe, where nine-tenths are baptized, is not the same as that in Nigeria where nine-tenths are not. In the United States, where Christians have tremendous political power in the affairs of the nation, their God-given duties in regard to national structures are great. Whereas in Andhra Province of India (where the church consists almost entirely of landless laborers, former Untouchables, and has very little political clout in either provincial or national affairs) the political duties of Christians are of an entirely different order—largely limited to what they can do in their families and villages.

While the Church is One and the Lord is One, the churches and their tasks are multitudinous. The tiny beginning church among the Tonga in Zambia could scarcely be more unlike the huge, old church among the English led by the Queen and the Archbishops. Sanity in mission will be advanced as speakers make clear whether they are talking about mission in Tongaland or England.

Possibly, therefore, the errors in these essays—and readers themselves will judge what these are—will turn out to be partly doctrinal and partly situational. In regard to doctrinal errors, there is no other way than to seek directives from the mainstream of God's revelation and guidance from the risen and reigning Lord—while regarding other Christians, whose understanding of the Word is not, we feel, as correct as ours, with tolerance and charity.

In regard to situational errors, however, the case is different. In these there is room for movement. Pronouncements of a worldwide nature will turn out to mean one thing in one context and something quite different in another. For instance, take the common pronouncement that the Church should minister to the whole man. For a mission (spending 90 percent of its resources for educational, medical, and agricultural services to a large receptive population in the midst of which there is a church of only a few hundreds) greatly to increase its emphasis on philanthropic services is probably wrong. By way of contrast, on Timor (where hundreds of thousands have recently become Christian and more are pouring in year by year) a greatly increased emphasis on education and medicine is probably right.

With these introductory comments, I now commend the documents themselves to the Christian public. The issues are grave. Discriminating reading is demanded. Christians should know what the modern options are and help direct their missions into correct channels. The debate concerns their very lives, the nature of their obedience, and the truest welfare of their brothers and sisters in every land.

NOTES

1. Richard McBrien, *Do We Need the Church?* (New York: Harper & Row, 1969), p. 206.
2. Ibid., p. 228.
3. *Evangelical Quarterly*, December 1969, p. 224.
4. Lesslie Newbigin, *The Finality of Christ* (Richmond: John Knox, 1969), p. 100.
5. In Gerald H. Anderson, ed., *The Theology of the Christian Mission* (New York: McGraw-Hill, 1961), p. 219.
6. William Ernest Hocking, *The Coming World Civilization* (New York: Humanities Press, 1958), pp. 148–49.
7. Norman Horner, ed., *Protestant Crosscurrents in Mission* (New York: Abingdon Press, 1969).
8. His article was first brought to my attention by a rabbi, head of the Anti-Defamation League, who on the strength of Hoffman's argument, told me with pleasure that Christians were at long last coming to see the sinfulnesses of their efforts to convert Jews and other non-Christians. He kindly sent me a copy of the article.

PART I

1964:
What Is Evangelism?

A. THE CALL TO EVANGELISM

J. C. Hoekendijk

It is impossible to ignore the call to evangelism, for it is being raised in so many quarters of the world. The Amsterdam Assembly expressed the conviction of the churches in these words:

> As we have studied evangelism in its ecumenical setting, we have been burdened by a sense of urgency. We have recaptured something of the spirit of the apostolic age, when the believers went everywhere preaching the Word. If the gospel really is a matter of life and death, it seems intolerable that any human being now in the world should live out his life without ever having had the chance to hear and receive it. . . . Now, not tomorrow, is the time to act.

This sense of urgency is echoed to an ever-growing extent. Recently, forty denominations in the United States launched a united evangelistic campaign. In the official statement we read:

> The time is urgent. The call to advance rests upon the seriousness of the day in which we live; upon the authority of Christ; and upon the necessity of new life for all men through obedience and faith in Him.

A similar call to advance is voiced in other parts of the world. Churches in Australia and Japan, in Hungary and Germany, in Great Britain and Canada, prepare a new and courageous evangelistic outreach into the areas lost to the church. And, meanwhile, the sober and less conspicuous evangelization in younger church areas is continued, without the clarion calls of a conquering army and without this heated crusading temper.

Let us begin by gratefully recognizing these facts. They are virtually a new feature in church history. The word "evangelism" has become an accepted part of our ecclesiastical vocabulary. We may use it now, without apology. The doors of some of our closed and stuffy churches have been flung open, and we breathe fresh air.

J. C. Hoekendijk is Professor of Missions, Union Theological Seminary, New York.

Even theologians—who in the past have been among the most unconquerable saboteurs of evangelism—seem to have rediscovered here and there its theological relevance. They realize that they jeopardize the biblical authenticity of their thinking if they go on refusing to acknowledge that the church is set in this world with the sole purpose of carrying the gospel to the ends of the earth. In some schools of Protestant as well as of Roman Catholic theology, the apostolate tends to become the all-pervading center of thinking—a total revolution in theology, with overwhelmingly wide perspectives.

Nor is it only in the life of the older churches that evangelism has come to the fore again. In recent missionary thinking, we note the same consciousness of the necessity for a new advance. For almost forty years now we have smiled at the old ambitious plans to "evangelize the world in this generation," somewhat embarrassed and compassionate. Many of us have revised our judgment. Even so dignified a meeting as that of the International Missionary Council at Whitby in 1947 stated that such a thing might be possible, after all.[1]

And now we are questioned from both sides. The home base asks us what has become of our pioneer missionaries [2] and of the tenacious will of our missionary forefathers. There may, of course, be some romanticism behind the question. It is easier to get excited about a Christian bushranger than about a dignified pastor serving the church in another part of the world. But when, from the other side, some of the younger churches [3] ask where now are our "sacred fools"—those reckless gamblers with life, so well known in the past—there is some bitter realism in the question. The missionary-pioneer has become a rarity. Our work has become so institutionalized that mobility and spontaneity are hampered.

It is sad but true that even in the younger churches the second generation of Christians becomes established and immobile. And for a next generation, Christian life has often already become an unexciting business of routine. The call to evangelism is consequently as necessary there as anywhere else. All over the world, the necessity of leaving our safe church harbors and of putting to sea again is indelibly printed in our minds. And yet, if we listen carefully, we often hear other undertones as well. We discern a note of anxiety lest the church should lose face or be outrun by its powerful rivals. A glance through evangelistic pamphlets confronts one with words like "communistic menace," "Muslim expansion," or—recently—even the atom bomb.[4]

To put it bluntly: the call to evangelism is often little else than a call to restore "Christendom," the *Corpus Christianum*, as a solid, well-integrated cultural complex, directed and dominated by the church. And the sense of urgency is often nothing but a nervous feeling of insecurity, with the established church endangered; a flurried activity to save the remnants of a time now irrevocably past.

These are some of the undisclosed motives. In fact, the word "evangelize" often means a biblical camouflage of what should rightly be called the reconquest of ecclesiastical influence. Hence this undue respect for statistics and this insatiable ecclesiastical hunger for ever more areas of life. We touch here upon one of the crucial problems of evangelism. We may approach it with a brief glance at the history of non-Roman Catholic evangelism.

Its main development coincided with the gradual breakdown of Christendom. This was natural. The Reformers presupposed the existence of Christendom.[5] This is one of the reasons, no doubt, why they did not develop a full doctrine of the church. Their purpose was, not to create new communities, but to reform those already in existence. They have therefore reduced the number of distinctive marks of the true church to one: the proclamation of the Word in its double form: the verbal and sacramental Word.[6]

Later generations maintained this position, but meanwhile the face of society changed. The presupposed foundation of Christendom sank away, and we simply continued with our reduced ecclesiology. The sermon and the Sacraments were placed in a void, and often, to our astonishment, missed their reforming power, for in fact there was no community to be reformed.

The remarkable fact is that it was those very groups in which the springs of modern evangelism are to be found that were most keenly aware of the total transformation that had come over society. Both the Pietists and the Methodists protested violently against the spirit of the age. They realized that individualism completely lacked the spiritual setting for their work. Yet they continued as if they still lived in Christendom. They tried to isolate individuals and assemble them in an island of the saved, floating on a flood of perdition.

Later on, not even the French Revolution and the Revolution of 1848 were enough to open people's eyes and to make them realize that Christendom was past. One year, even, after the 1848 revolution—one year after the Communist Manifesto—Wichern, the father of home missions, spoke of the aim of evangelism as "winning back those people in Christendom who have become a prey to sin in such a way that the organized church no longer reaches them."[7]

This intimate relation between evangelism and an ideology of

Christendom becomes even more clear as we look at missionary work. To assess realistically our present situation, we must try to disentangle the different motives. We will look at three examples:

1. Practice corrected theory very soon in pietistic missions. Only a few years after the death of Zinzendorf (1760), some of his Moravian brethren realized that they could not do effective work with their individualistic methods. Zinzendorf had instructed his missionaries to "gather individual souls" (*Seelen sammeln*) and "to stay away from all social and cultural work." Even schools were taboo.[8] The missionaries, however, discovered that their word needed a broad context. They tried to build up a form of what they called "Christian civilization" before they could begin to harvest the individual souls.[9]

2. Exactly one hundred years ago Missions-Inspector Karl Graul (1814–1864), of Leipzig, set out on his Indian tour. It became a decisive turning point in the development of evangelistic methods. In India, Graul became convinced that a person could not be converted unless his whole social context was Christianized at the same time. Hence *Volkschristianisierung* became as legitimate a part of evangelism as *Einzelbekehrung*.[10] Here again we find the intimate connection of Christendom and evangelism.

3. Suspect as they are, one may not neglect in this discussion the continuous stream of theologians in the nineteenth century from Schleiermacher to Troeltsch.[11] They stated with strong evidence that it would be impossible even to think of converting people without the simultaneous expansion of Western so-called Christian civilization, a point that was strongly put by Rothe: "One cannot make Christians with the Christian religion alone. Christian piety cannot be built in mid-air, but only on the foundation of christianized life."[12] It is clear that this point of view was an invitation to combine so-called Christian colonialism with missions; and much of Anglo-Saxon missions would seem to fall in this same category, with highlights in the nineteenth century in the persons of Alexander Duff and David Livingstone.[13]

How do we stand today? Gradually we begin to realize that we cannot grasp the real situation on the basis of our traditional categories. We have discovered that Zinzendorf and his men were too much akin to rationalist individualism; that Graul was too much influenced by romanticism; that Warneck was too outspoken a nineteenth-century bourgeois;[14] and that Livingstone believed too firmly in the reality of the Christian character of Western civilization. They cannot guide us any longer, because they all believe, in one way or another, in the possible realization of the *Corpus Christianum*, and our experiences with this kind of Christendom have been too bitter for us to follow them any farther.

Moreover (and I am aware of the heresy I am now going to commit), the ecclesiology of the Reformers is too one-sided, too time-conditioned; it needs too much further extension and development for us to be able to follow them without hesitation or criticism. So we must look for another way.

There is yet another reason that forces us to do so. When we try to grasp what this coordination of Christendom and church really means, we see that almost without exception a number of biblical concepts are distorted. I mention only three: the biblical concepts of the church, of the heathen, and of salvation.

1. As regards the concept of the church, we see that in this way of thinking, Christendom becomes a protective shell of the church. The church tends to be built into the vast realm of Christian-influenced society. Christendom becomes a shock breaker. Influences from outside are filtered; condemnations hurled at the church are intercepted; in this well-protected area the church can have its own style of life, speak its own language, determine its own time. The direct intercourse between church and world has ceased. The wolves are kept far from the little fold. A splendid (very Christian-tinged) isolation is possible. Life may change, but the church in this field of Christendom remains a bastion of the past, related to outworn social structures.

2. In consequence, we have distorted the biblical concept of the heathen. The church could see, from its safe distance, two kinds of people. I will call them moral pagans and intellectual pagans. Neither of them is conceived of as heathen. That would be too shocking a statement. The meaning of pagan is something quite different from heathen. It means something like a backward man (*paganus*), and this backwardness was generally located in his moral behavior or in his intellectual privateering. The drunkard and the skeptic have been the classical objects of evangelism. And therefore, in general, our evangelistic addresses have been either disgustingly moralistic or condescendingly apologetic. How deeply shocked we are, as evangelists, even after realistic expositions of what life without Christ must be, when we meet a man in total revolt who completely rejects our message. Our *Corpus Christianum* ideology has made us forget what heathen really are. In the safe environment of Christendom we could only think of moral and intellectual pagans.

3. And again, in consequence of this view, we have the distortion of the biblical view of salvation. To the drunkard we offered salvation as a way to a better moral rearmament, to the skeptic we offered wisdom. For the one, the forgiveness of sins meant ignoring a wild past; for the other, overlooking stupidity.

And now we realize, gradually, what an impossible outlook this has been. The world has come to the church's doorstep. The heathen can no longer—for our relief—be disguised as a moral or an intellectual pagan. And we are aware of the alarming fact that, after our moralistic advice and intellectual enlightenment, we have not proclaimed salvation, but have offered stones for bread.

If this analysis has any truth in it, the call to evangelism finds us unprepared. The ecumenical inquiry on evangelism begins by confessing that to many questions the only possible answer is, "We do not know." But we do know that we cannot continue as before. We need a new vision of evangelism, a disentanglement of all secular complexes and secret ideologies—a recovery, in short, of the biblical sense of evangelism.

Throughout the Bible, the evangelization of the heathen is seen as a possibility only in the Messianic days.[15] In the Old Testament it is the Messiah who gathers the nations. "Unto him shall the gathering of the people be" (Gen. 49:10). His will to save becomes so powerful that all resistance is overcome. "In the last days," i.e., in the days of the Messiah, the nations will come and praise God. In other words: the Messiah is the evangelist. Only to his power and his authority will men surrender.

It is written of the Son of Man (Dan. 7:13–14) that "there was given him dominion, and glory, and a kingdom, that all people . . . should serve him." In the New Testament we find this same context. Jesus dies without having given the explicit order to carry the promises of the gospel beyond the limits of Israel. Only after the Resurrection, after the Messiah has revealed himself in his power, victorious even over death, is the way to the heathen made free. The great commission in Matthew 28 is a reference to Daniel 7. Now, after the Resurrection, *now* only, Jesus says, "All power is given unto me in heaven and in earth. Go therefore and make all heathen my disciples." [16] Now the last days have dawned on you, you have entered the Messianic era, now you walk in the midst of the signs of coming glory. You are transplanted in the aeon where you live in the fellowship of the Kingdom which is to come.[17] And one of the decisive signs of the time, a token that the end is imminent—and yet some time *still* is given—is that the gospel of the Kingdom shall be preached in all the world for a witness to all heathen, and then shall the end come (cf. Matt. 24:14). This eschatological perspective has been one of the constant elements in our missionary thinking for a long time.[18] Two of the obvious consequences thereof have, however, only very seldom been drawn.

The first is that the Messiah (i.e., the Christ) is the subject of evangelism. Paul expresses this conviction in his epistles to the Corinthians, showing that the apostles can march only as conquered men in the triumphal procession of God (2 Cor. 2:14).

The second consequence is that the aim of evangelism can be nothing less than what Israel expected the Messiah to do, i.e., he will establish the shalom. And shalom is much more than personal salvation.[19] It is at once peace, integrity, community, harmony, and justice. Its rich content can be felt in Psalm 85, where we read that shalom is there, where "mercy and truth are met together; righteousness and peace have kissed each other. Truth shall spring out of the earth; and righteousness shall look down from heaven."

The Messiah is the prince of shalom (Isa. 9:6), he shall be the shalom (Mic. 5:5), he shall speak shalom unto the heathen (Zech. 9:10); or, in the prophecy of Jeremiah (29:11), he will realize the plans of shalom, which the Lord has in mind for us, to give us a future and hope.

In the New Testament, God's shalom is the most elementary expression of what life in the new aeon actually is.[20] Jesus leaves shalom with his disciples—"Shalom I leave with you, my shalom I give unto you" (John 14:27), and the preaching of the apostles is summarized as "preaching shalom through Jesus Christ" (Acts 10:36; cf. Isa. 52:7). "We are ambassadors therefore on behalf of Christ, . . . working together with him" to proclaim "now is the day of shalom" (2 Cor. 5:20; 6:1–2).

This concept in all its comprehensive richness should be our leitmotiv in Christian work. God intends the redemption of the whole of creation. He must reign until he has put all his enemies under his feet. In some segments of creation his sovereignty may be established already: shalom for all life; destruction of all solitude, obliteration of all injustice, "to give men a future and hope." Is this a utopian ideal? Or could it be apocalyptic realism? A superhuman task? Or is this the marching on of the victorious Son of Man? Is it not possible in what Dr. Minear has described as the *modus vivendi* of the new age—"the mood of expectant wonder, of ecstatic joy, of buoyant confidence"? [21] These are the kinds of questions we must answer before we can deal with problems of evangelistic method.

Evangelism can be nothing but the realization of hope, a function of expectancy. Throughout the history of the church, wherever this hope became once more the dominant note of Christian life, an outburst of evangelistic zeal followed. That should make us think, surrounded as we are by clamant calls to evangelism.

In *The Truth of Vision*, Dr. Warren writes:

> Any effective prosecution of the Church's primary task of evangelism in the world of our time must surely depend upon the nature of its hope. Incidentally, and as a corollary to that, we need to note that the nature of the hope will largely determine the character of evangelism.[22]

This Messianic conception of evangelism means a total rejection of two very well-known methods:

1. It means in the first place a total rejection of everything that tends to be propaganda.[23] I take this word in the meaning and with the content given to it by Martin Kähler, who distinguished very sharply between missions and propaganda. He clarified this distinction once in the image used by Paul in 1 Corinthians 15:36–38, where we read: "That which thou sowest is not quickened, except it die: . . . thou sowest not that body that shall be, but bare grain. . . . But God giveth it a body as it hath pleased him, and to every seed his own body." To evangelize is to sow and wait in respectful humility and in expectant hope: in humility, because the seed that we sow has to die; in hope, because we expect that God will quicken this seed and give it its proper body.

In propaganda, however, we imagine that we sow the body that will be. Propaganda's essential character is a lack of expectant hope and an absence of due humility. The propagandist has to impose himself. He has to resort to himself, to his word (verbosity being a characteristic of every propagandist). In short, the propagandist tries to make exact copies of himself. (*Er macht Wiederholungen, dessen was man selbst ist.*) He attempts to make man in his image and after his likeness.

It is not difficult to make this distinction in theory. It is, however, one of our most painful and most frequent experiences that evangelism is almost always concealed in a form of propaganda. Be it ever so lowly, through our witness of shalom, there sounds also a call: Follow me!

For example, do we really hope, and can we really expect, that God can give another than a Lutheran, or a Reformed, or an Anglican body to the seed that we sow? Do we not act as if God has thought out already all forms in which he may shape his shalom? And is not this confessional propaganda almost without exception the form in which our evangelization is concealed?

To let Christian hope determine our evangelism means that we move forward in a world with unlimited possibilities, a world in which we shall not be surprised when something unforeseen happens, but shall, rather, be really surprised at our little faith, which forbids us to expect the unprecedented.

2. In the second place, the Messianic conception of evangelism also means a complete rejection of another frequent misconception of evangelism. There is a stubborn tradition in our midst that interprets the aim of evangelism as the planting of the church (or even the extension of the church). This tradition has a respectable past. In the seventeenth century, Voetius defined as the aim of missions the *plantatio ecclesiae*.[24] It is certain that he borrowed this conception from Roman Catholicism, but it is one that has been adopted by many since. I am sure that many of us hold it.

What happens here is that missions are seen as the road from the church to the church. It is the outgoing activity of one church —it can remain as it was before—to a place in the world where again a church is planted. In principle, the task of missions is completed as soon as this church exists, in the same way as in Roman Catholic circles missions must withdraw as soon as the hierarchy is created.

It is possible to justify this position. But we should be aware of a temptation to take the church itself too seriously, to invite the church to see itself as well established, as God's secure bridgehead in the world, to think of itself as a *beatus possidens* which, having what others do not have, distributes its possession to others, until a new company of *possidentes* is formed.

We reach here a crucial issue. It is common to think of evangelism, to think of the apostolate, as a function of the church. *Credo ecclesiam apostolicam* is often interpreted as: "I believe in the church, which has an apostolic function." Would it not be truer to make a complete turnover here, and to say that this means: I believe in the church, which is a function of the apostolate, that is, an instrument of God's redemptive action in this world. Or to put it in terms we used here, the church is (nothing more, but also nothing less!) a means in God's hands to establish shalom in this world. It is taken into the triumphal procession of the glorified Son of Man, and on its way it discovers that it walks amid the tokens of the coming Kingdom. And, if this statement has any truth in it, it is also true that planting the church in this institutional way of thinking cannot be the aim of missions. Evangelism and *churchification* are not identical, and very often they are each other's bitterest enemies.

When Christian hope, the partaking of the coming Kingdom, has really to determine the character of our evangelism, it is impossible to think of the *plantatio ecclesiae* as the end of evangelism. It is too poor a conception and betrays too clearly a lack of expectant hope. It is too static a view of the church as a closed and definitive entity.

If, now, we try to find the right translation of Messianic shalom, we may take as our starting point Matthew 11. Jesus is asked there: Are you he that should come? That is, are you really the Messiah, who will establish his shalom? The answer is: "Go and show . . . those things which ye do hear and see: The blind receive their sight, . . . the lepers are cleansed, and the deaf hear, the dead are raised up, and the poor have the gospel preached to them" (Matt. 11:4, 5). This is the Messianic shalom in its abundant multiplicity.

1. This shalom is *proclaimed*. That is one aspect of evangelism. In the kerygma, that shalom is represented in the literal sense, it is made present.

2. This shalom is *lived*. That is another aspect of evangelism. It is lived in koinonia. We must not speak too quickly of community. Only insofar as men are partakers of the shalom, represented in the kerygma, do they live in mutual communion and fellowship.

3. There is a third aspect of evangelism. This shalom is *demonstrated* in humble service, diakonia. To partake of the shalom in koinonia means practically and realistically to act as a humble servant. Whosoever will be great among you shall be your servant. And whosoever will be the chiefest shall be servant of all (Mark 10:43-44).

These three aspects, kerygma, koinonia, and diakonia, should be integrated in our work of evangelism. Only so, are our methods of evangelism justified.

The kerygma is the proclamation that the shalom has come. Christ is there. We have not to look for another. We have entered upon the last days of total renewal. But, with the kerygma alone, in isolation, the evangelist soon becomes a more or less interesting orator. He needs the manifestation of the koinonia of which he is a part, and he has to justify himself as a witness of the Messiah-Servant in his diakonia.

The koinonia manifests the shalom, as it is present among men. But we need the continuous reminder of the kerygma, the interpretation of this shalom as the salvation of the Messiah, and the diakonia should prevent this shalom from being used in a self-sufficient way.

The diakonia translates the shalom into the language of humble service. But if we isolate this diakonia or give it an undue emphasis, then the evangelist soon becomes a sentimental philanthropist. He must never forget that he cannot render real service if he deprives man of the kerygma and leaves him outside the koinonia.

It is a remarkable fact that the call for evangelism is now, in so many parts of the world, a call for this comprehensive evangelism.[25] In this respect missions would seem to be far ahead of the older churches' areas. But there is a *rapprochement*. We should not overlook the fact that evangelistic work in Europe, for example, is beginning to acknowledge the need to learn of missionary methods. In the Netherlands, articles on rural evangelism contain frequent references to the missionary work in so-called primitive areas in Indonesia. In France, the Roman Catholic priests have taken as the pattern for their work in the industrial sub-proletariat the great missionary to Muslims, de Foucauld. In fact, one religious order, les Filles du Père Foucauld, has two branches, one working among the Muslims in North Africa and one among the industrial workers in Marseilles. In both branches they use in principle the same method. It is therefore neither new, nor followed in only half the world.

Let us try to study these three aspects somewhat more precisely.

1. Professor Dodd has shown that the apostolic preaching, the kerygma, was strictly objective.[26] For this history of God's great acts there was apparently no point of contact in our life. We cannot use our own experiences to interpret or to clarify what God has done. There is a notable lack of personal stories in the apostolic preaching. It is constantly affirmed that in the kerygma a history is proclaimed, of which all men are ignorant until it is announced as a revelation, things that "eye hath not seen, nor ear heard, neither have entered into the heart of man" (1 Cor. 2:9). All witness that neglects or minimizes this character of revelation is useless, for it is disobedient and unfaithful.

This point should be emphasized, for it is precisely in evangelistic work that we run the risk of minimizing this feature of revelation. The temptation to mask the mystery, to avoid the scandal of the gospel, becomes almost inevitable, once we are confronted with men who are perplexed by the absurdity of our message. We tend, then, to reduce the gospel to a few vague religious generalities, or the propagandist awakens in us, and we try to impose ourselves, with our personal experiences, which are obviously irrefutable. And through a false fidelity to the man before us, we tend to become unfaithful to Christ, who has committed unto us the proclamation of this scandalous, mysterious gospel.

This said, something else should be added. This fidelity is

quite different from any kind of rigidity. The representation of shalom is something quite different from a precise enumeration of all the shibboleths of orthodoxy. Merle Davis has recently given a remarkable example of this rigid proclamation.

> In Madagascar, after a generation of proclaiming Jesus as the Lamb of God who sits on the right hand of His Throne and whose blood alone can save from sin, the old chief of a tribe which has resisted the Christian message revealed the reason for his people's indifference. "We are a cattle-raising people; we despise sheep. Our clans asked the early missionaries whether there was a place on God's throne for a cow as well as for a sheep and when they were told 'no' they closed their hearts to the Christian Gospel." [27]

Any of us could enlarge on these examples. The hearers are not shocked by the fact that the message is incomprehensible, but they are scandalized by this inflexibility, by the fact that a man who has to proclaim freedom to the prisoners himself remains a prisoner. The gospel is not merely glad tidings to him, but rather, an ideology, to which he has to submit himself. That is why he repeats himself. The kerygma becomes a stereotyped recital, unrelated to the world where it is proclaimed. And so he tells the blind that the lame walk, and the lame that the blind receive their sight. To the bourgeois he bears witness to the shalom for the proletariat, and to the proletarians he gives a message in which they can recognize nothing but a bourgeois shalom.

To regain liberty and flexibility in our witness two things must happen: We must in the first place find ourselves fully at home in this strange new world of the Bible so that we can move familiarly about and concretize and articulate the shalom in a different way in different situations. And secondly, as the Reverend D. T. Jenkins puts it, we must

> be aware, from within, of the situation which the Gospel addresses in our own time. . . . We must strive to understand the whole religious, moral and intellectual setting in which people are placed. . . . Even those who appear most indifferent to the vital currents of thought going on in the world around them, and who certainly cannot understand them, come to sense after a time that the situation is different from what it used to be and adjust themselves accordingly. One of the reasons for the irrelevance of the Church's proclamation in recent times has been that it has been content to achieve communication on too narrow a front. We have expressed our Gospel too narrowly in terms of the conscious experience of the middle-class people in our pews, forgetting that even they lived in a world where they

were being unconsciously exposed to movements of thought very different from those which they themselves would naturally frame.[28]

2. The koinonia is the place where the shalom is already lived. As such, the Christian community belongs to the new age. That means that this fellowship of the partakers of the same salvation is nothing more in this world than a company of strangers and pilgrims (1 Pet. 2:11), a paroikia, or group of sojourners in the world, fully detached and therefore free to relate itself to every form of existence.

The Christian community, therefore, is (or should be) an open community, open to everyone who has become a partaker of the same shalom. In practice this is not the case. In an unconscious way the national churches have become closed, because they related Christian community and nationality too exclusively, and in the West the churches have become class churches, because they identified themselves too uncritically with one special group of society. It is nonsense to call these churches to evangelism, if we do not call them simultaneously to a radical revision of their life and a revolutionary change of their structure.

It is here that we are confronted in Europe with some of the most ardent problems of evangelism. When evangelists come together, one of their main topics of discussion is sure to be the creation of extra-church communities, groups serving as meeting —and mediating—centers between church and world.[29] It may be necessary to create them as an interim measure. But we should realize that as soon as these halfway communities between church and world become a permanent feature, we have in fact given up hope for the church. We conceive of it then as a body definitive and static, over against the world as the other static entity. And this is nothing less than to despair of establishing shalom in the church and of realizing the koinonia.

Another complex of questions lies in the field of the relation of existing human groups to the koinonia. As soon as we say that the koinonia is an open community, we imply that it can be realized in a variety of social structures. We deplore the breakdown of the primary social groups (family, neighborhood, etc.) in modern mass society. But at the same time many of us continue as if these were still the basic units. Koinonia, however, is so flexible that the unity of the modern city quarter, of the factory, of the trade-union or of the communist cell can be related to shalom (though this does not mean, of course, that these groups are thereby accepted). Some experiments have been made in this field. The work of the Roman Catholic priests among workers in

France (for example, in Marseilles) is directed toward the three contexts of the industrial worker's life—his factory, his living quarters, and his pub fellowship.[30]

The main and all-decisive function of the koinonia is, however, that it is the primary kerygmatic and diakonic unit, kerygmatic as the place where the shalom is really made present, diakonic because it has no other relation to the outside world than that of humble service. It is here that the call to evangelism becomes of biting actuality. It is no use stimulating to new and rapid advance while this work remains neutralized by the mockery of koinonia that our churches really are. "The acts of your koinonia speak so loudly that we cannot hear the words of your kerygma."

3. And finally, confronted with a state that sets out to care for man from the cradle to the grave, one has the feeling that the diakonia will be reduced on the one hand to charity, which is the diakonia of Matthew 25: give the thirsty to drink and clothe the naked; and on the other hand to prophecy, the service that one renders in accompanying life with the message of divine judgment, putting a lamp unto the feet, a light unto the path of the state (the diakonia of Ps. 119).[31] For this reason people outside the church see it both as a philanthropic agency, a body that escapes the fight for justice in condescending charity, and as a "factory for solemn statements."

There is, however, a third possibility, through which we can avoid this constant temptation to the church to speak when it should act. We may call it the level of the laboratory, the diakonia of a little group, living in a concrete situation, and serving each other and their environment by reforming the structure of a segment of society. Social problems are not solved at this level, but life is made more tolerable. The opposition to the Messianic shalom is not completely broken, but here and there it is tempered. It is not the Kingdom of God that is constructed, but some significant tokens are set up. An object lesson is given of what shalom should be.

NOTES

1. Charles W. Ranson, ed., *Renewal and Advance* (London: Edinburgh House Press, 1948), p. 215.
2. E. Kellerhals, "Sind wir noch Pionier-Mission?" *E.M.M.*, 1948, pp. 104ff.
3. Ecumenical Press Service, Nov. 26, 1948.
4. Cf. Frank Laubach, "How to Convert 1,200,000,000 People," in *Church of England Newspaper*, Oct. 7, 1949.

5. Cf. G. Wehrung, *Die Kirche nach evangelischem Verständnis* (1946), pp. 29ff.
6. *Verbum: unica perpetua et infallibilis ecclesiae nota* (Luther). Cf. E. Wolf, *Evangelische Theologie*, 1938, pp. 134ff.
7. *Innere Missions*, 1849. "Home missions is that total work, that love born from faith in Christ, which seeks to renew those *multitudes in Christendom* who have fallen prey to the power and the rule of all sorts of lost conditions, which directly or indirectly is the result of sin, but who are not reached by the existing ministries."
8. "Don't, under any conditions, get mixed up in outward things," Utendörfer, *Zinzendorfs Missions Instruktionen* (Herrnhut, 1913), p. 9.
9. In North America, especially David Zeisberger (1720–1808) (among the Indians), and in Antigua, Peter Braun.
10. G. Hermann, *Karl Graul und seine Bedeutung für die lutherische Mission* (Halle, 1867).
11. W. Kunze, *Der Missionsgedanke bei Schleiermacher* (1927); O. Kübler, *Mission und Theologie* (1929); E. zur Nieden, *Der Missionsgedanke in der systematischen Theologie seit Schleiermacher* (1928).
12. R. Rothe, *Theologische Ethik*, vol. V, p. 1178.
13. Cf. G. M. Young, ed., *Early Victorian England*, vol. 2 (New York and London: Oxford University Press, 1934), p. 392.
14. J. Dürr, *Sendende und werdende Kirche in der Missions-Theologie G. Warnecks* (Basel, 1947), p. 159.
15. "The expansion of belief in Yaweh among all nations is part of the Messianic expectation," A. G. Hebert, *The Throne of David* (New York: Morehouse-Barlow Co., 1942), p. 72.
16. O. Michel, "Menschensohn und Völkerwelt," *Evangelische Missions Zeitschrift*, 1941, pp. 257ff.
17. Max Warren, *The Truth of Vision* (London: Canterbury Press, 1948).
18. Cf. Oscar Cullmann, *Christus und die Zeit* (Zürich, 1946), pp. 138–153. For a Roman Catholic view, see Jean Daniélou, *Le Mystère du Salut des Nations* (1945), pp. 85–110.
19. Cf. Johannes Pedersen, *Israel: Its Life and Culture*, 2 vols. (New York and London: Oxford University Press, 1926, 1940), pp. 311ff.
20. Ethelbert Stauffer, *Die Theologie des N. T.* (Geneva, 1945), p. 123.
21. Paul S. Minear, *The Eyes of Faith* (New York: The Westminster Press, 1945), p. 267.
22. Warren, *op. cit.*, p. 57.
23. Martin Kähler, *Dogmatische Zeitfragen*, II, pp. 347–351; H. Frick, *Mission und Propaganda* (1927).
24. H. A. van Andel, *De zendingsleer van G. Voetius* (1912). Here and there is added *conversio gentium*.
25. J. Merle Davis, *New Buildings on Old Foundations* (International Missionary Council, 1945).
26. C. H. Dodd, *The Apostolic Preaching and Its Developments* (New York: Harper & Row, Publishers, Inc., 1936).
27. *International Review of Missions*, Oct. 1949, pp. 407–408.
28. D. T. Jenkins, "A Message to Ministers About the Communication of the Gospel," *Theology Today*, 1949, pp. 183–184.
29. Cf. Report of Bossey Conference on Evangelism, March, 1949.
30. R. Loew, *En Mission Prolétarienne* (1946).
31. Similar to what William Temple called "social witness." Cf. *Social Witness and Evangelism* (London: The Epworth Press, Publishers, 1943).

B. ESSENTIAL EVANGELISM
An Open Letter to Dr. Hoekendijk

Donald McGavran

Your "Call to Evangelism" in the April 1950 issue of the *International Review of Missions* (recently reprinted as *Occasional Paper*, Ser. II, No. 7, by the Department of Missionary Studies of the World Council of Churches) raises many questions for Christian mission. Your analysis of *evangelism* as the integration of three aspects of the shalom of God—kerygma, koinonia, and diakonia—has been widely and favorably quoted. In these revolutionary days when we know with certainty that the shape of tomorrow will be very different from that of today, your denunciation of an evangelism which merely reproduces Western churches and Western civilization is well taken. With much of what you say I find myself in hearty agreement, and yet the central message of that article seems to me so damaging to essential evangelism that I write this letter, hoping that your original article, this letter, your answer, and my rejoinder may be published. Such a debate ought to illuminate some of the vital issues of the day and (hopefully) find a common ground of agreement.

We are agreed, I believe, on the urgency of evangelism. You say theologians "jeopardize the biblical authenticity of their thinking if they go on refusing to acknowledge that *the church is set in this world with the sole purpose of carrying the gospel to the ends of the earth.*" [1] I do not put the matter quite as strongly as this. I content myself with saying, "A *chief* purpose of Christian mission is to proclaim Jesus Christ as divine and only Savior and persuade men to become His disciples and responsible members of His Church." My quarrel with the existing order is that the multiplicity of good activities carried on by the Church has made such proclamation and persuasion not "a sole," not even "a chief," but merely "one among many good things done by the Church." However, you and I both agree that evangelism is extremely urgent.

But from there on, as you probe the nature of evangelism and what it means for the Church today, I find myself increasingly uneasy. It is possible that I misunderstand you. We all face the problem of semantics. If so, please correct me. I want to understand.

Let us start with the concept of the Church. You contrast, I think, the state churches of Christendom with the real Church which you describe as the koinonia—the one a mixture of culture, state power, and Christian-influenced society with diluted koinonia, the other a "fellowship of the partakers of the same salvation . . . a company of strangers and pilgrims." [2] I am a "gathered church" man. I readily and deeply appreciate the contrast. I agree that the Church is ideally not a culture-church of any land. We handicap ourselves when we think it is. Yet the hard fact of the matter is that, from the first days of the Church to date, a culture-church is all there has ever been. But because of this, I cannot affirm that there has been no Church for 1930 years.

Evangelism proclaims Christ and persuades men to become His disciples and responsible members of His Church. Ideally it is His Church only. Practically "His Church" takes much of its color from the civilization in which it lives—and does so of necessity. It is not less the Church for it. The first koinonia "spake the word to none but Jews" but was a real Church nevertheless. Some of its members owned slaves and no doubt bought and sold human beings, but the members were nonetheless "in Christ."

To some extent I agree that evangelism is "a function of expectancy." [3] When the Christian believes profoundly that God will establish His rule (His shalom) and redeem the whole of creation, and reign till He has put all His enemies under His feet, including death, then an outburst of evangelistic zeal should normally follow. Granted. But how often in the long history of the Church has evangelistic zeal burst forth, with very little of this closely reasoned theology lying back of it! Suppose some section of the Church (and there are many which we in the ecumenical world accept as equally validly Church) had a different system of theology. Suppose it based its evangelism on different passages; and possibly even by-passed entirely the eschatological perspective. Would that mean that it had no valid evangelism? Here is a branch of the Church, which by proclaiming Christ to men and persuading them to become His disciples and responsible members of His Church, has established a cluster of congregations in which the Word is preached and the sacraments administered. Let us assume that the system of that branch of the Church is not as biblical as yours. Does this make its evangelism any less evangelism? Or its churches any less Church? Is not Christ greater than the systems by which we bring men to Him?

You make a strong point that true evangelism sows the seed and in humility lets God give the seed any body which pleases Him. You stigmatize as "propaganda" a Lutheran sowing seed and raising up a Lutheran church or the Baptist sowing seed which inevitably develops into Baptist churches. There is this truth in your distinction: we should not plant churches for the sake of denominational glory.

Yet can we use such black and white terms? Is it possible for a Lutheran missionary to do any other than plant Lutheran churches—the best kind he knows? Could Paul plant Judaizing churches—on the plea that if the seed he planted, led by the Holy Spirit, grew in the direction of circumcision, Paul had done his duty?

There is truly a sharp difference between propaganda and evangelism, but is it not possible for an ardent Anglican to be a true evangelist while planting genuine Anglican churches? And must there be "a total rejection of everything that tends to be propaganda"? [4] If so, how can God's obedient servants keep from spending their lives pondering whether a given course of action should be entered upon because some of its elements might tend to be propaganda? How do we get any evangelizing done in this world where the most common color is gray?

You insist that evangelism must not seek to reproduce the state churches of Europe. "They cannot guide us any longer, because they all believe, in one way or another, in the possible realization of the *Corpus Christianum,* and our experiences with this kind of Christendom have been too bitter for us to follow them any farther." [5] An evangelism which merely reproduced existing churches (European, American, or Afericasian) would certainly be less than ideal. But since both the state churches of Europe and the culture churches of America do transmit a knowledge of the Savior and the Holy Scriptures and have been used of God to raise up multitudes of Christian congregations in many lands, I would not dare call their evangelism "no evangelism." On the contrary, it appears to me to be genuine and good evangelism—which must become still better. The evangelism of the early church for the first twenty years made the renunciation of pork and the practice of circumcision essential marks of the Christian. This handicapped their evangelism among Gentiles, but enormously advantaged it among Jews. It may have been the will of God—for the first twenty years—for the Church to grow strong in one segment of society. Is it not possible that

God himself has been requiring the kind of evangelism which the past one hundred years has so greatly used?

You are emphatic that evangelism is *not* planting churches. You say, "It is impossible to think of the *plantatio ecclesiae* as the end of evangelism."[6] I could not help but think of the father of the ecumenical movement, John R. Mott, who with Robert E. Speer and Robert Wilder trumpeted abroad for decades that the basic purpose of Christian mission was the establishment of self-supporting, self-propagating and self-governing churches.

On the positive side you affirm that "the Church is (nothing more, but also nothing less!) a means in God's hands to establish shalom in this world," and you describe the right kind of evangelism as a combination of kerygma, koinonia, and diakonia[7] which we might call K.K.D., implying that this is vastly different from the multiplication of churches.

I dissent at this point. If the K.K.D. formula is merely a fresh way of speaking about the Church and what the Church should be, that is one thing. Ideally the Church should be all three. But since you systematically use the word koinonia for church and substitute "the shalom" (God's peace, rule, integrity, community, harmony, and justice, where mercy and truth are met together, and righteousness and peace have kissed each other) for "the Church," in effect you deny that the empirical Church is the Church at all. You qualify this stricture in a place or two (as in para. 3, page 54), but emphasize it so much that your qualifications tend to disappear.

Hence my dissent. The Lord God himself has not chosen to plant a disembodied shalom anywhere, nor to transmit the Christian faith without the Church. True, the shell is not the living germ in the egg; but the shell had better be there. The egg is living germ plus shell. I do not see how we can get away from the institution—the Church. We can easily get too much institution. This I devoutly believe. I am a "free church" man as were my fathers before me. But the faith and some form of the Church are inextricably intertwined.

Hence also my insistence that the aim of evangelism is the planting of churches. Christ is the Evangelist, and through His obedient servants, and by other means too, He plants multitudes of churches. The extent of *His* shalom is marked by a *multitude of His churches*. The closer the churches live to their Lord, the less will they desire that the multitude selfishly advantage the churches—though they can never divorce themselves from the fact that often it does. The closer they live to their Lord, the more they will desire that the multitude benefit others.

It would be a sorry kind of mission or evangelism which multiplied churches to aggrandize the fathering body. I say "it would be" because in all my studies of church growth in four continents I have yet to run across a Church so motivated. If we attack self-aggrandizement as a motive for modern Christian mission, we attack a straw man. Multiplying churches increases the burden of the multipliers. It does not work to their aggrandizement. Ask any missionary society.

You write, "It is nonsense to call these churches [class churches] to evangelism, if we do not call them simultaneously to a radical revision of their life and a revolutionary change of their structure." [8] I fear I must dissent. It is never nonsense to call a Christian church to evangelism, and, as it evangelizes, it will reform itself far more than it could while introverted. The ecumenical movement, which certainly calls for a radical revision of the life of the churches, arose out of the missionary movement. It would never have arisen except that the early missionaries had called their churches to evangelism without even suggesting ecumenicity in Europe and America. Another example comes from the field of race relationships. The Church is ideally an open community, open to everyone who has become a partaker in the same shalom of God-in-Christ. Under some circumstances it is imperative that the churches demonstrate and incarnate this openness. Under these circumstances if a church lags behind, closed and segregated, it should, indeed, be called to radical revision. But under other circumstances, for the Church to disregard sociological realities would betray both the gospel and the people. For example, if on the day of Pentecost, Peter had insisted that all believers, before they could be baptized into the koinonia, had to be willing to practice radical brotherhood—eat with pig-eaters and give daughters in marriage to uncircumcised believers—he would have killed the Church. Fortunately the Holy Spirit led him to keep the Church almost entirely Jewish for many years.

Since integration is a crucial issue in the United States today, let me explain exactly what this principle will mean here. In the United States today, segregation of God's children on the basis of race pride (the strong denying admission to God's house to the weak) is sinful. The churches have rightfully taken up the cudgels for brotherhood and integration. Ministers have rightfully marched in demonstrations and rightfully gone to jail. The right of any Christian to worship in any church must be fought for till it is established beyond question. The whole shameful system of second-class citizenship must be abolished.

Nevertheless, that men receive the gospel is tremendously important. So that when the extension of the Church is favored (as it was A.D. 30 to 50) by the fact that the gospel is flowing along cultural, racial, or linguistic lines, the Holy Spirit himself may still lead to the establishment of segregated churches. Swedish Lutherans might find that the gathering up of Swedish immigrants to Canada into churches like those in Sweden was helped by worship services in Swedish and fellowships fairly well limited to Swedish Lutherans. In the United States, Spanish-speaking churches made up almost exclusively of Puerto Ricans will (in the first generation or two) be better churches and will communicate Christ more effectively than those which attempt to mix Puerto Ricans and old Americans in English-speaking congregations.

Much depends on what segregation means. If it means deifying racial pride, it is sinful and must go. If it means an arrangement of convenience pleasing to some subculture or racial group and used of God to the conversion of the unsaved, it may, under some circumstances, be in harmony with God's will. As one who has been a member of a Negro church in the United States for some years, I believe devoutly in integration. As one concerned that the gospel spread mightily in every land, I want to leave the door wide open to people movements (caste-wise movements) which take in every member of a given people before becoming integrated. In New Testament terms, I do not want the pig-eating issue to prevent my brother Hebrews from seeing, desiring, and *obeying* the Lord. Till A.D. 50 I am on the side of Peter. After A.D. 50 I am on the side of Paul.

In the last three paragraphs I have not diverged from the subject. Each embodied church will pass through periods when action which seemed right to it in the past will seem less and less right to it and ultimately will seem wrong to it. Evangelism is equally its duty in all three periods. It is not nonsense to call a church in its period of tension to evangelism. During this tension God may also call it to "a radical revision" of its life and a "revolutionary change" of its structure, but seldom as a prerequisite to evangelism.

If I may summarize our disagreement, you seem to say, "If the ideal cannot be obtained, it is better to have no evangelism," whereas my conviction is that in this vale of tears we never obtain the ideal and must always evangelize, starting with the imperfect empirical church. We start with Peter and John and Mark and the uncircumcised Timothy. We carry on through the Judaizing controversy. The Great Evangelist uses us—poor human tools—and when we blunder, or frustrate His will by our unbelief, ignorance, or cowardice, He picks up the pieces and starts again. That the tools are mortal is no reason to cease to evangelize.

Pietists often say, "The Church can go no farther till it goes deeper." Sociologist Christians rejoin by saying "True in some places; but in others the Church can go no deeper till it goes farther." Until the Church grows to the place that an individual congregation is much more than a few Christians scattered across a thousand square miles of countryside, it is extremely difficult for it to achieve either real biblical knowledge or ardent faith—or to survive across the centuries. It must go farther before it can go deeper. It must grow in numbers before it can grow in grace.

Again you write, "It is no use stimulating to new and rapid advance while this work remains neutralized by the mockery of koinonia which our churches really are. 'The acts of your koinonia speak so loudly that we cannot hear the words of your kerygma.' " [9] I dissent vigorously. The Church in the years 300 to 750 lacked a great deal in koinonia, kerygma, and diakonia. Its expansion was constantly handicapped by the smug sense of Latin superiority. The spread of Islam through North Africa was accelerated by the fact that the rural masses—the Berbers—living in the shadow of the great Augustine and hundreds of bishops, had not become Christians chiefly because the Bible was in Latin and the worship of the churches was in Latin. North Europeans were openly called barbarians. Yet the Church, proud, impenitent, and chained to a dying culture, spread, often by crude methods, during those centuries through the north country. If it had not, Charles Martel would not have turned back the Moslems at the battle of Tours and you and I would have been Moslems not Christians.

If it is possible "to stimulate to new and rapid" extension of the Church, then we should not, I think, adduce our own imperfections as good reason for no evangelism. All evangelism proceeds from sinners on their way to the New Jerusalem. Those who reject the gospel sometimes say they do so because of the hypocrisy of some Christian, but often they lie. If the hypocrisy ends, rejecters still love the world and find some other convenient objection.

This, to be sure, is no reason for Christians remaining in their sins. The churches greatly need a further capturing of the mind of Christ and a reformation of their existing state. The more our church is a Household of God the more pleasing to our heavenly Father. The more Christian our acts, the more clearly can the kerygma be heard. Yet it is a dangerous overstatement to conclude from these truths that the empirical Church (whose koinonia is always less than God desires it to be) *cannot* communicate Christ. After all, we preach Him, not ourselves. If the Christian's gospel was only his own achievements in love and justice, he would of all men be the most miserable.

You understand evangelism to be rather complex—kerygma, koinonia, diakonia, proclamation of the shalom of Christ, and His redemption of the entire order by His death and Resurrection. Is this not needlessly involved? Will "the saints" in ordinary churches consider this a clarion call to evangelism? Can the illiterate multitudes understand this complicated concept? And is it biblical? I do not thus read my New Testament. In the New Testament Christ was proclaimed as Savior, Messiah, and Lord. Those who believed on Him were baptized into His Church. Commonly the missionaries or witnesses did not before or after the baptism serve the people to whom they proclaimed Christ. Converts were baptized for "salvation"—which they interpreted in various ways. They were given the Holy Spirit who gradually led them to become loving, kindly, just, pure, and God-worshiping people. The fruits of the Spirit were not usually adduced as the reason for belief. Peter or Paul would never have said, "The hollowness of your koinonia cancels the effectiveness of your kerygma. Stop and perfect yourselves before you say another word about Jesus Christ."

Does a basic cause of our difference lie in the new situation which has arisen regarding the younger churches? Mission is no longer the "Christian West" proclaiming Christ to the "non-Christian East." It is rather Christians everywhere, East and West, extending the gospel and reconciling unbelievers everywhere, East and West, to God in Christ.

It seems to me that some missiologists today on the basis of this undoubted fact go on to conclude that mission has therefore become, not intention to win men to Christ and multiply churches, but simply ardent Christian living. Understanding evangelism as K.K.D. would fit in here beautifully. Each congregation would be koinonia and would practice diakonia and proclaim the kerygma. A very neat system! But is it mission?

K.K.D. is one good description of normal Christian life. Most of the passages you use to support K.K.D. as evangelism were addressed to already established congregations urging them to live thoroughly Christian lives, to *be* what they in fact were, the redeemed of God. May we legitimately conclude from these passages, however, that evangelism is nothing more than living as Christians?

I have another difficulty with K.K.D. as evangelism. It is a rather too nice justification of the traditional triad of modern missions—evangelism, church, and service. K.K.D. fits a heavily institutionalized mission whose affiliated church of 3600 communicants in the midst of winnable multitudes is growing at a mere 20 percent a decade. This church and its assisting mission have an evangelistic department, a large educational and medical work, and fulfill all the requirements of K.K.D.—but they reconcile few to God. What Christian mission needs today across the continents and the denominations is not further biblical justification of the structures developed in the past hundred and fifty years by Western missions of Western empires. Missions today need courage, wisdom, and biblical authority to devise new ways, new budget proportions, new institutions, new modes of proclamation which make for better progress in discipling the nations—West as well as East, Germany as well as Japan or Oregon.

We must find a more biblical foundation for evangelism than K.K.D. It will lie, I think, in the passion of God for men's salvation. It will manifest itself in the life of Him who had no place to lay His head, came to seek and save sinners, and soon gave His life a ransom for many.

We must separate evangelism from other good Christian activities. For example, it has no necessary connection with diakonia —though diakonia is a fruit of the Spirit and may on occasion commend the gospel. An intelligent Christian will notice that diakonia is often a good preparation for the gospel, but he will also note that it was never consciously so used in the early church. Evangelism is also separate from koinonia. Evangelism is activity undertaken with the intent of communicating the good news. Koinonia is a fellowship of Christians which does many other things than communicate the gospel. True, all Christian life may communicate the gospel unintentionally. The honest Christian pays his taxes gladly and a non-Christian (under particular circumstances) may see this act and be led to Christian faith. This does not mean that paying taxes is evangelism. If we make everything evangelism there is grave danger that no intentional persuasion will be undertaken.

Furthermore you define and delimit evangelism theologically and schematically. For you, the concept of the Church must be theologically sound. The act of communication must be ideologically pure—no propaganda. Evangelism itself must not be too individualistic or too social. It must have the three divisions we have been discussing. It must proceed out of a true Church without spot or blemish or any wrinkle. While I cannot believe that such is your thinking, seemingly whether such evangelism finds any lost sheep is immaterial! Under this "ideal" evangelism, whether churches multiply or decline apparently makes no difference. If pushed to the logical extremity, the Church as an institution might actually vanish from the earth while such pure evangelism was in progress.

Is such a configuration pleasing to our Savior? Is this what the Bible really says? Is this the message from God recorded in the New Testament? Rather, is not the purpose of evangelism in the New Testament that the shalom of God *be extended*? When you say that "The church is set in the world with the sole purpose of carrying the gospel to the ends of the earth," [10] are you not much closer to the early church and the revelation of God than in the particular theology of evangelism you have developed thereafter?

I take as basic truth that God desires the salvation of multitudes of countable persons, who will be organized into multitudes of countable churches. Would you agree? Let us qualify this basic truth as we think best—churches must be spiritual; the institution must not dominate; justice, peace, and brotherhood must characterize the churches. Christ saves, not the Church—but let us continue to emphasize that the extension of His Body into every human society, every hamlet, every home, is His purpose and hence ours as obedient servants. There must be a church in every village in the world and in every section of every city. He sends us to reap in fields which He has ripened. Let us with zeal proceed to obey.

A section of Christian mission today is wandering in a maze. In this section no one knows quite what Christian mission is. In some circles, everything is called mission—feeding the hungry, educating the ignorant, healing the sick, building bridges of friendship between nations, and now, with the population explosion, campaigns of birth control and sale of contraceptives may be added. In other circles, correct theological doctrines are substituted for an objective reconciliation of men to God in the Church of Jesus Christ.

How can we find our directions again? The way out, it seems to me, is to recognize that the actual planting of countable churches is a chief end of mission. It is not the only end and not even *the* chief end; but it is *a chief end and it must always be sought*. We must communicate the gospel while doing the good deeds which the Christian sees needed both within and without the Church. When the Holy Spirit leads us to do good deeds, let us be responsive to Him. But over and above these good things— "the mission activities" Roland Allen describes in *The Ministry of the Spirit* [11]—let us see to it that the gospel is communicated *in fact.* The great Kirkpatrick at Columbia University in New York City used to say, "Where there is no learning there is no teaching." Similarly we Christians must learn to say, "Where there is no communication of the gospel, there is no evangelism."

Evangelism is not correct theory. Evangelism is seeking and saving sinners. Evangelism is not correct theology—though the closer evangelism remains to the truths of the Christian revelation, the more it will please God. Evangelism is finding lost children of God and bringing them rejoicing into the household of God. Evangelism is bringing lost men to the Savior. Evangelism is not a system—though knowledge about how God has acted to save men often gives guidance as to how He is likely to act in the future. Evangelism is actually grafting multitudes of wild olive branches into the Divine Tree. Evangelism is not purity of motive or of method—though God desires and blesses clean hands and a pure heart.

In fields white to harvest, evangelism is each bringing his quota of sheaves to the Master's threshing floor. Evangelism is Paul wishing himself accursed if only his kinsmen came to accept the Savior and planting churches all round the Mediterranean. Evangelism is not a nice weighing of rights and wrongs. Evangelism is an overwhelming conviction of the preeminence of Christ flowing through human life like a river in flood. Evangelism is not necessarily vocal—though God has commanded the foolishness of preaching and himself appeared as Word. Evangelism is all Christian acts done with intention to transmit the treasure we have in earthen vessels.

NOTES

1. See above, p. 42.
2. Ibid., p. 53.
3. Ibid., p. 47.
4. Ibid., p. 48.
5. Ibid., p. 44.
6. Ibid., pp. 49–50.
7. Ibid., p. 49.
8. Ibid., p. 53.
9. Ibid., p. 54.
10. Ibid., p. 42.
11. Roland Allen, *The Ministry of the Spirit* (Grand Rapids: Wm. B. Eerdmans, 1965).

PART II

1967:
Are Conversion Missions Outmoded?

A. YES! CONVERSION AND THE MISSION OF THE CHURCH

Ronan Hoffman

Christians used to think that through their mission work they would bring the whole of mankind into the Church some day. In past centuries the principal motive of mission activity was the evangelical one, common both to Protestants and Catholics, of saving as many souls from that eternal damnation which otherwise awaited them. Among nineteenth-century Protestants the slogan, "The evangelization of the world in our generation," stirred many souls to seek zealously the conversion of the entire human race to Jesus Christ. Even though more sober minds did not expect this to be accomplished within a single generation, nevertheless it was thought that the missionary effort was directed towards that ultimate goal of converting all mankind to Christianity.

This motivation was very powerful and it gave birth to the greatest missionary movement in history. Current Protestant and Catholic theology, however, no longer accepts this as the proper motivation. Missionary action, it is insisted, aims at something more than conversion and salvation of souls. Yet there is confusion and a lack of understanding on the aim of the mission and especially in regard to the matter of conversion.

In the past many Christian missionaries regarded everything in the non-Christian religions and cultures as evil, idolatrous, and superstitious, and they determined that these should be replaced by the Christian religion and cultural values. For this and other reasons, Christian missions have often been criticized. Innumerable Asians, for example, have maintained that there is no justification for them at all. They point to the present state of

---

Ronan Hoffman is Associate Professor of Missiology and Modern Church History at the School of Theology, Catholic University of America, Washington, D.C: This address was given at the 18th annual meeting of the Mission Sending Societies, Sept. 18, 1967, Washington, D.C., and was printed in the *Journal of Ecumenical Studies*, Winter 1967–68.

Christianity and ask, "Why have missions? The Christian nations are no better than we." In the view of Mahatma Gandhi, missions were an "intrusion into the sanctity of personality." He once wrote: "Every mission runs the risk of falling into a 'religious imperialism' dangerous to itself." From his point of view any conscious attempt to convert others by means of more or less rational arguments was an abuse of reason itself. The end desired ought to be, according to him, to make Christians better Christians, Moslems better Moslems, and Hindus better Hindus.[1]

In the face of such adverse criticism, Christians ought not simply spring to the defense of missions and become apologists for them. Rather, we should face these not always unfriendly criticisms honestly and squarely to see what validity there may be in them. We must be much more aware than we have been in the past that many non-Christians dislike intensely the idea that Christian missionaries should consider them as objects of conversion. In their eyes it appears that missionaries wish to destroy all that they cherish as sacred and holy.

What have the Church and theology said about conversion? It is an important question, for on the answer to it will depend in large part the practice of the Church in its missionary action in the future.

There is need for more understanding in this area, and so the scope of this paper will be to survey the way conversion was regarded in past centuries, why it was so regarded, and why some traditional assumptions are no longer tenable.

I

The sacred Scriptures contain the foundation for the universal mission of the Church, which was sent by God to carry the message of redemption and salvation to all mankind. The Old Testament tells us of a particularistic pact made between God and the people of Israel, a pact which however included the notion of teleological universalism. Indeed, the particular juridical covenant of God with the Jewish people was made in order to prepare the way for the universal salvation of all men. In the past, Catholic apologetics stressed the element of universality in order to justify the Church's universal mission. Recent scriptural studies have made us more aware of the need likewise of reflecting on the particularity of the covenant and of the theological significance in the paucity of numbers of the chosen people. Their minority status and the diaspora situation of the Israelite people in the Old Testament already suggest what appears also in the New Testament in regard to the size of the *ecclesia*.

The entire outlook of the New Testament indicates that the visible Church was intended to be a minority group within the whole human race, just as it always has been. The Church has always been the *pusillus grex*, as Christ spoke of it.[2] The parable of the sower and the seed was one of the few parables explained by Christ.[3] It seems to give the impression that only a fourth part of the gospel seed would grow and bear fruit, and from the parable of the weeds or cockle it would appear that even this fourth part would be seriously hindered in its progress and development.[4] St. John Chrysostom considered that by these parables Our Lord was trying to prepare the disciples for the humiliation and persecution which would be the lot of the Church.

The attitude of Our Lord towards conversion as sought by the scribes and Pharisees can be seen in His reproaching them as hypocrites for going around about land and sea to make but one convert.[5] It was not their desire to make converts but the absence of the right motives in making converts that Christ condemned. He reproached them not for their missionary zeal but because this zeal was animated less by a desire of promoting God's glory and the good of men than by the desire of self-aggrandizement and of boasting of the increase in the numbers of their sect.

We should take careful note of the fact that Christ did not send His disciples to convert the whole world to the Church but rather sent them out to teach or make disciples of all nations.[6] It would seem that not enough attention has been paid to the difference between evangelization of the nations and the attempt to convert all nations. One mission writer of the seventeenth century did point out this difference. Cardinal Brancati distinguished between the external work of preaching the gospel and the internal inspiration of God's calling which alone converts men to the faith. To the missionary is committed the external work alone but not the conversion itself, which is the work of God and His grace.[7] The Cardinal wrote this in order to give some comfort to those missionaries who, after a number of years and many labors in the missions, found little or no fruit, judged by the number of conversions. His counsel was that missionaries should not be disturbed by this apparent failure, provided they had carried out their ministry faithfully, because God had not committed to them the internal work of conversion but only the external work which might lead up to it. Such a wise counsel could prove to be of comfort to some missionaries today, who, regarding the goal of their work as that of conversion, might be disturbed at their apparent failure.

II

It should be noted that none of the Church Fathers composed any formal treatise on missionary activity, although many of them discussed questions bearing on it. The relationship of conversion to the Church and its mission, however, is not one of those discussed.

What strikes one in looking in the indices of patristic writings is the almost complete absence of references to "conversion" in the sense of external conversion to the Church. No doubt the principal reason for their not discussing this matter is that the Fathers generally tended to take for granted that the Church had already expanded "throughout the world," by which they meant of course the world around the Mediterranean basin. Well known is the typical and oft-quoted statement of Tertullian to the effect that Christians were only of yesterday but already had infiltrated into every class of society, even into the highest classes. Apart from St. John Chrysostom and a few others, the Fathers did not exhort the early Christians to go forth and seek the conversion of others.[8] Instead of urging future expansion and instead of exhorting Christians to convert others, the large majority of the Fathers stand as witnesses to the fact of universal expansion "throughout the world." With such a frame of reference, it is understandable that one searches in vain in patristic writings for doctrinal teaching in the relation of conversion to the mission of the Church.

Yet the fact is that, regardless of its rapid expansion, the Church was a minority group in the Roman Empire in the early centuries.

According to Harnack, the first and indeed the only Christian writer who bears witness to the relative fewness of Christians is Origen. He states that in his day there was no entirely Christian city; that the number of the Christians was small, and that there were many nations within and without the empire to which the gospel had not yet penetrated.[9] Even though Origen is apparently the only Christian writer to bring out this fact, still it seems very unlikely that the other Fathers were unaware of it. The significant thing is that they did not consider this numerical minority to be in any way incompatible with the universality of the Church. For apologetic reasons, they chose to stress the fact of actual expansion rather than exhort their readers to greater attempts to convert non-Christians. One must conclude from this that they evidently did not regard total conversion, or even the conversion of the majority of the empire, to be the goal envisioned in the universal mission of the Church. Patrology does not lend any foundation to the notion of total, or even general, conversion of mankind as being necessary in order that the Church be catholic or that it carry out its universal mission in the world.

III

When we come up to the modern mission era, however, we find a different spirit and outlook. The idea of converting all the inhabitants of the new lands discovered by the Spaniards and Portuguese appears clearly in the missionary writings of the fifteenth and sixteenth centuries. Yet, it is remarkable that there is little reference to scriptural injunctions in support of this goal apart from the usual "Go forth, teach." It is likewise remarkable that these documents differ both in content and tone from the Scriptures and the writings of the Fathers.

In the seventeenth century, high hopes arose that before long the Cross of Christ would be firmly planted in most areas of the world and the inhabitants of the world converted to Christianity. Nobody of that time—pope, bishop, priest, or lay persons—would have thought that any other objective could be admitted. For example, in the most influential missionary work of the early seventeenth century, Thomas a Jesu wrote explicitly on the propagation of the faith in the whole world, by which he understood the conversion of the whole world.[10]

It is worth noting that, despite this outlook, the purpose of the missions in the official documents of the early propaganda do not mention conversion. These documents refer to the propagation of the faith without any reference to the conversion of non-Christians.[11] The widespread assumption of general conversion did not come from the teaching of dogmatic theology. Nor did it come from the teachings of the general councils of the Church. The Second Vatican Council is the first council in history ever to discuss and publish a document on the missionary activity of the Church.

While on the one hand one might tend to deplore the fact that theology and the councils have had almost nothing to say directly about the missionary work of the Church, it is rather important to note this fact. For, in repudiating the deeply rooted notion that the Church is to seek the general conversion of the human race, it is important to understand that this is not a repudiation of any former teaching which might be found in the Scriptures, in patristic sources, or in the teachings of theology or the general councils. There is no such teaching; it has been merely an assumption, though admittedly widespread. Consequently, it is necessary to note carefully the absence of teaching on this point.

One can easily verify this by consulting the word "conversion" in theological dictionaries and encyclopedias. Traditionally, theology has generally considered conversion on an individual basis but has not treated the point under discussion here, namely, the notion of general conversion as an objective of the Church's missionary action.

Theologically, conversion signifies a change—a moral change, an orientation or a return to God, to the true religion, and it is in this sense that it has passed into modern languages. Thus, it is in this sense that we speak of the conversion of St. Paul, of St. Augustine, of Constantine, and so on. In the Middle Ages it also referred to those who left the world to enter religious life. In short, conversion has signified: (a) a change from infidelity to the Catholic faith, (b) a change from heresy or schism to the Roman Catholic Church, or (c) a change from a sinful or tepid life to a life of grace and fervor. It has always been considered by Catholic theologians as that act whereby one embraces integrally the faith of the Catholic Church and becomes a member of it by means of baptism.

This appears to be incomplete. It seems that Catholic theology must also consider a change from a nonreligious state to belief in the one true God (without further specification), and also a change from a nonreligious state to any one of the Christian churches. Otherwise, theology would simply overlook what must be acknowledged to be concrete realities, namely, the existence of "religious" but unchurched persons, as well as the many Orthodox and Protestant Christians. Simply to ignore them does not in any manner negate the fact of their existence, and an integral and complete treatment of conversion should take these types of conversion into account also.

Catholic theology can and ought to make a distinction between (a) conversion to God, (b) conversion to Christ, whom one accepts as his Lord, and (c) conversion to the Catholic Church by one who believes that this is the will of God for him. From what has been said, it is evident that Catholic theology has generally considered the first and third together as one thing and simply ignored the second. Moreover, conversion as a goal of missionary activity must always be regarded as dependent upon the inspiration of divine grace, and with the full realization that this is not absolutely demanded of any given individual either by the nature of Christianity or the requirements of individual salvation, and also that the religious freedom of all men must be scrupulously observed.

IV

When and how did the notion of winning over masses of people to the Church arise? It began at the beginning of the Middle Ages when the Church undertook the evangelization and Christianization of the Celtic and Germanic tribes of northern Europe. It is of great importance to recognize that the medieval missionary methodology was not only a radical departure from earlier thinking and methodology, but also that the reason for this change in methods was not based on Scripture or early tradition but on political and social considerations. The historical facts are well known, but their theological significance seems not to have been thought out fully.

The reason for the change in mission methods was due to the relationship of the Germanic people to their leaders which, among other things, demanded the submission of their will to that of the leaders in every respect, even in religious matters. Consequently, the early medieval mission took as its aim not so much the winning of individual persons as such, but rather the conversion of whole communities, that is, of the masses; and in working towards this end they first sought the conversion of princes and persons of importance.

Unfortunately, political and social factors became intermingled with religious convictions as the various European peoples became baptized Christians. Moreover, there was rarely absent in the medieval period a certain compulsion or coercion in these "conversions." Promises and threats, and even force and compulsion, were regarded as suitable means to bring about conversion. The close alliance between the state and the Church, between religion and politics, that was established with the founding and building up of the Frankish Kingdom explains how the notion of total conversion arose within the Church. This notion, which arose at an early stage in the history of European Christianity, was to give rise to a misunderstanding of the mission of the Church—a misunderstanding which unfortunately has perdured down to the present. It has caused too much attention to be paid to the quantitative growth of the Church without sufficient emphasis upon such an essential matter as the quality of the conversions thus effected.

These historical circumstances involved in the manner in which the medieval Church approached the northern Germanic tribes influenced the attitude and outlook in regard to future missionary policy. Since she could not approach these tribes individually, she had to approach them collectively. This led in time, in a very subtle and unchallenged manner, to the notion that membership in civil society necessarily required membership in the ecclesiastical society of the Church. It explains but does not justify the compulsory methods used to extort conversion. The practice was discountenanced and condemned in the writings of the most eminent churchmen and missionaries. In fact, ecclesiastical law has always stressed that conversion must be entirely voluntary, that there must never be any force or coercion of any kind used in order to induce non-Christians to enter the Church. Yet the history of the missions shows clearly that this law of the canonists was all too frequently breached in actual practice.

Moreover, to understand more clearly how the unscriptural notion of total conversion came to be generally accepted without any challenge, it is necessary to realize that in medieval society men felt themselves to be first and foremost members of Christendom rather than of any given political society. The Christian Church provided the only effective principle of social unity in the Middle Ages. In the light of this, it is easy to understand how the notion could arise that all men (in Europe) should be Christian and Catholic. This was certainly the attitude of medieval man; heretics or schismatics or atheists were not only destructive of religious unity but also of social unity, so closely united were Church and state. Likewise, it is easily understandable that this same mentality influenced the outlook of all those engaged in missionary activity during and after the Age of Discoveries.

In the modern Catholic missionary movement the methodology was too often based on the politics of colonization rather than the solid base of Scripture and tradition. Nowhere was there a closer identity between Church and state than in the two countries of the Iberian peninsula, which countries had a monopoly on the missionary work of the Church for over two centuries, during which the idea was firmly entrenched that the whole world had to be won for Christ and His Church. Thinking of the Kingdom of Christ too much after the manner of the kingdom of Spain and Portugal, it was concluded that just as every Indian in the New World and the Orient had to become a subject of his majesty, the Catholic king, so too every Indian had to become a subject of the Vicar of Christ in Rome.

Such a view, fundamental to the missionary methodology in the colonizing period, cannot be supported by the Bible or tradition. It is a political, not a theological, view. No one will deny that our image of the Church and her mission must be that of Christ rather than of man. Christ spoke of the Church as the "little flock" and as "the leaven in the mass," not the mass of mankind.

This in no way denies the truth that the Church has a universal vocation. It is, in the words of Vatican II, "the sacrament of salvation of the entire world." This phrase is fraught with missionary meaning. Even though the Church is destined to be "the little flock" of the gospel, nevertheless it is the sign and instrument of salvation for all mankind. God wills that all be saved, and it is through the action of the Christian Church that this comes about. Current ecclesiology requires that we place numbers and quantitative growth in the background rather than consider these as the criterion of "success," as we have been too wont to do. In the past we wrongly conceived the mission task in terms of converting as many as possible, overlooking the fact that Christ commanded the apostles to teach or make disciples of all nations, not to convert them. The difference between the two is significant, for it is not so much the external teaching of men as the internal inspiration of God-calling which converts men to the Christian faith. Faith is a gift of God, and God alone determines to whom He will give it. "Paul plants, Apollo waters, but God gives the increase." [12] To missionaries is committed the external work of preaching but not conversion itself, which is the work of God. It should be remembered that not even Christ himself converted all to whom He preached; much less then should His followers consider the number of conversions as the criterion of mission success. The servant is not above the master.

V

During the present century there have been several developments which have caused a gradual change in outlook upon mission activity. These developments are a growing recognition of the diaspora situation of Christianity in the world; a better understanding of the notion of catholicity; and a clarification of the goals of missionary activity. The results of these developments show up in the documents of Vatican II.

For example, a study of missionary documents of the Holy See between 1909–1946 reveals that conversion was spoken of as an important goal, although it was by no means as prominent in these documents as the ideas of preaching the gospel and the propagation of the faith. Nonetheless, the inclusion of conversion as a missionary goal in these documents makes all the more significant the fact that neither the Decree on Ecumenism nor the Declaration on Non-Christian Religions use the word "conversion" to signify outward embracing of the Catholic faith. In its place, the first document speaks about "the work of preparing and reconciling those individuals who wish for full Catholic communion." [13] It thus foresees realistically that some separated brethren will wish membership in the Catholic Church in the future. At the same time it notes that this is of its very nature distinct from ecumenical action, although not opposed to it.

It is also highly significant to note that a reference to "conversion" of the Jews was removed from an earlier version of the Declaration on Non-Christian Religions. An observation of the Protestant Dr. Claude Nelson is pertinent to our discussion. He writes:

> The Vatican Declaration avoided suggestions of conversion, confining itself to the hoped-for reunion of all believers at the end of history. A shift from Christian denunciation of Jews to a Christian strategy of their conversion, advocated and practiced by many Christians, would not improve relations and might exacerbate them. What is needed is that Christians learn and practice truly Christian attitudes and relationships, amounting not to a strategy but to the creation of a new climate.[14]

It should be noted that the newly revised prayers in the Good Friday liturgy have been changed from prayers for the conversion of the Jews and of others who do not believe in Christ simply to prayers *for* them. This is also significant, for *lex orandi est lex credendi*, and in this case we might add *lex agendi* also. A careful reading of these prayers indicates that conversion is not necessary for the accomplishment of that for which they ask. While conversion is not ruled out, it would be reading into them something not present in these prayers to conclude that they imply the notion of any wholesale conversion.

This seems to indicate an authoritative change of attitude on the part of the Catholic Church. In his encyclical *Ecclesiam Suam* Pope Paul VI, in speaking about dialogue as a method of accomplishing the apostolic mission, stated that "this approach does not aim at effecting the immediate conversion of the interlocutor, inasmuch as it respects both his dignity and his freedom." [15] Readers will note, of course, that remote conversion at the end of a courteous, non-polemical dialogue is not even mentioned. Yet who could quarrel with this if it comes about as a result of sincere interior conviction?

The Constitution on the Liturgy of Vatican II notes that before men can come to the liturgy, they must be called to faith and to conversion, hence the necessity of preaching in order to bring this about. It does not specify anything further except to say that the conversion spoken of there consists in repentance and mending of one's ways.[16]

The Decree on Missionary Activity, as one might suppose, has more to say on conversion:

> When the Holy Spirit opens their heart, non-Christians may believe and be freely converted to the Lord, and may sincerely cling to Him (Christ).... This conversion, to be sure, must be regarded as a beginning. Yet it is sufficient that a man realize that he has been snatched away from sin and led into the mystery of the love of God, who has called him to enter a personal relationship with him in Christ. For, by the workings of divine grace, the new convert sets out on a spiritual journey. Already sharing through faith in the mystery of Christ's death and resurrection, he journeys from the old man to the new one, perfected in Christ.[17]

The Decree simply says, "When the Holy Spirit opens their heart, non-Christians may believe and be freely converted to the Lord." Yet there is no indication here whether the Holy Spirit will open the hearts of many or of only a few, or for that matter of any. It simply states that *some* non-Christians may believe and be freely converted when (and if) the Holy Spirit opens their hearts. More to the point, nowhere does this document positively insist that Catholic missionaries should strive for a large number of converts, even if this might be hoped for as a result of their preaching of the gospel.

Admittedly, in the past, Catholics have been too prone to equate the notion of conversion with the idea of openly accepting membership in the Church and to consider this as *the,* or at least *a,* principal goal of missionary activity. This, however, overlooks the fact that the scriptural meaning of conversion refers to a sort of religious or moral transformation in which man turns to God. In the New Testament it refers not only to a change of attitude but also to the external expression of this change, such as the confession of guilt, fasting, etc. In general, the scriptural meaning is the conversion of a sinner to God in faith, hope, and love in response to God's merciful willingness to forgive him.[18] So far as the New Testament's meaning is concerned, we would have to add: "... God's merciful willingness to forgive him in Jesus Christ."

The recent Council has made an authoritative change in approach not only to other Christian churches and ecclesial communities but also to the non-Christian religions. For the first time in its history, the Catholic Church has officially taken cognizance of non-Christian religions and has declared that "she rejects nothing which is true and holy in them." In fact, the Church has stated:

She looks with sincere respect upon those ways of conduct and life, those rules and teachings which, though differing in many particulars from what she holds and sets forth, nevertheless often reflect a ray of that Truth which enlightens all men. . . . [Therefore] . . . The Church has this exhortation for her sons: prudently and lovingly, through dialogue and collaboration with the followers of other religions, and in witness of Christian faith and life, acknowledge, preserve, and promote the spiritual and moral goods found among these men, as well as the values in their society and culture.[19]

New ground was broken in this declaration, for never before has the Church spoken of non-Christian religions in such a respectful manner. One does not set out to destroy or even to minimize that which one respects. Accordingly, the Council exhorts Catholics to "acknowledge, preserve, and promote the spiritual and moral goods found among non-Christians."

In addition, it is necessary to consider the newly formulated position of the Catholic Church on religious freedom. On the one hand, the Declaration states that every man has the duty, and therefore the right, to seek the truth in matters religious and that all others must respect this right. It repeats the centuries-old official teaching of the Church that no one is to be forced to embrace the Christian faith against one's own will, for the reason that the act of faith is of its very nature a free act. Missionaries, following the example of Christ and His early disciples, can and should do no more than attract and invite men to embrace the Christian faith of their own free will.

The document acknowledges that in the very early days of the Church, the disciples of Christ strove to convert men to faith in Christ as the Lord—not, however, by the use of coercion or by devices unworthy of the gospel, but by the power above all of the Word of God. But in so doing, they showed the gentleness and respectfulness of Christ himself. The Church then and her missionaries are being faithful to the truth of the gospel, and are following the way of Christ and the apostles when she recognizes, and gives support to, the principle of religious freedom as befitting the dignity of man and as being in accord with divine revelation. Indeed, this principle must be held the more inviolable in that it derives not only from the natural law but also has roots in divine revelation.[20]

If religious freedom is to mean anything, then, it must mean that Catholics must defend it for non-Catholics as well as for themselves, for it applies with *equal* validity to all men. To assert less would be to minimize and water down the Council's declaration itself. And the meaning of this declaration will become known and apparent more through the deeds of the Church and her members than through her words, noble though they be.

VI

In the light of the foregoing, I should now like to address myself to some questions posed by Rabbi Abraham Heschel, who asks:

> Is it really the will of God that there be no more Judaism in the world? Would it really be the triumph of God if the Scrolls of the Torah would no more be taken out of the Ark and the Torah no more read in the Synagogue, our ancient Hebrew prayers in which Jesus himself worshipped no more recited, the Passover Seder no more celebrated in our lives, the law of Moses no more observed in our homes? Would it really be *ad majorem Dei gloriam* to have a world without Jews? [21]

These questions deserve an answer, and that answer must be unequivocally in the negative. Whatever good God himself permits to exist, no man should dare try to exterminate.

In this connection perhaps Christians should take another look at a certain passage in the Acts of the Apostles which has been quoted at times in defense of the divinity of Christianity. The apostles had been summoned before the Sanhedrin for interrogation about the new religion of Christianity. Realizing that some among the Sanhedrin might wish to put the apostles to death, the wise and prudent Gamaliel stood up and warned them to take care in what they were about to do to the apostles. He noted that previously certain false teachers had risen and had gained some followers, only to disappear from the scene after a short time, and he concluded:

> Keep away from these men and let them alone; for if this plan or this undertaking is of men, it will fail; but if it is of God, you will not be able to overthrow them. You might even be found opposing God! [22]

Is it not possible today for Christians to apply the words of Gamaliel to Judaism, just as he once applied them to Christianity? Judaism has existed for the most part within Christendom since the time of Christ and has often been the target of proselytizing activities on the part of Christians over the centuries. Judaism not only exists at present, it shows signs of continuing to exist permanently.

Despite the efforts of Christianity to convert the Jews over the centuries, Judaism remains firm. If it were merely the work of men, would it not have perished? Christianity has not been able to overthrow it. Must we not conclude then that it continues to exist precisely because Almighty God, for His own reasons, wishes it to continue? And would we not perhaps find ourselves opposing God himself if we were to try in the future to overthrow Judaism or any other non-Christian religion?

Again, consider this text from the Book of Micah:

> It shall come to pass in the latter days that the mountain of the house of the Lord shall be established as the highest of the mountains . . . and peoples shall flow to it, and many nations shall come and say: "Come, let us go up to the mountain of the Lord, to the house of the God of Jacob; that he may teach us his ways and we may walk in his paths. . . . All the peoples walk each in the name of its god, but we will walk in the name of the Lord our God for ever and ever." [23]

Does not this last verse mean that, even for Christians who believe that the Messianic era is already here, the "latter days" mentioned in the text, we must hold that many will "walk in the name of their god" without recrimination and in good faith and conscience, even as Christians do in the name of Christ their Lord? Would not the denial of this in effect amount to passing judgment upon those religious beliefs and practices cherished by men which God alone has the right and power to judge? I believe it does; moreover, I believe that Christians should repudiate absolutely anything and everything which smacks of intolerance for the religious beliefs and practices of others.

Does all this mean then that Christian missionary activity is no longer necessary or proper? No, but it does mean that it has to be understood in a different light and carried out in a different manner and spirit than sometimes in the past. Christian missions can no longer be considered as a crusade or conquest of souls for Christ. Still, the command of Christ to "teach all nations" remains and must be carried out until the end of time. And this too is important for both Catholics and non-Catholics to understand.

Both should try to understand that, according to Catholic theology, the Church is necessarily a missionary community. As the Second Vatican Council teaches, "the pilgrim Church is missionary by her very nature." [24] The Church is convinced that it has something to say to this world and to all its peoples. The Church believes that it has a missionary duty of spreading the good news of salvation, so that as many as are inspired by the grace of the Holy Spirit may come to believe in Christ and His teaching. Even if men do not accept this belief—and probably most men will not—the Church still believes its message of redemption is of value and assistance to them also.

Properly understood, this is not uncomplimentary to non-Christians. On the contrary, it is an implicit compliment, inasmuch as Christian missionaries are thus treating others as fellow human beings worth speaking to and worth trying to attract and invite to an acceptance of what the Church has to offer. Within due limitations, there is a natural right to try to communicate one's doctrine, as there is also a natural right to listen to the doctrine of others and then either to accept it and support it, or reject it and peacefully oppose it.

It must be admitted that Catholic missionary work often did not give the impression of bestowing a compliment on non-Christians; in fact, it often gave the opposite impression. The Vatican Council has frankly acknowledged that the Church's members have at times acted in a manner which was less in accord with the spirit of the gospel and even opposed to it.[25] It is of the utmost importance that these mistakes not be repeated, and that future missionary activity be undertaken according to the authentic spirit of the gospel.

Non-Christians must try to realize that, as Emil Brunner has put it so well, "mission work does not arise from any arrogance in the Christian Church; mission is its cause and its life. The Church exists by mission, just as fire exists by burning. Where there is no mission, there is no Church, and where there is neither Church nor mission, there is no faith."[26] So essential is mission to the Church that non-Christians would be asking the Church to give up its very existence if they were to ask it to give up its missionary activity.[27] The Church is missionary by its very nature and must ever strive to carry out the work of evangelization, namely, of presenting Jesus Christ so that as many men as possible may come to know Him, to accept Him as their Savior, and to serve Him and their fellowmen in Him.

Christians today are convinced that they face together a non-Christian world of vast proportions and therefore they must give due attention to ecumenical activities as well as to missionary activities. This means, I believe, that Catholics ought to assist other Christians in living more faithfully their form of Christianity. This appears to be merely a realistic appraisal of the situation obtaining in an inevitably pluralistic world. To become more Christian is surely the will of God for all who believe in Christ and are baptized, and by helping Christians within and without one's own church, we are helping them to enter more fully into God's plan for them.

There is a certain analogy between the spirit of Christian ecumenism and missionary activity, even though the two are distinct in their methods. Analogously, should we not go one step further and agree with Gandhi that while we should strive to make Christians better Christians, we ought also to make Moslems better Moslems, Hindus better Hindus, and Jews better Jews? From a realistic point of view, it is doubtful that Christians can really assist non-Christians to be better followers of their religion, even if they can help each other to some degree to be better Christians. Furthermore, non-Christians might consider such a presumption to be more than a bit arrogant.

What is important, however, is the attitude and spirit. Even though Christians might wish and hope and desire that all others might also, as they are, be followers of Christ, it is not at all contrary to Catholic teaching to want them to practice more faithfully that religion which they in good conscience believe to be the right religion for them, at least in those matters which we also consider to be true and good. It would be too much, however, to expect that we can conscientiously acknowledge and promote everything in every non-Christian religion, for there are some things unacceptable in the light of Catholic teaching.

Nevertheless, the above conclusion seems inescapable. At the same time it does not conflict with the notion of missionary activity rightly understood in terms of dialogue, in terms of a conversation in which there is a mutual giving and receiving, teaching and learning, in an atmosphere of mutual esteem and respect. Indeed, the Council exhorts Catholics to undertake dialogue with members of other religions.

But if at the end of the dialogue, non-Christians wish to retain their religion, Catholics must not only give in gracefully but, even further, let them know that they would sincerely like them to be better followers of their chosen religion and leave all matters to Almighty God. For "all the peoples walk each in the name of its god, but we still walk in the name of the Lord our God, Jesus Christ, for ever and ever."

In conclusion, it is important that Catholics and others come to a clearer understanding of the goals and objectives of Catholic missionary work. An adequate and systematic presentation of these goals is still lacking, but they can be summed up better under the headings of Christian witness and service rather than of proselytizing and conversion.

The missionary goals must be seen more clearly in the light of present theological teaching and attitudes in regard to ecumenism, religious freedom, the place of other religions in salvation history. It is no admission of defeat to acknowledge that we neither can nor should attempt to "convert the world." It is essential to realize that the mandate of Christ is to evangelize the world, not to convert it. The difference between the two must be clearly seen and not confused. Christians then will be enabled to rise to the task committed to them by the Lord: that of evangelizing the world, even as the early Christians evangelized the world known to them. Their small numbers did not deter the early struggling Christian community, for they did not suffer from the illusion that evangelizing was identified with converting, as later Christians did.

The Church must seek its end in directing man's vision upwards to higher things and not consider its success as commensurate with territorial or numerical expansion on the horizontal level. Its concern must not be on its own growth and expansion but rather on helping all men to realize better the goal for which all were created by an all-loving, all-merciful God. The mission must not seek to develop an earthly kingdom but to lead all men to the heavenly Kingdom.

Finally, it should be noted that the mission and conversion to God and to Christ must be understood in its eschatological aspect. The Council touched on the mystery involved in this when it declared:

> In company with the prophets and the Apostle Paul, the Church awaits that day, known to God alone, on which all peoples will address the Lord in a single voice and serve him with one accord.[28]

NOTES

1. Thomas Ohm, *Asia Looks at Western Christianity* (New York: Herder and Herder, 1959), pp. 201–202.
2. Luke 12:32.
3. Mark 4:3–9, 13–20; Luke 8:5–8, 11–15.
4. Matt. 13:24–30, 36–43.
5. Matt. 23:15.
6. Matt. 28:19–20.
7. Laurentius Brancati, *Commentaria in Tertium Librum Sententiarum Joannis Duns Scoti*, Tomus III, pars 2a, Romae 1673 (Typis Sacrae Congregationis de Propaganda Fide), Disp. XVIII, art. 10.
8. It might be noted also that neither does one find in St. Paul's epistles any exhortation to his readers to seek converts and the expansion of Christianity; on the contrary, he gives testimony to the fact that this was being done, and evidently in a satisfactory manner. The same can be said of the Fathers, who tended to assume the *de facto* universality of the Church.

9. Joseph Schmidlin, *Catholic Mission History*, trans. Matthias Braun, SVD (Techny, Ill.: Mission Press, 1933), p. 91.

10. Thomas a Jesu, *De Procuranda Salute Omnium Gentium* (Antverpiae, 1613), Lib. III, Cap. 3. "Hanc enim heri semitam ita voluit Deus, ut per religiosas familias, quae Christiani orbis fuere seminaria ab Apostolorum fere temporibus, maxime vero hac nostra aetate, ut supra demonstravimus, fere totius orbis conversio procuretur."

11. Cf. *Juris Pontificis de Propaganda Fide*, ed. Raphael de Martini (Romae, 1888), I, 2ff. and 87ff.

12. 1 Cor. 3:6.

13. *Decree on Ecumenism*, #4. This document uses the term "conversion" to signify interior renewal, not outward adherence to the Church.

14. Cf. Walter M. Abbott, S.J., gen. ed., *The Documents of Vatican II* (New York: Herder and Herder, 1966), p. 671.

15. *Ecclesiam Suam*, A.A.S., LVI, 644.

16. *Constitution on the Sacred Liturgy*, #9.

17. *Decree on Missionary Activity*, #13.

18. Cf. K. Rahner and H. Vorgrimler, *Theological Dictionary* (New York: Herder and Herder, 1965), p. 102.

19. *Declaration of the Relationship of the Church to Non-Christian Religions*, #2.

20. *Declaration on Religious Freedom*, #2–9.

21. Abraham Joshua Heschel, "No Religion is an Island," *Union Seminary Quarterly Review* 21, Vol. XXI, no. 2, part 1 (January 1966), 117–134.

22. Acts 5:38–39, RSV.

23. Micah 4:1–5, RSV.

24. *Decree on Missionary Activity*, #2.

25. *Declaration on Religious Freedom*, #12.

26. Emil Brunner, *The Word and the World*, 2nd ed. (London, 1932), p. 108. Quoted in Olav G. Myklebust, *The Study of Missions in Theological Education* (Oslo: Egede Instituttet, 1955), I, 27.

27. I would like to emphasize that in saying this, a clear distinction must be made between missionary action as essential to the Church and any given historical expression in the form of missionary movement. Missionary action is always necessary, yet we must disinherit many features of the past missionary movement.

28. *Declaration on the Relationship of the Church to Non-Christian Religions*, #4. Cf. Wisd. 3:9; Isa. 66:23; Ps. 65:4; Rom. 11:11–32.

B. NO! THE CHANGING NATURE OF MISSION

Avery Dulles

By way of introduction, I should mention that I am not a specialized missiologist, still less a missionary. But at a meeting such as this, some of you might wish to hear the views of a nonspecialist who has been making efforts to keep abreast of general developments in the larger theological picture. Missiologists today are keenly interested in this larger picture, because they are aware that the nature of mission has to be understood in the light of broader questions, such as the nature of grace, of salvation, and of the Church.

The topic to which I have been asked to speak is "The Changing Nature of Mission." The topic itself evidently presupposes two things: first, that the Church in any age is missionary in character, and secondly, that the manner in which mission is conducted must differ from one age to the next. It is important not to lose sight of either of these presuppositions.

The Church is essentially missionary because Christ's redemptive action, which constitutes the core of the Christian message, profoundly affects all men. The risen Christ made it clear to the apostles that the good news of salvation was to be preached all over the world till the end of time. If the Church ceased to be mission-oriented and restricted its ministries to a certain portion of the human race, it would cease to reflect the universal dimensions of Christ's redemptive love, and thus be false to its own essential nature as universal sacrament of salvation. Christianity lives off the recognition that, thanks to Jesus Christ, there is no longer any distinction between Jew and Gentile or between Greek and barbarian; for, as Paul put it, "here is the same Lord of all, rich towards all who call upon him" (Rom. 10:12).

On the other hand, we live in a changing world. The way in which the gospel was proclaimed in New Testament times was

---

Avery Dulles is Professor of Systematic Theology, Woodstock College, Maryland. This address was given at the 18th annual meeting of the Mission Sending Societies, Sept. 18, 1967, Washington, D.C.

entirely appropriate to the first century, but may not be equally appropriate to ours. For example, the resurrection of Christ was then a fresh piece of news about what God had done only a few years before, within the memory of living men. By today it is a story which has become almost trite for the retelling, and scarcely sounds like news either to believers or unbelievers. A man would make himself ridiculous if he came rushing on the scene shouting, "Christ is risen."

We must be careful, then, to present Christianity in terms which make sense to modern man and are adapted to the current world situation. In some ways this should not be too difficult. The universalism of Christianity has special relevance at a time when the various nations and continents are ceasing to enjoy their own particular histories and are being swept, whether they like it or not, into one common history in which each is affected by the problems of all the rest. Amid the present anxiety concerning world hunger, war, and dissension, men look spontaneously to Christianity, with its message of love and reconciliation, to make a contribution. By courageously sharing the joys and hopes, griefs and anxieties of men of our age, and seeking to apply everywhere the medicine of the gospel, Christianity can discharge its worldwide missionary responsibility in a new and significant way.

We are emerging from a period in which the Church felt itself to be encircled by hostile powers and reacted in a polemical fashion. In the Counter Reformation the Church took on some of the attributes of a closed society; it tended to become isolated, rigid, and narrow. Today, thanks in great part to Vatican II, the Church is seeking to reaffirm its true nature as an open society, positively related to all that is humanly good and true. In the conduct of the missions, this demands special care to avoid tactics that could seem to be importunate, arrogant, or disrespectful of human freedom. Paul VI in his great encyclical, *Ecclesiam Suam*, outlined a program of what he called "missionary dialogue." In the spirit of this encyclical I should like to suggest five areas in which the Church's missionary endeavor is being rapidly transformed under the influence of recent theological developments.

1. *Evangelization*

In the past it was commonly thought that those who did not come to explicit belief in Christ and receive sacramental baptism had at best a poor chance of saving their souls. Many respected theologians argued that this theological conviction was a necessary basis in the absence of which the Church's missionary effort would collapse. But as a result of the clear teaching of Vatican II, it is evident that all men—whether evangelized or not—receive the helps necessary for salvation, and that those who, without personal fault, do not arrive at explicit belief in God or in Christ, may nevertheless save their souls if, with the help of divine grace, they strive to live a good life (Cf. *Lumen gentium,* n. 16; *Gaudium et spes,* n. 22).

Convinced that God's grace is at work among all peoples, even those who do not believe in Him, missionaries today are not frantically concerned with statistics on baptisms, as if these were the primary measure of their success. On the other hand, the Church is newly conscious of its missionary responsibility toward the non-Christian who wishes to remain such. By word and example the missionary can sustain idealism and hope in situations where men might otherwise fall into cynicism and despair. He can stimulate non-Christians to live according to their highest ideals, and even to examine whether these ideals are high enough. In this way the missionary injects the leaven of the gospel into other civilizations and helps men everywhere to live in a manner more pleasing to God.

While the modern missionary is not ashamed to profess his faith when the occasion calls for forthright testimony, he avoids doing so in an aggressive way that would be tactless and offensive. Respecting the right of others to follow their conscience, and not wishing to restrict their full psychological freedom, he refrains from exerting pressure on potential converts by promises or threats. Vatican II in its Declaration on Religious Freedom explicitly discountenances "any manner of action which might seem to carry a hint of coercion or a kind of persuasion that would be dishonorable or unworthy, especially in dealing with poor or uneducated people" (n. 4).

2. *Religious Dialogue*

In the past it was generally held that religions other than Christianity, especially the nonbiblical religions, were idolatrous, displeasing to God, and incapable of mediating valid religious knowledge. St. Francis Xavier, like others in his time, took it for granted that the Hindus and Buddhists worshiped demons. But Vatican II, in its Declaration on the Non-Christian Religions, takes a much more optimistic view of these other faiths. It holds (n. 2) that they "often reflect a ray of that Truth which enlightens all men"—i.e., of Christ the eternal Word of God. Many theologians today hold that the great religions of the world contain authentic elements of divine revelation and should therefore be treated with great reverence, even though on some points they stand in need of correction.

As a result of this theological development, the missionary today is careful to avoid the domineering and arrogant attitudes which in the past have often provoked resentment, especially among the most highly cultured and deeply religious non-Christians. He considers it an essential part of his task to initiate respectful dialogue with these other faiths, not in a spirit of partisan debate, but with a humble desire to learn from them and to enrich them with whatever they can gain through contact with Christianity. He considers that Christianity itself has much to gain from hearing the questions and criticisms put to it by sincere adherents to other religions.

3. *Ecumenism*

Since the Reformation, the various branches of Christianity have engaged in a disedifying power struggle among themselves. They have often denigrated one another to impede each other's work. As Vatican II notes at the opening of its Decree on Ecumenism (n. 1), such discord "provides a stumbling block to the world and inflicts damage on the most holy cause of proclaiming the good news to every creature." In a very bold and constructive paragraph (n. 15), the Decree on Missionary Activity gives guidelines for cooperation with other Christian groups:

> To the extent that their beliefs are common, they can make before the nations a common profession of faith in God and in Jesus Christ. They can collaborate in social and in technical projects as well as in cultural and religious ones. Let them work together especially for the sake of Christ, their common Lord. Let His Name be the bond that unites them! This cooperation should be undertaken not only among private persons, but also, according to the judgment of the local Ordinary, among Churches and ecclesial Communities and their enterprises.

The precise degree of ecumenical collaboration has to be worked out prudently in each place according to local circumstances, but the general principles here laid down are making an important impact on the mission picture in every land.

4. *Cultural Pluralism*

Due to an insufficient historical consciousness and an understandable preoccupation with heresy, missionaries in the past few centuries were very rigid in imposing European—even Latin—forms of Christianity on other continents, thus awakening not wholly unjustified fears of spiritual colonialism. The efforts of a few farsighted missionaries in the seventeenth century to devise authentically Indian and Chinese ways of practicing Christianity were not approved by Roman authorities. But Vatican Council II has introduced a more positive approach. In the Decree on Missionary Activity (n. 22) it states that the younger churches in mission lands "take to themselves in a wonderful exchange of all the riches of the nations which were given to Christ as an inheritance (cf. Ps. 2:8). From the customs and traditions of their people, from their wisdom and their learning, from their arts and sciences, these churches borrow all those things which can contribute to the glory of their Creator, the revelation of the Savior's grace, or the proper arrangement of Christian life" (n. 22). Other Council documents stress the fact that cultural pluralism in the Church is a great aid to the achievement of true catholicity. The Constitution on the Liturgy recommends bold adaptations to make ecclesiastical rites and ceremonies more meaningful to people of various cultures.

The age when Asians and Africans are compelled to practice their Christianity in European dress and language is fast drawing to a close. It is important for the enrichment of the total Church that these peoples should not be culturally uprooted but should devise truly indigenous forms of Christianity. The unity of the Churches does not require, but rather forbids, mechanical uniformity in ways of speaking and acting. A plurality of traditions, and a dynamic interaction between all the local churches, will make it easier for the great Church to avoid imprisonment in its own past forms and to respond more creatively to the demands of the new age that is upon us.

5. *Service to the World*

In recent centuries missionary activity has most commonly been envisaged as a means of aggrandizing the Church by the accession of new members. While missionaries have worked diligently in the service of the Church, they were often less successful in showing forth the servant character of the Church itself. While they were generous in ministering to temporal needs, there was a tendency to regard such service as a mere means of gaining converts, and thus to neglect the point so pithily expressed by Bonhoeffer: "The Church is her true self only when she exists for humanity." [1]

In our day it will not do to depict the Church as a foreign substance, having its own life and purposes, unrelated to those of mankind at large. To appear at all as a gospel—as good tidings—Christianity must prove its ability to contribute to man's quest for a more human community on earth, in which men are bound together by mutual respect, freedom and love. If Christianity is presented as a faith that weakens men's solidarity with the world and their sense of responsibility for its future, men of good will will be repelled.

Vatican II, especially in its Constitution on the Church, teaches that the Church exists not in order to exalt itself but to transform the world more and more into the Kingdom of God (n. 9). From this it follows that the missions must seek not simply to promote the interests of the institutional Church but to make the world a better and holier place. This thought appears in the Decree on Missionary Activity (n. 8): "The gospel has truly been a leaven of liberty and progress in human history, even in its temporal sphere, and always proves itself to be a leaven of brotherhood, of unity, and of peace. Therefore, not without cause is Christ hailed as 'the expected of the nations and their Savior.'"

This new relationship of intimacy between the Church and the world raises many complex questions which I have no intention of discussing here. It will have to be asked, for instance, to what extent the Church should put its support behind worthy humanitarian causes and to what extent it should maintain its own charitable programs and institutions. But however these questions are resolved in particular cases, it is necessary that the Church should maintain an effective presence to instill its own vision of man. The convinced Christian, looking upon his neighbor as a child of God, called to eternal life and redeemed by the blood of Christ, will love and care for his fellow man in a distinctive way.

Today as always, the distinguishing marks of Christian missionary endeavor must be the attitudes of Christ himself, the pattern of missionaries. This comparison is eloquently developed in the Constitution on the Church (n. 8):

> Just as Christ carried out the work of redemption in poverty and under oppression, so the Church is called to follow the same path in communicating to men the fruits of salvation. Christ Jesus, "though he was by nature God, . . . emptied himself, taking on the nature of a slave" (Phil. 2:6), and "being rich, he became poor" (2 Cor. 8:9) for our sakes. Thus, although the Church needs human resources to carry out her mission, she is not set up to seek earthly glory, but to proclaim humility and self-sacrifice, even by her own example.

The missionary who abandons the comforts of home to go forth to the ends of the earth, and to spread the charity of Christ where there would otherwise be desolation and despair, perpetuates Christ's saving presence in the world. As long as Christianity has power to evoke this type of self-sacrificing love, there will be missionary vocations. And as long as missionaries are clearly animated by an altruistic love, such as faith alone can sustain, men of good will will be attracted to the Church and will seek to share in the dynamism of its life. If there are few converts it is generally because there are few such Christians. And where Christian missionaries generously spend themselves for others, they cannot help but radiate the peace and joy of Christ.

Since this talk was prepared before I had any knowledge of what Father Hoffman was going to say, I feel that I should add a few words to my prepared text to indicate the extent of my agreements and disagreements with him. He has made this easy by neatly dividing his address into four propositions, on each of which I shall comment briefly.

1. That the foreign missionary movement as we have known it is at an end. The statement seems to be ambiguous. Of course there are changes and adaptations needed for our times, but I do not see that we should speak of an "end." I do not agree that the purpose of the foreign missionary movement has already been achieved. There are huge parts of the globe where the gospel has as yet made practically no impression, and other parts where, for one reason or another, the local churches are in grave need of outside help for personnel and material resources.

2. That we should do away with the Church's missionary organization and structure in order that the whole Church may become missionary. I agree that the Church as a whole is missionary, though at some points in his talk Father Hoffman seems to say that the Church is not supposed to conduct missionary activity. But assuming that the Church, under God, should engage in mission, I think there will always be need for specialists and service organizations which deal with this branch of activity. It is quite true, as Father Hoffman says, that the Colonial Office is dead; but missionary activity is not colonization. A more apt parallel would be the Foreign Office. Every country today is heavily engaged in diplomatic activity, and needs persons and structures specializing in this. So likewise the Church needs missionary bureaus and personnel in order to maintain everywhere an intelligent interest in and support for the missionary task.

3. That the role of the clergy and religious in the missions is diminishing. I prefer to say that there is an increasing scope for lay missionaries. But if a person is to go abroad in the service of Christ and the gospel, I think that he or she is living a consecrated life, and I see no reason why such a person should not seal this inner consecration by an external profession which makes him or her a religious in the canonical sense. This canonical question is however of secondary importance. The main thing is that there should be missionaries who reflect the authentic features of Christ.

4. That the laity must assume a larger role. I agree. Let that role be as large as possible. But I do not agree with Father Hoffman's apparent conviction that the evolution of human society makes evangelization unnecessary. Since it is important that people should know and believe in their divine Redeemer, Christian missionaries must continue to bear witness to the fact that Jesus Christ is the Savior of the human race and that there is salvation in no other name under heaven. Evolution and development are excellent things, but it still remains true that men are in need of conversion. While the Church must indeed serve the world, it can best do so by performing its own distinctive kind of service, namely, to bring men the fruits of Christ's redemptive action through word and sacrament, teaching and example.

Father Hoffman says that ours is a revolutionary era. He is correct. But I should be very much afraid of any revolution which attempted to achieve the true good of humanity apart from the knowledge and love of God in Christ Jesus. And I would add that wherever that knowledge and love burn brightly, God is establishing His Church. Science and technology without Christ will never lead to the Kingdom of God. The permanent and indispensable task of the missions—which is to assist in the conversion of men to God in Christ, and to gather them together into the one Church of God—is as urgent today as it ever was. I conclude then, the Christian missionary effort should not be dismantled but greatly intensified, in a manner suited to the needs of the present hour.

NOTES

1. Dietrich Bonhoeffer, *Letters and Papers from Prison* (New York: The Macmillan Company, 1962), p. 239.

PART III

1965-1968: Church Growth and Mission Strategy

A. WRONG STRATEGY—THE REAL CRISIS IN MISSION

Donald McGavran

What is correct strategy in the Christian mission? This question stands at the heart of the missionary dilemma today. Until the major direction is determined and agreed, the effectiveness of the missionary enterprise is sorely diminished. No question is more important than this: What are the policies, patterns, goals and principles of highest urgency?

For many, mission is essentially seed-sowing from Europe and America to the ends of the earth. It has been this for a hundred and fifty years. The gospel must be proclaimed. Christian witness must be given. The light must penetrate. The Church must spread. The populations of mankind must hear. Bibles and Gospels must be translated into many languages. But the objective and measurable growth of churches must neither be expected nor counted as a criterion of effectiveness. Some followers of this strategy preach for a witness before the return of the Lord, not expecting many churches to be established. Others, not stressing the return of our Lord, working where little church growth has been seen, similarly work on, expecting little growth. For both, correct policy in mission is witness, seed-sowing, and confronting men with the reality and power of God's Kingdom—whether they heed the gospel or not.

For others, correct strategy consists in making those organizational adjustments in missions that will enable them to survive in the new age. Turning over responsibility and authority to nationals, transferring power from mission to church, merging several weak denominations to make one strong, becoming ecumenical, increasing the degree of unity between Christians—all these and similar actions are said to be the essential mission policies in this and succeeding decades.

For still others (bemused by intricate questions about how one gets men really to listen and learn, how one avoids conflict situa-

---

"Wrong Strategy" originally appeared in *The International Review of Missions,* October 1965.

tions in which Christians preach at others for generations to no effect), effective mission consists in the quiet Christian presence. Mission is not discipling, not witness and not church-planting; but rather, it is simply being there, as Charles de Foucald said, "with a presence willed and determined as a witness to the love of Christ." This quietism is powerfully reinforced by that branch of mission which has been laboring for decades in hostile populations, where to survive at all was victory. The service arms of the Church prefer this definition of mission and back this strategy. Some in this third camp are hesitant to use the word "strategy." They feel it is too aggressive. How would we feel toward communists, they ask, if they were using a "strategy" to displace our ideology with theirs?

A fourth multitude of mission leaders is searching for a common "mission to the world," which all Christians can carry out together. For this fourth camp, mission is partnership in obedience—any kind of obedience, to any kind of Christian end beyond the local church. Correct strategy is simply working together in any task committed to any Christian by the Lord of the Church. The following "strategy of the fifties" is what many missionary thinkers are saying today:

> The Christian mission to the world is simply this: to proclaim the whole gospel, to all of man, in all his needs, wherever he lives, whatever he does. The gospel must be addressed to the whole man to the geographical, political and economic ends of the earth. Every Christian and every church in all continents shares in the mission. Every church, according to the grace God has given it, and the circumstances in which it finds itself, is called to mission. Small and large, old and young—all churches are partners in obedience. They should all be united in carrying out "mission under God." Doing just this is correct strategy in mission today.

This statement includes each of the first three strategies stated above. It takes account of the ecumenical temper. It recognizes that this is the age of the Africasian churches. It can be used by quietists. It can be used by activists. It can be used by those preaching for a witness and engaged in seed-sowing evangelism and service. It has the most prestige of any concept of mission today. Phrased in many ways by many missiologists, this "strategy of the fifties" has achieved a position of unique authority. Many accept it as the consensus of intelligent thinking about Christian mission today. Their mission is conditioned by this strategy or (if that word is distasteful to them) these overriding policies and theological presuppositions.

It is time to raise the question whether, instead of being right, this strategy of the fifties is at best partial, at worst thoroughly wrong—a well-intentioned but misleading policy, a basic error. In 1943 President Franklin D. Roosevelt summoned General MacArthur to Pearl Harbor for a top-level conference. The story is told in MacArthur's reminiscences. The conference was to determine what strategy should govern the vast effort about to be made to win the war in the Pacific. The admirals were there with their staffs, advocating that the Philippines should be by-passed and a direct assault made on Japan itself. MacArthur, on the contrary, defended an island-hopping campaign culminating in the recapture of the Philippines, thus shutting off the stream of raw materials so essential to Japan's continued war effort. MacArthur's was the strategy adopted—to the enormous saving of life and the greater effectiveness of the campaign.

Christian missions have no Roosevelt to convene a strategy conference to decide what is the most effective course of action. Instead, each missionary and leader concerned with world mission thinks through missions today and comes to the position that he considers is God's will for him. Later, groups of individuals engaged in mission formulate what they consider essential policy. To these fellow laborers, this article is directed. Before them I lay the strategy of the fifties, and plead for a more up-to-date, effective, and biblical course of action. It seems to me that the strategy of the fifties has five serious defects.

First, it attempts to take in everything that the Church and the Christian faith ought to do. Let it be agreed that the Church (or some part of it) ought to do many tasks. The Church of Jesus Christ is a vast assemblage facing limitless needs and problems. Possibly the whole Church assembled in plenary session would formulate such a statement of its total task. But since the whole Church has never yet been assembled in plenary session and is not likely to be, surely it is rather too much to expect of divisions of world mission and evangelism, foreign missionary societies, overseas ministries and similar bodies that they should embrace every aspect of the Christian enterprise. Is there no danger that the task will become so broad that it becomes thin? Indeed, that this strategy of the fifties is in grave danger of becoming ineffective is obvious when one observes the inadequate church growth in country after country.

Secondly, this strategy includes church-planting as one of its many emphases, but steadfastly resists focusing on church-planting as partisan and narrow. It frequently does not even mention the multiplication of churches, seemingly assuming that, if various aspects of mission are carried out, church-planting of some sort will somehow result. Naturally, with a low view of church-planting, this strategy achieves little of it; and pessimistically defends small growth as good mission—theologically correct, all that Christians should aim for and, in any case, all they are likely to obtain.

Thirdly, this strategy has no answers to pressing problems. It has no answer to the population explosion, except that Christians resign themselves to coexistence with other religions. It has no answer to static younger churches, except to pour in more money. It has no answer to the harvesting of responsive populations, except to wonder whether talk of responsive populations is not greatly exaggerated.

Fourthly, this strategy is really a defense of the existing machine of mission, its departments, vested interests, bureaucracies, and massive service arms. These all shelter under slogans such as "the whole gospel," "all its fullness" and "the whole man." No one doubts that there is a whole gospel, but that is not the issue. The issue is whether the apostles shall wait on tables. The issue is whether Paul at Troas, hearing "Come over to Macedonia and help us," shall send over some specialists to enter into dialogue with the priests of Jove and Venus, and others to assist a revolt against Roman oppression and slaveholding. The issue is that, while we proclaim "the whole gospel" to "the whole man," opportunities for propagating the Christian religion are neglected. Opportunity after opportunity to win the winnable while they are winnable and to multiply churches in receptive populations is lost. Certainly, the whole gospel is good. Balanced rations for sheep are good—but the only sheep who can be fed with such rations are those that have first been found and brought into the fold. The whole gospel for all mankind means little, unless it is preceded by stupendous church-planting. The gospel is empty words until it is believed and obeyed. Christ died for all, but vast multitudes do not know this; and many who do know, reject Him. Only those who are baptized into Christ and become responsible members of His Body are made into new creatures.

In the fifth place, this strategy of the fifties is theologically and biblically wrong. It does not throb with Christ's passion for men's eternal redemption. It makes haste to point out that there are many kinds of redemption and appears equally in favor of all. It does not blaze with certainty that man, the immortal soul, was created in the image of God, is not in that image now, and must regain it through the saving work of Christ. It does not seem to know which part of the Christian religion is center and which is periphery. It loses the purpose for which the organization was created in maintaining the organization to carry out the purpose.

When it convenes its conferences, it frequently expends all its time on everything except the propagation of the Christian religion. It does not lack those who shudder at the thought of the propagation of the Christian religion, preferring to talk about confronting men with the cosmic Christ. For example, at a four-day conference to consider Asian missionaries, the East Asia Christian Council spent all its time talking about the relationship of Asian missionaries to existing churches and existing Christians, and said very little indeed about Asian missionaries propagating their faith.

The crisis in the Christian mission is that many expecting defeat today are backing a course of action that leads to defeat. The outcome is concealed behind the vast wealth and prestige of the churches of Europe and America, but can be readily seen if one notes the diminishing proportion of the world's population that calls itself Christian. It has become orthodox to adhere to a strategy which, with the best intentions, is nevertheless in grave danger of betraying the Christian mission. Mission has been jockeyed into a broad basic policy which cannot gain the very ends it devoutly desires. It lacks a bold, creative plan for propagating the gospel—and loves its lack. This is its crisis.

In the magazine *World Encounter* (February 1965, p. 12), Pierce Beaver recently wrote these words: "Evangelism is made in three forms: the spoken and printed Word, the dramatic Word of service, and the visible Word of Christian unity." This general statement is in danger of subordinating the spread of the gospel to the current sacred triad, *kerygma*, *diakonia*, and *koinonia*. Christian mission is intentionally, and constitutionally, by word and deed, proclaiming Christ as Lord and Savior and persuading sinful men to become His disciples. If it is not this, it is not Christian mission. Evangelism always *intends* to lead men to believe in Christ. Much of the "spoken and printed Word, the Word of service, and the visible Word of Christian unity" has no such intention. It spends all its effort in other directions. It insists that its effectiveness must not be measured by the number of those who become confessed Christians. On all these counts, the Word enshrined in innumerable good activities of the Church cannot be called Christian mission.

Make no mistake, these activities are good. Some of them are urgently necessary. But they are not evangelism. Worship, for example, is good; but worship is worship. It is not evangelism.

Seeing Christians worship, someone may occasionally be led to Jesus Christ, exactly as someone seeing a Christian pay his income-tax might be led to become a Christian. On the other hand, he might simply infer that paying income-tax is a prudent thing to do. When we call the multitude of good activities in which Christians must ever engage evangelism, we ensure that the particular Christian activity which intends that men shall believe on Him, die with Him in baptism, and rise with Him to newness of life will become less and less.

Good activities must be justified by their own rationale. They must stand on their own feet. They must neither masquerade as evangelism nor diminish evangelism. Good activities must be seen as such. Evangelism must appear as evangelism. This truth is especially germane to Christian mission which is always carried out in particular populations.

Let us take one particular population, a factory community. What does mission mean in it? Before we can answer, we must know more about the factory community. Is it 100 percent Hindu, Protestant or Roman Catholic? Are 60 percent of its people baptized, of whom a few are earnest Christians? Are the owners of the factory Christians or violently opposed to Christ? Is the problem renewal—getting the many existing Christians to carry their Christianity over from the worship service on Sunday to the shop meeting on Wednesday night? Or is it conversion—getting some of the Marxists or Hindus who make up the labor force to become baptized, practicing disciples of the Lord Jesus? Or is it social action—getting the Christian majority to devise and institute Christian solutions to human problems?

Again, let us take some instances of desirable social action. The village in West Irian which recently became Christian should deter girls from mutilating themselves after their brothers have died in battle. The *barrio* in the Philippines which has just become Christian should act corporately to outlaw the almost ritual gambling that keeps many desperately poor. Christians in the United States do well to conduct freedom schools in Mississippi and Chicago. The passive resistance of Christians in India to break the oppression of caste is good. Sharing knowledge by building and maintaining Christian schools and colleges is excellent. But in all these good things, we must first have some Christians: no Christians, none of these good things. And in millions of communities there are no Christians.

The crisis in missions is this: it is possible to wax enthusiastic about factory evangelism, confrontation, dialogue, the whole gospel, the whole man, and many other good things, without intending or achieving any planting of new churches, or winning any unbelievers to the Christian faith. Mission in the 1960s becomes renewal witness, outreach, rapprochement, penetration—there is no limit to the vague, elastic words which have only one thing in common: they do not require the baptism of bodies, the salvation of souls, and the building of visible new churches. Following one of these words too often becomes acceptable regular mission.

To be sure, regular mission (in which hundreds of thousands of Christians, nationals and missionaries, are each year engaged as professionals) issues here and there in a certain amount of church-planting, and occasionally in a dramatic surge of the Church into a new population. That it does so is often more a testimony to the vitality of the faith than to the intention of the protagonists.

To advocate this vague, inclusive program as the *esse* of Christian mission is wrong diagnosis and wrong strategy. What the world needs is not "more of everything, whether churches multiply or not." What the fantastically mounting population of this world needs is fantastically multiplying churches which will enable liberated populations, filled with the Holy Spirit, to generate their own Calvins, Wesleys, Wilberforces and Martin Luther Kings, and their own sober, godly and fruitful societies.

Partisan emphasis on peripheral aspects of the task, justifying them theologically as the whole and substituting them for an objective, measurable growth of the Church, is poison, not food. It is more likely to weaken the patient than to promote his abounding health.

So much for the wrong strategy. What are some of the outlines of today's right strategy?

Right strategy tailors mission to fit each of the thousands of separate communities, so that in it the Church may grow. There is no one strategy which is right everywhere. There is no one humanity in which the Church grows. The one world we often speak of is made up of numerous ethnic units, suddenly brought close together but not yet fused into one race. Nor are they likely to be so fused in the near future.

At this point, the cultural overhang from Europe and America must be recognized and rejected. It is common for Christian thinkers today, shamed by the wicked racial distinctions practiced in so many communities, to plead for brotherhood. One recent writer says, "If ethnic, political and class lines combine with denominational and confessional differences to serve as the basis of Christian congregations, the Church will continue to pay the price of impotence both in witnessing and in growth. There is no longer room or justification in Africa for tribal or colonial or racial churches."

The hard fact is, however, that by far the largest number of *growing* churches are growing *in* some tribe or segment of society. Thus, the tremendous increase of Pentecostals in Latin America is in large measure due to the fact that they are frankly Christians of the masses. They multiply churches in the masses, not the classes. Their churches are made up of the masses and appeal to people of the masses. They are not constantly trying to crawl up into the middle classes, nor do they take a special pride in the fact that some of their members are middle- or upper-class folk. Similarly, in the Sudan Interior Mission churches in Ethiopia (where communicants have increased from a few dozen in 1936 to perhaps a hundred thousand today), 95 percent of the growth has taken place in the Wallamo and Kambatta tribes—and could not have taken place on any except a tribal basis.

That church growth generally takes place in some one ethnic unit is no denial of brotherhood. Nor should it be used as a reason for continuing ethnic distinctions in discipled populations. The Lord will indeed break down the dividing wall of hostility between the Jews and Gentiles, but only between those Jews and those Gentiles who become Christians. This means that at the discipling stage, right strategy in Christian mission must establish ethnic churches, must let Christ ride the chariot of tribal allegiance into the heart of the tribe. It also means that at the perfecting stage, when ethnic or cultural units have been discipled, right strategy in Christian mission must press forward to full brotherhood. Only the short-sighted and emotional will confuse these two stages. Right strategy must be tailored to fit each of the thousands of separate communities in which the Church grows.

Right strategy will also take church growth with life-and-death seriousness. Right strategy will not so focus attention on "many good things to do" that church growth is not desired. Church growth is not something which automatically takes place when good church and mission work is carried on. It is less than wise to expect that if we are but faithful Christians in a pietistic sense, the Church will somehow begin to grow. Only those who live on the accumulated debris of decades of defeat would neglect the tremendous conscious effort at church-planting recounted in 2 Corinthians 10 and 11. The harvest is not granted to those living kindly Christian lives in ripe wheat-fields. The harvest is granted only to those who arrive sickle in hand, labor all day, and have carts ready at noon to carry in the piled sheaves.

The continual checking of every aspect of Christian mission against the church growth achieved is the *esse* of right strategy. Methods of church and mission work, systems of training missionaries, forms of ministerial and pastoral training, ways of producing tens of thousands of unpaid leaders, church mergers and cooperative enterprises of various kinds, institutional expressions of the faith—all these must be checked against the growth of the Church.

Only a poor theology of church growth closes its eyes to anthropological and sociological factors in church growth and stubbornly asserts that the Holy Spirit alone grants church growth. Of course, the Holy Spirit grants church growth. God the Holy Spirit is truly the Life of the Church, as God the Son is her Lord. Yet full recognition of this truth should aid us in observing how the Holy Spirit uses the regularities of society to achieve His will. Right strategy will have a right theology of church growth—thoroughly biblical and thoroughly scientific.

Right strategy will devise hard, bold plans for planting churches, and will put them into execution. Nothing inhibits the reconciliation of men to God today more than to imagine that Christian mission can be carried out without conscious planning for church growth. Mission is not beautiful, inclusive statements about mission. Mission is not a quiet Christian influence in the world. Mission is not simply bearing witness to the Lord by word and deed. Mission is neither worshiping God according to the ancient rubrics of our Church nor meeting to discuss church and mission problems. Mission is not serving our fellow men and binding up their wounds. All these are good activities—but they can be carried on for a thousand years without reconciling anyone to God in Christ. While the churches have been doing exactly these things, Europe has become post-Christian.

Hard, bold plans for proclaiming Christ and persuading men to become His disciples and responsible members of His Church are a *sine qua non* of Christian mission. Their boldness will be enhanced by their tender, sympathetic approach to the bewildered multitudes of every nation. They are essential to right strategy.

Right strategy will divide the world into cultural units—those where Christian mission is correctly seed-sowing and those where it is correctly harvesting. Both kinds of culture are found, and there is no clear line between them. Wrong strategy fails to note the difference between responsive and resistant segments of society. Right strategy not only notes the difference, but constantly explores to discover ways of identifying each variety of population and of fitting the missionary effort of the Church correctly to each variety. Since innumerable cultures, each at a stage of development different from that of its neighbor, are found in all the continents, right strategy is continually asking, "What kind of Christian mission is best calculated to propagate the gospel in this ethnic unit at this stage, when the fathering Church is itself at a specific stage and has a specific kind of mission?"

Right strategy will deal with both individuals and man-in-society. Where individualism has seized whole populations, men exist as lone units, and urbanization has destroyed lineage and kin, there right strategy will use discipling methods calculated to confront truncated men with Christ and to graft or integrate them one by one into the new community built on Him. Where persons already exist as parts of a larger whole and each man knows himself to be not so much a particular individual as a particular tribe or caste, there right strategy will develop a theology and methodology which will induct peoples or segments of peoples into the Body of Christ. It will take Matthew 28:19 literally, and go out to make disciples of *ta ethnē*—the social units of which humanity is composed.

Right strategy understands the words of John Collier:

> Colonizer, missionary, moralist, idealist, crusader for causes, it is to the hurt of all that you love, to the defeat of your own purpose and the ruin of men, if you, plunging toward your aim in terms of individuals, aggregations of individuals, or external material results, ignorantly or impatiently by-pass the society.

Right strategy recognizes that church growth is an exceedingly complex process and cannot be commanded. Since it deals with persons and is moved upon by God the Holy Spirit, it is never a mechanical sequence. There is no short cut to it. No single formula achieves it. All judgments concerning it are partial. Some are actually wrong and must be corrected in later generations.

All this notwithstanding, the Church can learn more about church growth today than ever before. Churches can rise above petty partisanship, station loyalties, and denominational pride in their church and mission work. They can coolly ask, "How much of the Lord's assignment in discipling the nations have we accomplished?" They can draw on the lessons of one country and one denomination to assist missions in another country. There is no need to repeat the mistakes of previous generations and other branches of the Church.

Church growth is not some obscure process wrapped in a riddle and hidden in the murky depths of a muddy pond. Administrators of missions and churches and missionaries, though inevitably limited by their cultural heritage, can learn what kind of church growth is possible and likely in each subculture where they have work. Of the many varieties of church growth, which one should be promoted at this particular time in this particular ethnic unit—this is the crucial question that each churchman concerned with propagating the faith should ask himself. Church growth can be learned. A body of knowledge concerning how churches grow and how they stagnate can be built up. We can discover reasons why churches have grown. We can isolate causes for church increases.

The Church can develop right strategy in mission. All she has to do is to observe what has taken place in the hundreds of matchless laboratories which a hundred and sixty years of modern missions have provided. By amassing knowledge, by pooling the common experience of missions and churches, by assembling the evidences of instances where the Church was planted, where it grew, where it stopped growing, and where it never even started, she can discern which processes in which specific circumstances receive God's blessing and which do not. Right strategy will spend large sums of money and the lives of some of its best men and women in intensive research into the most effective ways and means of reconciling men to God and of multiplying churches.

Right strategy can be discerned, learned, taught, and executed. When it is, the enormous potential in today's missions will be realized. When it is, the confusion and frustration that mark so much mission today will happily become a thing of the past.

B. ANSWERS FROM THE WHOLE WORLD
1. Church Growth: A Faulty American Strategy

Walter J. Hollenweger

"Church growth, a matter of enormous importance, should never be seen as self-aggrandizement, but always as faithfulness to God. God wants men saved. He commands bringing the nations to faith and obedience. St. Paul in Romans 16:25ff. tells us that the gospel was revealed to this very end. Yet only as churches multiply fantastically among the millions of men who have no other way of knowing the Savior, is it possible for them to come to 'faith and obedience.' " [1] This requires "the baptism of bodies, the salvation of souls, and the building of visible new churches." [2] Because it makes "an eternal difference whether a man believes in Jesus Christ as God and Savior and becomes His disciple and a responsible member of His Church," [3] "fantastic church growth" is necessary.

This is to be the priority of all Christians, for which the "right strategy" must be sought, e.g., to concentrate on the people who "are standing with outstretched arms begging for knowledge of the Savior," and not continually to increase churches in America and Europe or to "waste time in modes of mission like dialogue and presence" which assume non-Christians hostile or unwinnable. "Multitudes today welcome proclamation and persuasion." [4] Therefore let's persuade them! We have to fish where the fish are.

This is in short the position of Donald McGavran, Director of the Institute of Church Growth at Fuller Theological Seminary, which he has expressed in a number of articles and books. When, with a view to stimulating a discussion of this subject, we sent one such article to several persons, we expected to receive a variety of favorable, interpretative, and critical responses.

It is probably not the duty of a guest editor to evaluate the

---

Walter J. Hollenweger is Secretary for Evangelism, Division of World Mission and Evangelism of the World Council of Churches, Geneva. His chapter and the eight which follow appeared in *The International Review of Missions*, July 1968.

different contributions and thus to enter into the debate. Instead, I shall attempt to reveal some points where the lines of different commentators have converged. Most of them criticize McGavran. Mathew P. John from the Syrian Orthodox Church questions strongly whether McGavran's understanding of church growth stands up to his own criterion, i.e., faithfulness to God. The biblical evidence quoted by McGavran does not—according to John—lead to the priority of "fantastically growing churches," unless McGavran were to read in Luke 12:31ff. "Seek ye first church growth. . . ." "To state that the problem of population explosion is to be met and solved by an explosion of the number of churches is not only misleading but irresponsible." [5] In some respects, McGavran's strategy treats people "as less than human and justifies the non-Christian critics of mission who describe it as a form of imperialism and domination." [6] Because McGavran isolates service from his understanding of mission, his strategy can perhaps include "techniques of manipulating social groups to produce predetermined changes." To this, McGavran answers: "Multitudes today welcome proclamation and persuasion." But it does not convince the Roman Catholic missionary, Jordan Bishop. In order to exclude all manipulation he would suggest for a time cutting off all money from the so-called home-bases.[7] Even if people want to be persuaded, taking hold "of man precisely where he is not free, making use of economic, psychological and sociological pressures in order to 'persuade' him to become Christ's disciple may well be a false gospel" and may lead to exchanging "one kind of servitude for another, and perhaps a worse one." [8] Examples are at hand for Bishop in Latin America.

Therefore to reject the "questions such as the meaning of Christianity as 'peripheral' in favor of 'an objective measurable growth of the Church' takes entirely too much for granted." [9] We have to ask whether what we multiply is the Church, whether it preaches the gospel, whether the conversions are authentic ("freed, one should add, not only from economic but also from sociological and psychological pressures").[10] Furthermore, the problem remains of spelling out the consequences of this discipleship in a variety of concrete situations. ". . . we do not have a 'pure gospel,' entirely freed from cultural interferences." [11]

J. B. A. Kessler, former missionary to Peru, draws our attention to the fact that some churches like the Moravians have exercised a permanent influence in Europe and North America in spite of their small size.[12]

One of McGavran's main points is: let the churches grow, "which will enable liberated populations, filled with the Holy

Spirit, to generate their own Calvins, Wesleys, Wilberforces, and Martin Luther Kings. . . ." [13] In order to achieve social justice, peace, adequate medical care, better education, increased food production, etc., "we must first have some Christians: no Christians, none of these good things." [14] To this, Bishop replies: "The fact is that many of these good things have been achieved or initiated without the intervention of Christians, or, as in Cuba, in the face of Christian opposition." [15] McGavran's friend, J. B. A. Kessler, states on the basis of thorough investigation that even some churches which adopt McGavran's strategy do not grow. "It is remarkable how few churches which really did try to extend themselves succeeded in achieving that kind of growth for which Dr. McGavran is looking." [16] Where churches are growing, the reason is that they are able to meet real needs and that they manage to communicate on the level of the masses. This can be studied in the Brazilian and Chilean Pentecostals, and also among the South African Zionists and the Kimbanguists of the Congo.[17]

This fact is also recognized by John B. Housley's review of J. B. A. Kessler's thesis on Peru and Chile. But he goes on to ask whether it is possible for other forms of Protestantism to emulate the strategy of Chilean Pentecostalism. He considers this kind of church growth a "transitory phase of Christian presence leading to a genuine permeation of the culture." [18] But this is exactly the view of McGavran. First discipling and baptizing, and then leading on into the broader responsibility of Christian existence, a view which is also shared by the Pentecostal Melvin S. Hodges. But Hodges does not seem to expect much social involvement after conversion, as the imminent coming of the Lord will solve the social problems.

This of course is a process which has often been expected by missionary movements. However, when institutional and structural problems arose—and the Lord was tarrying, as He evidently still does, although some of us really think that His advent is overdue—they have had to seek durable solutions for social and political problems.

It is interesting to see Hodges' statement that the divine direction of mission, the spiritual strategy, includes variety for each local situation. This is necessary for all Pentecostal mission, as it relies mainly on the witness of the newly converted. Together with Marie-Louise Martin, Hodges stresses the "somatic" aspect of evangelism—Hodges through healing, Martin through diakonia.

J. G. Davies, an Anglican professor, has titled his contribution "A Critique." He criticizes the concept of church growth as "planting denominations," a point which is also taken up by Kessler, who thinks that, since Vatican II, missionaries have to ask themselves seriously whether they are carrying on mission or proselytism. And Marie-Louise Martin suggests that in order to overcome this difficulty, ecumenical teams recruited from different denominations might be created.

But even if we had a truly ecumenical Church, Davies would see in McGavran's strategy merely "a plan for survival" and not obedience to the Great Commission, because it isolates mission from the rest of Christian existence and from the life of the Church as a whole. The Church is a missionary Church or it is no Church.

What is such a missionary Church? David Gill, in his analysis of the 1928 Jerusalem Conference, has shown very clearly that at an early stage the IMC saw "Christ's presence in other religions." Paton contradicted at that time McGavran's "no Christians, none of these good things," when he wrote: "We are probably all familiar with men who not only make no profession of religious faith but have none; who are nevertheless among the foremost in the service of their fellow men for the removal of oppression and the succour of the weak." [19] The whole secularization debate seems to have been foreshadowed at Jerusalem, and points of view which have more recently become familiar through the works of Arend van Leeuwen and Harvey Cox were expressed forty years ago, e.g., that the scientific world-view "is heavily indebted to Christianity." And Gill reminds us: "Those who now seek to direct the ecumenical movement more towards the world are not perverting it but rather recalling it to a neglected dimension of its work."

I was interested to test the reaction of a man who had—together with Bonhoeffer—refused "the option taken by the majority of the German Christians, who were prepared to withhold their protest against the persecution of the Jews and against the Government's foreign policy, lest it should impede their opportunities for church growth and evangelism." [20] So, I gave McGavran's "American Concept" to Axel von dem Bussche, a Lutheran layman from West Germany, who is at present serving on the staff of the World Council of Churches. His special field, economic growth, includes such questions as development, the food gap, and population problems. During the Second World War he was active in the resistance movement against Hitler.[21] When asked about his reactions to Dr. McGavran's "Wrong Strategy," Mr. von dem Bussche replied along the following lines:

"Towards the end of this century, Christians will comprise no more than 8 percent of the world's population—assuming that present demographic growth will not be arrested in some unforeseen manner. This figure is, however, no indication of the quality of faith and witness, or of the 'Christian credibility' which we may expect to find in the world, as little as one generation hence.

"Even the best missionary strategy with a conventional approach to the field of church-planting and church growth will have no material effect upon this prognosis. More important still is the fact that this 8 percent will be mainly concentrated in the regions of the world now best known as the 'temperate zones.' In East and Southeast Asia, Christians will constitute a minority of under 1 percent, or less in sectors which are predominantly Muslim. We cannot predict the future of Christianity in the Soviet Union, where faith may be strong, despite its absence amongst the ruling 'classes.'

"In Latin America, one is tempted to forecast a new type of Christian spiritualism, which will bear the features of pre-Columbian culture, Marxist social ethics, and Roman Catholic liturgy, mingled with the 'leaven' of Protestantism.[22]

"The issues raised by Dr. McGavran are existential for every Christian. Although myself a layman, I should like to consider that I am a missionary—if the term could be freed from association with the nineteenth century. The article's deductions and conclusions stem from a serious and sincere attempt to cope with real problems. But like everybody, the author cannot avoid being marked by the framework of his cultural background, his hemisphere, even his nation. As a Central European, I know how difficult it is to outgrow or overcome such bonds—although I hasten to add that they vary greatly, owing to environmental, regional, emotional, historical—in short, 'tribal' factors.

"Hesitantly and with strong reservations, I am inclined therefore to link Dr. McGavran's approach with values and patterns which have developed and have remained unchallenged ever since the United States' founding fathers achieved independence: witness the drive towards the Pacific and into Mexico; contacts with Japan and the rest of Asia; involvement with Latin America; and unequalled contributions to freedom in Europe and other parts of the world. This story of almost unlimited success has conditioned historical thinking and business philosophy. Indeed, any firm which does not expand is thought of as going downhill. Growth at home and abroad, according to this school of thought, cannot be recognized unless it is tangible, visible, measurable.

"But this philosophy of growth, this triumphant view of development and progress, this 'success,' may now have reached its limit in international trade and foreign policy. It seems certain to be at an end *vis-à-vis* a vast portion of Asia. For this reason, many a reader of Dr. McGavran's, for whom this admirable sociohistorical pattern of the American outlook would seem to have been injected into certain theories of church growth and mission work, might mistakenly infer that the mission of the churches should play a secular expansionist role. They are aware that if this should take place, terrible and costly disappointments would be unavoidable. And it would soon be too late to undertake the painful process of rethinking the question of spiritual proportions, once those disappointments turned to frustrations."

Another lay-person—this time a laywoman—brings into the discussion our friends, our family, who belong "to that world which Dr. McGavran sees as having rejected Christ, and, therefore, as 'lost.'" [23] What is the Christian witness towards those people? Surely it is not to withhold from them the best that we have, i.e., the witness to our Lord. But Mme. Gouzée has experienced that this very witness to our Lord becomes falsified when made to serve the expansion of the Christian "party" to which we happen to belong (that is how our friends interpret the church growth program). Mme. Gouzée does not abandon witness to Christ: "I agree that it is not enough to serve incognito within the structures of the world. For one thing, what Christians do is not always immediately intelligible; like some comic strips in our newspapers, it requires verbal explanation in order to be properly understood." [24]

Was this not the case with the first apostles? Surely, the day of Pentecost was a "comic strip" for the Jews of Jerusalem: "They were all amazed and perplexed, saying to one another, 'What can this mean?'" (Acts 2:12, NEB). And then, but only *then*, did Peter give the verbal explanation of the mighty rushing wind, the tongues of fire. Then—and in this order—the people asked: "What shall we do?" After that, the church increased. Every chapter of the Book of Acts shows *this* order. Chapter 3 begins with the healing of a lame man, and subsequently provides a verbal interpretation.

The first Christians did not preach on the wonders of times past, but answered the question: What does *this* mean?

Those words do not form a declaration *against* church growth. "It would be a tragic mistake . . . if church growth strategy and Christian presence thinking were pitted against one another as competing points of view." [25] But it is a declaration which wants to be sure that it is the *Church* which grows, this Church which knows that its final goal is to become unnecessary. For the new earth and the new heaven no longer need a temple (Rev. 21:22).

The Church should always remember that it is provisional, yet for the time being necessary, a Church which heeds its own message: ". . . whoever would save his life will lose it, and whoever loses his life for my sake will find it" (Matt. 16:25, RSV). What will it profit a church, if it gains the whole world and forfeits its life?

NOTES

1. Donald McGavran, "Church Growth Strategy Continued," see below, p. 177.
2. Ibid., p. 178.
3. Ibid.
4. Ibid., p. 184.
5. Mathew P. John, "Evangelism and the Growth of the Church," see below, p. 118.
6. Ibid.
7. Jordan Bishop, O.P.: "Numerical Growth—An Adequate Criterion of Mission?" see below, pp. 122–23.
8. Ibid., pp. 124, 126.
9. Ibid., p. 122.
10. Ibid., p. 124.
11. Ibid., p. 125.
12. J. B. A. Kessler, "Hindrances to Church Growth," see below, p. 137.
13. Donald McGavran, "Wrong Strategy: The Real Crisis in Missions," see above, p. 103.
14. Ibid., p. 102.
15. Bishop, op. cit., p. 122.
16. Kessler, op. cit., p. 138.
17. Marie-Louise Martin, "Does the World Need Fantastically Growing Churches?" see below, p. 155.
18. John B. Housley, "Church Growth and Christian Mission" (review article), *International Review of Missions* (July 1968), p. 361.
19. David M. Gill: "The Secularization Debate Foreshadowed. Jerusalem 1928," *International Review of Missions* (July 1968), p. 347.
20. See the review by Dr. Hollenweger in *International Review of Missions* (July 1968), p. 377f.
21. See Eberhard Bethge: *Dietrich Bonhoeffer. Theologie, Christ, Zeitgenosse.* (Munich: Chr. Kaiser Verlag, 1967), p. 907.
22. In this context the prophecy of a Brazilian Pentecostal leader might indicate one of the many current trends of thought in Latin America: "Rome has brought to the world idolatry, Russia the terrors of Communism, the USA the demons of Capitalism; we Brazilians, nation of the poor, shall bring to the world the Gospel." *Ecumenical Review* (April 1968), pp. 164–65.
23. C. Gouzée: "Counterpoint," see below, p. 158.
24. Ibid., p. 163.
25. Herbert Neve: "Christian Presence and One of Its Critics," see below, p. 169.

B. ANSWERS FROM THE WHOLE WORLD
2. Evangelism and the Growth of the Church

Mathew P. John

In an important article under the title "Wrong Strategy: the Real Crisis in Mission," Dr. Donald McGavran has called for a reexamination of the "strategy of the fifties" which saw the essence of mission as "partnership in obedience . . . to any kind of Christian end beyond the local church." He wants a new strategy, the "right strategy" which "will have a right theology of church growth," "thoroughly biblical and thoroughly scientific." His proposal is for a strategy which "will spend large sums of money and the lives of some of its best men in intensive research into the most effective ways and means of reconciling men to God and multiplying churches."

It is not my intention to criticize the article in matters of detail, but to consider its main arguments, which seem to be the following:

1. The mission of the Church is an activity that should be seen as distinct from and independent of other activities of the Church, like worship and service.

2. The primary aim of mission is "church-planting," which consists in "the baptism of bodies, the salvation of souls, and the building of visible new churches."

3. The Christian answer to the problems of the world is more churches. "What the fantastically mounting population of this world needs is fantastically multiplying churches which will enable liberated populations, filled with the Holy Spirit, to generate their own Calvins, Wesleys, Wilberforces and Martin Luther Kings, and their own sober, godly and fruitful societies."

4. This can be achieved by (a) a survey and analysis of the factors and methods which have contributed to church growth in the various cultures and communities, using them as "matchless laboratories" and (b) the application of the right methods to particular situations.

Mathew P. John, of the Syrian Orthodox Church, is Professor of New Testament at Serampore College, Serampore, India.

5. The above procedure is justified and demanded by reasons of science as well as those of the Bible and theology.

Let us examine these points in order:

1. Within the wholeness of the life of the Church, the Bible recognizes different functions, as for example in 1 Corinthians 12:4–31 and Ephesians 4:11–16. But these passages are set within contexts that stress the unity of the Church and the interdependent character of the diverse functions. The attempt to isolate the "mission" of the Church from the rest of its life suggests that the saving message stands alone in proclamation, disembodied as it were, as a word that does not, and need not, become flesh in a redeemed-redeeming community that is turned to God in worship and to others in witness to the saving grace of God affecting the totality of human life, and within itself in disciplined obedience and fellowship.

It is to be recognized—in humility and penitence—that our life and witness as members of the community of faith has fallen short in many directions. Let us encourage all that is being done, and all that can be done for the renewal of the Church to make its witness to God's love more true and effective. A special emphasis on "mission" so entirely isolated from what Dr. McGavran calls "the current sacred triad, *kerygma, diakonia,* and *koinonia*" is not true to the Bible.

The author suggests that the question is whether the apostles should wait on tables. It is of course a vital question, but the answer given by the Book of Acts is nowhere near as definite as he suggests. Stephen would probably have lived long as an executive officer of the Church if he had kept his mouth shut except in committees. Philip, though appointed to "wait on tables," continues to be a highly successful evangelist. And Paul, who could say "woe unto me if I preach not the gospel," pays considerable attention to the collection for the saints for which he uses the significant term "grace" (1 Cor. 9:16; 2 Cor. 8:19; 9:8).

Again, Dr. McGavran says that "the issue is whether Paul at Troas, hearing 'Come over to Macedonia and help us,' shall send over some specialists to enter into dialogue with the priests of Jove and Venus, and others to assist a revolt against Roman oppression and slaveholding." It can equally well be said that the issue is *also* whether our response when face to face with a brother or sister who is ill-clad and in lack of food, is to say: "Jesus Christ is the Savior of your souls; go in peace."

Man's response to the revelation of God's saving grace in Christ has many facets, including worship, fellowship, witness, service, and internal transformation. It is within the context of such a many-sided response that the *kerygma* expresses itself in words and actions, and into which a man enters when he responds to the word of God in Christ in faith and obedience, through baptism.

2. It is possible that the author deliberately stated matters in a provocative manner to force our attention. It is natural for an enthusiast to put things strongly. Even making allowance for that, it is impossible to escape the fact that there appears to be much in the article that is questionable from a biblical point of view. The author puts together "reconciling men to God and multiplying churches" as though they were either synonymous or parallel. Jesus brought into being a community around himself. The Gospel records the saying about the building of the Church against which the gates of hell shall not prevail. Paul shows much concern for the churches in 2 Corinthians 10 and 11 and elsewhere. While all this is true, it is not at all clear that the multiplication of churches is the chief aim of the Christian mission. The consistent use of the plural "churches" implies a distance from an essential dimension of the meaning of the Church in the Bible. It may be meaningless to talk of an invisible Church except in the context of a visible one, but it is also relevant to remember that the visible church or churches share in the ambiguities of human existence and can become demonic like other human institutions (cf. "The Grand Inquisitor" in *The Brothers Karamazov*).

Some of the phrases that Dr. McGavran uses and the ideas behind them, though they have become traditional in large areas of the Church, do not belong to the distinctively biblical perspective. The concern for "man's immortal soul which is made in the image of God" hides the fact that according to the Bible it is man, the whole man—not merely his soul—that is said to be created in the image of God.

The author criticizes the understanding of mission as "partnership in obedience—any kind of obedience, to any kind of Christian end beyond the local church." Let us recognize that the concept of obedience can, just like a great many other concepts such as the saving of the heathen, redeeming the souls, or extending the Kingdom, become a disguise for motives that will not stand close scrutiny from a Christian point of view. But obedience is certainly to be understood in the light of Him to whom it is due; and in Paul's words, taking "every thought captive to obey Christ" and making the Corinthians' "obedience complete" was the aim of the mission for him (2 Cor. 10:5–6, RSV). The quest for unity that is present in the Church today may in some cases be a disguised form of self-assertion, but at its best it is certainly the response of the Church to the moving of the Spirit to make the Church obedient to its Lord at this time; and this is intrinsically bound up with the mission of the Church.

It is true that the life of Christians has often been a hindrance rather than an aid to the growth of the Church, and that we need to be called back to repentance and obedience. But the attempt to plant and multiply churches, as though this were our total missionary task, is likely to be self-defeating like the quest for "happiness" or "love."

3. The suggestion that the Christian answer to the problems of the world consists in an increase in the number of churches is unsatisfactory. To state that the problem of population explosion is to be met and solved by an explosion of the number of churches is not only misleading but irresponsible. If the quick growth of population is seen as a *problem*, the solution must be along the lines of making men face the responsibility of their actions and teaching and helping them to make the right decisions and choices. If the increase in the number of churches is *the* end of Christian mission, we ought to hail the "fantastically mounting population" as an enlargement of our harvest field and therefore a blessing without any qualification.

The gospel offers illumination on, and ways of solution to, the many problems that face man; but the answers of the gospel are not given as a cure-all which can be applied directly to the problems of societies and nations.

4. The study of social systems and evangelistic methods is in itself a valid and necessary part of missionary studies. Many have been helped and influenced by studies like those of Roland Allen. But the suggestion that former missionary situations are to be looked upon as "laboratories" is out of keeping with the motives of the missionaries and of the converts who turned to Christ and joined the Church often at considerable risk, and is disrespectful towards their memory. Dr. McGavran's proposals about classifying societies for the purpose of seeing what particular technique is to be applied to them to turn the raw material into churches, treats them as less than human and justifies the non-Christian critics of mission who describe it as a form of imperialism and domination.

If we follow the author's proposals, it would seem that evangelism can be computerized in the future with the certainty of success. Research and applied research can certainly serve the missionary enterprise, but the approach suggested in Dr. McGavran's article takes into account only the external, measurable aspects of what is essentially an internal and spiritual matter. An attempt to make churches grow by the application of the "right techniques" would be like hoping to increase true love by the researches of Kinsey or the experiments of Johnson and Masters.

The author has in more than one instance stated that it is the Holy Spirit that really makes the Church grow, and that "church growth is an exceedingly complex process and cannot be commanded." In some of his other writings he has given illustrations where prayerful preparation and planned witness bore fruit in visible ways. But in this article we seem to be moving towards a physical sciences approach of devising an experiment to produce predictable results. "Right strategy can be discerned, learned, taught, and executed. When it is, the enormous potential in today's missions will be realized. When it is, the confusion and frustration that mark so much of mission today will happily become a thing of the past."

5. Dr. McGavran's claim is that this approach is "thoroughly scientific and thoroughly biblical." The use of the word scientific in this context is very vague. Sociology is a scientific study, and can perhaps include the strategy and techniques of manipulating social groups to produce predetermined changes. We live under the threat that students of the bio-sciences will be able to condition human beings, or manufacture them according to required specifications, in the future. But certainly the gospel does not give us any warrant to do this to others.

No grounds are given for the claim that the proposed procedure is thoroughly biblical. The references to 2 Corinthians 10 and 11 and Matthew 28:19 are certainly insufficient to establish the claim. The clearest statement, in the Gospels, of the purpose of the Incarnation seems to be Mark 10:45, and that includes the ideal of service which Dr. McGavran would separate from the Christian mission. The sense that mission is not an isolated activity seems to be clear in many parts of the New Testament (e.g., Acts 2:43ff.; 5:1ff.; 6:1ff.; 1 Cor. 12–13; Eph. 4:11–16; James 2:14ff.)

Man's existence in societies is recognized in the Bible. We may hope for conversions of groups or of individuals, but the figure of Christ riding the "chariot of tribal allegiance into the heart of the tribe" appears to be not far from the words: "All these I will give you, if you will fall down and worship me." The hope that tribal loyalties can be used when the tribes are being "discipled" and left behind at the "perfecting" stage makes the questionable assumption of a measurable growth of spirituality affecting all members of a tribe equally. In areas where considerations of caste or tribe have been allowed in the Church, their removal even after one or two generations has proved difficult. It is, of course, possible to argue that they have not yet come to perfection.

The article isolates the mission of the Church from the rest of its life, and therefore understands it too narrowly. The mission of the Church is *to be the Church of Christ on the earth,* and in this the Godward direction in worship, the inward-directed quest for unity and renewal, and the outward-directed witness of proclamation and service, with a view to bringing all men into the fellowship of the redeemed-redeeming community in obedience and faith, are integrally involved. The quest for unity and renewal and the witness must go on even within the membership of the Church, in the individual and the social dimensions, in a perpetual process of transformation of character and growth in fellowship under the power and guidance of the Holy Spirit. If more men do not come to find faith in response to our witness, the cause may be the faults in our life and witness, and we ought continuously to seek renewal and strength. But to pursue the predictable and measurable success of our enterprise through the methods of sociology and statistics would be to reject the way of the Cross and to follow the path which our Lord rejected at His temptation.

B. ANSWERS FROM THE WHOLE WORLD
3. Numerical Growth—An Adequate Criterion of Mission?

Jordan Bishop, O. P.

Writing of a crisis in the Christian mission, Donald McGavran makes an eloquent appeal for a conscious strategy of mission, the criterion of which is quite simply the growth of the Church. The Church, sent by Christ to "make disciples of all nations," must plan her missionary effort in function of the numbers of people, obviously on the increase today, who have not heard or will not listen to the gospel of Jesus Christ.

The author is certainly not alone in his approach to mission in the Church. The same concern is manifest in an editorial published several years ago in the Roman Catholic Review *Christ to the World*,[1] where the editorialist laments the fact that the increase in adult baptisms is very weak with respect to population growth in the world today, and where we even find a criticism of the church-planting approach to mission in favor of a "direct apostolate," of "evangelizing non-Christians and saving souls." Here, as in McGavran's paper, the problem of numbers appears to be paramount, although the latter does not oppose this to planting the Church. In both cases there is a definite accent on the need for "strategy" or "planning" in the missionary effort of the Church; and in both cases the criteria appear to be quantitative, as if other criteria in the Church could, given the presence of committed Christian missionaries, be taken for granted.

It is precisely here that we are faced with what seems to this writer to be the greatest weakness of this approach to mission. There exists at the present time something of a crisis of meaning in the Church, a crisis of identity on the part of missioners themselves, so that to propose church growth as the primary criterion of mission risks evading serious theological problems, the answers to which are simply taken as given in strategies centered

---
Fr. Bishop is Professor of Church History in the National Seminary of Cochabamba, Bolivia. He has been associated with the review, *Parole et Mission* (Paris) and has published two books: *Latin America and Revolution* (London, 1965) and *Les théologiens et la mort de Dieu* (Paris, 1967).

on church growth or church-planting. While the author criticizes "partisan emphasis on peripheral aspects of the task" which he contends are justified theologically as the whole and substituted "for an objective measurable growth of the Church," he is certainly embarking on a courageous course of opposition to much of contemporary missionology. But to reject questions such as the meaning of Christianity as "peripheral" in favor of "an objective measurable growth of the Church" takes entirely too much for granted. Even as he states that "the cultural overhang from Europe and America must be recognized and rejected," this is subjected to the apparently unique criterion of church growth. Praising social initiatives, he goes on to state that "in all these good things, we must first have some Christians: no Christians, none of these good things." The fact is that many of these good things have been achieved or initiated without the intervention of Christians, or, as in Cuba, in the face of Christian opposition; and it is probable that such initiatives will continue. Freedom schools in Mississippi and Chicago or passive resistance in order to break caste systems, have no necessary relation to the institutionalized gospel, and the warning against European or North American cultural overhang surely cuts both ways: much of our missionary effort in the past has been prejudiced by the tendency to form ingroups modeled on European or North American cultural values other than those currently proclaimed in ecumenical circles.

On the other hand, it is certainly true that ethnic, political, and class lines are a part of the human reality to be confronted with the gospel of Jesus Christ. Interferences with European and North American colonialisms of one kind or another have added to the ambiguity of much modern missionary effort; and an artificial attempt to break down barriers between men by eliminating or bypassing national or tribal differences may in the end be another type of ecclesiastical colonialism, an attempt to impose patterns of life on new peoples for which they are not prepared. It is admittedly a dilemma: we must on the one hand respect this human reality, and on the other avoid the formation of closed, nationalistic or tribal churches such as we have sometimes experienced in modern Western Christianity. This, of course, must be taken seriously, and responsibility for local churches must be given to local leaders as soon as possible. One is tempted to add, "sooner than possible," since history has shown that we tend to be rather conservative in this respect. A Roman Catholic missioner from Africa has recently written: "My real answer would be to cut off all money from abroad, relax all the prescriptions of canon law, and then let the Church here by force of necessity work out structures suited to itself." [2]

On the whole, it appears that missioners today are more aware of the danger of cultural colonialism than were, for example, the Spanish missioners in the sixteenth century, whose *tabula rasa* approach to the missionary effort of the Church resulted in an endeavor to impose patterns of Spanish Christendom on the peoples of Latin America. This was unsuccessful, and already in the sixteenth century Toribio de Mogrovejo, third Archbishop of Lima, could speak of a "new" Christendom in the Americas, although institutions such as the *patronato real* impeded the growth of an authentically Latin American Christianity. At the present time a massive influx of missioners presents a new problem with a variety of cultural influences.[3]

While the old identification of Christian missioners with colonialism has broken down, the problem remains of identification with a new colonialism, the apparently benign economic power of aid to developing countries and social action programs whose net result is often closer to "pacification" than to development. This brings with it another problem with respect to evangelism measured in terms of church extension or growth: the gospel can easily become identified in the minds of the people with power, influence, or money. The word is addressed to man in his freedom, and the evangelizer who appears as identified with human power of one kind or another runs the risk of betraying the gospel to a new kind of idolatry, appealing to that which is unfree, and thus falsifying the Christian commitment. This is not to be read in simple moralistic terms or as a condemnation of the cruder forms of making "rice Christians"; the problem seems to this writer to run much deeper, and in its context one can see the value, or even the necessity, of an approach such as that of Charles de Foucauld or Albert Peyriguère. The charge of quietism would have to be examined in the context of every missionary situation.

There can be no question here of an appeal to some sort of "pure" Christianity, freed as it were from all cultural overhang. Nor can we propose some sort of "anonymous Christianity" as a norm. A Christianity which has no roots in a cultural situation is not possible, and a committed Christian cannot remain "anonymous." (It is interesting that Charles de Foucauld and Peyriguère did not.) But one cannot propose either "small growth" or "large growth" as good mission. It is difficult to see how we can evaluate missionary effort on any kind of quantitative basis, although given the presence of other criteria, church growth might be one sign among many of the gospel. Its value is certainly conditioned by the situation of the church or churches in question: the growth of the Church before Constantine would have a different meaning in this regard than that under Constantine or Charlemagne, and in any context the authenticity of conversion to Christ (freed, one should add, not only from economic but also from sociological and psychological pressures) is more important than the number of men converted or churches planted. In some situations a too-rapid numerical growth could create serious problems with respect both to the authenticity of Christianity and to the future development of the Church in a given area.

There is one difficulty with the current tendency to value the freedom of the individual in the Christian commitment: the fact that unredeemed man is in fact in a state of unfreedom. The gospel itself should free men from the bondage of sin. Nevertheless, this theological consideration can hardly justify preaching a "gospel" which takes hold of man precisely where he is not free, making use of economic, psychological or sociological pressures in order to "persuade" him to become Christ's disciple. Planning and strategy must not blind us to the fact that these interferences exist, and that a "gospel" which leans too heavily upon them may well be a false gospel, the church planted "nonchurch." Paul himself takes care to point out that he "did not come proclaiming to you the testimony of God in lofty words or wisdom . . . but in demonstration of the Spirit and power, that your faith might not rest in the wisdom of men but in the power of God" (1 Cor. 2:1, 4–5, RSV); "We have renounced disgraceful, underhanded ways; we refuse to practice cunning or to tamper with God's word, but by the open statement of the truth we would commend ourselves to every man's conscience in the sight of God. . . . For what we preach is not ourselves, but Jesus Christ as Lord, with ourselves as your servants for Jesus' sake" (2 Cor. 4:2, 5, RSV).

It is perhaps because of this that the East Asia Christian Council found it necessary to spend "all its time talking about the relationships of Asian missionaries to existing churches and existing Christians, and said very little indeed about Asian missionaries propagating their faith." In Latin America today the relationship between "missionaries" and "pastors," and between foreign and local clergy in the Roman communion, is one of the most urgent questions facing the churches in that area. It is certainly less "peripheral" than the question of church-planting and church growth, since it has to do with what the Church is to be, with the meaning of the gospel. It is all very well to speak of "proclaiming Christ as Lord and Savior and persuading sinful men to become His disciples," but the problem remains of spelling out the consequences of this discipleship in a variety of concrete situations.

Again, we do not have a "pure gospel," entirely freed from cultural interferences. Fear of syncretism led the Spanish missioners of the sixteenth century to take a *tabula rasa* approach to evangelism, so that the necessary intra-cultural dialogue between native Christians and others who shared their common culture never took place. There were no "native apologists" to reinterpret their culture in terms of the Christian commitment.[4] Donald McGavran is certainly aware of this need: it is a logical consequence of his insistence on the conversion of the *ethnē*, and his recognition of the fact that "there is no one humanity in which the Church grows." The question might be posed in terms of a double authenticity of the Church: fidelity to Jesus Christ and fidelity to the humanity in which the Church is planted. Neither can be adequately honored in contempt of the other, and numbers are not a criterion for either. If conversion to Christ implies cultural or religious alienation, our gospel is distorted, and we are, perhaps paradoxically, preaching a human gospel, imposing our own ethnocentrism on the peoples to whom we preach. Judged in terms of church growth, the Spanish evangelization of Latin America was certainly one of the most successful in history; yet there exists today an almost unanimous consensus to the effect that the evangelization of Latin America was never fully achieved.

A word should be said of the author's criticism of the "whole gospel" and similar terms: ". . . it attempts to take in everything that the Church and the Christian faith ought to do"; ". . . surely it is rather too much to expect of divisions of world mission and evangelism, foreign missionary societies, overseas ministries, and similar bodies, that they should embrace every aspect of the Christian enterprise. Is there no danger that the task will become so broad that it becomes thin? Indeed, that this strategy of the fifties is in grave danger of becoming ineffective is obvious when one observes the inadequate church growth in country after country." Aside from the fact that the criterion by which the judgment of "ineffective" is applied to this "strategy" is that of numbers, the obvious reply is simply that a church which concerns itself with anything less than "the whole gospel" is failing in its mission. It is true that we live in a specialized world and that effectiveness demands special ministries, organization and planning. On the other hand, foreign missionary societies, overseas ministries, etc., can hardly be described as those sectors of the Church whose specific function is church growth. These days, there will always be someone to ask: church growth *for what*?

These structures (and no doubt many of them are open to criticism) should rather be seen as organizations of the missionary church directed to a missionary presence of the Church in new areas or to helping new churches. As such their concern must be with the whole gospel, although this does not mean that the entire responsibility for the emergence of a New Humanity is to be borne by these ecclesiastical institutions. Needs vary from place to place, and the obedience of Christian communities, new or old, must be determined in accord with those needs which are discerned.

There is no doubt some danger that social action and other projects can eclipse the primary mission of the Church, that of proclaiming Jesus Christ and calling men to conversion. This danger is greatest when such projects are conceived in function of church growth. One sometimes hears the term "pre-evangelization" used in this sense, as if "one could not preach the gospel to empty stomachs," or as if we must "first" attend to "human needs" and then to the work of evangelism. "It is important to stress that this suffering service, this *diakonia,* is not an instrument of mission. All kinds of service, such as medical work, are embodiments of the gospel; they are signs not means." [5] It is not only possible, but necessary to "preach the gospel to the poor" (Matt. 11:5). On the other hand, it may be more difficult to preach the gospel to the poor when we are rich, since the danger of appealing to that which is unfree in men, of relying on human power and prestige rather than on the power of the Spirit, is proportionally greater. It is a sign of sensitivity to this that we have experienced a strong reaction against proselytism in our time. We do not *want* church growth based on human power and prestige. Social action as a presence and embodiment of the gospel can set men free; but if it appears as a *means* of gaining adherents to the Church, then we are simply exchanging one kind of servitude for another, and perhaps a worse one, since like the *encomienda* against which Las Casas fought, it is done in the name of the gospel.

At this juncture it is fairly obvious that this writer does not share Donald McGavran's views as to the correct strategy for Christian mission. Perhaps we have misunderstood him, but he appears to make church growth the final criterion of missionary activity. Coming from an area where most people are baptized and accept, at least in name, Jesus Christ as Lord and Savior, we are only too conscious of the need for evangelism in this situation, so that the authenticity of the Church, the meaning of the gospel, appear as the fundamental questions. At the present time, it hardly seems possible to accept these things as given in the institutional church in order to get on with the work of church growth, since there is a real danger that in our concern for numbers, our salt may lose its savor.

NOTES

1. Cf. *Christ to the World* 6 (1961), 161. For another Roman Catholic position, see *Parole et Mission* (Paris, October 1961), pp. 488–94.
2. Adrian Hastings, "A Missionary Correspondence," in *New Blackfriars* 48 (Cambridge, England, August 1967), 602.
3. Cf. Ivan Illich, "The Seamy Side of Charity," in *America* (New York) January 21, 1967; "The Vanishing Clergyman" in *The Critic* (Chicago) June–July, 1967.
4. Cf. E. Dussel, *Sintesis para una historia de la Iglesia en América latina* (Barcelona, 1967).
5. J. G. Davies, *Worship and Mission* (London: SCM Press, 1966), p. 34.

B. ANSWERS FROM THE WHOLE WORLD
4. Church Growth: A Critique

J. G. Davies

"Right strategy will . . . take church growth with life-and-death seriousness."[1] How simple it all seems! What a clear directive and how precise is this definition of Christian effort! Yet, I venture to suggest, upon analysis this apparently crystalline statement is basically ambiguous, and not only ambiguous but also misleading. What, after all, is the Church?

We can consider the Church from two aspects, theologically and empirically. If we approach the subject from the side of theology, we immediately encounter a disagreement between Christians. What the Church is for a Roman Catholic is not what it is for many Protestants. To a Roman Catholic there is only one true Church—all schism is outside it. That Church is to be identified with a hieratically structured community, holding a body of doctrines *de fide*, engaging in a uniform liturgical and devotional life and acknowledging the Pope as its head. On this premise, when the Roman Catholic speaks of "planting the Church," he knows exactly what he means; he refers to the extension of the Roman Catholic Church. Hence Roman Catholic missiology in the past has consistently interpreted mission as an action directed towards church (i.e., Roman Catholic) growth. The Protestant, however, cannot accept this premise. He believes that schism may be within the Church. He sees the Church as the dismembered body of Christ, fragmented into many denominations, some of which uphold different and indeed contradictory doctrines. When he speaks of planting the Church, he can only mean the planting of denominations. This immediately reduces such a definition of mission to well nigh an absurdity, as it would mean the increase of Methodists, Lutherans, etc. Can it seriously be maintained that this is God's purpose for the world? Is God's primary concern the multiplication of Congregationalists, Presbyterians, and the like? Is this not to reduce the living God of radical monotheism to a tribal

---

J. G. Davies is Head of the Department of Theology and Edward Cadbury Professor at the University of Birmingham, England.

deity? Considerations such as these make the statement about church growth essentially ambiguous. In saying this, I am not seeking to advance a debating point; I am in fact touching upon one of the central questions of theology today which, according to Dr. I. T. Ramsey, is "the problem of establishing its objective reference." [2] Hence the need also to consider the Church empirically.

We can define the Church not only by reproducing a series of biblical images—the Body of Christ, the Chosen People, etc.— but also by declaring what we find it to be in our experience. We can describe the Church as it *is*, and this description, if accurate, is a necessary part of any valid definition. Now it is the bitter experience of many people in England—to look no further than my own country—that the Church or churches is/are groups of inward-looking people, introverted to such a degree that their ecclesiastical interests are primary. They are also preoccupied with "religious" matters and regard worldly concerns as outside their purview. "No politics in the pulpit" is the cry. They maintain a dichotomy between their religion and everyday life; they split up reality into two spheres, the one supernatural and sacred where God is honored, and the other natural and profane where God is increasingly irrelevant. These groups are frequently judgmental, nonacceptive, conservative, and backward-looking. To many people their religious practices appear to belong to a dream world which has no point of contact with the real world. Their structures, devised in bygone days, have petrified, and institutional loyalty seems to command more respect than faithfulness to God.

Fortunately there are exceptions, but this is nevertheless not a caricature; it is an objective description of what *is*, of what many of us encounter day by day. Is this the Church whose growth we are to promote? If it is not, then to what really existing entity does our opening definition refer? What is the objective reference of this theological statement? It is useless to mouth such a word as *koinonia* and then assume that it is embodied in some Anglican or Methodist congregation. Time and again the evidence is plain that it is not so embodied. So what does the "growth of the Church" mean? A theology which is content to regard the Church as the community of the saved or as a community built upon Christ, and does not grapple with the relationship of such concepts to the empirical reality is inauthentic. To speak of the growth of the Church is, for me, to speak both ambiguously and misleadingly— but, perhaps more seriously, it is also to dangle before Christians a false goal for their endeavors.

Let us assume—and what an assumption it is—that the

churches are united; that we have indeed one Church and not a multiplicity of denominations. Let us assume further that this one Church is everything that the previous churches are not—open-minded, dynamic, outward-moving, concerned with the world, etc. Would it then be right to speak of church growth? I do not think so, for the following reasons: [3]

1. To define the goal of mission as church growth is to indulge in an ecclesiastical narrowing of the concept of the Kingdom of God. The Church is an instrument of the Kingdom, or should be; it may also be conceived as the first-fruits of the Kingdom; but it is not to be identified with the Kingdom, which is what we are doing if we rest content with church growth as our objective.

2. To think in terms of church growth is to plan for survival, and this is the antithesis of the pattern of life laid down for us by Christ. That life was one of service and suffering unto death, of self-giving and not self-aggrandizement, of acceptance of the Cross and not self-sufficiency.

3. The strategy of deliberately planned church growth is a limitation of the free activity of the Holy Spirit. Instead of subjecting ourselves to His action, instead of participating through Him in the mission of God, we substitute our program of planting churches which are in all important particulars identical with those that exist. We then manifest a lack of faith, in that the unprecedented is not expected.

4. To place church growth at the center of Christian concern is to provide that concern with an illegitimate goal because, as the New Testament makes quite plain, God's concern, which presumably the Christian should share, is the world and not the Church. The Church is an instrument, but not the only one, of God's action for and in the world; it is therefore not an end in itself, and to regard it as such is to turn ecclesiology into ecclesiolatry. This is to succumb to the temptation to which ancient Israel gave way. Israel's election was for the life of the world, but by Jesus' day this understanding had been largely lost, and indeed the two terms—Israel and world—had been reversed, so that it was held that the world had actually been created for the sake of Israel (2 Esd. 6:59). Mission which is aimed at church growth reproduces this post-exilic falsification, and for the New Testament concept of centrifugal action it substitutes a centripetal outlook.

The masked centripetalism that would appear to underlie Dr. McGavran's whole position breaks surface in a statement which he makes about worship: "Worship, for example, is good; but worship is worship. It is not evangelism." [4] In order to indicate what I believe to be the falsity of this approach, I must begin by drawing a contrast between the Old Testament understanding of Israel's vocation and the role that worship has to play within that vocation, and the New Testament understanding of the vocation of the Church and the role that worship has to play within that vocation. Briefly put, Israel's vocation is to be a holy people (Lev. 19:2), i.e., a people whose life is patterned after the very being of its holy God. In so far as this is achieved, Israel then becomes a "light to the Gentiles"; it is a witness before the nations to Yahweh in order that the nations themselves may come to acknowledge his universal Lordship. The function of worship in relation to this vocation is to enable Israel to be holy; it is a means of sanctification for the Chosen People, who are set apart for the worship of Yahweh (Exod. 19:6). The Temple cultus is both the guarantee of the purity of Yahwism and the center to which the nations are to come. It will be noticed that Israel's vocation is interpreted centripetally; Israel is not *sent* to the nations; instead they are to *come* to it, attracted by its life of worship and devotion. In exact conformity with this, Israelite worship is understood centripetally; it has its true center in a single place, viz., the Jerusalem Temple, and it is to this that all the nations are to come (Isa. 2:2, 3).

The New Testament presents a contrast—indeed an antithesis—to this view, in that the centripetal attitude is discarded and is replaced by a centrifugal one. The Church's vocation is to go out; it is to participate in the divine mission in order that the nations may acknowledge the Lordship of Christ. The Church's vocation then is to join in God's action in the world as He continues His movement of humanization, assisting man towards that maturity or fulness embodied in Christ. The function of worship in relation to this vocation is to celebrate God's action in the world and so "to proclaim the Lord's death until he come," this being involved in the eating of the bread and the drinking of the cup at the Eucharist (1 Cor. 11:26). Thus just as the Church's vocation is interpreted centrifugally, so is its worship; it does not have a center in a single place; anywhere is the place of encounter with God in the context of everyday life; and in so far as any temple continues to exist, this is not a building of stone but a community living in the world (2 Cor. 6:16). Hence the Old Testament is consistent in understanding both the vocation and the worship of Israel centripetally, while the New Testament is equally consistent but understands both the vocation and worship of the Church centrifugally.

To this contrast between the Old and New Testaments is to be added a third, viz., the contrast between the general understanding of Christians today of their vocation and worship, and that which we have just examined in the New Testament. As a consequence of the great missionary awakening of the eighteenth and nineteenth centuries, most Christians now understand the vocation of the Church centrifugally, but they still persist in viewing their cultic acts centripetally. They thus give up the logical consistency that is to be found both in the Old and New Testaments, and attempt to combine the Old Testament centripetal concept of worship, in terms of ingathering, with the New Testament centrifugal concept of vocation. Hence the relationship of worship and mission has for decades been defined in terms of gathering and sending.

The idea of gathering and sending was prominent in German missiological thought at the end of the last century, and is often represented today. According to this, worship is an occasion for the gathering together of the Christian community in order that its members may be strengthened to engage in mission. Through their sharing in the life-giving body and blood of Christ in the Eucharist, Christians are enabled to go out into the world as men and women charged with missionary participation. These cultic acts and missionary activity can then be compared to breathing in and breathing out, which are both necessary for life, and so both worship and mission—gathering and sending—are essential for the Church.

The analogy is a plausible one, and it is doubtful if it would have persisted so long if it were not; but is it accurate? In effect it merely associates centripetalism—breathing in—with centrifugalism—breathing out—and therefore it fails to resolve the basic tension between them. Moreover it involves the idea that the cultic acts are interruptions in the Church's participation in mission— ". . . worship is worship. It is not evangelism." When the Church ceases its centrifugal action in mission, for however brief the periods may be, in order to engage in centripetal actions of worship, it is no longer being missionary during those cultic actions, for, in terms of the analogy, you are either breathing in or breathing out; you cannot do the two at once. But if mission and worship are truly united, the cultic assembly must be understood within the context of mission; the coming together takes place in mission and it is not preparatory to mission. The Church is the Church when it is participating in the mission of God. If it is to fulfil its role constantly, it cannot disengage itself from mission in cultic activity. Church services must then not be conceived as halting places *in via* nor as iron rations on the way; they are an essential part of being on the way. So while the gathering and sending analogy does point to a relationship, it is not a relationship of unity, and this is precisely what we have to rediscover if we are to be true to the New Testament. Worship then is not a means of mission; nor is it a preparation for mission, since we worship in mission. The inadequacy of the analogy under consideration, which appears to justify the affirmation that worship is worship and not evangelism, should become more apparent if we now briefly examine what worship means from a centrifugal or missionary perspective.

Worship, as it is presented to us in the New Testament, is the joyful celebration of life in the world; it is the response of men to what God has done and is doing in history. Three examples will serve to illustrate this.

In Luke 17, we are told how Jesus is met by ten lepers who ask Him to have mercy on them. He accedes to this request and they are made whole. One of them, who is a Samaritan, recognizes in this the act of God and accordingly he worships—"praising God with a loud voice . . . he fell on his face at Jesus' feet, giving him thanks" (17:15–16, RSV). The man does not draw apart from the world in order to worship; the basis of his act of worship is his response to God's action in this secular world—his restoration to wholeness through Christ—and this takes the form of expressing thanks and giving praise.

Similarly in Acts 4, we are informed how Peter and John were arrested and how, after trial before the Sanhedrin, they were eventually released. They then "went to their friends and reported what the chief priests and the elders had said to them" (4:23, RSV). The reaction of the group to this was to join in prayer, i.e., they worshiped together on the basis of an incident which had taken place in the secular world.

The Lord's Supper itself, throughout the Apostolic Age, was also essentially a secular act, since it was an everyday meal, although one which, while not ceasing to be a source of bodily nourishment, was at the same time a vehicle of worship. Indeed the meaning of the Eucharist "cannot be understood without reference to the normal physical functions of eating and drinking." [5] Christians met from house to house, breaking bread together, presumably in the main living or dining room. Consequently it can be said that in New Testament times "worship, conceived as the joyful response of Christians to God's action in Jesus Christ, was not defined first and foremost in terms of what happened in a certain *place where* and at a certain *time when* Christians assembled. What happened on these occasions was understood within the context of response to God in their total existence." [6]

Here we have worship interpreted from a centrifugal position.

Just as the world is understood to be the sphere of mission, so it is also the sphere of worship which is to be offered in terms of the Christians' total existence. The Church of the Apostolic Age does not therefore withdraw from mission. It never ceases to be in mission in the secular world, whether it is preaching, serving or worshiping. There can therefore be no great center of worship, corresponding to the Jerusalem Temple. Cultic acts take place *in via*—they are centrifugally conceived in complete unity with mission itself. In the words of Gerhard Bassarak, which refer to the present day but which apply equally to the New Testament period: "The reality of the congregation materializes in the gathering of the two or three rather than through church-going."[7] Hence worship is a spontaneous response to God's action in the world, and it does not involve *reculer pour mieux sauter*.

To speak of God's action in the world is, however, to refer to mission, for mission is not something the Church "does"; it is a divine movement in which the Church has to be involved if it is true to its calling. The Church's role is not to concern itself about its own growth, but to facilitate, to identify, and to participate in this movement; and the function of worship as response is to be understood within this totality. Worship is not therefore just historical commemoration in the sense of the thankful recalling of what God has done and, in particular, of what God has done in Christ in Palestine two thousand years ago. It is also the celebration of what God is doing in contemporary history.

Unless worship is interpreted in terms of mission, we shall not be enabled as Christians to break out of our ghettos. Dr. McGavran therefore does less than service to the gospel when he contends that worship is worship and not evangelism, which I include within the concept of mission. It is only "not evangelism," if you interpret that word in the way that he does as directed towards church growth. Deny this definition and the whole subject becomes open-ended, which is what every theological subject should be.

NOTES

1. Donald McGavran, "Wrong Strategy: The Real Crisis in Missions," see above, p. 104.
2. Eric James, ed., *Spirituality for Today* (London: SMC Press, 1968), p. 79.
3. I have not attempted to elaborate these because I have done so twice already in *Worship and Mission* (London: SCM Press, 1966), pp. 46–53 and in *Dialogue with the World* (London: SCM Press, 1967), pp. 40–44.

4. McGavran, op. cit., see above, p. 101.
5. J. M. Gustafson, *Treasure in Earthen Vessels* (New York: Harper & Row, 1961), p. 18.
6. F. W. Young, in M. Shepherd, ed., *Worship in Scripture and Tradition* (London and New York: Oxford University Press, 1963), p. 77.
7. Z. K. Matthews, *Responsible Government in a Revolutionary Age* (London: SCM Press, 1966), p. 380.

B. ANSWERS FROM THE WHOLE WORLD
5. Hindrances to Church Growth

J. B. A. Kessler

In his article entitled "Wrong Strategy," Dr. Donald McGavran writes: "What the fantastically mounting population of this world needs is fantastically multiplying churches." To a European such words may well suggest a picture of a hard-driving North American businessman, armed with a sheaf of statistics, eager for new take-overs and determined to keep his concern within a category outlined by "growth companies." The European theologian then counters with a declaration that holy living and sound doctrine are more important than numerical growth; and in this way the basis has been laid for a misunderstanding. As one of the hindrances to church growth consists of the misunderstandings that have arisen on the subject, it is first of all necessary to examine what the Bible says about this matter and to ask oneself whether Dr. McGavran wishes to encourage quantitative growth (if need be at the expense of quality) or whether he is seeking recognition of numerical growth as an essential ingredient of the coming of God's Kingdom.

In Genesis 12:2–3, we read that the promise originally given to Abraham is destined for every inhabitant of the earth, and this implies a growth from the figure one to that of several thousand millions. According to the prophets, the Messianic government would increase its extent without limit (Isa. 9:7), and one of the essential points of Nebuchadnezzar's dream was that the universal growth for which the earthy empires had striven would be realized only in the Kingdom of God (Dan. 2:35). Whereas the Old Testament deals with growth as a whole, the New Testament pays more attention to the role which growth in quality has to play in the general increase. The apostles mention the need for an increase

---

Dr. Kessler served as a missionary in Peru under the Evangelical Union of South America (based in London) from 1949 until 1958, and subsequently undertook an extensive study of the older Protestant missions and churches in Peru and Chile, the results of which were published as a doctoral dissertation for the University of Utrecht. He is now Lecturer at the Netherlands Bible Institute, Zeist.

in faith (Luke 17:5; 2 Cor. 10:15 and 2 Thess. 1:3), in fruits of righteousness (2 Cor. 9:10), in the knowledge of God (Col. 1:10), in love (1 Thess. 3:12), in grace (2 Peter 3:18), as well as the need for more unity with Christ (Eph. 4:15–16 and Col. 2:19).

The Bible writers do not, however, mean to play off one factor against the other. The Old Testament does not ignore the need for improvement in quality, nor does the New overlook the importance of numerical growth. The parables of the mustard seed and of the leaven (Matt. 13:31–33) give an implied warning of the dangers attending numerical growth, but at the same time they confirm that such growth is characteristic of the Kingdom of God. An increase in the number of professing Christians does not necessarily mean that the Kingdom of God is coming, but wherever that Kingdom is really coming there will be a multiplication of believers and of churches.

Dr. McGavran would like to see the growth of the church on a mission field divided into two stages. Firstly, an attempt should be made to win the ethnic group as a whole to an allegiance to Christ; and secondly, this group must then be lifted to a condition of full brotherhood. The implication is, therefore, that the qualitative element only comes to the fore during the second stage, and that during the first stage quality is indeed sacrificed for quantity. Dr. McGavran accepts this on the grounds that an improvement in quality on a broad scale is only possible once the allegiance to Christ of a sizable group has been established.

At first sight, the history of the Protestant churches in Peru and Chile would appear to contradict this contention. It proved to be possible to establish small groups of devoted believers whose influence was quite out of proportion to their numbers. Yet a study of the older Protestant churches in these two countries shows that the smaller groups were unable to maintain their influence for long periods. The missionaries who planted these churches were so disturbed by the example of superficial Christianization given by the Roman Catholic Church that, generally speaking, they went to the other extreme and refused to adapt to local circumstances the moral standards which they had brought with them from their home churches. The establishment of relevant ethical patterns takes place only as a result of a long process, and to demand it straightaway in a young church dooms it to remaining ineffectively small.

We have, on the other hand, the example of the Moravian Church, which has exercised a permanent influence in Europe and North America in spite of its small size. But it must be remembered that large Protestant churches already existed in these areas which were prepared to learn from the newcomers, especially in the field of missionary endeavor. In this way the Moravians were able to stimulate growth in others, while remaining relatively small themselves. In Dutch Guiana, however, where Moravian missionaries were confronted with a spiritual vacuum, their work, together with that of the Roman Catholic mission, has become the largest in the country. Provided attention is restricted to mission fields, there do seem to be grounds for believing that the dogmatic attitude adopted generally by Protestant missions that growth in quality must precede growth in quantity has been a real hindrance to missionary progress, and that Dr. McGavran's reasoning, although not of universal application, must be seen as a healthy corrective in this respect.

A second valuable feature of Dr. McGavran's position is that he parts company with those who say that mission problems would soon sort themselves out, if those concerned could be lifted to a new level of spiritual experience. The danger of the latter assumption is that only the influence of spiritual attitudes upon the organization is taken into account, and not the influence of the organization upon those spiritual attitudes. The result is that the choice of methods becomes a matter of expediency, and that missionaries unwittingly adopt policies which not only give the native population among whom they are working a false impression of their intentions, but may also in the end affect the intentions themselves.

A third helpful point made by Dr. McGavran is that the comprehensive approach to missions, to which so many adhere today, has a tendency to overlook the need for concentrating attention on those problems which are holding up progress in a particular area. A missionary situation often resembles a log jam, in that only a very few logs may be impeding the movement of the whole.

It is in the assessment of missionary motivation that the weakness of Dr. McGavran's arguments would appear to lie. The impression gained from his writings is that the chief hindrance to progress is the fact that today many missions are not making advance in quantity a prime object of their policy. Certainly there is no evidence to suggest that churches which are not interested in expanding manage nevertheless to do so, but it is remarkable how few churches which really did try to extend themselves succeeded in achieving that kind of growth for which Dr. McGavran is looking. During most of their existence, the fourteen churches in Peru and Chile which we have studied endeavored to achieve rapid expansion, and yet only the Chilean Pentecostal movement succeeded in this.

To say that none of these fourteen churches achieved spectacular growth because they did not apply what Dr. McGavran describes as a "right strategy," would be a dangerous oversimplification. Several of them paid considerable attention to the policies they should apply, and for a time achieved encouraging growth; but none in any way matched the Pentecostal movement. Dr. McGavran writes: "The tremendous increase of Pentecostals in Latin America is in a large measure due to the fact that they are frankly Christians of the masses." But this cannot be substantiated. The Pentecostals in Peru directed their efforts towards the masses, but achieved less growth than the Adventists who aimed more at the lower middle classes. In Chile the Pentecostals certainly concentrated upon the masses, but so did several other churches.

The Pentecostals in Chile did adopt interesting methods, but there is nothing which indicates that these were decisively different from those used by others. We choose to believe that the important difference lay in the unique combination among the indigenous Chilean Pentecostals of an active lay ministry with an authoritarian form of church government, which made possible a self-propagating church among the masses. In turn this combination depended on the spiritual experience of these Pentecostals and on their maintenance of many of the traditions of the Methodist Episcopal Church from which they sprang. Church growth in this case was fostered by a synthesis of spiritual experience, retention of church traditions, and right methods. Dr. McGavran clearly sees the importance of the last factor, but devotes insufficient attention to the other two.

The influence of doctrine as a hindrance to church growth must also not be overlooked. We are convinced that several of the Protestant churches in Peru and Chile owe their slow rate of progress to the way in which they have presented the message of salvation. When they stated that Christ had already done everything for us and that all the sinner had to do was to receive this finished work, converts tended to become introverted and even selfish. When, on the contrary, the Pentecostals declared in effect that salvation was only complete with the baptism of the Spirit, which could only be experienced in the complete consecration of oneself to God, they were less prone to become supremely satisfied with their own salvation. This was an important factor in the development of their lay ministry.

Recently, doctrine has also been hindering church growth in Peru and Chile in another way. Dr. McGavran mentions those who "shudder at the thought of propagation of the Christian religion, preferring to talk about confronting men with the cosmic

Christ"; here we have the impression that he does not appreciate the extent to which this problem has recently had an influence even on missionaries from a conservative theological background. The proclamation of the gospel has so often been tinged with a desire to impose one's own views on other people, that it has become necessary for missionaries everywhere to question their right to proselytize. So long as the Roman Catholic Church in Peru and Chile refused to reckon with certain vital elements of the gospel, only a minority of the Protestant missionaries considered the problem of proselytism to be an acute one; but now in view of the Chilean Catholic Church's increased willingness to accept reform, and in view of the eagerness to read the Scriptures which Roman Catholics in Peru have demonstrated during the last two years, it is difficult for anybody to ignore this issue.

The impact of the problem has been different in the various groups. The so-called traditional Protestant churches in Peru and Chile, the first to recognize and openly to admit the danger of proselytism, have in effect side-stepped the issue by concentrating on social and education projects, and by attending to the needs of those who were already Protestants. With one exception, the general result has been that evangelism of those outside the Protestant fold has been given a secondary place or abandoned altogether (and this may be seen as a real hindrance to any further advance). Among those related to the faith mission group, the issue of proselytism has been largely suppressed by the conviction that the divine command to preach the gospel must be given preference over any human reasoning. People who hold this view have become suspicious of the rational approach to mission policy for which Dr. McGavran stands.

The example of the Pentecostal movement in Chile shows that a rational approach to missions is not a prerequisite to church growth, because these Pentecostals achieved their success through an unusual combination of spiritual and social factors. But the chance that such a combination will recur of itself is slight, and therefore missions must be prepared to study and to learn from each other. In either case, it will be seen that the practical effects of the reaction to proselytism will curb church growth. Still, the recent experience of the South American Missionary Society indicates that as far as Latin America is concerned the problem is by no means insuperable.

This society is an Anglican mission which started work among the unevangelized Araucanian Indians in southern Chile in 1895. After 1909, a spontaneous movement started among these Indians, which at first seemed full of promise. However, after a number of years, stagnation and then decline set in. The missionaries of the Society have probably been more aware of the dangers of proselytism than have any of their colleagues in the country, and yet in the 1950s they came to the conclusion that they had to extend their evangelistic outreach to the whole of the Chilean nation. Since that time, they have widened their scope still further to include Peru and Bolivia.

These Anglicans have, despite their reluctance to proselytize, been able to sustain an active evangelistic outreach, because they are quite prepared to remain small themselves provided that by their influence and testimony they can stimulate growth in the other churches—including the Roman Catholic Church. When it is remembered that according to recent estimates only 6 percent of nominal Roman Catholics in Peru actually take part in the religious exercises of their church, it becomes clear that one of the great frontiers for church growth in that country, as indeed in the whole of Latin America—both in a qualitative and a quantitative sense—lies within the Roman Catholic Church itself.

B. ANSWERS FROM THE WHOLE WORLD
6. *A Pentecostal's View of Mission Strategy*

Melvin L. Hodges

Pentecostals have their roots imbedded in *The Book*. They strive constantly to follow the New Testament in every aspect of faith and practice. It follows that Pentecostal missiology should be based on biblical doctrine, experience and methodology.

THE ROLE OF THE HOLY SPIRIT IN MISSION STRATEGY

Pentecostals are so called because they believe that the Holy Spirit will come to believers today as He came to the waiting disciples on the day of Pentecost. They recognize the Holy Spirit as the divine Agent of the Deity in the earth, without whom God's work of redemption through Jesus Christ cannot be realized. Since there can be no effective mission to reconcile men to God without the Holy Spirit, it follows that His leadership must be sought and His empowering presence must be in evident manifestation if there is to be any success in carrying out the Church's mission. Beyond His work in regenerating the believer, the Holy Spirit comes as a baptism to empower the believer for his role as a witness (Acts 1:5, 8); his body becomes a temple of the Holy Spirit (1 Cor. 6:19); and joined with other believers, he forms part of the Church, which is the temple of God for the habitation of God by the Spirit (Eph. 2:21, 22). This marvelous privilege is not reserved for the spiritual elite but is the heritage of every believer, regardless of age, sex, or social station. Even the servants (slaves) shall prophesy (Acts 2:17, 18). The Holy Spirit is poured out on the common man, and he finds an important place in the body of Christ according as the Holy Spirit grants His gifts and enablements (2 Cor. 12:4–13).

According to these concepts, the spiritual life of the believer

---

Melvin L. Hodges is Field Secretary of Latin America and West Indies for the Foreign Missions Department of the Assemblies of God, Springfield, Missouri, U.S.A.

and the activities of the Church are to be realized on a supernatural plane. The Church is to be directed by the Spirit; believers are to be led by the Spirit. The supernatural Presence should be manifested in healings, miracles, and answers to prayer. Is not Jesus the same today? Inspirational utterance will be given by the Spirit for the encouragement of the Church. Divine direction will be received through a Spirit-guided administration. The Holy Spirit is the Chief Strategist of the Church in evangelism and mission. Human planning is valid only as it reflects the Divine Mind. The Holy Spirit has a strategy for each age and place. It is the Church's responsibility to discern this and to put the strategy into effect. The Apostle Peter probably was not planning to evangelize the Gentiles, but in prayer the Holy Spirit showed him his next move and commanded him to go. He found himself shortly after in the house of Cornelius with the Gentiles turning to Christ and receiving the gift of the Spirit (Acts 10:19; 44–48). The church at Antioch would doubtless have desired to retain Paul and Barnabas as their chief ministers, but the Holy Spirit said: "Separate me Barnabas and Saul for the work whereunto I have called them" (Acts 13:2).

This prominence given to the role of the Holy Spirit should not lead us to believe that the human role is one of complete passivity. There is need for the engaging of all our mental, physical, material and spiritual powers in the planning and execution of God's work. Once the will of God is determined, we should set forth as did the apostles in an active effort to fulfil the divine commission. As the Holy Spirit corrected details in their planning as they went along, so we may also expect His continued guidance as we launch forth (Acts 16:6–10). As the Holy Spirit directs the strategy, and we respond, converts will be won and churches planted, as occurred in the apostles' ministry.

THE ROLE OF THE CHURCH IN MISSION STRATEGY

Since the Scriptures teach that the Church is the body of Christ and the temple of the Holy Spirit—the body that Christ directs and the temple through which the Holy Spirit manifests himself—Pentecostals see the missionary task as that of winning non-Christian men and women, whether they be civilized or pagan, to Christ, so that they can experience regeneration and become vital members in the living Body of Christ. Each local church (where two or three are gathered together in His name) becomes a living cell of the Body of Christ, and God's agent for the bringing of the message of reconciliation to its community. Therefore church-planting and church growth (cell multiplication) are of supreme importance in the Christian mission. Whatever other good things the Church may do, its success in promoting the Kingdom of God must be measured by the number of people it can bring into vital relationship with Christ and the number of local units of the body of Christ that it can produce.

STRATEGY FOR EVANGELISM AND CHURCH GROWTH

Pentecostal methodology for church growth emphasizes the importance of the individual believer's response to the Holy Spirit. Every Christian is called to be a witness and, upon receiving the gift of the Spirit, is empowered for this service (Acts 1:8). True converts do not have to be urged to witness, but overflow with zeal to share their experience with others. They do need to be taught and guided in order that their witness may be effective. Believers understand intuitively that as the "good seed of the Kingdom" they should multiply themselves by bringing others to a knowledge of Christ. This witness assumes many forms:

Local churches start new churches. In general practice, local churches make a systematic effort to reach their community. Lay workers are sent to open outstations with the expectation that they will develop into churches. When this is accomplished the new church in turn sends out its own local workers to open still other outstations. So the church grows by cell multiplication.

Laymen develop into pastors and evangelists. Most pastors begin their ministry as laymen in a local congregation, often by taking the responsibility for opening an outstation. Thus they receive practical "on-the-job" training under the supervision of a pastor and the local church board. As the outstation develops into a church, the lay worker may become a full-time pastor. Many attend a Bible school for a period of basic training in Christian doctrine and church administration, etc., but they would doubtless still be considered as laymen by some who insist on a highly trained clergy as the only qualified church leaders. Nevertheless, many of these men have been outstandingly endowed by the Spirit with gifts for ministry. They have the advantage of being close to their people and identified with the local culture. Without question they are as qualified as were many of the "elders" of the Primitive Church.

This work of developing outstations is supplemented by the forming of *branch Sunday schools* in the outstations. Also there are often organized efforts of *house-to-house visitation* by the members, both for the purpose of personal witness and for the *distribution of appropriate literature.* The object is to win men and women to Christ and bring them into the local church. *Street meetings,* where permitted, are a common and fruitful practice, and attract new people to the churches.

Emphasis on indigenous principles of self-propagation, self-government and self-support. In those cases where the Church has made notable advances in Latin America, it will be noted that without exception the Church has assumed the responsibility for its own decisions and has found within itself the resources necessary to maintain its operation and advance without dependence on foreign personnel or funds. There is a keen sense of responsibility among the national Christians for evangelizing their own people. There is an absence of "foreignness" in the atmosphere, the Church being rooted in the nation itself and prospering in its climate.

Mass evangelism. Pentecostals are interested in reaching the masses. Great evangelistic campaigns have been held in the large cities of Latin America, sometimes with scores of thousands in attendance. Emphasis is on the good news of salvation and healing. Such a campaign was held in San Salvador (El Salvador) in 1956. Thousands attended the open-air worship, standing during the entire service. At the end of four months, 375 new converts were selected for baptism. These all had attended a series of classes for new converts. At the beginning of the campaign, the Assemblies of God had one small organized church in the city. At the end of the year there were twelve congregations, either launched or already organized as churches. Within five years the numbers attending the churches or the branch Sunday schools had reached seven or eight thousand; and now, ten years after the campaign, the number of churches in the city has increased to about forty. The campaign gave this church growth its initial impetus; and the faithful, sacrificial work of pastors and laymen produced the multiplication of churches experienced after the initial campaign had terminated.

Literature, radio, and television evangelism. Literature has become an increasingly important instrument of evangelism. The use of radio is widespread, and television is gaining recognition as an effective medium.

Pentecostals believe that the gospel is for the masses and that it is God's will today, as in New Testament times, that multitudes should believe on the Lord, that the word of God should increase and the number of disciples multiply (Acts 5:14; 6:7).

Flexibility of strategy. Pentecostals would agree with Dr. McGavran that the strategy for missions must be kept flexible. Even so, certain principles are inviolable. The message we preach, the spiritual new birth of individuals, the control of the Holy Spirit in the believer's life and in the activities of the Church, the responsibility of Christians to form themselves into churches and to multiply themselves—all of these things are basic and must not be modified. The approach, however, must vary with the widely differing opportunities. If a particular tribe or section of society is "ripe for the harvest," the Church must be sufficiently flexible to find the means for taking advantage of the occasion. The Pentecostal's deep conviction that the guidance of the Holy Spirit must be sought for each situation makes for flexibility and ensures variety in method.

In one place an evangelistic campaign may be the means for opening the area to the gospel. Elsewhere the beginning will be made by opening a small outstation in a home, following up with literature saturation. Again the healing of a paralytic, or the restoring of sight to a blind person through the prayer of faith may be the means of stirring interest and founding the church. Pentecostal believers pray for their sick neighbors and lead them to Christ. The deliverance of an alcoholic or a narcotic addict may open the door in a community. Admittedly, all this may seem foreign to those who are accustomed to an institutional approach to the mission of the Church, but to Pentecostals such happenings are to be expected and are entirely in accord with the New Testament concept of the Church's mission.

PENTECOSTAL STRATEGY RESULTS IN CHURCH GROWTH

The Pentecostal movement has made rapid strides in its worldwide outreach since its humble beginnings at the turn of the century. Although Pentecostals have been labeled the *third force* in modern Christianity, they see themselves not as a "third force" or a "fringe movement" but as New Testament Christians returning to the simplicity, central truths, and vitality of the Apostolic Era. Pentecostals form a vital part of evangelical Christianity round the world. Without dispute, the Pentecostals stand at the front of the Evangelical [1] advance in Latin America.

One of the outstanding examples may be observed in Brazil. The Assemblies of God of Brazil began when two Swedish missionaries went to that country in 1910 in response to a definite guidance of the Holy Spirit. Beginning their work in Belem, a city at the mouth of the Amazon, they established a church which spread rapidly throughout the country until every city, town, and most hamlets had an Assemblies of God congregation or at least a sign of their foothold in the community. Today, estimates of membership in the Assemblies of God churches of Brazil is placed at one million or more. Probably there is an equal number to be found in the churches of sister Pentecostal organizations throughout the country. William Read, a United Presbyterian missionary, estimates that the Assemblies of God membership in Brazil is increasing at the rate of 250 percent every ten years.[2]

In Chile, the indigenous Pentecostal churches, represented by the Methodist Pentecostal Church and sister groups which grew out of a Pentecostal revival in the Methodist Church early in this century, have now grown until they dwarf in size the church from which they emerged. It is estimated that somewhere between 80 percent and 90 percent of all Evangelicals in Chile are Pentecostal, with a combined constituency of all Pentecostal groups in the country reaching a million or more. This has been accomplished without the help of missionary personnel or foreign funds, except for the guidance that Doctor Hoover, the Methodist missionary, gave in the beginning. Representatives of these groups are to be found everywhere in Chile; and like the Assemblies of God of Brazil, they have gone beyond their own borders in missionary effort, so that churches affiliated with them are now found in neighboring countries.

In passing it should be mentioned that Pentecostals also take the lead in several other Latin American countries, such as Peru, El Salvador, Guatemala, and the Dominican Republic.

PENTECOSTAL STRATEGY AND SOCIAL CONCERN

There are those who contend that the Pentecostals' view of Christian mission is too narrow, and that emphasis on evangelism and personal conversion leaves much to be desired in the area of men's physical and economic needs. To this, Pentecostals answer: Let us put first things first!

There is nothing as important as getting men's hearts right with God. The center must be put right before the periphery can be corrected. To try to remedy peripheral conditions leaving the heart unchanged is useless and deceiving. When a man is truly converted, he seeks a better life for himself and for his family. One has only to observe the families of Evangelical Christians over a period of a few years to note that spiritual conversion leads to improvement in every aspect of a convert's life.

When the Evangelical community gathers strength, the Christians themselves show concern for the betterment of their own people. For example, many of the larger Pentecostal churches establish day schools. In San Salvador, an Assemblies of God church has established a large school which now includes a junior college. This is entirely a local effort. In Brazil the churches have established orphanages and homes for elderly people. The larger churches have commissaries to aid the poor. All is carried on in an unassuming way, without fanfare, and with a minimum of outside help. The image of the Christian witness is not distorted by the political and cultural implications involved in a "rich America helping an underprivileged people."

It is interesting here to note the observations of William Read:

> Ceaseless migrations from rural to urban areas are occurring in Brazil. . . . Continuous uprooting and transplanting of a restless people driven by cultural changes of all types—inflation, drought, industrialization, illness, illiteracy, and idolatry—have created a great sociological void. . . . Of all the Evangelical Churches in Brazil, only the Assemblies and their sister Pentecostal Churches are in a position to take full advantage of the sociological receptivity of a people in revolution.[3]

And again:

> The Assemblies of God is a Church of and for the masses, and as long as it continues to minister to their needs it will grow. . . . There is a social revolution in Brazil today, and all governments are certain to make better and better provision for the common man. . . . The Assemblies under God are becoming the greatest upward movement of lower-class people in all Latin America. They are rising everywhere into new levels of character and godliness. God is blessing them with income, education and status.[4]

PENTECOSTAL STRATEGY AND ESCHATOLOGY

It should be observed that Pentecostals do not expect all the world to become Christian through the efforts of evangelism. Rather, they see that the remedy of many of earth's ills must await the Second Advent of the King of kings, for which they earnestly pray and wait. His coming will solve the problems of the social order. Until then, Christians must faithfully witness by life and word, and prepare that body of transformed men which is the very salt of the earth in this present age and which will form the nucleus of the redeemed race in the coming Kingdom. Converts must be won, churches planted and multiplied; Christian leaders called, prepared and sent forth until every soul on earth shall have had an opportunity to hear God's message of love and redemption in Christ Jesus.

NOTES

1. Latin American Christians dislike the term "Protestant," preferring to be known as "Evangelicals" without making a distinction between liberal and conservative theologies as is the case in North America.
2. William R. Read, *New Patterns of Church Growth in Brazil* (Grand Rapids: Wm. B. Eerdmans, 1965), p. 142.
3. Ibid., p. 130.
4. Ibid., p. 143.

B. ANSWERS FROM THE WHOLE WORLD
7. Does the World Need Fantastically Growing Churches?

Marie-Louise Martin

The statement that the world does in fact need fantastically growing churches sets one to thinking. These days many would say that the world needs above all peace, development of food production in view of the population explosion, hence development of educational standards, and a better distribution of the means of production. Does the world also need fantastically growing churches? What is the Church, after all? What is its function in the world? What is meant by church growth? When speaking of the Church in this part of the world, many people are unable to see what the Church has to do in the world, when for them it is a small corner where they find refuge from the storms and tempests of the world; they close doors and windows to shut the "evil world" out and deceive themselves, for a short while, with a heavenly mythology, to which they return about once a week. "Their church" must remain as it was established some 100–140 years ago; no changes may be made in the sacrosanct structure and organization. Only small, inevitable adaptations are permitted. We have, therefore, to pose the question anew:

1. *What is the Church?*

It is indeed a question which has to be answered by every generation, because the Church stands in a rapidly changing world and must relate to changing patterns of society. This does not mean that the character of the Church must also change. Modern theology has again taught us (what the New Testament writers knew so well!) that the center of the Church is the person of

---

Dr. Martin, an ordained minister of the Reformed Church in Basel (Switzerland), left her parish work in 1946 at the request of the Swiss Mission in South Africa to teach and serve as chaplain in Northern Transvaal. Since 1957 she has been Lecturer in Theology at Morija Theological School (Lesotho), as well as Lecturer and Chaplain and (since 1966) Reader in Theology at the University of Botswana, Lesotho and Swaziland, in Lesotho.

Jesus Christ. When we say Church, we say Jesus Christ. This takes the whole question of the Church out of the institutional and structural into the *personal* sphere which is so very important in a highly technological and impersonal world. Jesus Christ is not a dogma, a myth, an institution, but a living person. The Church is His people, His disciples, His friends, gathered round Him because He has called them. They hear His word and see Him acting and realize that in this man Jesus, God has come to seek and take care of man, to give him a home and guidance in a puzzling world. They realize that with Jesus they find true freedom, life, and joy, help to come to terms with their problems, and strength to bear the tensions, conflicts, sufferings, and frustrations of modern life. This fellowship is daily renewed through His word, made an actual and living word through the Spirit; it is renewed in the common meal of the Supper, the breaking of bread and the sharing of the cup. Those around Jesus are the Church.

We Westerners are used to thinking in terms of individualism. Easterners—amongst whom Jesus lived—as well as Africans, emphasize much more the community aspect. Jesus and his disciples form one "body." This is not an abstraction, because life is not lived in isolation but in relationships. The Church is a community of sharing in which Jesus shares His resurrection-life and His victory as well as His sufferings and His Cross with His disciples.

This then is the Church: Jesus Christ and His disciples. It is in the first instance the *local church,* the local community of Christians who meet to hear His word, to break the bread and to worship, pray and act. It is in the second instance a nation- and worldwide Church. We have thus described the Church in terms of *koinonia,* the "communion of saints."

2. *The task of the Church*

The Church is not an end in itself. Jesus came for all men as the "second Adam," the new man. In Him the whole of mankind has already moved into the new age which is the age of reconciliation and therefore of a new relationship with God. The Church is men and women who in fellowship with Jesus have recognized and acknowledged this fact; they have acknowledged it not because their own culture and religion were closer to the Christian truth than those of others, or because they were more responsive than others, but because God's grace has overcome all their resistance (cf. Eph. 2:1ff.). With Christ they are the "new man" and represent the whole of mankind. They are the first-fruits in this world. With this fact the task of the Church is given: to proclaim to all mankind—to all the world—that in Jesus all men find their true nature and destiny, their true freedom from evil, and fellowship with God, a fellowship that does not depend on human mediation other than Jesus Christ, a fellowship that does not depend either on human sacrifices, rituals, or conformity to a code of laws. It is based entirely on God's seeking and outgoing love in Christ.

Because of God's outgoing love the Church is not only a home for believers where they belong, a home where they find strength to bear the tensions and frustrations of modern life, but it is a "place" from which they are sent out into the world to share what they have received. The world needs the Church with this startling message: You are already God's through Christ. Acknowledge this fact and rejoice in it! Though the world may not be aware of it, it needs the Church, as Jesus' ambassador.

This then is the task of the Church: the *kerygma*, the proclamation of the good news by word and by accompanying signs which we can sum up in the term *diakonia*, service. If the word is to be believed, it must in some way be audio-visible. The life of new men and women, their actions, their readiness to forgive, their going-the-second-mile are signs that help to realize the contents of the message and confirm it. All this cannot be separated from evangelism, but cannot take the first place either, which belongs to the *kerygma*.

There must be concern for the poor, the underprivileged, for justice, peace, and better social and economic conditions for those nearby and those far away, but always in the name of Christ so that He may be made known as the great liberator. We agree therefore with Dr. McGavran that mere dialogue and Christian presence are not sufficient in themselves. This does not mean to participate in social efforts with the aim of "proselytism" only, but with the deep and yet tactful concern that men and women should receive not only the second-best, but the very best, their true humanity which is theirs in Christ. Much wisdom is needed, lest *diakonia* become a mere tool of evangelism, or—the other extreme—lest we abandon all mention of Christ because it looks like catching people in need and then creating "rice Christians."

Dr. McGavran attacks the "current sacred triad, *kerygma*, *diakonia*, and *koinonia*." This is unjustified, because it is biblical. We must, however, get the priorities right. *Kerygma* is decisive, it is the task of the *koinonia*; and *diakonia* is a demonstration of the contents of the *kerygma*.

To proclaim the good news is a tremendous task. It must

indeed be *good news* and not only, as one sometimes hears in Africa (and elsewhere), a myth of heaven, or a series of prescriptions and laws for "the good life" which weak and sinful men cannot attain. The message must be relevant and prophetic, related to the world, its conditions, anxieties, needs, and aspirations. If this is not the case, the Church is just another club, set up to satisfy the needs of a few pious people, and is useless for the world. Here we meet the immense problem of communication and actualization of the word.

3. *The relevance of the message*

Paul communicated the gospel to Greeks in different terms than to Jews. It was the same gospel, but proclaimed in the thought-forms, speech-forms, idioms, and even folklore and wisdom of the people to whom it was addressed. For example, the phrase that the blood of Jesus Christ cleanses us from all sins, may mean a lot to people of a culture where sacrifices are offered for the purpose of purification and reconciliation, but may be a completely empty phrase for people of another culture. In this latter case another image must be used to convey the same message.

Kerygma is not an easy task, but a very complex one. First the biblical message must be understood in the context of the old oriental cultures. The messenger must have an elementary knowledge of what biblical phrases, words, and images meant when they were used by a prophet, an apostle, a community that handed the message down orally until it was committed to writing. That is only one side. The other side is this: he must have a knowledge of the culture, the language, the images and idioms of the people to whom he has to preach. And above all he must know the conditions in which they live, their hopes and anxieties, their temptations, and he must have the vision to place all this in the context of the present world at large.

This is a tremendous effort which requires men and women of high caliber, not only intellectually, but first and foremost in terms of dedication, prophetic zeal, and openness. Such persons are lacking in our churches. Once a man has obtained his diploma, certificate, or degree, once he has been accepted by the church and ordained, he often settles down, preaches for fifty years in the same old-fashioned terms, and does not realize that his message is no longer related to the realities round about him. Sound strategy with regard to the task and mission of the Church is to attract the right kind of man—perhaps higher stipends have to be found for this purpose—then to train him most carefully and to help him to remain open, to enable him to continue studying and reading. Shortage of personnel, serious as it may be, must not be a reason to deny a man this possibility. To achieve it, much more cooperation between the denominations is naturally needed.

One might object that as the Holy Spirit is the teacher who leads into all the truth, all careful study of the biblical message and of the environment to which it has to be related, are not absolutely necessary. Still, the Holy Spirit is no *Deus ex machina* to replace serious study, thinking, and meditation. He will inspire and help those who take this task most seriously. Theological seminaries and university departments of theology have to cooperate by offering studies which are concentrated on the hermeneutical problem in its widest sense, including the background knowledge related to the biblical message, as well as to the present world and the people to whom it is proclaimed.

In order to preach the message to people of a certain culture and environment, Dr. McGavran proposes ethnic churches for the time being. I do not believe that ethnic churches will be the solution. They cannot cope with the problem of cultural change, nor can they view issues in world perspective. We have ample proof of this, quite apart from the theological problem which they pose.

4. *Who should proclaim the message?*

It is commonplace to state that every Christian is a "missionary," i.e., sent into the world to proclaim the gospel. We have stated the necessity of careful training for the service of the Church. We have thus pointed to the great importance of adequate leadership. Someone recently made the statement that the problem of church growth is the problem of dynamic and competent leadership. The Church, being in this world, cannot make headway without dynamic and well-equipped leaders. The more institutional any church becomes, the less it will produce and retain this type of leader, because there is hardly any place for him. He is on all sides hemmed in by the existing structure. Simon Kimbangu in the Congo might not have become the leader and symbol of a large prophetic (and at times messianic) movement if there had been a place for him in the existing church structure. The same might be said of Alice Lenshina in Zambia.

Dynamic and well-trained leaders are the men and women who will inspire the other disciples of Christ and make them His messengers in their immediate surroundings, in their homes, their professional life, their recreation clubs, their political parties, and trade unions. We see this process happening all the time in the African independent churches where the leader makes a strong impact on the members. The result is that from a body of such active members new leaders emerge. Young people like to get involved in a dynamic fellowship, but pull out of one which is half dead.

5. *Church-planting and church growth*

Church-planting, which is a result of the proclamation of the message, is not the planting of a particular denomination, though it is undertaken by men and women who belong to a denomination. In view of the greater realization today that what is important is the living Christ, and not an institution, could we not think of an ecumenical effort by a joint team in areas where church-planting has not yet taken place, and then leave it to the emerging fellowship of discipled men and women to find a structure, an organization, and a form of worship which express their response to the newly found fellowship with God through Christ? Or is this a utopia? Too heretical? Impracticable? Perhaps.

Planting is not enough. The new plant needs watering or else it dies. Paul says, "I planted, Apollos watered" (1 Cor. 3:6, RSV). Where the result of the Church's *kerygma* is the emergence of a new community of disciples, they must be attended to. They need further teaching, exhortation, guidance, and help, but not necessarily by the founder. They may at this stage need another type of leader. What is essential, however, is that "God gives growth." All our planting and watering, even the *best* missionary strategy and policy, cannot replace Him who alone gives growth.

At this juncture we are confronted by the puzzling question: Why is it that sometimes no church-planting follows the proclamation, or that the "plant" grows up to a certain height and then stops growing, or withers away in spite of all efforts to keep it alive? This is the situation of many churches in Africa. But next door to them, an African independent church springs up overnight, and another one just nearby. Today independent churches grow fast. They count two million members and adherents in South Africa alone. Many of them possess what the traditional churches lack: dynamic leaders. Moreover, they meet needs which were or are overlooked by churches who sent missionaries from abroad: the need of faith-healing, the need of African saints to replace the constant reference to Luther, Calvin, Wesley and others who remain strangers in Africa. Simon Kimbangu (to come back to him) would seem to fill this need in the *Église de Jésus Christ sur la terre par le prophète S. Kimbangu*. Independent churches give more scope for the expression of emotion in worship; they create a visible center for the new brotherhood, a city of God on earth, a new Jerusalem; and they see blessings in terms of prosperity. Here we find church growth, even fantastic church growth. This leads us, however, to the critical question: what is church growth? Do we underline *church* or *growth*?

6. *How can we determine church growth?*

Can it be determined by means of statistics? Yes and no. *Yes*, in so far as the task of the *kerygma* does lead the disciples to new places where churches grow up. Thus there ought to be numerical increase. Our answer must, however, also include *no* inasmuch as God alone can determine who is truly His. This applies to all churches, traditional and independent. Where Christ remains in the center, though certain teachings and above all certain ceremonies seem strange to Westerners, there is evidence that God is in the midst of the Church. But where the gospel disappears behind a new leader or messiah, or where structures, organizations, and forms of worship become more important than a living encounter and fellowship with Christ, where He is obscured under all sorts of popular religion and syncretism, there the Church is growing weak, despite numerical increase.

Another factor must be taken into account: a church may come under pressure and persecution and thus share in Christ's suffering and Cross. When the heat of persecution is turned on, many become weak and leave the church, and yet this church is infinitely stronger in its witness to Christ and in its life than a numerically strong church with members who in reality have moved away from Him. Moreover, trials and sifting can be the turning point where new numerical growth sets in.

This leads us to a last, critical issue. When speaking of church growth we are inclined to neglect the fact that the gospel of Jesus, the crucified and risen Lord, is not popular, but a "stumblingblock to Jews and folly to Greeks" (1 Cor. 1:23, RSV). We lose sight of the *skandalon* of the gospel. There is acceptance *and* rejection, and unless God gives His grace, no amount of dialogue and Christian presence will remove natural man's opposition to the gospel. We do need fantastically growing churches, it is true. But we cannot forget that ultimately this depends on God's grace to *raise the dead*. Between the old and the new man in Christ, there is no continuity. Between the two there is death, symbolized by baptism upon entry into the Church. Unless *God* works a miracle (1 Cor. 3:6) our best endeavors are doomed. But God "desires all men to be saved and to come to the knowledge of the truth" (1 Tim. 2:4, RSV). For this reason we must be thinking seriously about the question of church growth and adopting policies which will promote it—after getting our priorities right.

B. ANSWERS FROM THE WHOLE WORLD
8. Counterpoint

Mme. C. Gouzée

The invitation to contribute a nonspecialist comment on Dr. McGavran's article puts me in something of a quandary for several reasons, but particularly because that article is expressly directed to its author's "fellow laborers," to the "professional missionaries" who are his colleagues, and is clearly, in his view, no concern of mine. I am a lay-member of a Belgian church, and although I came into contact with Protestant missions during ten years spent in Africa (on account of my husband's job in industry), my contribution to their work never went beyond teaching French and conducting evening classes—activities which Dr. McGavran would regard as "good" in themselves but not as "evangelism." Obviously I do not qualify.

I might have been wiser, therefore, to hold my tongue and decline the invitation. Some readers of this specialist journal will undoubtedly be shocked by my naïve reactions to the article in question. No theologian will have the slightest difficulty in showing them to be heretical, nor any missionary in demonstrating their "irrelevance." In the last analysis, my views are merely symptomatic, a sample of the thinking of a fairly committed lay-member of a minority church. I hasten to add that it would have been very easy to find other Belgian lay people with views contrary to my own. To round off this brief introduction, may I say that, although I take an active part in the life of my church, I belong—by family, profession, friends, political concerns, and cultural interests—to that world which Dr. McGavran sees as having rejected Christ, and, therefore, as "lost." Indeed, considering my somewhat unorthodox attitude towards certain Christian dogmas, I think that this may perhaps be true of me as well. Let me even confess, since our theme is evangelism, that I often feel nearer to the evangelized than to the evangelizers!

Counterpoint—"Melody added as accompaniment to a given melody or plain-song." Also *fig.* "A contrary point in an argument" (*The Shorter Oxford English Dictionary*).

I begin then with a comment at an ordinary human level. I wonder whether people who take Dr. McGavran's view of "mission" do not in fact share a similar experience of the Church: the experience of a life of spiritual communion, of psychological stability, of friendship, of successful family life (I select at random), found within the bosom of a church and preceded perhaps by a disappointing and possibly distressing experience, *extra muros*, of loneliness, personal emptiness, failure or folly. By and large, it is in the Church that these people have found happiness, peace, their ideal, their friends and, above all, Jesus Christ. Their natural generosity impels them to devote their energies to add to the number of such choice places in the world.

But what if the reverse process takes place? What if—and this does happen—a happy person, coming from a generous, intelligent, open, integrated background, encounters Christ, is "converted" and then finds himself a member of a Christian community which becomes indispensable to his life and ideal of service, but which would seem to him to be narrower, more withdrawn and self-centered than that "world" with which he retains all his emotional links? How is such a person to live with the people he loves and whose views (unbelief apart) he shares, if he has to regard them as damned and himself as saved, and if his sole responsibility is to summon them to repentance? Can he have this attitude towards the rest of mankind if it is certainly not his attitude to his own family and friends? Can he possibly divide up the human race so as to number himself with the sheep who are often still strangers to him, and to place his friends among the goats who are rejected?

What I am driving at will now be clear. My purpose in beginning at this purely psychological level has been to try to explain to myself the nature of my first negative reaction to the article in question. But obviously the heart of the matter remains to be explored.

Dr. McGavran questions the correctness of the direction taken by much contemporary thinking about the objectives of missionary work which in his opinion often loses sight of the main objective, that is, to convert men and women, to baptize them, and so to create churches. He regrets that such missionary thinking tends to assume that the service and even the witness rendered by the missionary ought to be disinterested, innocent of any ulterior motivation to convert people, whereas, in his view, the entire missionary enterprise should be organized with an eye to its spiritual output, so to speak. He would say that there has also been too great a tendency to mistake all sorts of good works for the specific function of mission, namely, the planting of churches.

Would it be caricaturing his argument to conclude from it that he would, for example, reject the well-known slogan: "Let the world write the agenda," preferring to declare (with all due respect to many of the participants in the Church and Society Conference!): "Change men's hearts and you will change society"? Can we presume that he favors monologue rather than dialogue, both with men of other religions and with agnostics? Or that he is not persuaded that Christ speaks to Christians through these others? On the tactical level, does he mean that Christian missions should not select "points of tension" (revolutions, racial conflicts, confrontations with other major religions) but should choose rather the ethnic groups, classes, areas, where the opportunities for planting churches are greatest? Would he approve, for instance, of a missionary society which arrived in the Congo after Independence in search of promising sites for its hospitals but soon afterwards departed for more tranquil regions where its humanitarian work would be just as useful but its missionary work more fruitful?

Those who read *Drafts for Sections*, prepared for the Uppsala Assembly, and *The Church for Others* [1] will at once recognize the predilections of these authors for the strategy condemned by Dr. McGavran! Since it is always salutary for widely accepted views to be challenged (in this case, those expressed in ecumenical circles), we should be grateful to Dr. McGavran for compelling his opponents to ask themselves if they are not perhaps aiming in the wrong direction. He for his part is convinced that they are. But he has not asked himself (in the article in question, at least) the reasons which have led so many "missiologists," as well as a number of those at work "in the field," to pursue this mistaken strategy.

One basic question which we must raise concerns the relationship between faith and life. In a sense, the twentieth-century Christian, who is more of a moralist than a metaphysician, understands (even if he does not practice it) the way a man must live if he is to commend God's love to men, better than he understands how God, for instance, showed and continues to show His love to men in Jesus Christ. To serve his brothers, to open schools, to develop regions, to help revolutionaries, to combat racialism, or to look after lepers, it is necessary and it is enough for him to love men and to promote justice. He may love them because of Christ and believe that he is thereby helping to establish His Kingdom; but the questions such as how that Kingdom will be established, who Christ is, what is the origin of evil, what relation there is between Buddhism and Christianity, what will be the ultimate destiny of unbelievers—can be turned over and over again, or can be left to specialists, without producing any apparent effect upon the work in the field.

But if we are to proclaim the gospel, we must understand it; if we are to baptize, we have to be persuaded that baptism is essential; if we are to plant churches, we need at least a minimum of dogmas. In short, I wonder whether one reason for the "partisan emphasis on peripheral aspects of the task," to which Dr. McGavran refers, may not be the theological context in which we are living. Statistics would probably show that missionaries in the typical mold, those namely who have clung to a concept of mission close to McGavran's own, are mainly recruited from pietistic, fundamentalist societies or circles, which are almost completely proof against the great currents of uncertainty in our time. In other words, the "McGavran strategy" can only be accepted and implemented by those with simple faith. I have no doubt that such faith can still move mountains. I fear that it is no longer within the reach of many Christians today.

This crisis concerning the content of the Christian message goes, I believe, hand-in-hand with a crisis in language. Perhaps I have got things out of proportion by drawing general conclusions from what I have observed, for example, in theological quarters influenced by Bultmann, Bonhoeffer, Tillich, and others; in reactions throughout the world to the gallant but clumsy endeavors of Robinson; in the ferment within French university circles (see the spendid October 1967 issue of the review *Esprit* on the theme "New World and God's Word"); in the Vatican Council's discussions on the crisis of faith; and in more than one individual case known to me personally. But can it possibly be that missionaries do not experience the inability to find appropriate words to speak about God to a sick world, when we nonmissionary Christians encounter it every day of our lives? Is it really the old sin of "having ears but hearing not" that explains why so many people are closed to the communication of God's Word (in a language burdened with so much alien cultural dead weight)? Or should we not rather seek the explanation of this impermeability in the language itself, "shuttled between the cultural world of the witness to Revelation and our own cultural world"? [2]

Might we not go still further back and ask ourselves why we are passing through such crises? So far as the Christian mission is concerned, the position would seem to me to be as follows, expressed in broad outline:

1. In Christendom, where everyone is looked upon as Christian, Jesus' command, "Go and teach," is carried out in distant lands. And history, because it moves so very slowly, is treated as static and empty. Thus the time between the Ascension and the Parousia constitutes a historical vacuum in which the only thing that can happen is testimony concerning the past event of the Incarnation and the future event of Christ's Coming (see *The Church for Others*). All that can be done is to extract man from the sphere of damnation in which the world's history continues and to bring him into the sphere of salvation which is identified with the Church. This is the work of the "missionaries," namely, Christians specially called to this task as members of the clergy or as their equivalents.

It is easy to see how this point of view could have inspired the work of a missionary confronted by a primitive or Asiatic civilization, the history of which might indeed have appeared to him to have been arrested before the Christian mission's arrival on the scene, or even when he was confronted by the besotted miner, who could only be rescued from his sin and hopeless misery by inclusion in a Christian community. But that missionary also lived in a world where words, whether written or spoken, still kept their value and weight. Moreover, he was almost always dealing with theists and often with people less "cultured" than himself.

2. We now leap several decades forward. Where are the theists today? Not always within the Church! Civilization? Everywhere— or nowhere! Language? It proliferates, wants to say everything, and is valued only as it influences action. Where are the "mission fields"? Everywhere. Clearly, France as *"pays de mission"* bears little resemblance to those "dark shores of pagan lands" of which our missionary hymns speak so grandly! Finally, although a Livingstone might still possibly think that nothing important, nothing of significance to God, could happen in the world between the Ascension and the Parousia except the increase of His Church, will any missionary of 1968 who reads his newspapers dare to continue enclosing his work within so brittle and inadequate an ivory tower?

This situation, along with many other factors, has produced a theology of mission (for example, in the works of Hollenweger, Casalis, Keller, and Hoekendijk) which stresses the absence of any frontier between the Church and the world, the idea of Christ reigning openly in the Church and incognito outside it, and the transformation of the world by the leaven (identified with the Kingdom, not with the Church!). The Church is a witness, but is not God's sole instrument. And it must be aware of the fact.

This situation, along with the democratization of social and political institutions and the discovery of the duty of responsibility in addition to that of obedience, has accelerated the decline of clericalism in the Church and the discovery of the missionary role of every member. Now, lay people have various gifts, not always those required for preaching; and, as a rule, they have remained far more independent of the institutional church than have the clergy.

Lastly, once-powerful churches have become aware of their minority position in the world. In face of the "free thinkers," who have so often shown it the path of justice and truth, the Church no longer claims the right to any monopoly of these things. Hence the realization that the conditions for genuine dialogue exist, namely, "readiness to be changed as well as to influence others." [3]

It is this complex of factors which has produced the "strategy" that attracts Dr. McGavran's critical fire.

A rapid reader may view what I have written so far as a defense of the "strategy of the fifties," and may imagine that I am pleading extenuating circumstances by arguing that because of our "little faith" and our twentieth-century context, this is the most that can be done at present.

I must therefore make it clear before I conclude, that while I regard some of the main issues in Dr. McGavran's case as extremely important and rightly drawn to our attention, I find it impossible to share his standpoint.

1. I agree that it is undoubtedly necessary that bodies such as the overseas missionary societies should not try to move in all directions at once, but should realize that the main emphasis must still be placed upon explicit witness. I agree that it is not enough to serve incognito within the structures of the world. For one thing, what Christians do is not always immediately intelligible; like some comic strips in our newspapers, it requires verbal explanation in order to be properly understood. For another thing, we have to bear in mind St. Paul's question: "How could they have faith in one they had never heard of?"

2. I agree that we must heed the sociologists and anthropologists, and relate our missionary activity to the characteristics of the society in which we are working. My only regret in this connection is that Dr. McGavran has not provided us with an

illustration of what he calls "hard, bold plans for planting churches." The examples he does give of classifications for types of society leave us somewhat in the air.

3. I agree that it is a good thing to study past missionary experience and to compare what is attempted with what has been achieved.

4. I agree, finally, that "church growth is an exceedingly complex process and cannot be commanded."

Yet Dr. McGavran sometimes gives us the impression that churches will automatically increase and multiply, provided the right strategy is employed. His answer would, I suppose, be that church growth is only granted to those who, "sickle in hand, labor all day and have carts ready . . . to carry in the piled sheaves"; that church growth is a "measure" by which to verify whether or not one is on the right lines; and that merely preaching the gospel or living as "faithful Christians in a pietistic sense" and leaving it to the Spirit to convert people, is certainly not to proceed on the right lines.

This last point hits the nail on the head. Indeed, as I see it, it is this which constitutes the real scandal: that the "quiet pietistic lives" of so many Christians and of so many missionaries should be so indistinguishable from the lives of atheists that they clearly could never be a challenge to anyone. Once and for all, Christians must realize in this age of militant communists, of young people voluntarily serving their brothers in the developing countries, of the Guevaras and Régis Debrays, that they no longer have any monopoly of commitment or heroism, and that God frequently employs people outside His visible Church to hasten the coming of His Kingdom of justice.

Certainly "mission is not beautiful inclusive statements about mission." Certainly "the gospel is empty words until it is believed and obeyed." But precisely because it is no longer obeyed (and we only genuinely believe those whom we obey), it no longer gets much of a hearing in a world where it is in a fair way of becoming "empty words."

Does church growth prove that one is on the right lines? Is our present situation evidence of a mistaken strategy? I find such questions impossible to answer. My inclination would be to attach more importance to the quality of existing or developing churches than to their number; to the way Christians live than to their status as baptized persons; to their involvement in the world than to their participation in the Church. For one thing, the metaphors of the leaven, the salt, and the light seem to indicate that Christians are destined to be in a minority. Moreover, it appears to me contrary to the spirit of the gospel to look for visible signs of success, even and perhaps especially, in this field. Such an attitude is reminiscent of the view of those Puritans who regarded economic success as a mark of divine approval.

I should like to end with three quotations:

> Christ already dwells and works in this world. Incognito He accompanies all men on their journey. . . . Sent by Him, we go from Him to the world . . . as those who know, alongside those who do not. . . . And since Christ has preceded us among our brothers, in going to them we go to meet Him. We do not think of Him as imprisoned in our churches but as wandering and working throughout the entire world. Whether their agents are Christians or not, whether the Church backs them or not, all struggles for peace, all sacrifices for justice, all acts of love, have God as their hidden Mover and the victory of Christ as their ultimate goal. It is, therefore, not our business to bring salvation to a world already saved. . . . We have to recognize and greet Christ's presence at the heart of the world, to discover there the evidence of His activity, to decipher and to produce there the signs of His rule." [4]

> There are varieties of gifts, but the same Spirit. . . . Are all apostles? (1 Cor. 12:4, 29, RSV).

> We act as if everything depended on us but we pray as if everything depended on God; we know full well that it is not we who make the Kingdom which is coming; but we also know that what we do has a hidden connexion with that Kingdom. The practical problem of hope arises only when we have put behind us this disastrous and purely speculative alternative. On the other hand, the most orthodox statements we can make about the Kingdom of God and the Lordship of Jesus Christ remain null and void if we do not venture their meaning in some action in progress; on the other hand, our most effective actions are also meaningless if we fail to relate them to our profession of faith (Paul Ricoeur).

NOTES

1. *The Church for Others: Two Reports on the Missionary Structure of the Congregation*, prepared by the Western European and North American working groups of the Department on Studies in Evangelism (Geneva: WCC, 1967).
2. See *Esprit*, October 1967.
3. *Drafts for Sections*, p. 41.
4. Michel Philibert: *Assemblée du protestantism français*, 1963.

B. ANSWERS FROM THE WHOLE WORLD
9. Christian Presence and One of Its Critics

Herbert Neve

Currently a sharp distinction between two different types of mission is being articulated. The writer of this article agrees and disagrees with both of them at certain points. He therefore feels compelled to assume the role of a referee, although he recognizes that this involves a number of risks.[1] Donald McGavran has highlighted the issue by stressing "church growth" as the primary criterion for mission, in contrast to a trend towards the "Christian presence" school of thought. It is not difficult to suppose that the church growth strategy has a large circle of potential sympathizers and adherents, even if it does not yet represent the official attitude of most church mission boards. The "strategy of the fifties," as McGavran calls the Christian presence theory, has no doubt gained the dominant position in the minds of many mission policymakers. It is the latter approach which has been prevalent in ecumenical circles in recent years.[2]

Neither of these views has had the opportunity to develop enough to be presented in clear-cut theoretical outline. McGavran's ideas in particular are put forward in a rather stark manner, without much awareness of the nuances in contemporary theology. Such references as "the immortal soul" of man, "opportunities for propagating the Christian religion," and "fantastically multiplying churches" force many people to wonder about the thinking which undergirds his proposals. It is characteristic of McGavran that he employs very little theology upon which to base his new strategy. That which he does use is very simple and direct. He is obviously a man of action. Motivation for mission should "throb with Christ's passion for men's eternal redemption" and it should "blaze with certainty" about the central and universal truths of salvation. More than this does not seem to be required. One looks for more substance in his understanding of the Church, salvation, redemption, worship, mission and evange-

---

Herbert Neve is the Study Secretary of the Secretariat for Stewardship and Evangelism of the Lutheran World Federation, Geneva.

lism. It is not quite clear why further clarification of these points is omitted. He should state his reasons for this, and if he intentionally avoids explaining these words, then it is clear that one very important difference already exists between "church growth" strategy and "Christian presence" thinking. A continuing process of reflection on missionary action is an essential part of the latter.

McGavran is right in asserting that a direct approach in mission is still required in many parts of our world. Therefore, the Christian presence approach cannot expect to answer the universal need for mission in our day. He writes: ". . . in millions of communities there are no Christians." Here he alludes to large areas in Asia, Africa and Latin America which are entirely unevangelized. Under such circumstances it is true that an aggressive, self-conscious, planned approach must be employed. McGavran is an unabashed and forthright advocate of attempting to join the tools of modern science with the work of the Holy Spirit in the shaping of missionary policy. This undoubtedly offends the sensitivities of many. He claims that his orientation is essentially the same as that employed in the Primitive Church. The difference is that it would be carried out through the additional use of modern sociological and technical know-how. It should not be too difficult to agree with McGavran that in those places where the gospel has not yet been heard at all, the forthright style so typical of proclamation in the New Testament kerygma is quite in order. This pertains especially to those primitive tribes and subcultures to which he often refers.

If it is true, as is claimed, that there are still major portions of the world living in much the same circumstances as they lived in the ancient world, then the apologetic style of Christian presence may be a needless waste of time. McGavran admits, however, that in much of the non-Christian world, "seed" would have to be sown before the people would be responsive. This would be the case, for example, in those vast areas in the Middle East where, over the centuries, Islam has become immune to Christianity. It is a serious question whether having "Christ ride the chariot of tribal allegiance into the heart of the tribe" would work in that part of the globe. In spite of the disunity of the Arab world, it has a certain kind of solidarity, part of which is rooted in a firm stand against the Church's interpretation of the divinity of Christ. There the Church faces a strong segment of the non-Christian world where Christian presence in the best sense might be more effective than a growth strategy.

The refreshing thing about the church growth strategy is its sense of direction. Despite its simplistic theology and its strident methods, there is earnest commitment to a cause. This has been lacking for some time. It is difficult to become attracted to the "wholistic" approach of Christian presence because it tends to be ambiguous. What McGavran calls for is a program of mission where enormous amounts of money, human talent, information, scientific methods, and Christian commitment are to be organized efficiently to accomplish one single purpose, namely, to complete the evangelization of the world. This unquestionably has a strong appeal in contrast to the endless work of carrying on dialogue with the world without foreseeing any conclusion. And whereas Christian presence thinking has attempted to make concrete proposals about changes in church structures in order that the Church may become the Church-in-Mission, McGavran almost steals the show by speaking the language of experienced administrators who must formulate and carry out specific plans.

What church growth strategy gains by bending everything to meet the demands for "fantastically multiplying churches," it inevitably stands to lose in the task of assisting these churches to make the transition towards the new life in Christ. There is a distinct inconsistency in McGavran's thought at this point. He says that the task of bringing newly founded churches together into one brotherhood in Christ must wait for the "perfecting stage, when ethnic or cultural units have been discipled." There is no hint of provision for finding and effecting the "right strategy" for this task. Yet he admits that it is necessary for cultural units which have recently been converted immediately to begin adapting their customs to a new way of life. Granted that making disciples should take the first priority in initial missionary efforts, it would be a serious mistake to neglect the specific problems of social action which demand immediate attention. There is a definite lack of realism in missionary strategy which counts on a time lag between the "discipling stage" and the "perfecting stage." Both the internal requirements from within the cultural unit and the external influence of modern technological society combine in pressures for change which can be extremely sudden. The full mobilization of all the power of the Church behind the church growth strategy would help to precipitate this crisis. Many of the hard-won insights of Christian presence thinking would no doubt help to offset this glaring mistake.

What is most disconcerting about the church growth strategy is that it deliberately sets out to establish a set of false alternatives and attempts to force a choice between them. It even goes so far as to claim that Africa, Latin America, and Asia (Africasia) form a geographical bloc where church growth strategy should be employed exclusively. Europe and America (Eurica) comprise another entirely different geographical area where Christian presence thinking has arisen, and seems to be best applicable. Whether he feels that the latter assertion is true or not, McGavran has not clearly stated. In any event, he is certain that Christian presence should not be exported from Eurica to Africasia.

It is true that Christian presence thinking is uniquely a product of the West, formerly Christian, and now secular. It is based on the presupposition that in a post-Christian culture, mission must take the form of renewal regardless of whether this be of a revolutionary or of an evolutionary kind. McGavran is entirely justified in his criticism that its proponents during the last two decades have not taken the needs of Africasia seriously enough. His proposals therefore come as a certain corrective to the onesidedness of present-day missionary thinking.

It would be a tragic mistake, however, if church growth strategy and Christian presence thinking were pitted against one another as competing points of view. They are not mutually exclusive, but complementary. Even if it were to be established that the primary stress in Africasia is to be on church growth and that Christian presence is best suited for Eurica, this does not mean that they can be set one against the other. In simple terms, the one is mission as direct evangelistic outreach suited to certain needs, and the other is mission as church renewal suited to other requirements. Although the theories and strategies which belong to each appear on the surface to be at odds, in the light of the demands of the situation, they are not. Despite the different ways of saying and doing things, the emphasis of the church growth strategy is on justification (or conversion), and in Christian presence it is on sanctification (or the Christian life). Although particular emphasis may need to be made on one or the other in any given context, under no circumstances can they be torn apart.

If McGavran's criticism of Christian presence thinking introduces some discussion between adherents of the two alternatives, as he has formulated them, all well and good. It would be regrettable, however, if we were now led into accepting his apparent presupposition that there could be no way to reconcile them. One would hope that it will be possible to develop thinking and strategy of these two different types which might complement one another, while each maintains its own integrity and validity.

This approach will avoid the ambiguity of "wholism." At the same time it will provide a healthy atmosphere wherein resources for mission can be wisely deployed in the future.

NOTES

1. Some of the writer's own views are taken up in more detail in *Sources for Change* (Geneva: World Council of Churches, 1968).
2. See *The Church for Others* (Geneva: World Council of Churches, 1967).

C. THE GROWTH OF THE CHURCH
The Iberville Statement

WCC Department of Missionary Studies

1. *The Church's mandate*

The Church of Jesus Christ has been commanded by her Lord to proclaim the gospel to men and women in every human situation. Her mandate is nothing less than the making of all nations His disciples. In her inner life, the Church offers herself daily to God; in the world she is to live for those who have not yet heard or received the gospel. It is her very nature to be an outward-looking fellowship of witness. "That which we have seen and heard we proclaim also to you, so that you may have fellowship with us" (1 John 1:3, RSV). The Church must therefore seek to be ever growing in numbers, as well as in the grace and knowledge of her Lord and Savior—not for reasons of self-aggrandizement, but in pursuance of God's desire that all men should be saved. So great a commission requires a total dedication of the Church's resources, a working recognition of the unity of God's people and of the unity of the task, and above all, complete dependence upon and obedience to the Holy Spirit. It calls for a constant, self-forgetful concern for the world for which Christ died.

2. *Her sin is introversion*

The vast increase of the world's population today outpaces the growth of the Christian Church. In spite of this tremendous challenge, we have to confess that churches are often introverted, and missions frequently unfruitful. There are notable exceptions, but in far too many places Christians seem to have lost all ex-

---

This text, drawn up by a special consultation convened by the WCC Department of Missionary Studies at Iberville, Quebec, July 31–August 2, 1963, represents only an initial statement, arising from a particular concern, and makes no attempt to cover other special contemporary situations, such as those in America or Germany. It was reprinted in the *International Review of Missions*, July 1968.

pectation that the multitudes can be converted or that churches will significantly increase in size. Such introversion has its roots in the egocentricity of the natural man, still unchanged into the likeness of Christ's selfless care for others. Its lack of expectancy not only betrays weakness of faith, it is also evidence of a profound misunderstanding of the measure of God's redemptive purpose. For the Church is called into being not merely as a saved community, but as a saving community. It is more even than a manifestation of Christ's gathering into one all the scattered children of God. It lives as a witness to, and a servant of, God's plan to reconcile, and to sum up, in Christ all things in heaven and on earth. Thus a church without a dynamic missionary purpose belies its own true nature.

3. *A call to renewal*

Only constant reformation and renewal, through the power of God's Spirit, can save the churches from self-centered piety, and from this tendency to live as beneficiaries of the gospel only, instead of as benefactors, through a loving sharing of its blessings with others. Static and introverted churches are to be found in every continent. Why are the questions raised by absence of church growth so seldom squarely faced? We appeal for self-examination, in a spirit of penitence and hope. It was when churches in Chile asked themselves whether they could not reproduce the life of the New Testament Church that they won New Testament experiences, and started a remarkable movement which has persisted for half a century.

4. *"Now is the acceptable time"*

There are many indications that there will be abundant opportunities for winning men and women to faith in Christ in the years immediately ahead. There remain, as there have always been, difficult and unresponsive areas in the world. Missionary endeavor from the West, moreover, is likely to experience increasing handicaps in other lands. But the home base of the Church's mission is everywhere, and every church must answer for its use or neglect of the special opportunities which are given to it.

5. *Study each situation*

In surveying the world missionary situation, generalities are of little help. Each population presents its own distinctive problems regarding church growth, and solutions from one area must not be naïvely projected, without examination, into another. Analytical techniques can help immensely towards recognition and understanding of the facts, and at this point careful statistics are of great use. If we are willing to replace defensive prejudices by comparative study of situations in which the churches have or have not grown, we shall find much to learn.

6. *God gives the increase*

We fully recognize that it is God who "gives the increase." It is the Holy Spirit who converts men to Christ, not we. But not only are planting and watering committed to us, so also is reaping in the times of harvest which God gives. Often, however, when there has been a movement of the Spirit, churches have been slow to perceive it, and fearful to cooperate. Instances have been known of whole communities turning towards God, yet of churches being unwilling to baptize, or, having baptized, of failing to provide resources for a proper shepherding of the ingathered flock. Opportunities have thus been tragically lost.

7. *A discerning strategy*

Emphasis upon care for the times and places of special opportunity for church growth does not imply the abandoning of unfruitful fields. It does imply a waiting and watching for such movements among people, and an obedient readiness to deploy, in a properly ecumenical spirit and strategy, the resources of personnel and funds required for true cooperation with the Spirit's work. What God asks of us is creative expectancy and faithful obedience in His service. When both have been forthcoming, wonderful events have taken place among responsive populations.

8. *Expectancy creates expectancy*

We have to confess that we have often failed in both expectancy and obedience. One reason for this is that, though churches which are not themselves dynamically engaged in evangelism may send missionaries to other lands, such missionaries are liable to reproduce the same contentment with static church life. It is truly missionary churches which are most likely to plant missionary churches. On the other hand, churches which are not winning fresh converts are by that very fact on the way to becoming more introverted. When people are won to Christ, they should immediately be led to realize that they are themselves called to participate in the Church's task of witness and service. If the creation of a special class of paid evangelists shows itself as weakening the sense of evangelistic responsibility that all church members should feel, the cause of church growth is in fact retarded, however faithfully such evangelists may serve. Every Christian needs to be trained for missionary service, each according to his own gifts and opportunities.

9. *The crucial question*

Is the Church growing, or not; and if not, why not? This is the fundamental question which ought to be asked in every situation. Numerical expansion and quality of Christian life are not alternatives, but correlatives, inasmuch as each is vitally related with the other. Again and again, it has been shown that the spontaneous expansion of a church quickens its own spiritual life; on the other hand, a church which is truly growing in grace thereby grows in concern for its missionary outreach. It is through seeking to share his knowledge of Christ with someone else that each Christian grows most surely in his own apprehension of the faith.

10. *Past mistakes*

Experience has demonstrated that many missionary methods used in the past are wrong, yet these continue to be repeated and defended, because they are not honestly examined in the light of their results. Sometimes, for example, the strategy adopted has been primarily to approach the most influential members of the community, although these may actually have good reason to be ardent defenders of the status quo. Again, the convert has often been isolated from his natural community; what has been intended as a protection has thus frequently itself become an additional ground for hostility, and anyway has had the devastating result of preventing the new Christian from witnessing in daily life to his own people. Missions have bought land and built houses before any church has been gathered; in consequence the missionary has felt unable to respond to the opportunities created by the Spirit in unforseen localities. Although teaching, healing and other ways of meeting basic human needs have always been an integral and vital part of witness to God's Kingdom, yet an overemphasis upon institutions has often retarded rather than forwarded the missionary cause. Especially has this been so when teaching and healing have become divorced from preaching—though it is equally important that proclamation of the gospel should make clear its relationship to the whole world in which men live. Institutions tend to absorb a disproportionate amount of the churches' resources for their mission, and to be regarded as created for the benefit of Christians rather than for the service of others in Christ's name. A more personalized care for the sick and the uneducated would be more truly Christian. Much of what is being undertaken by missions, with foreign resources, would be immeasurably more effective as a witness to the gospel if spontaneously undertaken, according to their own means, by members of the local church.

11. *Discipling and nurturing are two stages*

In situations where whole communities have been ready to turn to Christ, the mistake has often been made of implying that qualifications other than repentance and faith are required for entry into the Christian community. The New Testament shows that discipling, the winning of an understanding allegiance to Christ, comes first, and that this must be followed by careful nurture in personal faith and in personal Christian life. Churches need to place fuller reliance upon the power and wisdom of the Holy Spirit. To demand evidence of Christian growth before a convert is brought into the fellowship of the Church is a denial of the meaning of the gospel, and one of many reasons why churches fail to grow as they should. What is required is far greater emphasis upon post-baptismal training, in which help in making immediate and sustained witness to Christ is extremely important.

12. *A need for research*

At our Consultation here, we have considered many illustrations of factors which favor or retard church growth, of the complexities which require examination before situations can be adequately understood, and of the prevalence of mistaken ideas on this subject which call for radical correction. These have left us more than ever convinced of the need for scientific research into many different matters, some related to sociology, anthropology, and similar disciplines, others to church administration and structures, all to the strategy of the Church's mission. What, for example, is the effect of financial aid upon the churches' capacity and willingness to witness? How is pastoral training related to church growth? What are the reasons for taking great heed of the different strata within any unit of a population? Have marriages between Christians and non-Christians in fact served more to spread the gospel than to hinder it? These and many other questions call for study, area by area, study which could most fruitfully be undertaken by the churches in cooperation with one another. We welcome the pioneering work of the Institute of Church Growth in Eugene, Oregon (USA), and desire to see similar centers established in time in Asia, Africa, and Latin America. Reliable information concerning areas of special need and opportunity as regards church growth ought to be constantly collated and circulated. We urge earnest consideration of these matters by the WCC Division of World Mission and Evangelism, and by such bodies as the East Asia Christian Conference and the All Africa Conference of Churches. The object of this is that churches and mission boards in every part of the world may be stimulated to give to study of questions of church growth the importance which belongs to a subject so essential for fulfillment of the Church's mission in the world.

D. CHURCH GROWTH STRATEGY CONTINUED

Donald McGavran

I am pleased that my article of October 1965 has stirred up this worldwide discussion of church growth, and grateful to those who have contributed these articles testifying to the present embattled state of church growth thinking. My special thanks go to the *International Review of Missions* editor for the privilege of further comment.

Church growth, a matter of enormous importance, should never be seen as self-aggrandizement, but always as faithfulness to God. *God* wants men saved. *He* commands bringing the nations to faith and obedience. St. Paul in Romans 16:25ff. tells us that the gospel was revealed to this very end. Yet only as churches multiply fantastically amongst the millions of men who have no other way of knowing the Savior, is it possible for them to come to "faith and obedience."

In 1963, in connection with the Montreal meetings, the Department of Missionary Studies of the World Council of Churches convened a four-day consultation at Iberville, where representatives from all six continents drew up a *Statement on the Growth of the Church*.[1] It is essential reading for all who have to do with the world mission. A few brief quotations suffice to indicate its scope:

> The Church must seek to be ever growing in numbers, as well as in the grace and knowledge of her Lord and Savior. . . . There are many indications that there will be abundant opportunities for winning men and women to faith in Christ in the years immediately ahead. . . . We fully recognize that it is God who "gives the increase." . . . But not only are planting and watering committed to us, so also is reaping in the times of harvest which God gives. . . . We have to confess that we have often failed in both expectancy and obedience. . . . Is the church growing, or not; and if not, why not? This is the fundamental question which ought to be asked in every situation.[2]

This chapter originally appeared in the *International Review of Missions*, July 1968.

Since church growth is important, mission strategy ought to be giving more attention to it. The strategy of the fifties by-passed the unbelieving myriads: growth strategy restores an emphasis on their evangelization. The strategy of the fifties did not see the multitude of little-growing churches in Africasia which remain impotent at a few hundred or thousand communicants for decades, while receiving much mission aid: growth strategy is speaking about them. To be particular, it is speaking about little-growing churches in lands *where other churches are growing vigorously*. No one objects to churches in Arabia which do not grow, but in most Africasian lands nongrowth is a disease which can be cured. Enough attention should be paid to it so that it *is* cured.

As to the responses to my 1965 article—I was surprised at the depth and thrust of the anti-church growth sentiment in several of them. Their authors may have been reacting excessively. They had evidently not read the Iberville Statement. When they see their combined and enthusiastic opposition to the growth of Christ's Church, they themselves may be surprised and possibly dismayed. Church growth is not the only end of mission, but it is generally held to be a chief and irreplaceable end. It is like the physical growth of children. A Christian wants his son to grow in wisdom and grace, but he would be very worried if little Johnny remained at thirty pounds for ten years!

Perhaps I should not have been surprised at the anti-church growth sentiment. After all, such critical responses validate my thesis that mission strategies of the fifties and sixties were notably lacking in growth emphasis. Those who hold the current wrong strategy might have been expected to react vigorously to a dispassionate description of it.

In the original article, I wrote "The crisis in missions is this: it is possible to wax enthusiastic about factory evangelism, confrontation, dialogue, the whole gospel, the whole man, and many other good things, without intending or achieving any planting of new churches, or winning any unbelievers to the Christian faith. Mission in the 1960s becomes renewal, witness, outreach, rapprochement, penetration—there is no limit to the vague, elastic words which have only one thing in common: they do not require the baptism of bodies, the salvation of souls, and the building of visible new churches. Following one of these words too often becomes acceptable mission."[3] I am grieved that this July 1968 issue of the *Review* records with such clarity that so many, from so many parts of the world, on so many "impeccable grounds" are against church-planting mission and defend a program of renewing existing churches as the *esse* of Christian mission. It is sad that such a large part of the missionary movement, dominated by Europe and confused by the rapid changes of the last thirty years, should be so indifferent to the spiritual needs of the Afericasian millions and deaf to the cries of the younger churches to help them evangelize the exploding populations of Asia, Africa, and Latin America.

I want to write into the record that, my worthy critics notwithstanding, the majority of Christians today advocate church-planting mission and are opposed to the strategy of the fifties with its anxious insistence that renewal is mission. Vatican II affirms that the purpose of mission is to win the world for Christ and His Church. Vatican II makes vigorous pronouncements on social justice, peace, and other duties of the Christian and the Church, but does not substitute these for mission—for the redemption of sinful, unbelieving men. In the Protestant wing of the Church, too, an increasing number are turning from the comfortable doctrine that everything the Church ought to do outside her four walls is mission, and are concentrating their attention on the redemption of the two billion men and women who owe no allegiance whatever to Jesus Christ, and do not even know His name. In North America the "old-line" boards, who for the most part follow the strategy of the fifties, now send out about eleven thousand missionaries, whereas the "new-line" boards, who for the most part follow an evangelical policy and program, now send out over fourteen thousand.

My response is divided into two parts: (1) theological considerations which underlie the strategy of mission, and (2) practical considerations which have a close bearing upon it. Both speak to my correspondents' arguments, to which—alas—confined by the word-limit allowed me, I shall not be able to reply point by point. As readers ponder over my original article, this article, and the Iberville Statement, however, they will find that these points have been taken into account.

1. *Strategy in mission—and the theological watershed*

Any reflection upon right strategy in mission must give consideration to today's theological watershed. Of the elements which make up this watershed I mention two. First comes the authority of the Bible and of those passages which command discipling or make it the *esse* of mission (such as Matt. 28:19; Rom. 1:5; John 14:6; Acts 4:12; 1 John 5:12; Rom. 10:11–15; and 2 Cor. 5:18ff.). The central thrust of the New Testament wells up in these and scores of similar passages. *How authoritative are they?* Second comes the value of belief in Jesus Christ. *Does it make an eternal difference whether a man believes in Jesus Christ as God and Savior and becomes His disciple and a responsible member of His Church?* These are precisely the questions which constitute the continental divide.

a) Those who stand on the "south side" of the watershed immediately say, "Of course we accept the authority of the Scriptures. Of course it makes a difference whether a man believes in Jesus Christ. We agree with you as to the ends. We are *one* in praying and working that every man on earth may have the chance to say *yes* to Jesus Christ and become a faithful member of His Church. That means fantastic church growth. In regard to the means for achieving the ends, however, we sometimes have differences with you. We are *many* in the means which seem suitable for progressing towards the end. What we advocate may seem inadequate to you, and what you advocate may seem inadequate to us. There is room for difference of opinion." Yet, on the south side of the divide, Christians hold generally similar theological opinions, of which I mention four:

i) *The reality of salvation.* Because we believe in the authority of the Christian Scriptures and adhere to the doctrines there revealed, we accept the lostness of men without the Savior and the salvation which God has provided in Jesus' death and resurrection for all who believe.

ii) *Mission is to the real world.* All strategies of mission should be brought into line with the real world. This means many things, for the world is complex; but one is this: over two billion for whom Christ died do not know His name. Those astronomical multitudes have no chance to believe on Him in whom is life abundant and eternal.

When we reflect on the fact that the Lord Jesus is the Way, the Truth, and the Life, without whom no one comes to the Father, what do these billions mean? What is our strategy of mission? How much emphasis, for example, does God want us to place on renewing the faith of the baptized in Eurica, and how much on giving the countless Africasian millions their first real chance to opt for Jesus Christ? In Eurica every unbeliever passes the doors of a dozen churches every day. Often he has some professing Christian in his family. In Africasia, hundreds of millions never hear the gospel, never see a church, never talk to a Christian, and never see a Bible. Under these circumstances our answer is that a major part of Christian mission must be devoted to reconciling the Africasian billions to God in the Church of Jesus Christ.

iii) *The whole man is saved.* Faith in Jesus Christ and responsible membership in His Church are necessary to achieving a just, brotherly, and peaceful social order. Church growth men are not advocating basic policy with their eyes fixed solely on the souls of men. They *are* interested in souls, but also in bodies, societies, and institutions. They are inclined to believe that the normal order is "root first and fruit later." As they read their New Testament they see the Holy Spirit multiplying churches in which *then* men began to live as brothers and to practice forgiveness, justice, and peace.

iv) *The Church's unchanging core and changing periphery.* The Church, stripped her cultural accretions, alone with her Book and obedient to her Lord, is the unchanging core. But her periphery changes. When, for example, by the year 2000 there are 100,000,000 Christians in Africa,[4] we may be sure that the Church will appear in many African guises. She will not speak English and French, but a thousand languages. She will be housed in a million village churches. Although thoroughly grounded in a thousand tribes and appearing as linguistic denominations, she will be breaking down the walls of hostility and pressing on to supra-tribal unity. Since the denomination is the form the Church takes in the twentieth century, her congregations will group themselves into many African denominations of many colorful names. Movements to Christian unity will surge through the denominations, and regroupings will appear again and again. The periphery will change; but since these denominations will be local manifestations of the Church of Jesus Christ against which the gates of hell shall not prevail, the core will not change. And the whole Church will multiply exceedingly.

b) Those on the chilly "north side" of the watershed differ with us as to ends, and therefore necessarily as to means. It is useless to discuss mission policy with them. While using biblical words, they define mission in humanistic terms. They do not believe that it makes an eternal difference whether men accept the Lord Jesus and are baptized in His name. They do not believe that in the Bible we have the authoritative, infallible Word of God. They cannot but oppose church growth strategy: their theology allows them to take neither the Church nor the salvation of men's souls seriously. They use the right words but with such a radical reinterpretation of meaning that they no longer speak about historic Christianity. Those on the north side naturally find fault with church growth and its theological presuppositions. They find it ambiguous, simplistic, unaware of modern scholarship, behind the times, out of touch with reality, and wrong on a thousand counts!

Of the respondents to this discussion, who (if any) are on the north side? No one can say. In the articles, theological positions are inextricably combined with philosophies of mission, experience of living in moribund churches, Eurican and Africasian outlooks, and special interests. Nevertheless, certain arguments in favor of the vague inclusive strategy of the fifties or against church growth are natural to north-siders. And if one does differ as to ends, one will certainly differ as to means.

2. *Sources of unity for south-siders: some practical considerations*

Not all who believe that "Christ should be proclaimed as divine and only Savior and (that) men should be persuaded to become His disciples and responsible members of His Church" agree with the means which I have advanced. This is scarcely surprising. Each man forms his convictions about Christian mission out of his knowledge and experience of it. Nevertheless, some of the disagreement is unnecessary. A greater degree of unity is possible. We shall see more clearly what policies will serve God's purpose if we eliminate four sources of confusion and emphasize four sources of unity.

Humanity is composed of thousands of peoples and tongues, kindreds and lineages, cultures and subcultures. The function of the Church is not primarily to unify these segments of society, but rather to disciple them and to help them preserve the riches of their heritage. While the Church no doubt is intentionally and constitutionally One, the empirical churches are many. Swahili-speaking Roman Catholics in Tanzania, for example, could scarcely be more different from English-speaking Roman Catholics in Los Angeles.

The Church as she spreads into the cultures of the world will inevitably take on many colors. Each piece of the mosaic becomes "Church" at its own rate and in its own way. As she brings the good news, the strategy of the Church will vary. This means that (a) so long as the end is that the peoples be discipled, Christians can expect a great variation in means, and (b) methods and means must constantly be measured to see whether they further discipling *in that particular piece of the mosaic.*

Eurican cultural overhang must be rejected. Christian mission, despite its valiant efforts to adopt Asian and African viewpoints, is still largely run by Euricans and Africasians trained by them. This has been inevitable and is in no sense blameworthy, but it does mean that what looks like "good mission" to Eurica is often projected as "good mission" everywhere. Fashions in mission start in Eurica and roll round the world. In the thirties it was rural reconstruction; in the forties it was literacy; and at present it is an "evangelism" designed for post-Christian Europe to be carried on in a baptized population! It is "renewal of existing churches" masquerading as "evangelism and mission."

Theology of mission today is being written by men thoroughly immersed in the Eurican scene. Some of them have had a few years in Uganda, Japan, Indonesia, or Iran, but their thought-processes are formed in Holland, Germany, New York, or Chicago under the tutelage of Eurican theologians. Most nationals who write on the theology of mission have been well trained in the theological lore of Eurica.

This factor is rendered particularly pernicious by the slogan, "Mission has ceased to be from the Christian West to the non-Christian East and is now from Christians East and West to non-Christians West and East." Like many slogans, this has its values. But baptized Eurican pagans (highly literate, individualistic, and Christian-connected) need radically different mission from our non-Christian friends in Nigeria, Sumatra, Algeria, and Taiwan. To the great loss of the two billion who owe no allegiance to Jesus Christ, ecumenical mission to Africasia has in the last twenty years been captured by the theologians of "mission to Eurica," and made to march obediently at their chariot wheel. Mission to Eurica manifests no concern to communicate the Christian faith to Africasian multitudes and so, wonderful to relate, neither does mission to Africasia!

Parochial knowledge of mission must be surmounted. Limited knowledge of one field is a prolific source of confusion concerning strategy. It can be seen again and again in this issue of *IRM*. What writers believe to be good mission in their own fields, they project as generally true. My good friend Dr. Kessler gently suggests that approach to the masses has not been a factor in Pentecostal growth in Latin America (because in Peru, where he labored, the Pentecostals approached the masses and did not grow); Melvin Hodges, secretary for Latin America for the Assemblies of God, in the same issue affirms that his church has grown *because it has approached the masses!* Hodges' position is abundantly supported by independent studies in Argentina, Brazil, El Salvador, Mexico, and other lands.

Limited knowledge can now be ended and mission policies determined in the light of what God has blessed to the growth of His churches. Effective communication of the gospel can be fitted to each piece of the mosaic. It is no longer necessary to defend decades of defeat in one field as good mission everywhere!

The assumption of a universally hostile world must be abandoned. This assumption, underlying much theology and methodology of mission today and many of the responses in this issue, is gravely in error. True, there are some resistant peoples and nations; but thousands of pieces of the mosaic in scores of countries are *responsive*. In them, the multitudes are becoming members of Christ's Church. Mr. John, writing on the assumption which is quite reasonable in Serampore, India, feels that hostile men will resent any church being considered a laboratory wherein we can see what mode of presence and proclamation best communicates the gospel. But where, instead of being hostile, people are standing with outstretched arms begging for knowledge of the Savior, there surely they would welcome it if God's faithful servants examined each separate experiment in gospel proclamation to see which best sped life-giving water to thirsty multitudes.

We face the most winnable populations which ever existed. More men today want to know about Jesus Christ; more people are being baptized from non-Christian religions; more churches are being built; more congregations are being established; and the mind of Christ is being incorporated more into human society than ever before. Christians preoccupied with domestic problems and denominational housekeeping, or face to face with some hostile population, often fail to see the mighty church growth which God is continually bringing to pass. Some Christians, surprised at its size and spread, may even doubt its reality. But, like Mount Everest, it is there.

Much criticism of church growth strategy arises from a failure to see that *millions want to be told of the Savior and persuaded to believe in Him*. The hypercautious strategy of the fifties, suited to "mission" in Europe, and assuming non-Christians always to be hostile to the gospel, no longer applies in half of the world. In many populations, it is neither necessary nor advisable. It wastes time in modes of mission like "dialogue" and "presence." Multitudes today welcome proclamation and persuasion. Multitudes are winnable, waiting to be won.

Conclusion

Since this exchange of opinion on church growth and essential policy in mission occurs on the eve of the Fourth Assembly of the World Council of Churches, I have examined the preparatory documents with care. Section Two of *Drafts for Sections, Uppsala 1968*, entitled "Renewal in Mission," is the only draft dealing with Christian mission. It says precisely nothing about presenting the gospel to the two billion who now owe Jesus no allegiance. What it says about mission may or may not be germane to Eurica, but is irrelevant to the receptive multitudes of Africasia. Section Two portrays the strategy of the fifties better than the texts to which I had access in 1965. The Division of World Mission and Evangelism in session at Uppsala should remedy this tragic lack in her preparatory documents. Uppsala should make plans for church growth and the evangelization of earth's myriads to match God's mandate. Not to do so would be deliberately to espouse wrong strategy. Not to do so would be to betray earth's multitudes and our Lord.

NOTES

1. The statement is reproduced in the immediately preceding section.
2. See above, points 1, 4, 6, 8, 9.
3. See above, pp. 102–103.
4. ". . . on the most sober estimate, the Christian is reasonably entitled to think that by the end of the twentieth century, Africa south of the Sahara will be in the main a Christian continent." Stephen Neill: *A History of Christian Missions* (London and Baltimore: Penguin Books, 1964), pp. 568–69.

PART IV

1968: Presence and Proclamation as Forms of Mission

A. PRESENCE AND PROCLAMATION

Max Warren

Recently, in Westminster Abbey, a course of Lent lectures was given under the general title *1984?* The purpose of these lectures was not so much to attempt prophecy as to take a serious look at present tendencies in Christian thought and practice. As one of those taking part in this course it fell to me to take as my subtitle "1984? The Church East of Suez." Although I then confined what I had to say to a consideration of the Church in Asia I had in mind, of course, the Church south of the Sahara, the Church in Latin America, the Church in the Pacific, and no less the Church in Europe and North America—in a word the Church Militant here on earth.

I suggest that for our present purpose we might do well to have a similar perspective. Let me offer you two reasons for doing so, two reasons which have their own bearing upon what I will attempt to say on the subject allotted to me.

My *first* reason is based on a deep conviction that we are meeting at a turning point in the history of missions, and that means of course a turning point in history. We are all familiar with the fact that the colonial era in its nineteenth-century form has come decisively to an end. What may be less familiar is the thought that all of us, whether living and thinking "East" or "West" of Suez, have been, all of us, survivors of the colonial age. Our thinking as individuals and the pattern of all our institutions were formed during the colonial age, which, need I remind you, though a particular phenomenon of the nineteenth century, survived everywhere until after World War II. We may have been in revolt against the colonial past, or on the defensive about it, but we were all shaped by it. And this shaping did not end in 1945. It is still very much a part of our thought world. And the structures of our

---

Max Warren is the General Secretary Emeritus, The Church Missionary Society, London. His chapter was originally a paper read at the European Consultation on Mission Studies held at Selly Oak Colleges, Birmingham, England, April 1968.

churches and our missionary enterprise still reflect the past, as of necessity they must do.

What I want to suggest is that this "shadow" of the colonial age is a temporary phenomenon. It is passing away. We are moving into a new era. Already a generation has grown up and is standing knocking on the gates of power, a generation which has no personal recollections of living under an alien "raj." The preoccupations of this new generation are no longer with the pursuit of political independence. The legacy of economic poverty, the awareness that such poverty is no longer an inescapable fact of life, a mounting resentment that affluence is limited to one section of the human race, and the undercurrent of fear which accompanies the population explosion, fear of unemployment, fear of hunger—these are the preoccupations which are shaping the outlook of those now on the threshold of power in Asia, in Africa, and in many other places as well. Theoretically, academically, we of the West may understand these preoccupations. But emotionally we hardly feel them at all—as yet.

Now it is these preoccupations which will more and more determine the thinking and the actions of the less economically privileged peoples of the world. They will likewise exert a profound impact upon our fellow Christians of these countries. Whereas in the past, being a Christian, linked by religious allegiance to those in authority, was a source of prestige, this condition has already largely disappeared. Where being the member of an international society (the Christian Church) and the recipient of substantial foreign aid strengthened the position of the Christian minority, tomorrow it is more and more likely to make Christians the objects of suspicion. This is already happening.

We must then be prepared for quite a new kind of challenge both to the Church as an institution and to the individual Christian as a member of that institution. Whether the pattern of events in China is going to prevail elsewhere or not, it can be safely assumed that we are going forward into an era in which none of the material or social securities of the past can be assumed. As a friend wrote me recently on this whole subject, both the Church and the individual Christian have got to be prepared for what, he called, a new "nakedness." In the colonial era both Church and individual Christians were "clothed," often inappropriately no doubt but nevertheless clothed. Perhaps now they have to be "unclothed," both for their own salvation and future resurrection and also for their equipment for mission.

It is, I believe, urgent that we should be aware of this new era into which we are moving forward so fast.

My *second* reason for urging a perspective which takes the future seriously is that, as Christians, and as those committed to the Church's mission to all mankind, we need to discover how, in a new way, we can give expression to that common humanity which we share with all mankind. Despite all the violence and cruelty and hatred which are tearing our world to pieces there is yet observable a steadily increasing sense of our common humanity. Indeed, not a little of the violence and cruelty and hatred which we find around us is derived from precisely that old insularity which the new humanitarianism of our time is attacking.

The sources of this new sense of a common humanity are various. Thanks to modern means of communication we are discovering each other—discovering how much, in fact, we have in common. The new sciences of psychology and social anthropology are demonstrating in a quite new way our essential human community. That very imperialism, against which the world is in revolt today, made its own contribution, however ambiguous, to an awareness that we all belong together. And it would be unhistorical to underestimate the extent to which the Christian missionary enterprise itself has made towards one world.

What, however, we need to think about rather more than we have done is how, as Christians, we can more adequately express our genuine sense of being *with* others who are not Christians. Would it be going too far to say that in a real sense the missionary movement, for instance, has been so concerned to be *for* others that it has, albeit with the best intentions, been paternalistic and even patronizing? At any rate, we of the West will sadly misjudge the present situation, and our future possibilities in the service of the gospel, if we ignore the fact that much of our endeavor is *felt* to be paternalistic and patronizing. In the next twenty years the missionary, whether he comes from the West to the East or, as we may hope increasingly, from the East to the West, will need to have achieved something of a real self-emptying. He will no longer be a distributor of Christian Aid. Only in so far as he can be a witness to a Christian "presence" will he be genuinely welcome, valued for what he is and represents and not for what he brings. Our missionary vocabulary, as well as much in the shape of our missionary organizations, will have to change. Anyone who has ever attempted to interpret the meaning of "change" to a missionary constituency will be aware of what a formidable task lies ahead. I am half inclined to believe that the task is impossible, and that missionary strategy today should be devoted to searching out patterns of flexible action, while the old static structures slowly wither and die. Posterity may well discern an organic relationship between the new patterns and the old structures. That will be as may be. The future demands flexibility. The price to be paid for this is likely to be very costly indeed—costly in confusion, misunderstanding and loss of financial support. The reward might be a great new age of mission.

Without that preamble I could not proceed responsibly to present my more theological argument as I seek to consider the subject of "Presence and Proclamation." Both "Presence" and "Proclamation" assume a context. What I have attempted so far has been to indicate the context in which, in the coming days, "Presence" must be interpreted and "Proclamations" made.

I propose to handle my subject under three heads:
1. Proclaiming the Christ who is "present"
2. The "present" Church proclaiming Christ
3. The "present" individual proclaiming Christ.

In each case the word "present" is to be read as within inverted commas, indicating that the word "present" has a special meaning associated with the idea of "Presence."

PROCLAIMING THE CHRIST WHO IS "PRESENT"

For the purposes of this paper I must limit my subject very drastically indeed. Believing as I do that God the creator hates nothing that He has made, I must be world-affirming. I find God at work everywhere, often working very strangely by my limited human understanding, but working nevertheless.

I seek to trace His footsteps in the world-shaking events of our time. I am sure that He is to be found at work in the discoveries of modern science. He it is who makes men sensitive to the ethical problems posed by some of these discoveries. *Nihil humani a me alienum puto* is to me an axiom which follows from my belief in God who refused to treat humankind as alien, but himself became Man.

Within that broad context of convictions, and only within that context, I am ready to consider the problem of Christology, and indeed of theodicy, posed by the existence of man's many religions. I have used the word theodicy deliberately because I think that in the Christian mission we have tended to underestimate the problems raised by the very existence of other faiths, some of them far older in time than the Christian faith itself. What was in Paul's mind when in Athens, after dismissing the statues in the *agora* with a wave of the hand and also querying the misapplication of the "art and imagination of man" in the Parthenon, he went on to say, "The times of ignorance God overlooked, but now he commands all men everywhere to repent?" [1]

We cannot be sure of what he meant. But it is beyond question that he acknowledged genuineness in pagan worship. Some while before in Lystra he had used another phrase to describe the past religious history of his audience. " 'In past generations,' " he said, " 'he [God] allowed all the nations to walk in their own ways; yet he did not leave himself without witness, for he did good and gave you from heaven rains and fruitful seasons, satisfying your hearts with food and gladness.' " [2]

Again, we will not make too much of that reference. But remembering that Paul was a "Hebrew of the Hebrews" and a profound student of the Old Testament, the phrase that God "allowed all the nations to walk in their own ways" is an extremely interesting comment on the Old Testament teaching about idolatry, as we shall see.

My dictionary defines "theodicy" as a theory "justifying the ways of God to men." It is a very proper activity of the Christian mind, indeed it is quite indispensable if we are to communicate what we believe about God to those who are not of "the household of faith." Nor is it unlikely that for some within the "household" a theodicy is also called for. Much of the New Testament is itself just such a "justification of God." *A fortiori* we must take seriously the action of God in relation to those living in what Paul called "the age of ignorance."

There are certain questions which insist on an answer. What was God doing when the Vedas were being handed down? When the Gautama sought for the truth and sacrificed so much to pursue it, was God about? In that cave outside Mecca when the man Muhammad was overwhelmed by the certainty that there was only one point of reference in the universe to which man ought to address himself, was that an accident? There should be no ambiguity in our answer to those questions. The righteousness of God is at stake.

I am not, however, concerned to argue a theodicy. All I want to do is to point out that a theodicy is necessary for our obedience to mission. Here I want, rather, to consider a possible Christology, a way of understanding to be explored.

The *New English Bible* translation of Colossians 1:19–20 speaks of Christ as follows:

> . . . in him the complete being of God, by God's own choice, came to dwell. Through him God chose to reconcile the whole universe

to himself, making peace through the shedding of his blood upon the Cross—to reconcile all things, whether on earth or in heaven, through him alone.

In the next chapter Paul continues: "For it is in Christ that the complete being of the Godhead dwells embodied, and in him you have been brought to completion. Every power and authority in the universe is subject to him as Head." [3]

The headship of Christ is inclusive. Nothing is *outside* the sphere of His sovereignty, nothing in the present no less than in the future. As surely we have to look at man's past as well, to say nothing of Christ's role in creation. The writer to the Hebrews is very bold when he says:

> ... he has spoken to us in the Son ... through whom he created all orders of existence: the Son who is the effulgence of God's splendour and the stamp of God's very being, and sustains the universe by his word of power.[4]

If this be conceded then we have warrant in finding a reference to Christ, implicit if not explicit, in the words with which Paul ends his own attempt at a theodicy in Romans 9–11: "For from him and through him and to him are all things. To him be glory for ever. Amen." [5] Or, as the *New English Bible* expresses it with more dramatic force, "Source, Guide, and Goal of all that is—to him be glory for ever! Amen."

In passing let us note how emphatic the New Testament is that "the being" of God is embodied in Christ. Now, as we all know well, "being" for the Hebrew mind is not a philosophical term at all. That God *is* is known by what God *does*. And what God does in relation to man, within the historic process, is to reconcile man to his Creator, to his environment, and to himself. This reconciling ministry of God which even to the Hebrew people was *polumerōs kai polutropōs*,[6] can hardly have been manifested in less various fashion to the rest of mankind.

In the sense, then, that we are to understand the Christ as God active in reconciliation, we have to understand Christ as universally "present." And that means "present" in some real sense in all of mankind's search for truth, "present" certainly in mercy and in guidance, if also "present" in judgment and correction.

Now it is at this point in the argument that many, who are deeply concerned with the Christian mission and completely committed to it, become anxious. There is an uneasy feeling that much biblical evidence is being trifled with. In particular we are asked if we are taking seriously the Bible's "vigorous attack on idolatry and unequivocal assertion of the Lordship of the God of Abraham, Isaac and Jacob, the God and Father of our Lord Jesus Christ." [7]

That this strand of the biblical testimony is one to be taken seriously cannot be doubted. But it needs to be understood. If by the word "unequivocal" we are to understand "unambiguous" and therefore "readily applicable" to our Christian encounter with Buddhism, Hinduism, Islam, and other faiths, then we must think again. For what is surely clear from the indubitably unambiguous witness of the Old Testament prophets and other writers to the evil of idolatry is that the sin of idolatry lies in the fact that it is a breaking of the Covenant between God and Israel. A representative passage is Jeremiah 3, where the accent is laid upon Israel's faithlessness to the God of the Covenant. Jeremiah 11:3 explicitly speaks of the breaking of the Covenant. In Jeremiah 18:15 there is the cry from the heart of God, "My people have forgotten me." These are typical passages from the whole prophetic tradition. The horror of idolatry is well expressed by Ezekiel who hears God's verdict that "these men have taken their idols into their hearts." [8] This is the real inwardness of the prophetic complaint that Israel has "played the harlot." The marriage settlement of the Covenant has been repudiated.

In comparison to the "unambiguous" and "unequivocal" denunciation of idolatry on the part of Israel it is, in fact, remarkable how reserved the Old Testament is about idolatry outside the Covenant people. There is prophetic scorn for the foolishness of idolatry particularly in Isaiah, in five passages in Jeremiah, in one passage in Hosea, Habakkuk, and Jonah. [9]

What is more striking and worthy of some study is the number of passages where the idols of the nations are in fact conceived as symbols of the nations. This is clearly the case in a series of passages in Jeremiah 46–51. The same idea is present in a few passages in Isaiah, Jeremiah, Ezekiel, and Nahum. [10]

Such, I would suggest, is the testimony of the Old Testament about idolatry. Essentially it is a testimony about the relationship of the people of the Covenant with their Covenant-making God. It is, I suggest, a very precarious argument to draw any inference from this testimony to what should be our understanding of the work of Christ, God the reconciler, in the world outside the Covenant with Israel.

We do most surely, as Christians, accept that the God of Abraham, Isaac, and Jacob is one with the God and Father of our Lord Jesus Christ. We may and we do reckon that, as Christians we are members of a Covenant people, a new Covenant sealed in Christ's blood. But in and through our understanding of that blood shed for us and for all mankind we have a view of the reconciling work of God which is not present in the Old Testament. The abiding value of the Old Testament is to be found in its witness to the character of God and his righteousness. Indeed, much of the prophetic attack on idolatry is strictly subordinated to the denunciation of the people for their sins against social righteousness. Much of the indictment of idolatry was due to the experience that idolatry provided an easy escape from social responsibility.

I add that, because the importance of the Old Testament for Christian faith and practice cannot be exaggerated. It is from the Old Testament's insistence on the character of God and his righteousness, and of man's proper response, that in the Christian mission we have a right to ask men to consider the claims of such a God. The gospel of the New Covenant is rooted in the gospel of the old Covenant.

Now it is within the compass of this understanding of the biblical testimony that I would refer you back to that passage from Colossians and my earlier argument about the universal sovereignty of Christ. That very word "universal" argues a Christ who transcends the Covenant. We can well see how the Christ of the New Testament is indeed a covenanted Christ. He fulfills the promises of the Old Covenant. But there is a dimension to his reconciling work which is right outside the Covenant "made with the fathers."

There is an uncovenanted Christ with whom we have to do. Perhaps, indeed, it is a Christ whom we have got to discover or rather rediscover. For Paul was certainly giving us some remarkable hints about Him. And here let me say that I am not thinking only of great passages like the one already quoted from Colossians, or Ephesians 1:10 with its visions of "the universe, all in heaven and on earth . . . brought into a unity in Christ." [11] I have in mind the whole argument of Romans 5, the very heart of Paul's gospel. What he is writing about there is the uncovenanted Christ no less than the covenanted Christ. Paul was almost as much interested in Adam as he was in Abraham!

In that same letter to the Romans, Paul quite clearly sees the work of salvation as operating outside the confines of the Covenant people—

> When Gentiles who do not possess the law carry out its precepts by the light of nature, then, although they have no law, they are their own law, for they display the effect of the law inscribed on their hearts. Their conscience is called as witness, and their own thoughts argue the case on either side, against them or even for them, on the day when God judges the secrets of human hearts through Christ Jesus. So my Gospel declares.[12]

The judge of human hearts is Jesus Christ. That is the gospel. And that judge passes His judgment outside the Covenant. We who are within the Covenant must also stand before the judgment seat of Christ. But that is another matter. What we have here is a Christ who is a searcher of the hearts of all men. As the apostle goes on to say: "The true Jew is he who is such inwardly, and the true circumcision is of the heart, directed not by written precepts but by the Spirit; such a man receives his commendation not from men but from God." [13]

There is then a Covenant of Grace within which all men stand. And the mediator of that Covenant is Jesus, the Lord. To the chosen people of the Old Covenant, as to the elect people of the New, Jesus, the Lord, is the Covenanted Savior. But, in our mission to the great world outside the Covenant people, we have strong biblical support for a spirit of expectancy as we go to discover in those of other Faiths the prevenient grace of the uncovenanted Christ.

In his book with the suggestive title *The Unknown Christ of Hinduism*, Raymond Panikkar has said: "The Christian attitude is not ultimately one of bringing Christ *in,* but of bringing him *forth,* of discovering Christ; not one of command but of service. Or, in other words, Christ died and rose for all men—before and after him —his redemption is universal and unique." And later in the same paragraph he adds:

> The Christian instinctively falls in love with the positive aspects of other religions . . . because he believes that he discovers there the footprints of God's redemption, and some veiled sometimes disfigured grace which he believes he must unveil and reformulate, out of love for his neighbour and a sense of responsibility for the faith God has given him.[14]

Such a view is not the vestibule to the temple of syncretism. It is the unequivocal unambiguous assertion of the universal Saviorhood and Lordship of Jesus Christ. There is indeed "no salvation in anyone else at all, for there is no other name under heaven granted to men, by which we may receive salvation." [15]

What we need to bear in mind, as we quote that text, is that the *name* signified in ancient thought the nature of the bearer of the *name,* and by association, his power. Wherever then we discern truth, recognize what Raymond Panikkar calls "the footprints of God's redemption," there we are in the presence of the power of the uncovenanted Christ. God-the-reconciler. We do well to take off our shoes for we are on holy ground.

Along some such lines as these, I submit, we can discover a Christology which will equip us for our mission in the religiously pluralistic world in which our task is set. For it is in this kind of world that we have to proclaim the Christ who is "present."

THE "PRESENT" CHURCH PROCLAIMING CHRIST

The word "present" remains in inverted commas. The Church which has to proclaim Christ may be the outward and visible community of those professing to be Christians. Such a community will have a recognized standing. Varying according to circumstances it will possess certain rights in law. It may be a privileged community, what in European history and experience is known as an established church. It may be scarcely less privileged when as in North America, in Australia and New Zealand, and in parts of Africa, the greater part of the population are church members. It may be a very unprivileged community, its rights very strictly circumscribed, as for instance in a number of Muslim countries. In some countries it may be a suspect community, flotsam and jetsam left on the shore by a receding tide of imperialism, a community whose loyalty to the newly independent nation-state is not taken for granted.

Nevertheless, however diverse the circumstances in which the Church is a visible community under the law, it is everywhere a "present" community. It is "there." By the manner of its life, by the fashion of its worship, by the way in which it bears witness to the transcendent reality of God, this community, this Church is proclaiming Christ. The proclamation may be muted; it may be equivocal; it may be tragically distorted by divisions within the Church. Yet, however imperfect, it is "present," and within it prayer is made to God, sacraments are administered, the Word of God is read, and above all the Holy Spirit is at work.

We must never despair of the Church even when it is dead. Even when the last vestiges of the *visible* Church have disappeared we cannot possibly judge in what strange ways the proclamation of the Church may have infiltrated the life of society, planting seeds which in God's time will germinate.

That is an important conviction for all involved in mission. It is an important aspect of our faith in God.

The visible Church has two dangers to which it has to be alert. It can become so assimilated to its environment that the Christ it proclaims is no longer a transcendent Lord but a national fetish. This is a very great danger wherever the Church allows its national character to deny its universal dimension. In religious terms this can find expression in religious syncretism or in what is, in effect, religious tribalism. The pressures of national loyalties are very heavy pressures indeed. Both religious syncretism and religious tribalism are temptations to the Church everywhere, in Europe and North America as much as in Asia or Africa or Latin America.

The other danger is that of a withdrawal into a ghetto. A ghetto is a state of mind into which you allow yourself to be driven, whether it is a place or not. And a ghetto is a place, and a state of mind, from which others are excluded. A Christian community may have freedom under the law. But if such a community repels rather than welcomes enquirers, it is a ghetto. There are a disturbing number of Christian communities in the world which are ghettos.

Where these dangers are not avoided, the Church may be present as a statistic in the census reports. It is not "present" as proclaiming Christ.

But there is another way in which the Church can be "present" even where there is no outward and visible community of professing Christians. There are many places in the world today, there are indeed circumstances in every country, where the Christian man or woman must live and work for the greater part of their time without any visible means of spiritual support. The structures of industrial and commercial life often appear to conspire to insulate the individual from any other life whatever. And the pressure of the industrial or commercial activity does not end when the man leaves the factory or the office.

This means that the Christian man or woman so insulated has to discover what it means to be a Christian in this setting. It may or may not be easier to do this in Birmingham than in Bombay, in Liverpool than in Lagos, in Chicago than in Cairo. Nowhere is it easy. The Church as a visible community needs to become at once more flexible in its thinking about the way its members live and much more humble about its responsibilities for them. For these men and women are working on a very difficult evangelistic frontier. But unless they are faithful at that point, not least by way of courageous experiment, there will be no other means of proclaiming Christ in those particular circumstances, circumstances which are becoming more and more determinative for the whole life of mankind.

We need to accept without reserve the truth that *ubi Christianus ibi Christus, ubi Christus ibi ecclesia.* And this will become an ever increasing reality in proportion as the visible community is flexible in its thinking, and ensures that its own inner life of devotion, its ministering through Word and Sacrament is directly related to its members whose lives are "hidden" in the world.

At this point it may be pertinent to ask ourselves if our fellow Christians in China, being out of sight are also out of mind and, so, out of our prayers. Certainly the Church in China, *qua* institution is, as far as the most recent reports can be relied upon, largely the Church invisible. And that is a state of affairs which could happen anywhere. There is no Church anywhere in the world which can afford to dismiss such a possibility with the words "It can't happen here."

Flexibility in thinking, flexibility in structure, then, are the two most urgent needs of the Church in all its obedience to mission.

THE "PRESENT" INDIVIDUAL PROCLAIMING CHRIST

The word "present" is again in inverted commas, and that for the all-important reason that Christ is present in that individual and therefore the Church is present. Something of what may be involved for the "present" individual, the man or woman through whose presence the Christ and His Church may become visibly present, we have already seen.

I want, however, to give to this closing section of my paper a specific reference which links it directly to the Christology which we considered earlier. I want to consider the "present" individual in his encounter with the man of another faith.

At the very heart of the Christology which I attempted to outline was an insistence upon Christ, our Lord, as personally active in reconciliation. It is impossible to exaggerate the degree to which the Christian faith lays its stress upon the personal activity of a God who can best be conceived in the categories of "personalness" and who is known to us in and through the person of Jesus Christ. This "personalness" of the divine Being and of all divine action is vital for all thinking about the encounter between Christians and those of other faiths. And it follows from this that the encounter of religions is fundamentally an encounter between religious men, or it is not an encounter. Christianity, for instance, cannot encounter Buddhism. No doubt certain doctrines can be set down in parallel columns denoting similarities and differences. But this is an academic exercise all too easily lacking the breath of life. It is, indeed, a dangerous oversimplification to imagine that we can understand another religion by virtue of our knowledge of its sacred writings, its philosophy, its doctrines. We understand another religion only when we enter, in some genuine measure, into the experience of the man who lives by the other religion. What then we have to seek to explore is the way by which a person-to-person meeting can be achieved. To say this is not to belittle the hard work involved in becoming familiar with the symbols of the other man's faith, to be aware of the sacred writings which he reverences, to have some understanding of the complex of history, culture and personal experience which have gone to make him the man he is. The hard work is imperative for some. It cannot be undertaken by all.

Manifestly, a person-to-person encounter, such as I have suggested, can proceed at very different levels. In many cases, indeed in the vast majority of cases, the encounter will come through some service offered by the Christian to the other man, or through some service in which both cooperate, to meet some human need. This is the way of *diakonia*. The Christian and the other man meet in the realm of *agape*. Their understanding of each other proceeds from this experience and will be governed by it.

Sometimes, however, the Christian will find himself confronted by such barriers of suspicion and mistrust that only with infinite patience will he be admitted to a place where encounter is possible. Von Hugel has a passage which can be directly applied to such a situation even though the original context is slightly different. He wrote:

> Man attains in religion, as truly as elsewhere—once given his whole-hearted striving—in proportion as he seeks not too directly, not feverishly and strainingly, but in a largely subconscious, waiting, genial, expansive, endlessly patient, sunny manner.[16]

That is the costly way of friendship, of a friendship which will brook no refusal.

But sometimes the Christian will find the man of another faith ready for a genuine meeting of minds. It is to this possibility of a genuine meeting of minds that, so I believe, we ought strictly to confine the use of the word "dialogue." At the moment the word is being used very loosely indeed to the general confusion of Christian thinking. Dialogue is a difficult exercise and it is probably true that comparatively few people are called to attempt it. But all concerned in mission ought to understand its principles. What are these principles? The best statement of which I know comes in a book by a Canadian, Roland de Corneille, who is active in the field of Christian-Jewish relations.

The principles which he called "rules of dialogue" are as follows:

1. "Each partner must believe that the other is speaking in good faith. . . . Any dialogue must assume a common devotion to truth."
2. "Each partner must have a clear understanding of his own faith. This implies an eagerness to articulate his position and a willingness to have it scrutinized."
3. "Each partner must strive for a clear understanding of the faith of the other."
   This has two corollaries:
   (a) "a willingness to interpret the faith of the other in its best light rather than its worst."
   (b) "each partner must maintain a continual willingness to revise his understanding of the faith of the other."
4. "Each partner must accept responsibility in humility and penitence, for what his group has done, and is doing, to foster and perpetuate unnecessary divisions."
5. "Each partner must forthrightly face the issues which cause separation, as well as those which create unity."
6. "Each partner must recognize that all that can be done with the dialogue is to offer it up to God." [17]

The first three of those rules are theological and can be said to be fundamental to any genuine dialogue. The fourth and fifth have an obvious relevance to the encounter between Christian and Jews, and in any community in which there are immigrant groups. The fourth and fifth rules are, in a word, sociological in character. The sixth rule is a very important one in that it recognizes an inherent limitation in the use of "dialogue." Essentially "dialogue" is a way of understanding. It is not an essay in conversion. In so far as it leads to mutual understanding and respect, "dialogue" is self-justifying. The phrase "to offer it up to God" obviously refers primarily to what can be done between partners who believe in God. The phrase must find its interpretation in the setting of the dialogue. But axiomatically it will apply to the Christian who in this, as in everything else, is "under the will of God revealed in Christ."

"Dialogue" is not evangelism. Properly speaking it is not even preevangelism, a *preparatio evangelica*. It is an activity in its own right. It is in its very essence an attempt at mutual "listening," listening in order to understand. Understanding is its reward. Even in the attempt to articulate his own faith each partner is "listening" to see how far the articulation is communication. Evangelism, on the other hand, is the deliberate attempt so to present Christ as to persuade the other man to become a disciple, to join the community of faith. Evangelism so understood is the very heart of mission. Where this is lacking there is no obedience to mission as the New Testament understands it. Let "dialogue" and "evangelism" be distinguished the one from the other.

In conclusion I ask myself the question: Assuming that the "present" individual feels called to "dialogue" and to "evangelism" must he live in a painful tension? Tension may, indeed, be painful but I believe that tension there must be for such a Christian, and I also believe that it is spiritually creative for the Christian and for his whole witness. In the first place it will keep him humble which is the precondition both for "dialogue" and for "evangelism." For without humility there can be no "meeting" of minds, nor can there be persuasive communication. Further to this, the tension is necessary to prevent confusion between "dialogue" and evangelism. That said, it can surely be maintained that both in his approach to "dialogue," as in his approach to evangelism, the Christian is proclaiming Christ, in the sense of unveiling him, implicitly in "dialogue," explicitly in evangelism.

Dwell on that thought of the "present" individual unveiling the "present Christ." When I go to meet the man of another faith I do not, in any sense whatever, precede Christ. He is there before me. He has been at work in that other man, as He has been at work in me. In all kinds of ways beyond my understanding. Always He is the Way, the Truth, and the Life. There is no other way, no other truth, no other life but He. This follows, surely, from our deep Christian conviction about the sovereignty of Christ. With the Psalmist the "present" individual can offer up his own praise:

> Bless the Lord, all his works,
>   in all places of his dominion.
> Bless the Lord, O my soul.[18]

NOTES

1. Acts 17:30, RSV.
2. Acts 14:16–17, RSV.
3. Col. 1:19–20; 2:9–10, NEB.
4. Heb. 1:1–3, NEB.
5. Rom. 11:36, RSV.
6. Heb. 1:1—"In many and various ways" (RSV).
7. From the Report of a Working Group on Inter-Faith Services as presented to the British Council of Churches at its meeting in April 1968.
8. Ezek. 14:3, RSV.

9. Hos. 8:6, Hab. 2:18–19; Jon. 2:8.
10. Isa. 10:10; 19:1; 21:9; Jer. 43:12; Ezek. 30:13; Nah. 1:14.
11. New English Bible translation.
12. Rom. 2:14–16, NEB.
13. Rom. 2:29, NEB.
14. Raymond Panikkar, *The Unknown Christ of Hinduism* (London: Darton, Longman & Todd, 1964), pp. 45–46.
15. Acts 4:12, NEB.
16. Von Hugel, *Essays and Addresses on the Philosophy of Religion, Second Series* (London: J. M. Dent & Sons, 1926), p. 60.
17. Roland de Corneille, *Christians and Jews—the tragic past and the hopeful future* (New York: Harper & Row), see pp. 88–89.
18. Ps. 103:22, RSV.

B. PRESENCE AND PROCLAMATION IN CHRISTIAN MISSION

Donald McGavran

For over a hundred years Christian mission has been understood to be very largely proclamation. The Presbyterian Church in the United States of America has declared that "the supreme and controlling purpose of the Christian Mission to the world is to proclaim Christ as divine and only Savior" and this declaration is typical of those made by scores of missionary societies. Recently, the word "proclamation" has seemed to some in ecumenical circles too harsh, direct, and ineffective, and they have begun to use the word "presence" as the normal mode of mission. Proclamation needs little explanation, for it is thoroughly biblical and its messages are clear. Presence, on the contrary, is so new and so fashionable that it is used in many ways and with many meanings. Christian mission, too, has come to be a slippery term. Its meaning thirty years ago was clear, but today, in the process of being captured by one wing of the Church, it has developed many meanings. Both words—presence and mission—need careful definition.

I use "mission" in the classical sense—namely as that complex of activities whose chief purpose is "to make Jesus Christ known as Lord and Savior and to persuade men to become His disciples and responsible members of His Church." This has been the well-nigh universal meaning of mission. Whether by European or Asian churches, as long as the purpose was to invite men into a redemptive relationship with God through Jesus Christ, the activity was called Christian mission. The unfortunate turn of events of the last twenty years by which "mission" is taken by some to mean "everything Christians do outside the four walls of their church" contributes nothing but confusion. Today, according to some, who speak with eyes fixed on European and American churches, the Church, doing anything at all which may be considered the will of God, is dubbed "the Church in mission." What our fathers

---

This chapter was originally a paper read at the European Consultation on Mission Studies held at Selly Oak Colleges, Birmingham, England, April 1968.

called simply and adequately "doing God's will" is today in grandiose phrase called "sharing in the missio Dei."

Coming now to the word "presence," its *history* can be touched on only briefly. Leighton Ford says:

> The term has been made current since World War II, particularly perhaps by the "worker priests" in France. For French Catholics, "presence in the world" has meant a kind of evangelistic re-entry to renew contact with geographical and social sectors, such as the laboring world, from which the Church has been found to be absent due to the deChristianization and secularization of society. In western intellectual circles the term has been expanded to include involvement in the concrete political and cultural structures of society. Recent World Council of Churches evangelism studies have concentrated on the presence of Christians in the world. A recommendation has been made that major WCC evangelism and mission studies following Uppsala should be given to "structures of missionary presence." [1]

Definition of the term "presence" will take longer. Eszard Roland declares that the slogan Christian presence is "so abstract, so vague, that each of us can take it to mean something different." [2] Some, attempting to give the word theological depth, point out the rather obvious fact that God is *present* in the world, and hence that we also should be *present*. Some describe "presence" as a way of life, others as the center of our faith, and some as a program of the Church. Colin Williams says that "presence replaces the common view of mission, with a recognition that mission is first a being there—a servant-presence in love on behalf of Christ." [3]

A statement approved by the General Committee of the World Student Christian Federation appeared in the July 1964 issue of *Student World*, and a subsequent issue (Third Quarter, 1965) was given to responses, which included an editorial by Philip Potter. These two issues of *Student World* indicate how the word "presence" is being used by Christian students in Europe who appear to be little concerned about propagating the gospel in Asia, Africa, and Latin America, but deeply interested in how to talk about and demonstrate their faith to the student next door who may be a Marxist, a positivist, or a secular materialist. Though I cannot spend time on the *Student World* position, I do call it to your attention. It is one of the reasons I have reservations about "presence." The statement approved by the General Committee reads as follows:

> The Federation has always been concerned with making Jesus Christ known in the academic world. "Evangelization," "wit-

ness," and "mission" have long been among the words used to describe this task. But these words have now become problems for many students. This dissatisfaction springs from the historical burden which they carry and suggests a Christian behaviour of speaking before listening, of calling people away from their natural communities into a Christian grouping, and of a preoccupation with souls at the expense of the whole of life. Even when "witness" and "mission" are properly understood, many students feel that they are too big and too definite. They suggest a certainty of faith and purpose and an ability to conceptualize faith in terms which create difficulty for many people, not least for those most committed to Christ and his gospel.

When we try to find words . . . to describe the task of the Christian community in the academic world, we seek to give expression to the same realities as our forefathers knew, i.e., to witness to our belief that in Jesus Christ God has reconciled the world to himself. In this document, therefore, we use the word "presence" for that reality.[4]

Here we are told that students find the words "evangelization" and "mission" "too big and too definite." Indeed, the student, having little certainty of faith, apparently blushes even to witness to his belief in Jesus Christ. He feels much more comfortable in simply being present. I would like to spend the rest of this paper discussing this approved statement of the General Committee of World Student Christian Federation; but since it concerns primarily Europe and by definition I am discussing mission in the sense of communicating the faith to non-Christians, the great majority, but by no means all, of whom live in Asia, Africa, and Latin America, I pass on to Christian presence as a mode of mission.

Here we cannot do better than to turn to Canon Warren's concise definition of what he means by the term. This definition has been repeated a number of times in the Presence Series. I shall take the four books authored by Cragg, Appleton, Hammer, and Taylor, 1959, 1961, 1962, and 1963 respectively,[5] as the base from which to proceed, and Canon Warren's standard introduction to each of them as the definitive statement of "Christian Presence."

Back of the presence school of thought, says Canon Warren, lie three great challenges being thrown out by the peoples of Asia and Africa in their revolt against domination by the West. "First, a critical evaluation of the Christian religion . . . as something inherently Western. . . . Second, can Christians of the West accept the fact that the expression which Christianity will receive in its Asian and African forms . . . almost certainly will be in many respects very different indeed from what we know in the West?"

Challenges one and two are background. I shall, therefore, pass them by. Challenge three asks, "Can the Christian Church coexist with other religions?" This question is the matrix of the concept "presence." Let us, therefore, focus attention on challenge three. Warren says,

> The Christian Church has not yet seriously faced the theological problem of "co-existence" with other religions. The very term seems to imply the acceptance of some limitation of the universal relevance of the Gospel. Can that be accepted? . . . the answer must be "no." [6]

Canon Warren then goes on to say:

> Are we then shut up to . . . what in some disguise or other must be an aggressive attack on the deeply held convictions of those who live by other faiths than our own? [7]

This question is the mother of "presence." One way or another, this underlies the concept and all its related concepts. As we meet other religions and proclaim the gospel to men of other faiths, *are we shut up to aggressive attack?* Canon Warren says we are not, and proposes the complex way of missions summed up in "presence," as the via media lying between aggressive attack and coexistence. There are several essential parts to this way.

Before I get to them, may I inject a parenthesis?

Many are using the word "presence." Its twin sister "dialogue" is even more commonly used. Presence-dialogue is a very large umbrella. None of the other uses, however, is as well defined, and as consistent over several publications as Canon Warren's. None has sought so faithfully to be true to classical mission. Consequently, I have concentrated on his rather extended definition.

At the widest, advocates of "presence" are pleading for a respectful approach to non-Christian religions. They plead from several different grounds.

a) That presence is the *Christian* attitude toward other religions. Christians would want their own religion to be so treated. One must be scrupulously fair to others. Only as Christians put themselves in another man's shoes can they really understand the depths of his religion. Until one feels the reasonableness and the attraction of the secularists' position, for example, he does not really understand secularism, nor has he treated it fairly in confronting it with his own religion. Until one looks at Islam through the eyes of a Moslem and permits himself to glory in its grandeur, he has not been Christian toward it.

b) Others plead for the respectful approach from pragmatic

grounds. When Europe ruled the world, they say, we might count on our ideas being accepted, but when we look out at more than a hundred sovereign states, we must at all costs avoid setting ourselves over against them. We must not appear to them to be a hostile camp from which we shout out the gospel. If we appear to occupy that position, non-Christians will automatically reject our message, because it comes from the enemy. Running through much of the presence and dialogue apologetic is the pragmatic need to establish and maintain communication, as essential to any transmission of the gospel.

c) I wonder whether some missiologists advocate presence on a prudential basis—it is the only safe stance. Christians are tiny minorities in many lands and will remain so for generations. They will not be permitted to *proclaim* the gospel. They can speak of Christ—if at all—only in the form of dialogue or presence, where the claim "no other name" is muted.

It is noteworthy that a very early user of the term "presence" was Charles de Foucauld, a Roman Catholic missionary to North Africa. He defined a missionary as "one who is there with a presence willed and determined as a witness to the love of God in Christ." A very good definition of a mission, too—in a land where your throat will be cut before morning if you preach effectively for conversion. Such presence is all that is possible. I call this the prudent ground for advocating presence.

Speaking as an evangelical, I see no problem in "presence" on any of these three grounds. As long as the goal is *not* coexistence in any form or disguise, as long as the goal is that Jesus Christ according to the Scriptures be accepted, and the respectful approach is a means to that end, it is biblical. The *Christian* attitude to other religions, the use of methods which offer maximum communications, keep Christians from preaching the gospel *at* others, and give Christians a chance to live long enough to preach it effectively, are all defensible. Indeed it would be easy to illustrate each one from the history of mission, and probably from the history of any given mission.

Please note that I endorse presence *when the goal* is that Jesus Christ *according to the Scriptures* be believed, loved, obeyed, and followed into the waters of baptism. I like the World Council of Churches' formula for membership—that all may belong who accept Jesus Christ as God and Savior according to the Scriptures. That is a biblical test for becoming a Christian. Of course, because we are walking in days like those of Athanasius, we too may have to add definitive words and phrases to that simple, biblical statement so as to exclude those who do *not* believe in "Jesus Christ as God and Savior according to the Scriptures" and yet who smoothly join the World Council or want to be counted as Christians. Here the parenthesis ends.

Four Acts

Let me now take up Canon Warren's four beautifully clear acts which comprise the way of presence. I shall indicate the places where I agree heartily with him and those others where I have reservations.

The first act is that we gladly accept "the new situation in which the Christian Faith can everywhere be distinguished from its past historical association with Western political, economic and cultural aggression." I have nothing but cordial approbation of this part of the program. I agree that much of the churchly life known in Eurica is the Christian Faith dressed in Eurican garments. The Eurican garments do not fit Africasia. Christian mission should, indeed, require nothing of Africasian Christians (or of Eurican Christians for that matter) but what can be proved from the Bible. Everything else is adiaphora.

The second act is "deep humility. We must lay aside all feelings of superiority of culture, race, or nation." Evangelicals agree entirely that the missionary must renounce all pride in *his* personal, racial, or national attributes. He has nothing but what God has given him and there is no scientific reason to judge his race superior to all others. All feelings of white superiority, American superiority, Japanese superiority, or high caste superiority are sinful. All such pride and arrogance must go.

But there is one point at which evangelicals demur. The *treasure* we have (in admittedly earthen vessels) *is* superior to everything which natural man possesses, whether he be white, brown, yellow, or red. It is at this point that D. T. Niles' famous statement errs. Once the beggar has found food, he is no longer hungry; once he has found the treasure he is no longer a beggar. The Galilean Peter remains a Galilean peasant, true; but in Christ he is one of a chosen race, a royal priesthood, a holy nation. He *has come out*. To commend Christ to others, he must not falsely maintain that he is still in darkness. Is the Christian not in danger of being hypocritical if the protests that he is just one beggar telling another where to find food? How to separate the treasure from the vessel and how to speak of the vessel as we should without demeaning the treasure—that is the problem here.

In the third act Warren says, "We must approach the man of another faith than our own in a spirit of expectancy to find how God has been speaking to him and what new understandings of grace and love of God we may ourselves discover in this encounter . . . God was there before we arrived." I welcome wholeheartedly what the presence school of thought seeks to achieve. Cordial appreciation of the good in Hinduism, Marxism, Buddhism, secularism, and all other ancient and modern religions is so reasonable, so Christian, and in the presentation of the gospel, so necessary, that how anyone can object to it I do not know.

But the presence school gives a theological ground for the appreciative attitude—that is a different thing entirely. For example, many good counsels and clear insights as to man and God can be found in Tulsi Das's Ramayan (which was the common scripture in the part of India where I was a missionary) but there is also much that is mistaken, some that is foolish, and a little that is gross. We who are gathered here today, no matter what attitude we take toward the presence school of thought, would never dream of teaching Tulsi's Ramayan to our children as Scripture—what God has revealed. In what sense then can we sit down with our Hindu friend in a spirit of expectancy to find how *God*—the God and Father of our Lord Jesus Christ—has been speaking to him *through the Ramayan*. Does God speak out of both sides of His mouth? Is He the Author of double talk—affirming to the Theravada Buddhist that there is no God and to the Christian that God *is* and is intensely personal?

Let us see what biblical base there is for grounding our appreciation of other religions and systems of thought in an alleged revelation by God of himself in those religions. Paul's address on Mars Hill shows clearly how he dealt with the matter. He announced the solidarity of the human family and affirmed that God is not far from each one of us for in Him we live and move and have our being. He suggested that " 'in the hope that [men] might feel after him and find him,' " God made man with religious longings.

After this Paul did *not* proceed to explore Socrates, Plato, Aristotle, and others to find what *God* had told them. Instead, Paul with magnificent honesty says, with a wave of the hand toward the temples which crowned the Acropolis:

> "we ought not to think that the Deity is like gold, or silver, or stone, a representation by the art and imagination of man. The times of ignorance God overlooked, but now he commands all men everywhere to repent, because he has fixed a day on which he will judge the world in righteousness by [the resurrected and living Jesus]" (Acts 17:29–30, RSV).

Paul no doubt appreciated the high and noble principles, the philosophical framework of Greek thought, and the true insights which eventually flowered into the sciences of the West; but Paul never gave his appreciation a theological ground. He never suggested that Greek religion had in any sense been revealed by God, nor that it was a witness to God.

In the famous passage (Acts 14:17) where Paul says that God has not left himself without "witness," he specifically does *not* mean "witness" *in* the religions of mankind. These he sums up as "vain things," and as "men walking in their own ways" (v. 15–16). This witness passage should always be read in the light of its later clauses: " 'yet he did not leave himself without witness for he did good and gave you from heaven rains and fruitful seasons, satisfying your hearts with food and gladness' " (RSV). What bore witness to God was the natural fruitfulness of earth—rains and sunshine. We have a similar passage in Romans 1:18–23 (RSV).

> For the wrath of God is revealed from heaven against all ungodliness and wickedness of men who by their wickedness suppress the truth. For what can be known about God is plain to them, because God has shown it to them. Ever since the creation of the world his invisible nature, namely, his eternal power and deity, has been clearly perceived *in the things that have been made*. So they are without excuse; for although they knew God, they did not honor him as God or give thanks to him, but they became futile in their thinking and their senseless minds were darkened. Claiming to be wise, they became fools, and exchanged the glory of the immortal God for images resembling mortal man or birds or animals or reptiles.

It is of first importance to read this passage aright. What God has revealed to man, *that* is precisely *not* what the religions say about God. What the religions say about God, Paul calls "futile thinking." Their propositions about God are propositions of "senseless, darkened minds." What God was saying to them, what "he has clearly shown to them," this they rejected entirely or distorted so badly that it elicited the sternest rebuke of which Paul was capable.

True, the idols are not all there are to non-Christian faith—and Islam passionately rejects idols of all sorts. Nevertheless, the existence of a passage such as this—and there are many others in the Bible—must give us serious pause in any attempt to give theological ground for appreciation.

In the fourth act, Warren says, "we have to ask what is the authentic religious content in the experience of Buddhist, Hindu, Shintoist, Moslem, or Marxist." Here again the evangelical both agrees and disagrees. He agrees on two grounds, first, that in order to talk intelligently, we must have much knowledge of the other man's religion. Often in order to win the right to talk, we must demonstrate reasonable familiarity with the thought system of our friends. Yes, we must indeed appreciate what is the authentic religious content in the experience of the other man.

Second, evangelicals agree that man is the great discoverer. He seeks to understand. He projects theories to explain the world in which he lives. He constructs ideologies, myths, theorems, and formulae. Many of his discoveries are correct. They adequately explain reality. Many others are ingenious or partially correct. They serve as working hypotheses, until later discoveries closer to the mark, supplant them. The evangelical has no difficulty at all in honoring man's religious longings or affirming that he is made in the image of God, fallen and defaced but nevertheless in God's image. Evangelicals pay full respect to man the discoverer. Many of his moral judgments in the fields of theology and some of his religious judgments come close to the mark. Most religions, for example, inveigh against adultery, robbery, and murder. Many religions affirm men's need for some kind of god, for power greater than himself, for more *mana* than he possesses, or more divine favor, however that may be interpreted. Hindu theologians discovered the two basic views in soteriology and expressed them in the cat and monkey theories of salvation. Theravada Buddhists probed deep into the psychological aspect of salvation. If all this is what is meant by "the authentic religious content of the experience of the man of other faith," then evangelicals have no difficulty in agreeing that we ought to find out as much about it as we can.

Evangelicals disagree with this proposal on two grounds. First, if we define "authentic religious content of the experience of the man of other faith" as "the longing which is behind the myths and symbols" then evangelicals demur. The game of ascribing religious content to myths and symbols can be played by many different people. The content which Sigmund Freud ascribes would be one thing, that ascribed by Malinowski would be another, and that by some kindly missionary seeking desperately a little common ground with a man of another faith, and generously resolving to put the highest possible interpretation on myth, dogma, image, and custom, would be something very different.

For example, there are some high meanings in suttee, for those few widows who really loved their husbands and were genuinely devoted to philosophical Hinduism; but for those many widows who were dragged and shoved screaming and protesting on to the funeral pyre, suttee had low and sinful meanings. "Finding the authentic religious content" may become a hypocritical game in which Christians, to find common ground adduce high and noble meanings to myths, dogmas, customs, and images, which on the whole are much less than ideal.

Second, if by "authentic religious content" we mean something which the God and Father of our Lord Jesus Christ has been saying to these men of other faith, other than what He has revealed through the Holy Bible, then the evangelical dissents. New light, to be sure, will always break forth from the Scripture. Over the door of Zwingli's church in Switzerland, I am told, is carved in stone the statement, "If you give the Word of God to the people of God, God will speak to His people through His Word, the message they need on that Day." God is sovereign. His Word is sharp and living. The Holy Spirit guides men in the very different circumstances in which they live. But the Holy Spirit proceeds ever from the Father *and from the Son;* that is to say, the Holy Spirit does not and by His nature cannot lead in a direction out of harmony with the basic revelation in Jesus Christ the Son who was born of the Virgin Mary, was crucified, dead, buried, and rose again.

Leaving Canon Warren's four acts, which comprise the way of presence, let me now take up two aspects of "presence" which it shares with many other mission methods. First, it fits special situations; it should be selectively applied. Unless we are careful, we are likely to consider "presence" equally applicable everywhere. This it is not. Consider, for instance, the presence technique of entering "sympathetically into the pains and griefs and joy and history of our non-Christian friends and seeing how these have determined the premise of their argument."

The evangelical would, I think, agree that the presence mode of mission was required in the case of men of other religions who had set themselves like flint against the Christian gospel. As the Christian seeks for ways to proclaim the gospel to *such* men, he must look carefully into the genesis of the hatreds and fears and hostilities which block understanding. He must imagine how he would feel were he in the other man's shoes. The presence approach may be the only one possible.

But with the responsive, the case is entirely otherwise. When men are standing with arms outstretched begging for the gospel, then the main task is to give them the gospel quickly and completely. There is then no need to enter "sympathetically into the pains and griefs and joys and history of our non-Christian friends" or to find out "how these have determined the premise of their argument" against Christ. They are advancing no argument against Christ. They are ready to hear about Him. They want not a glorification of the faith they are leaving, but an introduction to the Savior they are accepting.

Second, presence, or identification (like all methods and means) should be used only to achieve a correct and chosen end. When Paul says that he became all things to all men, we must remember that he did this *"in order to win some."* He would immediately have rejected the idea of becoming a Jew so thoroughly that the desire to win the Jew to Christ was diminished. Identification is desirable to the degree that it *wins some* but should never be idolized. Evangelicals are particularly wary of a muddle-headed identification and presence which destroys the very desire to win.

Four Conclusions

1. Evangelicals agree with presence and proclamation as means, but reject them as ends. The end is that men accept Jesus Christ as Lord and Savior and be found in Him. Evangelicals have always practiced both proclamation and presence *as means* and have always shied away from them as *ends*.

Proclamation, mind you, can become an end. In Japan there used to be a band of missionaries whose members passed from town to town, set up a loud speaker, blared forth the gospel for an hour, then put away their equipment and proceeded to the next town to "preach the gospel." With these missionaries, apparently voicing the words of gospel was the end and whether any lost son came back to his Father's house was immaterial.

Presence also easily becomes an end in itself. It is hard to keep it means. With presence, the goal tends to become *being* humble, *remembering* that God was there before you got there, *looking* for the good in other religions, *appreciating* the religious longings of men of other faiths, and *putting* the most Christian interpretation possible on myths, images, doctrines, and customs. And doing all this *whether the man for whom Christ died becomes a disciple of His or not.*

Frequently "presence" is inexorably transformed—even against the will of the Christian—from means to end. As the Christian resolves to be present with his non-Christian friend, he inches over into religious relativism. The process is as follows. He starts out by saying, "I respect you. I want to understand you. And I want you to understand me. Let us talk together. God has been speaking to you. You tell me what He has said to you, and I shall tell you what He has said to me. Let us be mutually edified." But then by degrees the Christian shifts to a new position saying, "Of course, what God has said to you is as valid as what He has said to me." Finally the Christian says, "Let us agree that the goal is not that you become a Christian or I become a Marxist. These both are ways to God."

Let me say bluntly that mission misconceives its end when it considers either proclamation or presence its basic task. The basic task is, for the glory of God, to bring men into redemptive relationship to Jesus Christ. The missionary yields himself body and soul *to be the instrument of the Holy Spirit in winning men into a life-giving faithful relationship to the crucified and risen Lord.* Neither proclamation nor presence, but *that* is Christian mission.

2. Both proclamation and presence suffer from excessive intellectual emphasis. Both imagine that men come to faith in Jesus Christ for exclusively ideological, theological, or intellectual reasons. Populations like those in Lydda and Sharon, those on the day of Pentecost, those which *have* turned in great numbers, and will turn in still greater numbers, do not become Christians because they have considered all the reasons and find that ABC is more *rational* than XYZ. They are not argued into Christian faith. The hammer of logic does not beat them into submission. Rather, all kinds of reasons—social, economic, political, religious, rational, and biblical—combine to lead them to place their faith intelligently on Jesus Christ. Again and again in the New Testament we read that it was the sign the Lord gave them, or the power which went forth from Him, which convinced them. The twelve apostles followed Him for three years largely because they expected him to drive out the Romans and install himself as an earthly Messiah. Their patriotism and their hatred of the Romans together with the signs which they saw and the words of wisdom they heard *all combined* to keep them close to His side.

3. An objection to presence, which cannot be leveled against proclamation, is that presence is not a biblical concept. The respectful approach to other religions is not found in the Old Testament. On many occasions, God's messengers spoke and acted very roughly about the Baals and Asherahs. The word presence occurs nearly two hundred times in the Bible, but never as a mode of mission. Something much more direct was practiced by our Lord and His apostles. We do not see Peter on the day of Pentecost appreciating all that was good in the Jewish religion. Stephen was not making a sympathetic approach to the Jews. Paul before Agrippa, after telling about Jesus Christ, says bluntly that he wants all those noble, cultured, and powerful men who had gathered to hear him, to become Christians.

There is good reason for this absence of the presence mode of mission in the New Testament. In those days, the gospel was being presented to receptive multitudes. Great people movements were going on. There was no need for the long, patient approach. New Testament Christians were not laying siege to rebellious and resistant peoples. Hence presence was not consciously used. Presence is a means of communicating the gospel and is particularly useful to those who seek to win the resistant. Granting this, it is still a striking fact that the presence mode of missions is notable by its absence in the Bible. This absence must not be understood as biblical condemnation, but should warn us that the presence method should be used with care, as a servant not a master, a means, not an end.

4. Presence is beyond doubt the way of new, indigenous Christians. Without any minister or missionary teaching them to do so, they sit down with their kinsmen who are still in the old faith and talk endlessly to them about the new religion and the old religion. At that level, cross-fertilization goes on ceaselessly, resulting in both advance and vitality: and heresy and debility. Cross-fertilization went on during patristic days. Christianity, Gnosticism, Mithraism, and other religions interacted and practiced "presence" for three hundred years in mutual efforts to win men and women to their ways of life. But not as a self-conscious mode of mission.

As Christianity becomes the religion of more and more men across the world, we shall not have to stress presence. Presence will be there in every living church. We cannot prevent the practice of Christian presence. As the Church advances in each non-Christian subculture, she swims in a sea of presence. Whether we advocate or deprecate it, presence is there and will continue to be there. But not as a self-conscious mode of mission.

What Christians, as they carry out mission, must do is to remember that they are sent into the world to find God's lost sons and daughters. That is their task. God's greatest rejoicing does not occur when lost sons and daughters hear the gospel with their ears, experience it through social action, or sense it through Christian presence. God most greatly rejoices when lost sons and daughters walk back through the front door of His House saying, "Father I have sinned, make me as one of your hired servants." He rejoices even more when, redeemed and restored, the saved sons and daughters go back out and, through proclamation when that is effective and through presence when that is, start living as Christians and bringing sinners to a saving faith in Christ and membership in His Church.

NOTES

1. Leighton Ford, Theological Consultation on Evangelism, September 29, 1967, Liberty Corner, N.J.
2. Eszard Roland in *Student World* 53, no. 3, p. 215.

3. Colin Williams, *Faith in a Secular Age* (London and Glasgow, 1966), p. 12.

4. *Student World*, July 1964.

5. Kenneth Cragg, *Sandals at the Mosque: Christian Presence amid Islam* (London and New York: Oxford University Press, 1959). George Appleton, *On the Eightfold Path: Christian Presence amid Buddhism* (London and New York: Oxford University Press, 1961). Raymond Hammer, *Japan's Religious Ferment: Christian Presence amid Faiths Old and New* (London and New York: Oxford University Press, 1962). John V. Taylor, *The Primal Vision: Christian Presence amid African Religion* (London and New York: Oxford University Press, 1963).

6. Taylor, op. cit., p. 9.

7. Ibid.

C. PRESENCE AND PROCLAMATION

Hans J. Margull

I

During the last two months we had some, if however brief, reports about an attempt at presence in Saigon. These were reports about a young Japanese Christian, his name by the way being Funato Yoshitaka, a member of one of the teams of Asian Christian Service, the Vietnam aid agency operated by the East Asia Christian Conference.

Funato is a graduate of Tokyo's Union Theological Seminary and a minister of the United Church of Christ in Japan. In the English news bulletin of his church the following notice was given:

> His present assignment is to provide help for the shoeshine orphans of Cholon, a Saigon suburb. To do this he lives with them most of each day and every night. The only time he leaves the boys is in the morning when he joins other Asian Christian Service team members for devotions. He shares the boys' meager food, their street fights, their one-room shed with its plank beds and myriad pests. Most of the time he roams Saigon's cluttered, clattering streets, one or more boys at his side looking for potential customers in the sidewalk cafes and bustling markets. Like all thirty-five of the shoeshine boys (whom he was able to pick up and to gather), he carries in his hand a small wooden box containing polish and brushes. The only thing that differentiates him from the other boys is the wording on his box. On one of its sides are written the words "Funato—Asian Christian Service," (on the other one) "Pray for peace." [1]

Later reports said that Funato had to be withdrawn due to the intense street fighting during the Vietcong Tet offensive in Febru-

---

Hans J. Margull has been on the staff of the World Council of Churches, Geneva. He is now Professor of Missions and Ecumenics at Hamburg University. His chapter was a paper read at the Europeon Consultation on Mission Studies held at Selly Oak Colleges, Birmingham, England, April 1968.

ary 1968. They also indicated dangers of his being gravely misused by Vietcong forces. His work, however, one learned, would be resumed at the earliest possible hour.

Missiologically, this is a simple attempt at presence which should not be overestimated. After all, only a beginning was made as many a beginning was made in the history of missions. Only one person was involved, perhaps an extraordinarily suitable person. Neither the person's reflections nor his proclamation have fully come out, nor is anything known about the reactions of the shoeshine boys, nor about the comments by other team members and by observers—that is, the attempt was made for too short a time. However, the attempt should not be overlooked. It signalizes necessities and opportunities in this and other present situations. It shows in a promising way the possibility of a fresh assessment of missionary tasks in our historical hour, and it points to a tradition.

I should like to call it the tradition of Christian presence. This simple attempt at presence among a host of homeless boys in the notorious quarters of Saigon's Cholon reminds one of Kagawa Toyohiko and those who are following his path today in Japan's Kansai area, in Osaka's Kamagasaki district, in Tokyo's Sanya quarter and in some of the local branches of the Japanese labor movement.[2] It reminds one of the group of worker priests in Paris and in the other cities of France, of Henri Godin, who died by a fire in his shabby room the night before work in the Paris suburbs commenced, of Henri Perrin who lived through labor camps in wartime Germany and died during his mission in a motorcycle accident— to mention only two of the names waiting to be included in the history of Christian missions.

It causes one to remember Charles de Foucauld and makes one aware of the manifold presence of the Little Brothers of Jesus in a dark mining town near Lille or in Charleroi, in Hamburg, in Algiers, in Casablanca, in Marrakech, in Lima, in Santiago de Chile, in Saigon, and elsewhere. It brings to mind again William Booth who resolved to go and to stay where other Christians had not gone, attempting a presence in a particular form demanded by a particular hour. It recalls certainly all the singularities, all the onesidedness, all the dangers, all the shortcomings, all the problems of those who throughout many centuries chose presence. It also recalls, viewed in all soberness, the long and broad line of many a classic missionary who did not simply go (and even the going is not simple), but who went and were led to meet the challenge of not returning, of identifying in the name of their Lord who identified, of being present in the hope that they as witnesses would be where the Savior would have been or would have them now be. (After all, was it not Christ Jesus who in an unsurpassable way took man seriously?) Many of their names we know. And we cherish the work of these whose intention is best exemplified in the desire of the two Moravians who willed to be slaves among the slaves for the Savior's sake.

In this tradition of Christian presence a good number of missionaries may not have debated the goal, perhaps however the strategy, "to win the winnable while they are winnable and to multiply churches in receptive populations." [3] Yet we find in this tradition men and women wholly geared to be among and to live for the least winnable, to work out their hope among and in service to the unreceptive. In the wide range of their attempts at presence, say, among the cultured men at Madurai and Peking as well as among the pagans of New Guinea, the life for the least winnable seems to be precisely the foremost characteristic of the presence tradition. We find it again in Saigon.

The report on Funato's attempt calls attention to the wording on his small and used shoeshine box. His name is written on the box. He has identified himself. He is Japanese. When he was born the Japanese army were in Saigon. A war of now twenty years had already begun. When the boys were born the French had come back and were soon to be repelled. Inner strife began, the Americans and some others came, the boys' parents died or disappeared or changed sides. There is no escape from history, either for those boys or for a witness. A historical situation in which men are ever living has to be met and it has to be met boldly. Boldly, that is, both by clearly identifying oneself, being ready for repentance, and by participating unreservedly in the history of a group to which the path of the witness was led. Readiness to do this under all costs of suffering is the step into Christian presence.

The Japanese, Funato, is identified as a Christian. "Asian Christian Service" is written beneath his name. In this case a question currently raised in some discussions about the anonymity of Christians in social affairs and services as well as a problem for some in the tradition of Christian presence has been clearly answered. The boys know from where this fellow who lives and works with them comes, and they know that he who has come to serve as a Christian shall speak. The Christian himself, however, knows that he will only be able to speak once his presence has been accepted.

The other side of his box bears the word he is hoping to speak: "Pray for Peace." It is or rather will be his proclamation. It isn't the proclamation yet. The question has not yet been raised by the group of boys to whom the prayer possibly could be directed and what the meaning of peace could ultimately be. But the direction is given and the next and most necessary action is being called for. The greatest need in the Vietnam situation is acknowledged, and it is acknowledged by someone who could have his peace outside Vietnam and did not have it. Who is this man who is so much concerned? The hour of proclamation will have come when this question has emerged.

Attempts at presence are being made under the conditions of history. Many a presence, particularly in our time, was attempted at outstanding points of tension, and it was exactly those points where what we call Christian presence was formed. They were points or situations into which Christians were attempting to enter, knowing that there would be no chance or no early chance for them to master the historical forces producing the tension or even to setting the terms for a quick change of the situation in favor of a Christian influence. Funato went into the streets of Saigon, accepted the situation, and used one of the cracks in the hard and big wall of the Saigon situation as his opportunity and place of presence—as long as the situation would allow him to do so. In many cases Christian presence is presence in the face of the very limited possibilities of a historical hour. Not to see and not to use them will not lead to even that little bit of presence. To see and to use them, however, will lead to a presence which may soon come to its end. In Funato's case he has had to be withdrawn, although only temporarily. Thus far on one contemporary attempt at Christian presence.

II

The very fact that the simple attempt by Funato was reported immediately and widely indicates both an unusualness in mission and an expectation concerning the churches' response in our days. One is reminded of the publicity which the attempt at presence of some worker priests found immediately after their surprising move from their churches, convents, and seminaries into the factories and into some of the distressing laborers' flats. In the beginning of 1947 there were not more than ten of them. At the end of 1947 the group of the Mission de Paris consisted of only twenty-five priests, and not all of them in the front line. Yet it sounded as if an enormous number of properly dedicated men had been involved in an exodus long and properly expected of the Church. Documents from that time show a strong sense of liberation being felt among many who were burdened by the wide gap between an immobile church both structurally and doctrinally petrified, on the one side, and a society on the other side which was in an ever faster movement towards a future for which the church apparently had no concern. The open presence of some Christians in present times was felt as a sign of hope and equally understood for what it actually was—an act in and of hope. A signal was given for a need now to be met. Historians of Christian missions may one day register this signal as being of equal importance in history as the signals once sounded by men like Francis Xavier or Count Zinzendorf or William Carey or Hudson Taylor. The first strong use of the word presence in its current theological and most of all missiological meaning was made at that time. It was through the French Student Christian Movement that what we may call the "presential" thinking together with the term *presence* came into the discussion of many a Protestant group. The intensity of the discussion did not prove in the first place the emergence of theological and ecclesiastical problems but the existence of a need. The need is a growing absence.

We are currently involved in identifying prominent cases of absence and in defining their reasons. Apart from the overall language problem in the widening postreligious *Selbstverstandamt* of our time, the major case and a case in all churches around the world has been for a time the parochial or local congregation of Christians—parochial in the double sense of the word. It was this case that D. T. Niles brought to ecumenical attention by proposing a worldwide study on what would in the present time be a missionary congregation. The overall answer reached in this study was that a missionary congregation in all situations is a presential congregation. The answer reflects the need of absence.

On the whole it is an absence caused by the rapid and strong changes in the societies of our time. A congregation of Christians still present yesterday in a village or in a neighborhood, in a nation or in a tribe, still meeting the questions of the people around them, still aware of their deepest needs, still speaking the language of the people, still having their attention, still being able to communicate God's word in sharing fully an hour of despair or rebellion yesterday, may find itself today in a marginal position or belonging only to a group of people who up till now is still the same. This may be and is the case in a European parochial congregation which until yesterday was a presential structure and in the process of the Christianization of Europe was a highly missionary structure. It may be and is the case with a congregation in New Guinea which finds that it has lost contact with those modern men who move into towns and take up jobs. The question always is if church structures correspond to social structures—the term structure now being used to cover the dimension of organization as well as of communication. Indigenization was felt to be the primary need for rooting a Christian community in a certain culture so that a whole culture could be challenged and be changed. Presently we see the need of a new indigenization in areas where churches had already been or were about to be indigenous. And the necessity of this new indigenization into the realm of urbanized and industrialized, and consequently more and more secularized, societies or parts of them overtakes many an attempt at a traditional indigenization based on traditional religio-cultural grounds. Japan would be a case in point.

The task of a new indigenization is a worldwide task. For the changes we experience are worldwide changes. The question of a missionary congregation witnessing in the joy of the gospel to a Lord calling all men and invoking all things to be changed is being raised by all and in all situations of change. It is always a question of presence calling for responses in a manifold and flexible way, inviting an imaginative love and an experimental living according to the biblical promises, pointing towards other men and their actual agendas today, leaving behind that which once was necessary and good, embarking for a voyage towards, what only some days ago Martin Luther King was still calling, the promised land.

After much and sometimes bewildering debate and after some battle in theology as well as in matters of polity we eventually found in the study on "The Missionary Structure of the Congregation" that it was our task to let Christians speak who here and there were attempting presence amid situations of change and need, rather than to design on theoretical principles a church capable of responding to present challenges. Those men of presence, those communities in the pursuit of new indigenizations, those pioneering in particular new situations, those attempting the language for the gospel today, we discovered, were to be seen and to be accepted as the pathfinders of a new missionary era in a new stage of human and world history. It dawned upon us that He who leads history and in history leads His Church also, is leading all over the world and in all churches committed men to the paths on which before long the churches will walk.

To assess and to discuss attempts at presence all over the world has become, as it seems to me, a prominent and most urgent task of missiology. I think we would have agreed with Max Warren's wise reference to General Jack's diary and the sound observations contained therein. General Jack, a front-line officer in the First World War, Max Warren summarizes, was "writing of the need, for regimental morale to be maintained in the monotony of trench warfare, of always having a number of men going out prospecting the enemy's position. In a word, pioneering by some is indispensable for the morale of the whole. But at the same time [General Jack] insists that the 'pioneers,' those probing the enemy's position, can only function satisfactorily against the background of a regiment observing the strictest and highest discipline in the course of its largely routine activities." [4] And we would have disagreed with the inherent suggestion that the Church, as also being "a hospital for those being healed from sin, a community in which men and women grow to be saints," cannot "*qua* institution, discharge its total missionary task." We would have talked about a possibility of the promised breakthrough and a sudden order for the "regiment" to leave the trench, to raise their heads, to stand up and to march.

Will the Church be prepared or will she, even living "at concert pitch" be content with "those probing the enemy's position"? Will more people than the few pioneers know how to move and to act in an unknown territory? Will they be able to adapt to ever changing situations? Will they be ready after the stifling life in the trenches to march continually? For it will not only be a day long that they must move, not only one change has to be taken into account, not only the change in church life is necessary which would bring churches up to date with a change that had happened yesterday. We were convinced in saying:

> It is not the task with which Christians are faced today merely to recognize that the world in which they live is no longer the world of 1920. Nor are they called simply to discard beloved conceptions and entrenched customs in order to make themselves at home in a changed world. The task reaches further. We shall have to face up to the fact that change is part of our situation in the world and that, as far as we can see, there will never be stable conditions anymore. We shall have to understand how in the midst of a continually changing world to keep faith, to exercise love and to walk humbly, to the praise of God and to the pleasing of men.[5]

And the continual change, we ventured to say, has to be understood Christologically. "The revelation of the gospel of Jesus Christ (Rom. 1:17) marks not only a decisive point but also a series of irreversible steps and an irresistible movement in human history." [6] All men are caught in this movement, whether aware of it or not, and Christians are witnesses of this movement —in their capacity, one may say, as changed men and as present interpreters of the great change behind the many confusing and often utterly confused changes in history. The question remains of their presence in history, and of their presence in all kinds of mostly momentary situations in the wide flux of our time—a time uniquely shaped by change.

III

But does presence mean simply to be there where we are no longer or where we are not yet?

"It does not mean that we are simply there," has been stated in the WSCF paper on "The Christian Community in the Academic World." The term "missionary presence," clearly used in other parts of recent ecumenical discussion, is lacking in this paper, but the attempts at presence of a new generation are clearly conceived of as a contemporary participation in the mission of God.[7] The word "presence," it is said, "tries to describe the adventure of being there in the name of Christ," to which is significantly and not at all rashly added, "often anonymously, listening before we speak, hoping that men will recognize Jesus for what he is and stay where they are, involved in the fierce fight against all that dehumanizes, ready to act against demonic powers, to identify with the outcast, merciless in ridiculing modern idols and new myths." To that we would comment that the biblical act of ridiculing everything and everybody who tries to occupy the place of God and thereby eventually dehumanizes men and their communities, can only come about in the face of the real idols and myths of our time once they have been experienced. And it is exactly in such a presence that the nature of God is revealed affirmatively to Christians and non-Christians alike.

What I am trying to point at can best be shown by an experience of some Christians and some young Marxists at one of their conferences in Prague. The conference was on the commandment, "Thou shalt not make unto thee any graven image" (Exod. 20:4), and the Marxist participants were taking an active part in the Bible studies. "During the summing up of the results," it was reported, "a young Marxist said that the necessity of a study of the Old Testament had been clearly shown to him, because a firmly established image of man and his future were a danger both to man as well as to the future." [8]

In this connection a term and with the term a whole new trend of thinking has to be appropriated. The term is "proexistence." Again it has its origin in the Student Christian Movement, in this case in East Germany where some ten years ago it was born in one of the many discussions about the place and the task of the Church in a socialist country. Those were the days when the new political slogan of coexistence was propagated, and many a Christian under the given circumstances was reflecting about a coexistential solution of the church-and-ideology problem. The solution was rejected in a number of Christian student groups which had just been the subject of a strong ideological repression resulting in some of their leading members being jailed. It was rejected, as we may say, as a wrong solution, not leading to presence but petrifying absence. And in the discussions about the temptation of a Church living absentially in coexistence with a society or with the world in general, the new word "proexistence" was born.[9] It became a watchword for a faith to be lived in presence and a formula for a theology that strove to overcome an absential trend in Christendom.

The theology was derived from Dietrich Bonhoeffer's Christological and ecclesiological thoughts as expressed in a draft written in 1944.[10] "Who is God?" was Bonhoeffer's question. Any possibility of speaking of God in terms of a general faith in God's omnipotence (which actually would also mean his nonhistoricity) was contested. Meeting Jesus Christ was given as the answer. In Jesus Christ, Bonhoeffer wrote, a conversion of all that it means to be human is given by the life of one man who lived a life for other men. In Jesus' being there for others, read the statement, lies the transcendental experience, whereby faith in God as revealed in "the man for other men" makes for a new life in living for others. The ecclesiological consequence followed in the uncompromising words: "The Church is only Church if she is existing for others." "Proexistence" was a summary of this epochal theological design; it also became the lead word for a theological development in which the word "pro" achieved or is about to achieve a quality like or comparable to the quality of the reformer's "*sola.*" Or in terms of the biblical background, here is a stream in theology in which Romans 3:28 is actualized and thereby deepened by a newly appropriated Philippians 2:5–8. This actualization, by the way, characterizes the present stream in its responsible parts, of a theological renewal in which, I should think, missiology had a task and a great opportunity to participate.

Proexistence demands presence, and presence is the expression of a faith leading to proexistence. One cannot live for others being far away from them, geographically, culturally, existentially, theologically. There can be no proclamation without presence, presence precedes proclamation. Missiologically we have always known this; it was at least in missiology that Hendrik Kraemer's classical solution of the problem of the foreignness of the gospel in man's world emerged in the statement "that there is only one point of contact" and "this one point of contact is the disposition and the attitude of the missionary." [11] Proexistence in presence, however, also determines the proclamation of the missionary (whether he for himself cherishes this name or now tries, rightly or wrongly, to avoid it) in the sense of the question of when and how to speak about Jesus. Here again missiology has its material. Christian Keysser of New Guinea more than once remarked that as a seminarian he was taught to proclaim the Word among the heathen just as it was proclaimed in a Lutheran village back home in Bavaria, and that he found this utterly false and impossible after he became present among men in New Guinea. In his attempt at presence during the early time of the New Guinea mission, the proclamation of the Savior turned out to be a proclamation of power.[12]

But now the problem is deepened. Usually we were dealing with "proclamation events" like this one under methodological aspects, often marveling at the skill of some missionaries in introducing Jesus without finally altering or permitting the modification of the inherited doctrinal picture of the Savior and Lord. The task now, however, as it seems to come up, is no longer simply one of missionary methodology but of missional theology. Who is Jesus, witnessed to in the New Testament by men of Palestinian and Hellenistic presences, if he is to be proclaimed in a presence amid shoeshine boys in Saigon or in many a presence among men more and more becoming conscious of what has been called a planetary world? [13] The question for many different situations and situations of a world living in a world history is if there can be a legitimate theological morphology of the proclamation in acts attempted as acts of presence in the name of the proclaimed one. This is not a new question, but it is not being solved by letting it grow older. Attempts at presence for and in dialogue make this task more urgent every day. And I for one would have been glad for some case studies in this field on which a reflection on presence and proclamation could have drawn.

Proclamation always is proclamation in situation. The situation is made up by those who may listen, by those who are expectant to speak, and by those from whom the missionary is coming. The latter ones in their history pose one of the foremost problems in an hour when those who may listen know already, correctly or incorrectly or insufficiently, something about the Christianity with which the missionary is connected. God's Word does not depend, as we believe and know, on a saintly presentation by Christians. But we also experience and know that present missionaries, or any Christian anywhere, are constantly and exhaustingly challenged first of all to inform people of what Christianity is not. We are living in a late hour of the expansion of Christianity, and we are known around the world. In referring to the Church in Germany at a time which some have called her finest hour, the years of the Confessing Church, Bonhoeffer is able to remark that this church has only fought for her self-preservation as if she were an end in herself, and thereby has lost her authority to proclaim the reconciling and redemptive word for mankind and the world.

In reference to many a church and the missionary movement John V. Taylor speaks of our "possessiveness." [14] Bonhoeffer concluded that for such a reason only two things remain for a Christian to do—prayer and acts of justice among men. But he also expresses hope. It is the hope that the day shall come when men are called again to pronounce the Word of God in such a way that it will change and renew the world. He thought of a new language, perhaps entirely nonreligious, yet liberating and redeeming, received among Christians who are now going to pray and to act justly and in doing so to await God's time.[15] The accent is on presence awaiting God's time—a time that may certainly be now in some situations or it may be later in others, if it will be later at all. There is at least China to be remembered. And there can no longer be any easy talk of an aggressive and possessive missionary spirit. As John V. Taylor in his reflection on Christian presence amid African religion has put it: "The Christian, whoever he may be, who stands in that world in the name of Christ, has nothing to offer unless he offers to be present, really and totally present, really and totally in the present."[16] That is, unpossessive and expectant. And this is the kind of role we have to will in the present hour of mission above all.

Not that we should not go forward. There is a grave misunderstanding of the presential thinking in missiology if it is now concluded that we should remain where we are or that we should be silent at the places to which we are going. The call to presence is a call to action, and even silence, if it has to be this way, can be an action, a witness, a proclamation. What is being said here is intended for us to take the proclamation of the gospel as seriously as it is demanded in our time. We may lose the word for this and the next hour if we now as always want to win. There remains to be remembered that God's very (or should we say real) presence among men as the Man-for-others (as we are now come to believe in him) was and is the proclamation. This presence had to be articulated, and it was articulated in deeds and words of a faith being born in the face of this presence: "In the name of Jesus Christ of Nazareth, walk" (Acts 3:6, RSV)— "You are the Messiah" (Mark 8:29, NEB). There are certainly situations, particularly in our time, in which the simple presence (but presence is not simple) is in itself the proclamation. And such a presence will find its articulation eventually as a response by those among whom the presence has happened. The question of how we should think about and teach mission today and tomorrow, depends for its solution on our highest and most open attention to those attempts at presence which in themselves are proclamation.

NOTES

1. Kyodan News Letter (Tokyo), February 20, 1968.
2. H. J. Margull, Versuche "Christlicher Präsenz" in der japanischen Arbeitswelt, *Evangelische Missions Zeitschrift* 23 (1966), 227ff.
3. Donald McGavran, "Wrong Strategy," see above, p. 100.
4. Max Warren, "The Christian World Mission in a Technological Era," *Ecumenical Review* 17 (1965) 221.
5. *Planning for Mission,* ed. by Thomas Wieser (New York: U.S. Conference for the World Council of Churches, 1966), p. 70. (Written by Hans Schmidt, Hamburg.)
6. Ibid., p. 78 (drafted by Theophil Vogt, Zurich).
7. *The Christian Community in the Academic World* (Geneva: World Student Christian Federation, 1964), p. 8.
8. M. Heryan, "The Ministry of Dialogue," CONCEPT XII, (Geneva: WCC, Dec. 1966), 27.
9. Elisabeth Adler, *Pro-Existenz* . . .
10. Dietrich Bonhoeffer, *Widerstand und Ergebung* (Munich: Chr. Kaiser Verlag, 1955), pp. 257–62.
11. Hendrik Kraemer, *The Christian Message in a Non-Christian World,* 1938, 140.
12. Christian Keysser, *Das bin bloss ich* (Neuendettelsau: Freimund Verlag, 1966).
13. A. van Leeuwen, *Christianity in World History* (London: Edinburgh House Press, 1964), pp. 399ff.
14. John V. Taylor, *The Primal Vision* (London: SCM Press, 1963), p. 199.
15. Ibid., p. 207.
16. Ibid., p. 197.

PART V

1968:
The Uppsala Controversy on Mission

A. CRITICISM OF THE WCC WORKING DRAFT ON MISSION

1. Will Uppsala Betray the Two Billion?

Donald McGavran

By Uppsala I mean, of course, the Fourth Assembly of the World Council of Churches which is to be held at Uppsala, Sweden, in July 1968. By "the two billion" I mean "that great number of men, at least two billion, who either have never heard of Jesus Christ or have no real chance to believe on Him as Lord and Savior." These inconceivable multitudes live and die in a famine of the Word of God, more terrible by far than the sporadic physical famines which occur in unfortunate lands.

The Church, to be relevant, to discharge her humane duty to the masses of mankind, to act with justice, and to manifest compassion, must plan her activity, marshall her forces, carry on her campaign of mercy and liberation, and be faithful to her Lord *with the two billion in mind.* If the sufferings of a few million in Vietnam, South Africa, Jordan, Buchenwald, or the slums of Rio de Janeiro or Detroit rightly excite the indignation and compassion of the Church, how much more should the spiritual sufferings of two thousand million move her to bring multitudes of them out of darkness into God's wonderful light. The Church to be relevant must augment her program to carry the bread of life to starving multitudes and to dig wide, deep channels through which the water of life may flow to "the two billion" perishing of thirst.

By "betray" I mean any course of action which substitutes ashes for bread, fixes the attention of Christians on temporal palliatives instead of eternal remedies, and deceives God's children with the flesh when they long for the spirit. By "betray" I mean planning courses of action whose sure outcome will be that the two billion will remain in their sins and in their darkness, chained by false and inadequate ideas of God and man. Uppsala will betray the two billion if she, to whom God has given the leadership of such a proportion of the Church, plans a program

---

The comments in Part V, section A, appeared in the *Church Growth Bulletin,* Special Uppsala Issue, May 1968.

which leads her affiliated churches away from the precise issues on which Christians need to speak today, away from spreading the knowledge of their Savior to as many of the two billion as it is possible to do.

Will Uppsala betray the two billion? Why is it necessary to ask the question? Why suppose that Uppsala will do anything else but plan a strategy for the seventies which will meet the world's deepest needs, which will assuage the thirst of the two billion? The answer is clear. Because, as the Fourth Assembly of the World Council of Churches meets, its agenda says nothing about the two billion. Its agenda in the form of a 136-page book called *Drafts for Sections: Uppsala '68* has been published and is being studied by thousands of congregations, boards of mission, study groups, and others. This book is available from the World Council of Churches through the Geneva, New York, or London offices.

It should be clearly understood that these "drafts for sections" are *not* pronouncements made by the World Council of Churches. They are study documents drawn up by committees. In his Foreword, the General Secretary, Eugene Carson Blake, says that these committees have been directed to set forth "the precise issues on which we need to speak today . . . the relatively few subjects which we find most relevant to the contemporary situation and tasks of the Ecumenical Movement." The papers thus prepared were subsequently "twice subjected to discussion by widely representative groups of persons involved in World Council work." These six preparatory drafts then are sent out to be earnestly and prayerfully studied by participants and churches. This article in the *Church Growth Bulletin* is part of that study process.

Church Growth Bulletin is concerned with Section Two (the second Draft) only—that on mission, prepared for the Division of World Mission and Evangelism. The Church, enormously concerned with her mission to the two billion, should study "Section Two—Renewal in Mission." Christians everywhere should be asking themselves: did those who prepared this draft rightly discern "the precise issues" concerning the unsaved world on which the Church needs to speak today? When the Division of World Mission and Evangelism meets in Uppsala, it may depart entirely from this study document and draw up a new statement to guide the churches as they consider their mission during the seventies. Indeed this article is written in the hope that Uppsala will write another draft germane to the real issues of the day.

On what grounds can we judge this preparatory document a betrayal of the two billion? First, according to the clear teaching of the New Testament, it is necessary for men to believe on

Jesus Christ as Lord and Savior in order to be saved. How can they believe if they have not heard? And how can they hear without messengers carrying the word of life to them? Section Two says nothing about the necessity of faith, nothing about the two billion, and nothing about sending messengers.

In the place of this, we are treated to about six hundred words of involved theological dicta like the following: "We long for our personal life to be renewed. Nations and families, fishes and birds, trees and flowers also yearn eagerly for the day when the new man will be revealed." The strange passage, Romans 8:19–22, concerning whose meaning there is no common agreement among Christians, is used as the biblical justification for this nonsense that fishes and flowers and trees (and why not rocks and volcanoes, white dwarfs and neutrons?) yearn eagerly for the day when the new man will be revealed.

Section Two neglects the plain meaning of the Cross and of the Resurrection amply testified to by dozens of clear passages. He that believes shall be saved and he that does not believe shall be damned. . . . He who has the Son has the Father and he who does not have the Son does not have the Father. . . . That whosoever believeth on Him should not perish. . . . No man cometh to the Father but by Him. . . . Therefore we are justified by faith. All these passages and many more are strangely absent in the theological system set forth as the basis for renewal in mission. The entire draft says nothing about the two billion unbelievers, the need to believe on Jesus Christ, or the mandate to disciple the nations. Not a sentence, not a line, not a word. Nothing!

Second, from beginning to end the document is studded with the word *mission*. It is entitled "Renewal in *Mission*." Its first sentence reads, "God has set out on His *mission* to men in Jesus, the man from Nazareth." Its second main subsection is entitled "Freedom for *Mission*," and affirms that "Renewal for *mission* is the work of the Spirit." But, while the word *mission* is repeatedly used, its meaning is *nowhere* that of communicating the good news of Jesus Christ to unbelieving men in order that they might believe and live. Classical mission has been the carrying out of the great commission. Most missionary societies today have constitutions in which this classical purpose is specified. The United Presbyterian Church in the United States of America has a statement which begins as follows: "The supreme and compelling purpose of the Christian Mission to the world is to proclaim Jesus Christ as divine and only Savior and to encourage men to become His disciples and responsible members of His Church." Section Two sets forth a sophisticated theory and theology of mission which the vast majority of Christians and biblical scholars will not accept as the clear will of God toward the world of unbelievers.

Third, a deliberate purpose to divert attention *away from* men's need to hear about Christ, to confess Him as Savior, to obey Him as Lord, and to proclaim Him as Redeemer and King marks the document in all the critical passages. For example, subsection 5 is headed "Communicating the good news implies dialogue." Its emphasis is that the Christian must "listen to artists and scientists, to men of other faiths, and to agnostics to learn what news Christ has for him through them." Let us agree for the moment that the Christian is a courteous listener and can learn much from his fellow men. But is communicating the good news exhausted in listening? Suppose dialogue *is* one mode of communicating the good news to some kinds of men. Suppose it comprises one-tenth of all gospel proclamation. This preparatory document was supposed to devote itself to "the precise issues on which we need to speak today." What about the responsive millions who cannot wait for the tedious processes of dialogue, who want to be told about the gospel at once, that they and their children may enter into life now while they yet live. The real issue of today is not dialogue with the resistant, but encouragement of the responsive to accept the Lord as their personal Savior and enter at once into abundant and eternal life.

Fourth, the chief thrust of Section Two of the Uppsala Drafts is concerned not with mission but with renewing existing churches and getting them involved with all of life in points of tension, revolutionary movements, critical points of society and "the agenda of the world" (to use a bit of current ecumenical jargon).

To be sure, about one hundred fifty words are devoted to "Dialogue with Non-Christians." But if one hopes that here the spiritual thirst of the two billion will be assuaged, he will be sharply disappointed. "Dialogue with Non-Christians" asserts that "Christians can (through dialogue) affirm their common understanding of man which will lead to a fuller apprehension of truth. Such dialogue also involves a deeper understanding of our relation to our own culture, or to the different cultures to which we belong." That seems to say, that, in dialogue with non-Christians, the *Christian* may be benefited. He will realize that he too is a man and may receive some cultural development in himself. To the authors of Section Two dialogue seems to be not feeding those dying in the great famine of the Word of God but cultural improvements of Christians.

Fifth, in the Draft for Section Two, Uppsala will have its sole opportunity to consider the impartation of the gospel to the lost. Other Drafts, prepared for other sections (such as those for the

"World Economic and Social Development," "Justice and Peace in International Affairs," and the "Worship of God in a Secular Age") present other aspects of the human scene with which the Church should deal. We rejoice in the wide scope of the Church's business. We are proud to belong to a Church which meets humanity's need at so many places. But, without forgetting leprosy, disease, illiteracy, race pride, poverty, war and other temporal scourges, an obedient Christian walking according to his great Head must remember the salvation of his two billion brothers. It makes an eternal difference whether a man believes on Jesus Christ or not, and two billion do not know enough about Him to believe on Him. Section Two is the only section which can deal with the two billion—and Section Two has apparently resolved to say nothing about them or about their need to know Jesus Christ and be found in Him.

Instead, Section Two systematically uses the old words, which for a hundred and fifty years have meant one thing to the Church, with a radically new meaning. The procedure cannot be attributed to chance. The preparation of this draft, dealing with the enormously important subject of mission, it seems to me, has fallen into the hands of a small band of men determined to change the course of mission. They employ the simple expedient of using the classical words, heavily freighted with emotion, with an entirely new purpose. These men do not point out the changes they are making. They do not inform the Church that they are launching a radically new system and are directing mission away from the two billion into new channels. Whether this amounts to perpetrating a pious fraud or not the reader will have to judge.

For example, on page 32, the "Commentary" on the Draft has as its first heading "The Missionary God." In three substantial paragraphs about the "missionary" God, *not a word* is said about the two billion who have no knowledge of Jesus Christ as God and Savior according to the Scriptures. Instead, the reinterpretation proposes that the missionary God "in the person of Jesus is present with power. His words and deeds bring unrest into the world (Matt. 13:33; Mark 2:22). They bring a new movement; they introduce a new beginning in a dynamic way. This change has two aspects: it has already taken place—the old order has gone and a new order has already begun (1 Cor. 5:17), and it is still taking place—history is experienced as change. . . . Participation in God's mission is therefore entering into partnership with God in history. . . . The central question then becomes to what extent is what we have inherited still serving the mission of God?"

Quite on the contrary, for the Division of World Mission and

Evangelism (DWME) and all Christian churches, the *central question* is: How many of the lost are we bringing back to the fold? How obedient are we to our Lord's command to disciple the nations? How faithful are we to the mission of God, the mission to which our Lord gave His life?

Section Two has not been thrown together hurriedly or by accident. During the last twenty years, a new theology has been forged which apparently intends to have no place for mission from the Church in one land to non-Christians in other lands. It intends to divert the whole missionary movement into the movement toward Christian unity on the one hand and Christian behavior toward one's close neighbors on the other. In the latter, Christianizing the social order is also included. Christian unity and Christian neighborliness are good ends, to be sure, but they are not mission and should not masquerade as such. Granted that new light does break out of God's word from time to time, still is it not remarkable that none of the great leaders of the Church, none of the devout students of the Bible, none of the great theologians glimpsed this theology till these wise men discerned it after 1948?

The attempt on theological grounds to direct the missionary enterprise of the Church into channels not even remotely connected with bringing the nations to faith and obedience (Romans 1:5 and 16:25) or reconciling men to God in the Church of Jesus Christ (2 Cor. 5:18ff.) must excite the suspicion and will earn the rejection of Christians everywhere. It affirms that "the central question is to what extent is what we have inherited (existing missionary societies and their goals of world evangelization) still serving the mission of God." It asserts that they "are transitory forms of obedience to the missio Dei." It proposes that Christians must be "ready to abandon them and replace them with new ones."

Christians should, of course, be ready to abandon any instrument which ceases to serve the mission of God in the salvation of the two billion. But this is not what this Draft proposes. It proposes that the two billion do not need redemption at all and that mission must be concerned about *other things* which God is at work doing, "in history," of course!

Again and again this Draft insists that the Church must be concerned with the world's agenda. Indeed one heading is "The World's Agenda—Our Business." In plain English this means that the mission of the Church is to meet needs *of which the world is conscious*. Since it is not keenly conscious of the need to believe on Jesus Christ, proclaiming the gospel should be dropped from the tasks of the Church. This is not said, mind you; but it is a legitimate deduction for everything else is stressed and proclamation of the gospel is not even mentioned.

Does this mean that those who prepared the Draft for Section Two intended to capture the institutions and machinery of present day missions, together with the treasury which has an annual income of well over two hundred million dollars a year? Do they intend to direct the whole complex enterprise away from discipling the nations, away from the preaching of the gospel, away from the multiplication of churches of baptized believers, and into various forms of revivifying the Church? By this last phrase do they mean getting the Church to act more like the Church in every aspect of its being—*except the persuasion of men to become disciples of the Lord of Life?*

If I am wrong in this assumption, all Uppsala needs to do is to introduce into the official World Council of Churches statement, which will be drawn up, a strong section which calls on all churches to augment proclaiming the gospel, to increase discipling receptive peoples, to answer the calls from all Macedonias, and to multiply churches of Christ everywhere, in order that God may be glorified, His will may be done and thanksgiving to the glory of God may increase (2 Cor. 4:15). *Church Growth Bulletin* will rejoice in such revision and give it special coverage.

What shall we say if some one were to object as follows? "Dr. Blake's foreword specifically says that these Drafts for Sections are not to go on repeating 'what past Assemblies have said,' but should instead concentrate 'on the relatively few subjects which are most relevant to the contemporary situation.' Past Assemblies spoke of the need for winning the multitudes of mankind to Christian faith. The Church will, of course, proceed with that kind of mission. At Uppsala we are simply adding a new factor, which needs to be stressed during the seventies."

The answer is twofold. First, the committee which drew up this statement was straitly charged to formulate a draft concerning "the precise issues on which we need to speak today." The salvation of two billion children of God is *the precise issue* on which the Division of World Mission and Evangelism needs to speak. Nothing is more precise or more contemporary. Second, the whole tenor of Section Two is *not* a cordial acknowledgement that the discipling of the nations is a chief and irreplaceable purpose of Christian mission. The clear intent of Section Two is to substitute a totally new concept of mission for the old concept which Section Two considers outworn.

The committee which drew up this Draft is apparently unaware of the fact that today in many lands of Asia, Africa, and Latin America, an unprecedented receptivity to the gospel exists. Much greater receptivity exists than would have been deemed possible twenty years ago. According to the World Christian Handbooks, the Christian population of Africa south of the Sahara increased from twenty million in 1950 to fifty million in 1968. It is likely to increase to a hundred million by 1990. The precise issue in 1968 when the World Council will meet at Uppsala is this: how can the Christian Church carry the gospel faster and better to the multitudes who want to become Christians? The chief issue is not dialogue with hostile non-Christians. In the days of His flesh, our Lord instructed His disciples to by-pass indifferent and hostile villages and hurry on to the receptive. Such days have again come. This is a time to emphasize discipling, not to turn from it. This is not a time to betray the two billion but to reconcile as many as possible of them to God in the Church of Jesus Christ. For the peace of the world, for justice between men and nations, for advance in learning, for breaking down hostilities between peoples, for the spiritual health of countless individuals and the corporate welfare of mankind *this is a time to disciple the nations, baptizing them in the name of the Father, Son, and Holy Spirit and teaching them whatsoever our Lord has commanded us.*

Throughout history, the mission of the Church to non-Christians in other lands has been carried forward by companies of the concerned, not by the whole Church. It was not Jerusalem that dispatched Barnabas and Saul on the first missionary journey, but a group of specially concerned men in the church at Antioch. The evangelization of north Europe depended on monastic orders. Bands of the devout, the specially concerned, i.e., the orders, furnished Rome's missionaries. Among Protestants too, the missionary movement was launched not by the whole Church but by bands of specially concerned Christians—who often carried on their mission against the active opposition of the Church.

Of recent years, missionary societies have been so prospered by God and have so well fitted the era of European dominance, that some Protestant churches *as churches* have espoused missions. During the last fifty years many missionary societies have appeared to be *church societies.* If the denomination had only one missionary society, it was difficult for it to appear like anything else but "the missionary division of the whole denomination." It is significant that scarcely has this process gotten under way, scarcely has mission appeared to be the business of the whole Church, than the Church has begun to subvert the mission to her own service. Mission to carry the gospel to the two billion is becoming any good activity at home or abroad which anyone declares to be the will of God. Phoning lonely old ladies of the Church was recently given as a meaningful contemporary form of mission! And now the great quadrennial gathering of the World Council of Churches sends out a preparatory draft on mission (Section Two of Uppsala '68) which concentrates its entire attention on renewing existing churches in mission. By which Section Two does *not* mean renewing churches so that they will proclaim the gospel both here at home and abroad.

Church Growth Bulletin cannot believe that Section Two represents advanced missionary thinking of the great churches affiliated with the World Council of Churches. We cannot believe that the renowned and honored missionary societies which together make up DWME will allow any such draft to be set forth as expressing their 1968 purpose in mission. We cannot believe that this great missionary planning session can neglect so completely both Vatican II on Mission and the Wheaton Congress of 1966.

We prayerfully hope that more Christian counsels will prevail and the two billion will not be betrayed. We shall look forward with hope and support Uppsala with prayer, confident that Section Two is not the will of God and will be rejected, or revised, modified, and brought more into harmony with the experience and understanding of the universal Church, the clear intent of the Bible, and the express statements of Jesus Christ our Lord.

A. CRITICISM OF THE WCC WORKING DRAFT ON MISSION

2. Further Comment on "Drafts for Sections"

Ralph D. Winter

Drafts for Sections is both fascinating and weighty. No one mind could have put into 136 pages so much so closely reasoned and so diversely concerned. And it was produced under pressure—it is quite distracting to find different systems of cross reference between the six brief "Draft Documents" and the "Commentaries" that immediately follow them. But a great amount of keen, hard thinking is packed into this little book.

However, sitting back and looking once again at the document after reading it from cover to cover, one has a sinking feeling. Good as it is, profound as it is at many points, engagingly diverse as it is in subject matter—all of it relevant to the Christian—it is clearly no more than the best that could be done by an unreasonably small Genevan staff in consultation with the part-time attention of a representative number of other thinkers. One would guess that the production of this document was a painfully difficult work of "supererogation" piled on top of staff people who already had schedules full of normal duties.

Another widely published handicap the drafting group labored under, of course, was the internal tension within the WCC itself. When the Mexico Report talks about crossing confessional frontiers in mission, there have to be footnotes indicating non-agreement on the part of the Greek Orthodox members of that section. In view of such formidable obstacles (will the Greek Orthodox be persuaded to go to Uppsala after all?) it is no wonder really that this section is, shall we say, somewhat selective.

Zeroing in on the Section Two, "Renewal in Mission," we find a five-page "Draft Document" and then twenty pages of "Commentary." This is the section one might suppose to be of greatest interest to missionaries. Actually, as Dr. McGavran has pointed out, it says nothing at all in conventional language about missions, and there is no evidence of any practical, concrete concern about

---

Dr. Winter is Associate Professor of the History of the Expansion of Christianity, School of Missions and Institute of Church Growth, of Fuller Theological Seminary, Pasadena, Calif.

winning what Vatican II's *Ad Gentes* highlighted as "the two billion." And, while the twenty-page commentary makes many interesting quotes from many documents, there is no reference whatsoever to the 1963 Iberville, Quebec, *Statement on Church Growth*. That statement, drawn up at a consultation sponsored by the WCC's own Department of Missionary Studies calls church growth "a subject . . . essential for the fulfillment of the Church's mission in the world," and urges "earnest consideration of these matters by the WCC-DWME."

It is strange also that only two quite peripheral references are made to the DWME's own Mexico meeting late in 1963, which was its first full meeting following the International Missionary Council's merger with the WCC. I refer to the 200-page report, *Witness in Six Continents*. Neither of those references are to the "Helping Churches Grow" section. We can take that, maybe, but why is there also not a single reference in this Uppsala draft to the Vatican II document? Is this dialogue?

The problem of this document is not merely Geneva's tiny staff, nor the WCC membership's internal indigestion. Despite the impressive number of churches on their roll, as far as missions are concerned the largest two blocks are still outside the Council (in sheer number of missionaries): the Roman Catholics and the evangelicals outside of member churches—and there is hardly a trace of the thinking of these two groups in the document.

It is ironic that council people would speak so sincerely about dialoguing with other faiths and yet engage in so little dialoguing with those who are much closer. While it is a tribute to the solid work in WCC publications that evangelicals are more likely to be up on WCC thinking than vice versa, yet this fact does not illuminate the WCC staff.

Correspondingly, council people groping for new structures show little knowledge of the decentralized mission apparatus that has served the Roman communion so well. Or, they speak of "internationalization" of missions with nary a glance at existing Roman Catholic and especially evangelical missions that are truly international. They talk about a nonresidence locus for Christian fellowship and mission, but with little awareness of dozens of evangelical structures that for decades have simply been "invisible" to churchly spokesmen. Again, Hans Küng, in anticipating Vatican II, urged a new, more drastic adaptation to non-Western social customs (even to the review of the Chinese Rites dispute), while this document loftily but vaguely speaks of the Church's mission as "the breaking down of walls which divide human beings by race, speech, and culture."

Understandably, then, the section of "Renewal in Mission" tends strongly to be preoccupied with the single passion of a single Christian subgroup. The phrase "the new humanity" (or equivalent phrases: *new mankind, true humanity, mature manhood, renewed mankind*, etc. occurs eighteen times in the five-page Draft. Most of this theme song is found in Ronald Gregor Smith's *The New Man* (Harper, 1955), but it is appealingly restated. In part it all means that we should not be so excited any more about building the church but rather about building society. The church structure has been the scaffolding which now can be dismantled. With friends like these does the Church need enemies?

It is true of course that in early times the monastic structures provided a sanctuary, a haven to which people could retreat from a world in which there was outright physical danger to believers (as is the case in places today). From these refuges, outstanding leaders were recruited for "secular" duties, like the jobs to which Augustin and Martin of Tours were called.

Later when self-protection was no longer so great a problem, the "gathered" church pattern offered a part-time sanctuary and permitted members to return to the world during the week on a sort of out-patient basis. Even the Friars marked a notably new step forward in regard to their attitude toward the world. Hope began to be conceived for the world itself. The change of structure was not due to a better understanding of the will of God which made the earlier strategy inferior by comparison, but was due to a change in the nature of society itself due to the influence of the Christian faith. Over the centuries countless changes in social structures, sporadic but cumulative for the most part, were effected by these "gathered" religious subcommunities despite their continued exclusiveness.

But now the village-church relationship is passing away under the pressure of the multi-valence life of the city, and now it becomes convenient to shift our attention away from the church itself to the remaining problems of the world. The great need, it is said, is not to pull people into a dying church structure but to push dead church members out into their mission in the world. This is neither so new nor so amazingly helpful, since, as mentioned above, evangelicals have dozens of organizations already that "fit the shape of the world" and deal with the "agenda of the world," whether the locus is the campus or the business or government community, or the problem is drug addiction (e.g., the Pentecostal *Teen Challenge* recently praised by a Jesuit study in *America*, March 30, 1968). Rightly understood this document is prestigious encouragement to every kind of activity in this dimension of "mission."

But this vision for social justice and direct mission in the world seems out of place in nominal church circles. Perhaps that is why it often leads the exponents to reject the Church itself. Is it possible that this passion neither revives the dead church nor logically faults the live church? None of this emphasis really means that the young, growing church along traditional lines isn't necessary any more, or that such a church can't provide a vital sanctuary both for the prime movers in social renovation and also for the new, shell-shocked believers who really need to flee the world before they can go back to work on it. Quite likely there must always be that same old "where two or three are gathered together *in my name*" which has been the vital, essential structure in one form or another throughout history. And this brings us back to church growth.

A. CRITICISM OF THE WCC WORKING DRAFT ON MISSION
3. For Uppsala to Consider

Alan R. Tippett

I have been asked to express some opinions on *Drafts for Sections: Uppsala '68*. I do this only because the booklet itself invites our contributions before the Assembly meets. My comments are meant to be constructive. The "Foreword" says, "We should avoid repetition of what past Assemblies have said, unless our words have new topical significance. . . ." I feel this was unfortunate. The things which past Assemblies have said repeatedly are surely the abiding things which need restatement. They continue to be relevant, in spite of change. Their absence distorts the totality of the study and exposes it to criticism.

With the world in its present state, with processes of extremely rapid change, secularization, new dimensions in the fight for human rights, the passing of colonialism and a new emphasis on generation gaps, we are not surprised that these will be discussed. This is as it should be.

I agree that both the *role* and *form* of the Church in our day should be related to the conditions of our times and be socially relevant, and that this seems to call for modifications of both forms (e.g., the structure of the congregation) and communication techniques in the face of this cultural change. I also agree that there is in our midst much social injustice that urgently needs correction, and that the Church should concern itself with this business. I believe the agenda does focus attention on many of these issues, and the theses of its "Program for Action" are rightly to be brought before the Assembly. The corresponding theses in the section on worship are substantially sound, but persons from different Christian traditions will react differently to them. I feel they reflect the composers' presuppositions and would have been better posed as questions.

The section on "Renewal in Mission" causes me some concern. The authors seem to have been quite unaware of one fact of global

---

Dr. Tippett is Professor of Missionary Anthropology, Fuller Theological Seminary, Pasadena, California.

significance—that the great animist world is "turning over" like an iceberg in our day, and taking up a new position, which may be a determinative factor in world history for the next century. Whether we like it or not, millions of people are changing from something old to something new—maybe Islam, maybe Communism, or maybe Christianity. Culturally and spiritually this is their "fullness of time." Now what does this say to the Church, or to Uppsala? Do we hear those words again—"Behold the field is already white unto harvest"? The drafts and commentaries devote much space to discussing *dialogue*, stressing that dialogue includes listening; but in the last analysis the drafts admit that the relation of dialogue to *proclamation* still calls for much deeper reflection. It is high time this issue was resolved. I should have thought this Assembly would have devoted a session to the question of how to *proclaim* the gospel *for acceptance* in the light of the current opportunity, which, in all probability, will have passed by before the next Assembly meets.

Probably the most difficult problem before the Assembly will be the task of bringing the "contending" theologies of the members into harmony. The potential for tension is already reflected in the drafts and commentaries. First there is the desired unity for the world Church. Is it to be sought in confessional or organic terms? Is it to ramify through the different kindreds and tribes and tongues, or is it to be a uniformity breaking down these diversities? Then we are concerned, especially in this *Bulletin*, with the contending concepts of *mission* and *communication*. In Section One the Christian is related to man in general, as he himself is also a citizen of the world, confronting the hopes and despair of the world. Here "the members of Christ and his Church have a unique opportunity and task." This is stated in terms of "preaching" and "the *need for repentance* and *faith in Christ*," classical terminology. In Section Two, mission is the work of the "renewal of mankind," "the achievement of a truly human existence in a just society." In this particular statement of the "New Humanity in Christ" the commentary declares, "we have lifted up humanization as the goal of mission." This *humanization* is so stated as to meet the needs of our time. The draft recognizes this as a theological shift away from "assuming that the purpose of mission was Christianization, bringing man to God through Christ and his church." "Today," says this document, "the dominant concern of the missionary congregation must therefore be to point to the humanity in Christ as the goal of mission." My comments in this limited space do injustice to both viewpoints, but I mention them, not to resolve the argument, but to show the conflict is already in the draft. The Assembly will have to work out its own system of dialogue, within its own meetings, to resolve these theological differences.

To achieve harmony, one of these apparently irreconcilable views will have to give way. The theological orientation and presuppositions of one are theocentric, the other appears to be anthropocentric; one is definite, the other vague; one has a clear-cut Christology of mission, the other is open to various interpretations (including rationalization, universalism, and syncretism). "Humanization" is not the only vague word in this theology. "Renewal" is equally hard to pin down with meaning. Likewise the phrase "World's Agenda"! Many evangelicals will react against this. "To make the world's agenda our business," however explained in the draft (which the average Christian will not have, although he will hear the term), will suggest that the world determines the program of the Church. The question will be asked: why not seek to know God's agenda for the present world situation?

One recognizes the importance of stressing the urban and industrial problems of our day, but one hopes the communal societies will receive more consideration than the drafts seem to suggest. One hopes also the Assembly will recognize in foreign service projects the danger of establishing a new form of paternalism, and recommend the direction of funds and personnel to projects that train for selfhood. Finally I hope that the Assembly will not be so taken up with unity for the world, that it overlooks the fact that thousands of unique communities await the gospel in an indigenous form they can understand. Uppsala confronts some mighty issues. We pray that she will be equal to her opportunity and that God will bless her in her sessions and guide her findings.

B. RENEWAL IN MISSION
The World Council's Final Pronouncement on Mission

[*The pronouncement on mission issued by the Division of World Mission and Evangelism passed through two main phases. First was Draft One—two years in preparation—which was placed before the Division at Uppsala and which set the direction in which Geneva believed mission ought to go during the seventies. Second is the final draft, Draft Two (reproduced in this section), the outcome of revision at Uppsala in committee and on the floor of the World Council. What follows is the Report as adopted by the Assembly.* ED.]

I. A MANDATE FOR MISSION

1. We belong to a humanity that cries passionately and articulately for a fully human life. Yet the very humanity of man and of his societies is threatened by a greater variety of destructive forces than ever. And the acutest moral problems all hinge upon the question: What is man? We Christians know that we are in this worldwide struggle for meaning, dignity, freedom, and love, and we cannot stand aloof. We have been charged with a message and a ministry that have to do with more than material needs, but we can never be content to treat our concern for physical and social needs as merely secondary to our responsibility for the needs of the spirit. There is a burning relevance today in describing the mission of God, in which we participate, as the gift of a new creation which is a radical renewal of the old and the invitation to men to grow up into their full humanity in the new man, Jesus Christ.

2. Men can know their true nature only if they see themselves as sons of God, answerable to their Father for one another and for

---

"Renewal in Mission" was reprinted in the *Church Growth Bulletin*, Uppsala Issue Number Two, September 1968, and in *The Ecumenical Review*, October 1969, in the same form as it appears here.

the world. But because man refuses both the obedience and the responsibility of sonship, his God-given dominion is turned into exploitation, and harmony into alienation in all his relationships. In this condition man, with all his amazing power, suffers an inescapable dread of his own helplessness and his deepest cry, often unrecognized, is for the Triune God.

3. Jesus Christ, incarnate, crucified and risen, is the new man. In him was revealed the image of God as he glorified his Father in a perfect obedience. In his total availability for others, his absolute involvement and absolute freedom, his penetrating truth and his triumphant acceptance of suffering and death, we see what man is meant to be. Through that death on the Cross, man's alienation is overcome. The unconditioned love and mercy of God offers all men forgiveness from guilt and freedom for each other. The way is opened for the restoration of all men to their sonship. In the resurrection of Jesus a new creation was born, and the final goal of history was assured, when Christ as head of that new humanity will sum up all things.

4. But the new manhood is not only a goal. It is also a gift and like all God's gifts it has to be appropriated by a response of faith. The Holy Spirit offers this gift to men in a variety of moments of decision. It is the Holy Spirit who takes the Word of God and makes it a living, converting word to men. Our part in evangelism might be described as bringing about the occasions for men's response to Jesus Christ. Often the turning point does not appear as a religious choice at all. Yet it is a new birth. It sets a pattern of dying and rising which will continually be repeated. For we have to be torn out of the restricted and perverted life of "the old man." We have to "put on the new man" and this change is always embodied in some actual change of attitude and relationship. For there is no turning to God which does not at the same time bring a man face to face with his fellow men in a new way. The new life frees men for community enabling them to break through racial, national, religious and other barriers that divide the unity of mankind.

5. Mission bears fruit as people find their true life in the Body of Christ, in the Church's life of Word and Sacrament, fellowship in the Spirit and existence for others. There the signs of the new humanity are experienced and the People of God reach out in solidarity with the whole of mankind in service and witness. The growth of the Church, therefore, both inward and outward, is of urgent importance. Yet our ultimate hope is not set upon this progress, but on the mystery of the final event which remains in the hand of God.

6. The meeting with men of other faiths or of no faith must lead to dialogue. A Christian's dialogue with another implies neither a denial of the uniqueness of Christ, nor any loss of his own commitment to Christ, but rather that a genuinely Christian approach to others must be human, personal, relevant and humble. In dialogue we share our common humanity, its dignity and fallenness, and express our common concern for that humanity. It opens the possibility of sharing in new forms of community and common service. Each meets and challenges the other; witnessing from the depths of his existence to the ultimate concerns that come to expression in word and action. As Christians we believe that Christ speaks in this dialogue, revealing himself to those who do not know him and correcting the limited and distorted knowledge of those who do. Dialogue and proclamation are not the same. The one complements the other in a total witness. But sometimes Christians are not able to engage either in open dialogue or proclamation. Witness is then a silent one of living the Christian life and suffering for Christ.

7. Man is one indivisible whole. Science today furnishes us with constantly increasing knowledge about man's inner being and his interdependence with society. We must see achievements of greater justice, freedom and dignity as a part of the restoration of true manhood in Christ. This calls for a more open and humble partnership with all who work for these goals even when they do not share the same assumptions as ourselves. But it also calls for a clearer acceptance of the diversity of gifts of the Spirit within the Church. "He gave some to be apostles"—the bearers and strategists of the Gospel in a modern age, "some to be prophets"— to equip the saints for their ministry in the world and to be the protesting conscience of society, "some to be pastors"—to heal spiritual and psychological ills, "some to be evangelists"—the interpreters of the Gospel for the secular man or the man of another faith, "some to be teachers"—equipped with biblical light on contemporary perplexities. Each, knowing his need of the gifts of the others, contributes his own in a single, saving outreach to bring men to the measure of the fullness of the stature of Christ.

II. OPPORTUNITIES FOR MISSION

1. *The Church in mission is the Church for others.*

The Church in mission is for all people everywhere. It has an unchanging responsibility to make known the Gospel of the forgiveness of God in Christ to the hundreds of millions who have not heard it; for those who name his name and yet turn away from his mission; for those who, unknowing, serve the "man for others"; and even for those who reject the church, and yet continue to wait for the new humanity.

Since the Church is for others, its mission must both challenge and include men and women where they are:

—a Reformed banker in Zurich and his Roman Catholic colleague in Buenos Aires
—a Baptist policeman in the Congo, an Orthodox teacher in India
—a Methodist professor at Columbia, a Lutheran art student at the Sorbonne
—a pastor evangelist in New Guinea, a minister in industrial Tokyo
—a Spanish migrant worker in Holland, a West Indian bus conductor in London
—a nurse in Johannesburg, an interpreter in Moscow
—a hungry child in Rio, an unemployed farm worker in Mississippi.

Localities for mission are rich in variety and setting—where there is human need, an expanding population, tension, forces in movement, institutional rigidities, decision-making about the priorities and uses of power, and even open human conflict.

2. *Here we describe a few priority situations for mission today.*

   a) *Centers of power*

   Centers of power control human life for good or evil. Increasingly men struggle over this control. For example, the mass media can be employed for either powerful communication or deceitful manipulation. All existing centers of power such as government, business, industry, military establishments, labor, and the churches, must be called to account for their uses of power, especially by those affected. Frustration grows in proportion to human powerlessness and lack of dignity. For the sake of the new humanity the powerless must exercise power.

   b) *Revolutionary movements*

   The longing for a just society is causing revolutions all over the world. Since many Christians are deeply rooted in the status quo they tend to be primarily concerned for the maintenance of law and order. Where the maintenance of order is an obstacle to a *just* order, some will decide for revolutionary action against that injustice, struggling for a just society without which the new humanity cannot fully come. The Christian community must decide whether it can recognize the validity of their decision and support them.

c) The University everywhere is in change
The quest for a just society and a meaningful life ahead is erupting in all places of higher learning and research. Student rebellions reflect the insistence that maturing students share in decisions about the form and content of university life. In the intellectual centers of an emerging world culture, such movements require Christian presence and witness.

d) Rapid urbanization and industrialization
All over the world men are on the move from tribal village to township, from rural area to urban sprawl. The migrant worker, the sufferer from racial prejudice in housing, the child in a crowded school, the lonely student in his crowded dormitory, the watchers of the TV screens, the inmates, nurses and medical specialists of the hospital wards—all these make the emerging urban centers a locality for mission.

The material handler shifting ingots of steel; the woman assembling a transistor; the manager racing against time and spending his Sunday planning production targets—all these are in need of seeing the interrelatedness of their role with that of others in building a just industrial society.

e) Suburbia, rural areas
The pupil in rural areas, starving for education; the village pastor, looking for his young people who have moved to the town; the farmer struggling to develop intermediate agricultural technology; the prematurely aged laborer in an area of famine—*and* the prematurely retired and bored pensioner; suburban dwellers insulated from the challenging issues of the world around them—these too constitute localities for mission where there are pressures for conformity, social prejudice and the threat of a clouded future.

f) Relations between developed and developing countries
Centers of decision and forces of public opinion influencing the relations between the developing countries and the developed countries are a locality for mission, which demands new motivations and a new international missionary strategy.

g) The churches as an arena for mission
The words of proclamation are doubted when the church's own life fails to embody the marks of the new humanity and when it is preoccupied with its own numerical and institutional strength.

Too many of our discussions are about the internal concerns of our fellowship; too many statistical forms ask only about the budget and fluctuations in attendance and not about outreach and service. Too often we send only doctors and teachers where today's need calls also for town planners. Traditional mission board structures tend to commit the churches to institutional continuity. Too many traditional churches neglect relationships with independent, rapidly growing indigenous Christian movements. The Christian community desperately needs renewal, lest it become a spiritual ghetto, unaware of its true responsibilities. It is called the servant body of Christ given to and for the world.

3. *How to find criteria for missionary priorities.*

Because the world is changing, it is always necessary to evaluate missionary activities as to whether they bear witness to Jesus Christ in contemporary and persuasive terms. That evaluation will often require willingness to face loss in prestige and finance and detachment from monuments of faithfulness in mission localities of the past. We suggest the following criteria for such evaluation:

—do they place the church alongside the poor, the defenseless, the abused, the forgotten, the bored?
—do they allow Christians to enter the concerns of others to accept their issues and their structures as vehicles of involvement?
—are they the best situations for discerning with other men the signs of the times, and for moving with history towards the coming of the new humanity?

III. FREEDOM FOR MISSION

A New Stance Needed in Church Life

Mobilizing the people of God for mission today means releasing them from structures that inhibit them in the Church and enabling them to open out in much more flexible ways to the world in which they live. In this world we need to meet others, across all the frontiers, in new relationships that mean both listening and responding, both giving and receiving. This necessitates:

1. A continuing reexamination of the structures of church life at all levels, i.e., the local parish, the denominational synods and conferences and their agencies, the councils of churches at national, regional and world levels. All these must ask, not "Have we the right structures for mission?" but "Are we totally structured for mission?"

2. A reexamination of the variety of tasks to which the people are called in their ministry to the world. Laymen and women express their full commitment to mission, not primarily through the service they give within the church structures, but preeminently through the ways in which they use their professional skills and competence in their daily work and public service. We need to

employ all the gifts God has given to his people—whether it be gifts of proclamation, or healing, or political activity, or administration, or running a home, etc. We need to explore how, in the diverse roles in which we find ourselves, we can creatively and with integrity express our full humanity—whether it be as young people, or women, or members of minority groups, or people in positions of authority, and so on. In all these, we need to recognize what is our Christian obedience in the total ministry of the Church.

3. A reexamination of the whole scope and purpose of theological education. This is to be seen as preparation of the whole people of God for their ministry in the world. The training of the clergy cannot be considered apart from the training of the laity and both should be understood as one enterprise. This means:

a) Clergy need to be trained in an understanding of the world in which the people will minister and in their own responsibility for pointing the people to that ministry and equipping them for it.

b) Lay training needs to be understood in terms of preparing the people for the increasing complexity of their ministry in the world.

c) Provision must be made for training both clergy and laity for specialized tasks.

The Church in the Local Situation

Though some believe that the basic structures of church life are given and therefore unchangeable, others are convinced that all institutional forms of church life are provisional and open to change. In a given locality the mission of the church may be exercised in many forms, including congregations, chaplaincies, health and welfare services, youth projects, political and economic pressure groups, functional and professional groups and others. These have often inherited a pattern of life which was the response of a past generation to a situation which is now fast changing. In all the contemporary localities of mission, we must find new and effective ways in which the Gospel can be proclaimed today and understood in all these areas of life. This will mean:

1. That the congregation must recognize its own missionary role in proclaiming the Gospel in word and deed and as a caring community for all whom they meet across the different frontiers. Related to this community there need to be groups which will help individuals to feel accepted and to accept others. There people will find through dialogue a common basis for their task and be encouraged to develop new forms of service within the social structures for the sake of their fellow men.

2. That there will be a program of education which at all levels

directs people toward their ministry in the world. This needs to be rooted in a biblical understanding of mission, so that people share the encouragement and insights which Bible study can give. If a congregation is engaged in mission, it needs biblical nurture; if it is opposed or persecuted, it needs biblical encouragement; if it fails in missionary calling, it needs biblical vision. A congregation can be a living letter of Christ only in so far as it is rooted in the Gospel.

3. That we get to know the social structures in order to cooperate with all the forces working for good and to discover new tasks needing to be done.

4. That we discover the creative possibilities in the points of tension, conflict and decision in society, and try to make real our profession of love through the active pursuit of justice.

5. That teams come together to undertake specific tasks appropriate to the priorities of mission.

6. That we encourage a global understanding of the ministry of the Church.

No local situation or ministry is sufficient unto itself. No local group can isolate itself from the larger structures of planning and decision-making in society. It is in response to these that the Church needs to express its ministry in new ways, for example:

a) The need for specialization is recognized in areas of special concern such as education, rural development, industry, leisure, automation, the mass media.

b) Specialization without coordination is useless. There need to be joint planning and action between the diverse agencies involved in the localities as part of a total coordinated strategy of mission.

The Worldwide Situation

The missionary societies originated in a response of a past generation to the call to take the Gospel to the ends of the earth. Changing political, economic and ecclesiastical circumstances demand new responses and new relationships. Our understanding of the mission in six continents means that the resources of the whole Church in terms of men, money and expertise are available for the use of the whole Church. Their deployment must be determined by need and not by historic relationships or traditional procedures. This means in terms of structures and relationships:

1. Experiments in new forms of witness and service must be encouraged. Initiatives for such experiments may come from any quarter, but should, where possible, be carried through by joint consultation and strategy.

2. The old division between sending and receiving churches is now breaking down. More creative relationships between churches, and between churches and mission boards have developed. Now we must move to multilateral relations and decision making. These relations will be of many kinds, some national, some regional and some worldwide.

3. Where people and resources come from outside a community they must be related to the needs of that community and incorporated into its life. Mutual understanding and relationships have to be built up between the Church in the local situation and those who bring the resources of skill and technical knowledge from outside. In this sharing the unity of all Christians in each place can be deepened, tested and realized.

Never Go It Alone

There is but one mission on all six continents. This makes it now imperative that Christians engage effectively in joint planning and action in both local and international situations. Only ecumenical cooperation can be adequate for the immensity of our task.

Some joint action for mission has already taken place, but the churches are still too reluctant to implement the call to joint action sounded so strongly in 1963 at the Mexico City Meeting of the Commission of World Mission and Evangelism. Present structures obviously do not provide adequate vehicles for developing joint strategy. We must determine to find ways in which joint action can become operative. We urge consultation with regional and national councils, mission boards and societies and churches, resolved to find ways and means for such joint planning and action. We recommend that more specific areas be marked out as soon as possible for experiments in ecumenical action.

In fact, we find it impossible to envisage any situation where it would not be more effective to act together across all frontiers rather than go it alone.

In a world where the whole of mankind is struggling to realize its common humanity, facing common despairs and sharing common hopes, the Christian Church must identify itself with the whole community in expressing its ministry of witness and service, and in a responsible stewardship of our total resources.

The Certain Hope

Called as we are to take up our responsibility for mission in the future which God opens up before us, we do so in the firm and certain hope that the new humanity revealed in our risen Lord and Savior will surely come to its glorious fulfillment in him. So we humbly serve, in patience and in joy, confidently expecting his final victory.

C. DEFENSE AND FURTHER DEBATE
1. "Renewal in Mission"

Eugene L. Smith

[*One of the most important issues before all branches of the Church and missionary societies is the relationship between bringing men through belief on Jesus Christ to responsible membership in His Church and the relevant good works in the contemporary world which every Christian and every congregation ought to do. The important pronouncement on mission issued by the Uppsala Assembly of the World Council of Churches, under the title "Section Two: Renewal in Mission," presents one view as to what that relationship is.*

In this section we present four comments on "Renewal in Mission" by four eminent leaders of the Church, all of whom were at Uppsala, the first two as leaders of the Council, the last two as consultants, followed by a brief comment by the editor.

What is being discussed is the official *"Section Two: Renewal in Mission," and not the* tentative *Section Two, which first came out in* Drafts for Sections: Uppsala '68, *and was criticized in the May issue of the* Church Growth Bulletin. ED.]

The official draft of Renewal in Mission as passed by the Uppsala Assembly of the World Council of Churches was published in the September issue of the *Church Growth Bulletin*. I call attention to several implications for church growth in this historic document.

1. The Uppsala document "Renewal in Mission" reflects a deep hesitation about drawing a clear line between the two billion who do not know Christ, and the many millions who bear his name, but whose lives deny his Saviorhood and his Lordship. The great need of these "nominal" or "lapsed" or "unsaved" Christians is to encounter the living Christ, repent and be saved. The service they need from a renewed church is both education and evangelism. An evangelistic call which focuses on the two billion, but forgets these lapsed millions, is tragically inadequate.

Dr. Smith is Executive Secretary of the World Council in New York. The comments in Part V, section C, appeared in the *Church Growth Bulletin*, Uppsala Issue Number Three, November 1968.

Moreover, such a call leads with dangerous ease into assumptions of white superiority. A considerable proportion of the white population is composed of nominal Christians. Most of the colored people are not Christian. Is there no need for true evangelism among the white "Christians" of South Africa who support apartheid; among the white "Christians" in Latin America who maintain corrupt, feudal oligarchies; among the "Christians" who support the neo-nazi movement in Germany? An interpretation of the Christian mission which implies—even indirectly—that the nominal white Christian has no need for repentance and rebirth in Christ, while the great majority of colored persons do need to repent and be saved arouses hostilities to the Christian mission among those it seeks to reach. It produces mission doomed to failure.

2. Renewal in Mission reflects an intense concern for the growth of the church spiritually, with a related distrust of "statistical Christianity." It grows in part out of a refusal to measure the results of evangelism by numbers. The evangelization of Africa (or any continent) will have to be done for the most part, on the human side by the Christians that are there. An essential of the mission of God in Africa is an African church alive in mission, continually renewed in Christ. Without continual renewal in Christ, there is no continuing effectiveness in mission.

3. It reflects a reaction against the kind of evangelism which focuses excessively on the individual and his private morality. It performs a needed service to the cause of evangelism by building upon the biblical awareness that personality has both individual and communal dimension, and that the total person must be won for Christ. Thus it uses the biblical phrase of "the new man," with its clear implication that this "new creature" lives in Christ and no less in the community which He creates. The "new humanity" is more than a group of converted individuals, held together by loyalty of individuals to Christ. It is a new creation and the source of its existence is Christ himself.

4. It reflects a deep concern for human suffering, both for lack of knowledge of Christ, and for lack of justice and food. One kind of such need does not have to be denied to affirm the other. The Church must do her mission thinking in the light of (1) the known fact that one-third of the children of the world now are being stunted permanently in growth for lack of food, and (2) the unmistakable message of Matthew 25.

5. It reflects the single, most remarkable achievement of the Fourth Assembly, which was the openness it showed to the human suffering of this hour. In no world gathering of the religious

"establishment" has there been so keen a concern for the agony of the disestablished. Not for centuries, if ever, have the titular leaders of churches taken so seriously the parable of Dives and Lazarus. At this point, the Uppsala meeting showed the cumulative results of study groups over twenty years, involving key persons in many countries, under the themes of "The Responsible Society," "Rapid Social Change," and "Christian Response to Social and Technological Revolution." This sensitivity to suffering by the "establishment" represents a major victory of God in our time, and stands in illuminating contrast to the reactionary preoccupation with the vested interests of the institutional church which has characterized so much church history.

6. It reflects the prevailing uncertainty found among Christian groups everywhere, about the relationship between the Church's obligation to evangelize, and the Church's obligation to seek justice for all. Some try to evade this problem by denying responsibility of the Church for justice, and limiting it only to Christian individuals. Invariably, this denial makes the Church an agency of reaction, defending its own institutional interests.

Much basic scriptural study needs to be done on the relation to the biblical call for evangelism, and the biblical call for justice. Both calls focus on the obligation of the covenant community.

Most traditional calls to individualistic evangelism are inadequate to our present challenge. There is nausea, widespread and justified, about the kind of evangelism which calls a man to an altar and tells him he has met Christ, but sends him out with segregationist racial attitudes unchallenged and unchanged. "By their fruits ye shall know them." By that test it is clear that such a man has not met the living Christ, who died for all. It is partly in reaction against such false evangelism, that many who are concerned with the biblical summons to justice become cold to programs labeled "evangelism."

Impelled both by the biblical imperative and by the nature of human need, our task is to be used by Christ in shaping a pattern of witness as broad in vision of justice as the prophets, as deep in power as Pentecost. Development of it will require, on our part, among other things, a deep willingness on the part of those particularly concerned with justice, and those particularly concerned with evangelism, to learn from each other and move out together in joint witness to Him who is both Savior and Lord.

7. Withal, it is a committee document possessing the ambiguities and unevenness of such authorship. Every reader probably will feel, as probably each member of the Section felt, that it does not say some things as one would wish.

C. DEFENSE AND FURTHER DEBATE
2. "Renewal in Mission"

Philip Potter

It is gratifying that the final document of the Fourth Assembly of the World Council of Churches at Uppsala on "Renewal in Mission" has been published in the September *Church Growth Bulletin* and now these comments are being made. Dr. Eugene Smith has already commented on some of the basic emphases made in the document. I am happy to be given this opportunity to add something further.

1. Readers must bear in mind that this document was produced and sent forth by a representative body of *the whole Christian community*. Not only North Americans and Europeans, but also Asians, Africans, and Latin Americans were involved in the discussion. Moreover, it is addressed to the whole Church, and not just to traditional Western missionary circles. Only when we read it in this perspective will we fully appreciate what it is trying to say. The fundamental assumption underlying the report is that every congregation of the people of God is the basis of mission to its neighborhood and to the ends of the earth.

2. The first part, "A Mandate for Mission," seeks to define mission in terms of the Christian challenge and response to the longings of the three billion inhabitants on our globe. The question which men everywhere are asking is: What is Man? "There is a burning relevance today in describing the mission of God, in which we participate, as the gift of a new creation which is a radical renewal of the old and the invitation to men to grow up into their full humanity in the new man, Jesus Christ." This is a thoroughly biblical understanding of the gospel and takes up the purpose of the creation of man in God's image (Gen. 1–4), fulfilled in flesh and blood in Christ as the New Man, Adam, and waiting to be fulfilled in one renewed humanity, offering to God an open, constant worship which includes a life of shared freedom and well being (Rev. 21). The great Epistles of St. Paul to the Colos-

---

The Rev. Philip Potter is Director of the Division of World Mission and Evangelism, World Council of Churches, Geneva.

sians and to the Ephesians sum up his preaching and teaching precisely in this sense.

3. In the second part, "Opportunities for Mission," the Church's mission is indeed directed to the hundreds of millions who have not heard the gospel of the forgiveness of God in Christ. But it is also addressed to "those who name his name and yet turn away from his mission," and also to those who either do not know him or who reject the Church and yet unknowing serve him and wait for the new humanity. Illustrations are then given of people in different situations who have to be challenged to commitment to Christ within those situations.

The document goes on to list some situations which call for the Church's mission today—centers of which control human life for good *or* evil; revolutionary movements seeking social justice; universities the world over; urban and industrial localities, as well as rural areas and suburbia. The criterion of faithful missionary activities is "whether they bear witness to Jesus Christ in contemporary and persuasive terms."

4. The third part, "Freedom for Mission," calls for a radical change in the structures of our churches and missionary agencies so that the whole people of God can be mobilized, equipped, and deployed for effective mission to the neighborhood and to all lands. This is why the whole document lays so much stress on the need for the Church to be renewed. "The Christian community desperately needs renewal lest it become a spiritual ghetto, unaware of its true responsibilities. It is called to be the servant body of Christ given to and for the world."

5. Obviously, the document shows traces of debate and disagreement on some important issues. First, there is the issue of whether God works through the events of history and the words and actions of men to achieve his purpose of restoring man to his true being in Christ. While the document is in no doubt that man can only be renewed by Christ in faith, it also states: "We must see achievements of greater justice, freedom and dignity as part of the restoration of true manhood in Christ. This calls for a more open and humble partnership with all who work for these goals even when they do not share the same assumptions as ourselves." Similarly in the dialogue of the Christian with a man of another faith or of no faith, we are told: "Each meets and challenges the other; witnessing from the depths of his existence to the ultimate concerns that come to expression in word and action."

Secondly, the document refuses to put the stress only on mission to the two billion who have never heard the gospel, over against the one billion who have either heard it or dwell in an environment where it may be heard. We live today in one world where millions of people now constitute "the generation of rising expectations." They may not have been personally confronted by the gospel but they certainly experience the actions and attitudes of nations, groups and individuals who vaunt their Christian heritage but deny by their attitudes and acts the very heart of the gospel. Moreover, these peoples will only hear the gospel today in terms of the things which matter most—their longing for human dignity in which racial and ethnic barriers are broken down; their struggles for social justice; their eagerness to overcome the enslaving ties of ignorance, disease and hunger. It is in this context that the good news of the kingdom of God and his righteousness can be properly heard today throughout the world.

Thirdly, there is the debate about the place of the Church in the mission of God. This debate has oscillated between the extremes of the classical Roman Catholic position which seemed to equate the Church with the kingdom of God and of those who would say that God's concern is primarily for the world and the Church is simply his instrument for carrying his word of truth and love to the world. The latter would even go so far as to say that God can by-pass the Church and use others—the Cyruses of this world—to accomplish his will. The document acknowledges the necessity of membership in the Body of Christ and states that "The growth of the Church, therefore, both inward and outward, is of urgent importance." And yet, it also speaks of the churches as an arena of mission: "The words of proclamation are doubted when the Church's own life fails to embody the marks of the new humanity and when it is preoccupied with its own numerical and institutional strength." Christian communities which operate racial and social segregation and which support economic and political systems which oppress their fellow men cannot be true vehicles of God's grace. They themselves need conversion in the depths of their being. This is the burden of the preaching of the prophets and of Jesus to the Jewish people, and the writing of Paul, Peter and John to the young churches in the Roman Empire.

Charles Wesley has taught Christian believers to sing:

> Show me, as my soul can bear,
>   The depth of inbred sins;
> All the unbelief declare,
>   The pride that lurks within;
> Take me, whom Thyself has bought,
>   Bring into captivity
> Every high aspiring thought
>   That would not stoop to Thee.

This is a word which we need to heed personally and corporately if we are to be renewed for mission. But we can only utter this prayer as we plunge into those situations and places in which we are most exposed. Only thus can we be renewed *in* mission.

C. DEFENSE AND FURTHER DEBATE
3. *Does Section Two Provide Sufficient Emphasis on World Evangelism?*

John R. W. Stott

The simple answer to the question which Dr. McGavran has put to me is "no." Section Two does *not* provide sufficient emphasis on world evangelism.

The reason is not far to seek. Section Two is a hodgepodge, a compromise document, a variegated patchwork quilt sewn together out of bits and pieces contributed by delegates and advisers whose convictions were in fundamental disagreement.

Mind you, the final version of Section Two might have been a lot worse than in the end it was. As a result of pressure from evangelicals (usually misnamed "traditionalists" and then regarded with the appropriate contumely), a number of important additions were made. Bishop Lesslie Newbigin got in a reference to the new birth, Canon John Taylor the fine description of the man Christ Jesus in I, 3, beginning "in his total availability for others . . . ," and Archbishop Donald Coggan of York the mention of "biblical nurture . . . biblical encouragement . . . biblical vision" (III, "The Church in the Local Situation," 2). There is also the welcome acknowledgment of the need for proclamation as well as dialogue (I, 6) and for the spread of "the Gospel of the forgiveness of God in Christ to the hundreds of millions who have not heard it" (II, 1).

Nevertheless, it must be confessed with shame and sorrow that these are rather isolated concessions to evangelical pressure. The document as a whole not only expresses no coherent theology of mission but is actually self-contradictory. For instance ·

a) "Jesus Christ . . . is the new man," in his resurrection "a new creation was born" (I, 3), and "the new manhood . . . is a gift . . . to be appropriated . . ." (I, 4); yet, without "revolutionary action" and "struggling for a just society . . . the new humanity cannot fully come" (II, 2, b).

b) All God's gifts "including the new manhood" have to be

The Rev. John R. W. Stott is the rector of All Souls Church, London.

"appropriated by a response of faith" (I, 4); yet, through Christ's "death on the Cross, man's alienation is overcome" (I, 3).

c) The Church "has an unchanging responsibility to make known the Gospel . . ."; yet, there are apparently already those "who, unknowing, serve the 'man for others' " (II, 1).

d) Men and women are to "bear witness to Jesus Christ in contemporary and persuasive terms" (II, 3); yet they "express their full commitment to mission . . . preeminently through the ways in which they use their professional skills and competence in their daily work and public service" (III, "A New Stance," 2).

Each of these couplets contains an unresolved contradiction, and forces one to ask uncomfortable questions. Is the new humanity, experienced as the result of a personal new creation ("if any one is in Christ, he is a new creation" 2 Cor. 5:17, RSV) or as a result of the establishment of justice and peace in society? Is the gift of "new manhood" or of "reconciliation" bestowed indiscriminately on all mankind through Christ, or is it received by faith? Do people become Christians by conscious commitment to a Christ made known to them, or are many non-Christians in reality incognito Christians, serving a Christ they neither know, nor profess? Is Christian witness a testimony to Christ in word and deed (that is, in words corroborated by deeds) or is it merely a silent professional competence?

These inner contradictions are all, in their different ways, expressions of a more fundamental cleavage of opinion which Uppsala left unhealed. Precisely what is "mission"? The word occurs in many places in Section Two, but it nowhere is clearly defined. Evangelicals have something to learn here. We have too easily assumed that "mission" and "evangelism" (like the cognate adjectives "missionary" and "evangelistic") are interchangeable synonyms. But is this so? Would we not be more biblical if we maintained that "mission"—what God is doing in the world, what He sent Christ to do, what He wants us to do—is wider than evangelism? Jesus applied Isaiah 61:1-2 to himself and asserted that the Spirit had anointed Him not only "to preach good news to the poor" but also "to set at liberty those who are oppressed" (including the blind and the captives). I would not want to spiritualize the concepts of oppression, blindness, and captivity. Certainly, the earthly ministry of Jesus was marked by a compassion which did not exhaust itself in bringing salvation to sinners. He came to serve and to give His life. So then, I think, evangelicals should proclaim the equation that "mission = witness + service."

If that be granted, the problem concerns what the relation is between the two. God is both Creator and Redeemer. He is active in both the world and the Church. He is at work in history as well as in salvation and is concerned for social justice as well as individual redemption. So, too, the Church. We should not deny that we have a responsibility as Christians for social action as well as the proclamation of the Gospel. But what is the relation between the two? Mexico 1966 stated the dilemma, but then its participants agreed to disagree.

Dr. Visser 't Hooft, in a fine address before the Assembly began its sectional work, pointed the way: "I believe that with regard to the great tension between the vertical interpretation of the gospel as essentially concerned with God's saving action in the life of individuals and the horizontal interpretation of it as mainly concerned with human relationships in the world, we must get out of that rather primitive oscillating movement of going from one extreme to the other. . . . A Christianity which has lost its vertical dimension has lost its salt and is not only insipid in itself, but useless for the world. But a Christianity which would use the vertical preoccupation as a means to escape from its responsibility for, and in, the common life of man is a denial of the incarnation, of God's love for the world manifested in Christ."

However, as the work of Section Two progressed (was it progress?), there was a tragic failure to come to grips with the issue. Ecumenicals and evangelicals (if one may thus categorize the two main viewpoints) sparred with one another, and contrived to get included in the final draft some expression of their basic convictions. But there was no real meeting of minds, no genuine dialogue, no apparent willingness to listen and understand as well as speak and instruct. I for one ardently hope that where Mexico 1966 and Uppsala 1968 have failed, Madras 1969/70 may yet succeed.

Meanwhile, to return to Dr. McGavran's question, Section Two does *not* provide sufficient emphasis on world evangelism. The assembly was preoccupied with the hunger, poverty, and injustices of the contemporary world. I myself was deeply moved and challenged by it. And I do not want to see it diminished. What worried me is that I found no comparable compassion or concern for the spiritual hunger of the unevangelized millions. As I ventured to remind the Assembly, the World Council of Churches professes to acknowledge Jesus Christ as Lord. This Lord sent His Church to preach good news and make disciples; but I did not see the Assembly eager to obey this command of His. This same Lord wept over the impenitent city which had rejected Him; but I did not see that Assembly weeping any similar tears.

C. DEFENSE AND FURTHER DEBATE
4. The Theology of Section Two

David Allan Hubbard

Brief theological statements are the hardest to make. Theology itself is a seamless garment and suffers sorely when cut up. Yet no statement of whatever length can say everything about everything. It is understandable, then, that the drafters of Section Two would seek one theme to stress, one note to rally around in the statement on mission. Not that this is easy because the mission of God in Scripture embraces his election of Israel, his revelation in Christ, the great events of the Incarnation—the Cross, Resurrection and Ascension, the sending of the Spirit, the birth and growth of the Church, and the fulfillment of the mission at the End.

The rallying point chosen was a happy one—the "New Humanity." Theologically, it spans the whole sweep of biblical history from the creation and fall of the first Adam through the perfect obedience and full redemption of the last Adam to the triumph of the new humanity in the full manifestation of the new age. Tactically, it lifts the Christian message above the limitations of provincialism and affirms the worldwide character of the faith. Furthermore, it speaks cogently to the sharpest, most pervasive contemporary problem—what does it mean really to be human?

If the attempt to write an effective theological statement did not quite come off, as the inconsistencies pointed out by John Stott among other evidences suggest, the reasons are several. Since they stem from the nature of the World Council itself, they merit more than passing attention.

The first reason for the uneven, inconsistent statement is the *method of drafting*. The inadequacy of the working draft published before Uppsala was pointed out not only in an earlier issue of the *Church Growth Bulletin* but in the two alternate drafts with which German and Scandinavian delegates came armed to the Assembly. The fact that the draft was altered al-

---

Dr. Hubbard is President of Fuller Theological Seminary, Pasadena, California.

most beyond recognition at Uppsala proves that the pre-Assembly committee was in no way representative of the Council. The large almost unwieldy committee at Uppsala was forced to start from scratch and in a week's time to produce a major document while still carrying on a crammed schedule of Assembly activities. Only heroic effort by Canon John Taylor and other drafters saved the committee from frustration and failure.

The second reason for the inadequate statement is *the heterogeneous nature of the World Council*. Any temptation to see the struggle as a simple contest between liberals and conservative evangelicals will be misleading. The approach to evangelism of the older state churches, whether Lutheran or Orthodox, means that their contributions to a statement on mission will take a different tack from those of either social activists or conservative evangelicals. All the statements drafted at Uppsala reflect the compromise, the theological trading, that is the strength and weakness of ecumenical pronouncements.

The third explanation of the statement's inadequacy and especially of its inconsistency was *a basic conflict in definition of and approach to mission*. It is a simple fact that some of the delegates adamantly resisted attempts to give priority to evangelical emphases like zeal for the glory of God, church growth, personal decision, the spiritual needs of the unreached, the lostness of men apart from Christ, and the centrality of gospel proclamation.

Impatience with biblically based theological statement was not restricted to the youth participants. To have the statement turn out with as much evangelical insight as it did was no small wonder, given the original draft and the overwhelming preoccupation with social action on the part of some. If any group would be faulted for narrowness it was the activists. I heard no evangelical voice lifted against the social action statement. We tried to make clear that we share the concern for the abused and afflicted, the poor and the oppressed around the world. Yet our attempt to see both evangelism and social concern as essential, unchanging, binding obligations upon the Church in every age was not always reciprocated. To be honest, I found myself baffled as to why we had to work so hard in a Christian assembly to agree on things that are such basic Christian affirmations.

Undoubtedly it will seem to many that *the theological introduction to Section Two lacks urgency*. Father Schutte, who headed up the section of mission in Vatican II, pointed this out at Uppsala. The links between the description of the new humanity and the mandate to make the message known could have been tightened. The Assembly felt the burden of many pressures—Biafra, Vietnam, South Africa—and responded with a sense of urgency and compassion. But fields white unto harvest were not given high priority. Indeed, they were dragged in as afterthoughts and then only after much badgering.

If the pressures of time had been different, more of the theological portion of Section Two might have rubbed off on the rest of the document. "Might," I say, because I have no assurance that the drafters and subcommittees who worked on "Opportunities for Mission" and "Freedom for Mission" had a vested interest in building their sections consciously and deliberately on the theological basis laid by their fellow subcommittee. At any rate the priorities of subsection two show little connection with the emphasis on the gospel spelled out in subsection one.

All in all the theology of "Renewal in Missions" is better than it might have been and not as good as it ought to be. I can only echo John Stott's wish that discussion in the future may come to grips with the deep cleavages in the theology of evangelism and the wide chasms in the definition of mission. Documents which salute various views even when they are almost mutually exclusive may have been the best that Uppsala could do. But no one within or without the WCC can seriously allow the situation to rest there.

The next assembly may be crucial. The influence of the Orthodox churches can only increase as they apply to ecumenical deliberations skills in protocol learned over centuries of negotiating with governments. While the Orthodox share our regard for the doctrines of the early creeds, they view mission and evangelism in terms of nurturing their own families, not reaching out to others. Roman Catholic impact will intensify and may bring a church growth emphasis among animistic peoples but will becloud issues in Latin America. One could hope that the younger churches will play a greater role in shaping a theology and strategy of mission. I gained the distinct impression that their contribution at Uppsala was muffled by lack of facility in the official (Western) languages and crippled by their unfamiliarity with European approaches to negotiating.

I for one was not discouraged by the reception that conservative evangelicals received at Uppsala. Four hopes press upon me as I look forward: First, that a number of Pentecostal groups from Latin America will bring their emphases on conversion and evangelism into conciliar discussion as a helpful counterbalance to the Orthodox and Lutheran emphases on Christian nurture. The Latin Pentecostals can remind the North American activists that the Church is growing by leaps and bounds even amid deplorable poverty and oppression. Second, that conservative evangelicals within conciliar churches will insist that evangelism and church growth bulk large in the thinking and programs of their denominational boards. Third, that scores of young people who are related to conciliar churches and yet are committed to the evangelistic emphases of Inter-Varsity Christian Fellowship, Campus Crusade, Youth for Christ, and Young Life will take part in ecumenical gatherings to balance the social and political extremism of the Uppsala youth participation. Fourth, that evangelicals outside the council will earnestly endeavor to work out avenues of further theological discussion. It would be a pity for us to needle the WCC for theological flabbiness after we have refused to help plan the proper exercises.

C. DEFENSE AND FURTHER DEBATE
5. Uppsala's "Program for Mission" and Church Growth

Donald McGavran

Since John Stott and David Hubbard have spoken to subsection one, my comment will be largely confined to the second and third subsections, which comprise the great bulk of "Renewal in Mission." For brevity I shall call these "two and three" or "the program of mission."

The telegram from Eugene Smith which started the assembling of this issue read: "Section Two contains important implications for church growth which need to be pointed out. In fairness to WCC and DWME, as well as to your readers, you will want this to be done." I acceded to his proposal and in September wrote, "The November *Bulletin* will carry two articles by World Council Staff on Implications for Church Growth in Section Two and two by the editors of CGB."

Despite the telegram, Philip Potter and Eugene Smith have said very little about church growth, confining themselves instead to an exposition and defense of Section Two. In fairness to the readers of this bulletin, however, I feel I must discuss the meaning for church growth of Uppsala's "program for mission."

First, comes the sentence, "The Church . . . has an unchanging responsibility to make known the Gospel of the forgiveness of God in Christ to the hundreds of millions who have not heard it." The sentence is brief but, if the will is there, can be made to carry much freight. Much church growth will occur if this unchanging responsibility is taken with life-and-death seriousness by Africasian and Eurican churches. Since Jesus Christ died on the cross for the sins of mankind—an atonement made effective through faith in Him—the program for mission must begin here and emphasize this.

After this one sentence, however, nothing further is said in the whole of Uppsala's "program for mission" as to how this all-important duty is to be carried out. How such an oversight could have occurred is difficult to imagine. While one must not argue that such a summary dismissal of the proclamation of the gospel means that Uppsala had *no* faith in evangelism, it is legitimate to conclude that Uppsala considered it very much more important at this time to help people, and with them engage in the multitude of things that need to be done in every community and nation, than it is to proclaim Christ and persuade men to become His followers and dependable members of His Church. When Eugene Smith and Philip Potter defend the document, they do so on the ground *not* that it will lead to much evangelism and much finding of eternal life, but that the thousand and one activities "two and three" propose are necessary in today's needy world. The fact is that implications for church growth in Uppsala's program are few indeed. My position is that the proportion between evangelism and service displayed in "the program of mission" is totally unacceptable to Christians.

Mind you, it is not as if Uppsala, after penning this one sentence, had gone on to say, "All churches are now carrying out a great program of evangelism to men both within and without the Church. The gospel is being preached by word and deed, multitudes are being brought to commit themselves to the Savior and become dependable members of His Body. Hundreds of thousands of earnest Christians, laymen and ministers, in innumerable ways are beseeching men to be reconciled to God in Christ. We urge the Church to continue and augment this essential program. However, there is another emphasis to which the Church should be giving some of its attention during the decade ahead and we devote the rest of our 'program for mission' to this." CGB proposed that such a statement be inserted.[1] It would have united the Church and made "two and three" a much better and truer document. Even now the evangelical world would welcome a clear statement from Geneva that such a statement has all along been assumed.

Section Two does the World Council a grave injustice. The great churches which make up the Council with few exceptions are carrying out vigorous programs of conversion mission. Unless they do in fact intend to phase these out, Section Two misrepresents them. They had a right to expect from the World Council a "program of mission" which would include a vast array of activities by which multitudes in tens of thousands of societies might hear of the Savior, put their trust in Him, and become His disciples.

One reason why the propagation of the gospel has been so seriously slighted is that while in places at least subsection one defines the "new humanity" biblically, the program which "two and three" set forth aims at a "new humanity" which is a "humane order" or a "just society." It is difficult to avoid the conclusion that the drafters of "two and three" intended to subordinate evangelism to service. The new humanity of "two and three" is concerned chiefly if not solely with the relationship of men with men. It sees Matthew 25 and is blind to John 3. "Two and three" would be an excellent description of the mission of the Church if there were no Savior, no Cross, no "believe on the Lord Jesus Christ and thou shalt be saved."

Truly, part of mission should be to the physical, social, educational, and political needs of the world. At this point, Uppsala's program serves the two billion well. But the mission of every congregation should also be to the spiritual needs of lost men. Men are, to be sure, bodies, but they are also immortal souls who, if they truly believe on the Lord Jesus Christ and abide in Him are saved and if they do not, are lost. Every congregation, which as Philip Potter says is the basis of mission, has a "soul-saving" mission, which can never be omitted, to Euricans and Afericasians, rich and poor, born Christians and born non-Christians. At this point, "Uppsala two and three" short-changes both the hundreds of millions and the nominal multitudes of the Christian billion, too.

Mr. Potter says "two and three" set forth "illustrations of people in different situations who have to be challenged to commitment to Christ within these situations." I have searched "two and three" and fail to find where anyone is challenged to commit himself to Christ. Maybe committing oneself to Christ (believing on Him, being baptized in His Name, being united to His Church) was intended, but to a simple man like me what "two and three" talk about exclusively and at length is justice, welfare, interrelatedness, and the like.

Again Mr. Potter, explaining the document, says, that the whole purpose is so to change "the structures of churches and missionary agencies that the whole people of God can be mobilized, equipped, and deployed for effective mission." If this "effective mission" is invariably to include offering the water of life to multitudes perishing of thirst, I heartily agree with the purpose. But, alas, "two and three" say nothing about assuaging anyone's thirst through joyful following of the Lord Jesus.

Uppsala betrayed biblical mission especially by implying that, when the Church engages in great commission mission, "it is preoccupied with its own numerical and institutional strength." This is to distort the truth. Self-aggrandizement has seldom, indeed, been the motive of mission. Tens of thousands of missionaries who gave themselves to advance the gospel and tens of millions who prayed for and supported the work had no thought of advantaging their churches or themselves. Planting churches brings no strength but anxiety and weakness. Daughter churches are noted for not bringing wealth, peace, comfort or "institutional strength" to their parents.

An odd aspect of "Renewal in Mission" is that "the program" does not fit the real situation in Africasia. It assumes that churches and missions there are too largely concerned with an other worldly evangelism and should instead be concerned with relevant "outreach and service." How comical! The fact is exactly the opposite. For example, of the $200,000,000 going annually out of North America for mission in Europe, Asia, Africa, and Latin America, at least $150,000,000 already goes to service *highly relevant to the situation* and not into evangelism. Have the drafters of "two and three" never heard of the enormous mission effort devoted to leprosy, literacy, primary education, secondary education, colleges, universities, seminaries, agricultural demonstration centers, dispensaries, hospitals, medical schools, heifer projects, rescue homes, orphanages, and the like? The WCC affiliated missions are particularly likely to spend most of their resources in such truly "relevant aid." Tragically they are also the very ones most likely to heed the Uppsala line and substitute service for evangelism even more rigorously.

How could the honorable Christians who drafted "the program," so thoroughly concerned with men's horizontal relationships, have failed to stress the tremendous need of sinful men through faith in Christ to be born again? An answer which I fear some will give is that, in the theology of the drafters, God is dead and the two billion (animist, Hindu, Marxist, Moslem) need justice, brotherhood, peace, and plenty rather than the supposed benefits of repentance, faith, confession, baptism, and living in Christ. This is not my answer. A more plausible answer, it seems to me, is that these good men have been swallowed up by Eurica, and see most vividly the inadequacies of the Eurican churches. They assume large Christian populations. Reading, seeing, thinking, breathing Eurica, they see powerful and numerous churches who "really ought to do something about the terrible conditions in the world today." The program they propose makes sense when I consider the revolution which Christians in North America ought to make within their own orbits and responsibilities. There "two and three" describe practical and reasonable actions.

Why then find fault? Simply because, in addition to "doing good to all men" Christians and churches are commanded to give every living person a real chance to accept Jesus Christ as Lord and Savior. As St. Luke and Dr. t' Hooft have emphasized, there is "no other name." Therefore, in addition to all efforts to improve man's relationship with man, it is incumbent on Christians ceaselessly and lovingly to press the claims of Christ on all who do not believe in Him. Since Uppsala's program in "two and three" devotes itself almost entirely to improving horizontal relationships and apparently considers of minor importance that men develop vertical relationships with God, it must be said that at the point of the greatest need of the masses and in the hour of their greatest hunger, Uppsala misled them by so largely substituting the flesh for the Spirit.

As I read "two and three" I am reminded of what some selfish Christians used to say in the churches across America when I pled for their cooperation in the worldwide mission. "We have too much to do at home," they said, "to go halfway round the world. First, let us convert the heathen here, first build this hundred thousand dollar church, first raise our own budget and feed our own poor, and then, if anything is left, we shall give you a few dollars." Are we hearing a similar refrain in "the program"? Under the cudgeling of contemporary crises in Eurica, are the leaders of mission urging all churches to pay more attention to Christians than to non-Christians, to the one billion than to the two, to their own neighborhoods where the poor ride in automobiles than to other lands where the poor cannot even buy shoes, and to those "of no faith" who pass the doors of a dozen churches every day rather than to those who never see a church, a Christian, or a Bible?

Under these circumstances, what should ministers and missionaries of the gospel and their supporting churches and boards do during the decade ahead? I counsel four actions.

1. Refuse to accept this ambiguous truncated document from Uppsala as an adequate guideline for mission during the seventies.

2. Press ahead with the program of service and evangelism which God has blessed in the past, adjusting the amounts of service and evangelism so that the greatest good of mankind and the maximum discipling of the nations occurs. No one proportion will fit all cases. The "mix" which fits European state churches will be poison for large younger churches whose illiteracy amounts to more than 50 percent. It will be virulent poison for hundreds of younger churches numbering a few hundred or thousand communicants.

3. In determining the proportion, hold fast to the example of our Lord. He regarded temporal needs as real and urgent, but also said, "What shall it profit a man if he gain the whole world

and lose his own soul?" And He stopped feeding and healing men after a short ministry and went to the Cross as the propitiation for sins, to be appropriated "through faith in his blood."

4. Let us help the next Assembly make a pronouncement on mission which better represents the whole Church, avoids the confusion inherent in defining mission as "everything which Christians ought to do," and take seriously both the salvation of men's souls and the healing of their bodies and societies. In the next few years when the World Council writes a new document on mission, we hope this exchange of opinion will help bring forth a balanced pronouncement which will preserve the values of classical biblical mission, while adjusting it to the vastly more receptive populations of today and their vastly increased physical and social needs.

Our discussion of Section Two, which began with the May issue of *Church Growth Bulletin*, ended with this November issue. We have gladly given Dr. Potter and Dr. Smith space so that the strengths as well as the weaknesses of the document could be perceived. They have spoken frankly and so have we. Since we honestly think Section Two has grave weaknesses, we have said so. We may be mistaken. Readers have been given Section Two—the final official version—and will have to judge for themselves. They will be considering one of the most important issues in modern missions.

ADDENDUM

Dear Dr. McGavran:

You are performing a very useful service by publishing in the *Church Growth Bulletin* the text of the statement of the World Council of Churches, "Renewal in Mission." I am grateful for the opportunity to participate in the written discussion.

At the same time, there is need to express concern about some of the statements in the article, "Will Uppsala Betray the Two Million?" published in your May issue. With much of what you wrote, I agree. Some misunderstandings, however, you would want me to correct.

The article quotes a heading in the draft statement, "The World's Agenda—Our Business," and then states, "In plain English this means that the mission of the church is to meet needs *of which the world is conscious.*" No document of the World Council of Churches has ever so interpreted that phrase. "The World's Agenda" refers to the needs of the world—and for those needs Christ died. Those needs are the business of the Church.

The article states, "Section Two neglects the plain meaning of the Cross and of the Resurrection." The reader who saw only the analysis and not the draft was disadvantaged in not being able to read the statements in that draft, "He died, yet lives among us." "He brought hope by dying on an ambiguous Cross." ("Ambiguous" means the fact that the world sees the Cross as a disgrace; while we in the light of Christian faith see it as a supreme symbol of God's love.)

Other illustrations of misunderstanding in the article could be cited without denying weaknesses in the draft. It is notable, however, that every misunderstanding was on the negative side. In many conservative evangelical circles there is today a seemingly eager exaggeration of the negative in any discussion of the World Council of Churches. The conciliar movement has its weaknesses, and the World Council of Churches its faults. Pointing out these failings is a useful function. It will be done much more convincingly, and more usefully to all on all sides, when there is freedom from exaggeration of the negative. Love rejoices not in unrighteousness, or the semblance of it, but in the truth. It will be a great gain for all interested in the truth of Christ when more conservative evangelical publications report the contributions of the conciliar movement with an enthusiasm equal to that with which they now point out any apparent sign of weakness.

Very truly,
Eugene L. Smith
Executive Secretary

Note: I am happy to publish this courteous letter from Dr. Smith, noting merely that in discussing a document of the importance of Section Two, concerning which Christian brothers have such deep conviction on both sides, it is not remarkable that there should be disagreement. I see no profit in defending any of my particular phrases. The main goal to be kept in mind is that Christian mission, its theology and its program, must serve the two billion at the point of both physical/social needs *and their eternal salvation.* Though these two are not coequal, the Church has resources to meet them both.

Donald McGavran

NOTES

1. *Church Growth Bulletin,* May 1968. See *Eye of the Storm,* pp. 233ff.

PART VI

1970:
The Frankfurt Declaration
on Mission

A. BACKGROUND OF THE DECLARATION

Donald McGavran

The great debate on mission raging in the churches today and to a degree set forth in the twenty-nine preceding essays, climaxes in the Frankfurt Declaration. The issues which have occupied our attention have been given classic expression by Dr. Peter Beyerhaus and a group of distinguished German theologians.

The "closing speech" in *Eye of the Storm* is, therefore, the magnificent Frankfurt Declaration. It is brilliantly aware of the contemporary world and the current hot issues in missions. It is competently theological. It turns the spotlight of truth on both positions and then, on solid biblical grounds, espouses the one and opposes the other. It should be contrasted with the new position on mission which influences the conciliar participants in this debate, dominates the World Council's pronouncement on mission (in Part V), and is briefly stated so clearly in Mme. C. Gouzée's "Counterpoint" (in Part III).

Dr. Peter Beyerhaus, author with Henry Lefever of *The Responsible Church and the Foreign Mission* [1] and director of the Institute of the Discipline of Missions and Ecumenical Theology of the University of Tübingen in Germany, has been greatly disturbed at the humanistic turn the World Council of Churches missions have taken. Feeling that the Uppsala statement on missions was no mere surface ripple but signaled a profound change of direction, he wrote *Humanisierung—Einzige Hoffnung der Welt?* ("humanization—the only hope of the world?"). As soon as I read it, I wrote Dr. Beyerhaus about publication of the work in English. I also urged him to gather together German theologians of like precious faith and issue a declaration calling Christians and churches to a thoroughly sound and Christian concept of missions. Dr. Beyerhaus replied:

You will be interested to hear that in German churches and

Both the Background (with the exception of the first two paragraphs) and the Text of the Frankfurt Declaration appeared in *Christianity Today*, June 19, 1970.

missionary societies a deep unrest caused by the present departure from what we believe to be the genuine motives and goals of missions has developed. It is similar to the unrest which led to the appearance of the Wheaton Declaration. I was asked by an association of confession-minded theologians, "The Theological Convention," to write a first draft for such a declaration. This paper was discussed thoroughly at our meeting on 4 March 1970 in Frankfurt and at the end unanimously accepted after slight revisions. It is now being printed in several German publications, and invitations for signatures have been sent to persons in key positions. Many have already responded positively.

Knowing your vital concern for the upholding of a clear biblical motivation and practice of mission, I am sure you will rejoice in this venture. We have now prepared an English translation which will serve as a basis for deliberation with missionary leaders on an international level. Perhaps American theologians will be interested to join our German adventure.

Among the first signers of the Frankfurt Declaration are:
Professor P. Beyerhaus, Th.D., Tübingen
Professor W. Böld, Th.D., Saarbrücken
Professor H. Engelland, Th.D., Kiel
Professor H. Frey, Th.D., Bethel
Professor J. Heubach, Th.D., Lauenburg
Herr Dr. A. Kimme, Th.D., Leipzig
Professor W. Künneth, Th.D., Ph.D., D.D., Erlangen
Professor O. Michel, Th.D., Tübingen
Professor W. Mundle, Th.D., Marburg
Professor H. Rohrbach, Ph.D., Mainz
Professor G. Stählin, Th.D., Mainz
Professor G. Vicedom, Th.D., D.D., Neuendettelsau
Professor U. Wickert, Th.D., Tübingen
Professor J. W. Winterhager, Th.D., Berlin

Signatures are pouring in to Dr. Beyerhaus. On May 11 he wrote me again, saying, "The declaration has stirred up commotion in the whole German-speaking missionary world. The reaction differs between enthusiastic support and passionate rejection! But the supporters seem to be in the majority."

The official English translation has just reached me, and I make haste to share it with Christians in North America. Although it arose quite independently, like the Wheaton Declaration,[2] it speaks to "a fundamental crisis" in missions. It is a tremendous pronouncement issued to "clarify the true missionary motives and goals of the Church of Jesus Christ." It rings true to the Bible.

It rings true to historic missions. It will cheer all those engaged in world evangelization and confound the enemies of the gospel.

In Germany most missionary societies are aligned with the World Council of Churches. In the Frankfurt Declaration, the conservative elements in the churches appeal to Geneva to reverse its stand that horizontal reconciliation is the only suitable mission strategy for our day. How far Geneva will yield remains to be seen.

In North America many churches are similarly aligned with the WCC. Indeed, since they are also aligned with the NCC, they are somewhat to the left of Europe's churches. The Frankfurt Declaration gives the conservative elements in each church (the silent majority?) a chance to appoint someone to receive signatures and to flood denominational headquarters with them, demanding emphasis on vertical reconciliation.

However, in North America many churches and many congregations and hundreds of thousands of individuals are unaligned with the WCC and the NCC. They are already sending abroad more than twenty thousand missionaries through societies holding substantially the position of the Frankfurt Declaration. They may deal with the statement in one of two ways:

1. Watch what happens within the WCC–NCC-aligned bodies.
2. Declare themselves in favor of the biblical position taken by these confession-minded German theologians and missiologists. I would like to see every missionary society of the Evangelical Foreign Missions Association and the Interdenominational Foreign Mission Association plus independent missionary societies by the score promptly sign the declaration, making it known that "this defines our unshakable position on mission. If you want to do this kind of missions, do it through us."

In view of the multiform nature of the missionary societies of North America—their many denominational affiliations, alliances, shades of theological opinion, sources of income, and types of work—I cannot suggest that readers send signatures to any common address. But those who agree with the statement should joyfully stand up and be counted. This is a time to act; a widespread signing of the Frankfurt Declaration by theologians and missionary-minded Christians is in order. Readers will know where to send signatures—probably to missionary societies or to denominational headquarters. Let each tell his or her missionary society or church that he believes in this kind of mission and will support it.

Let us keep pace with our fellow Christians in Germany. Two months from now, may we, like Professor Beyerhaus, be able to say: "The reaction differs between enthusiastic support and passionate rejection, but the supporters seem to be in the majority."

NOTES

1. Peter Beyerhaus and Henry Lefever, *The Responsible Church and the Foreign Mission* (Grand Rapids: Wm. B. Eerdmans, 1964).
2. Published in *The Church's Worldwide Mission*, Harold Lindsell, ed. (Waco, Tex.: Word Books, 1966).

B. TEXT OF THE DECLARATION

Frankfurt Theological Convention

The Church of Jesus Christ has the sacred privilege and irrevocable obligation to participate in the mission of the triune God, a mission which must extend into all the world. Through the Church's outreach, His name shall be glorified among all people, mankind shall be saved from His future wrath and led to a new life, and the lordship of His Son Jesus Christ shall be established in the expectation of His second coming.

This is the way that Christianity has always understood the Great Commission of Christ, though, we must confess, not always with the same degree of fidelity and clarity. The recognition of the task and the total missionary obligation of the Church led to the endeavor to integrate missions into the German Protestant churches and the World Council of Churches, whose Commission and Division of World Mission and Evangelism was established in 1961. It is the goal of this division, by the terms of its constitution, to insure "the proclamation to the whole world of the gospel of Jesus Christ, to the end that all men may believe in Him and be saved." It is our conviction that this definition reflects the basic apostolic concern of the New Testament and restores the understanding of mission held by the fathers of the Protestant missionary movement.

Today, however, organized Christian world missions is shaken by a fundamental crisis. Outer opposition and the weakening spiritual power of our churches and missionary societies are not solely to blame. More dangerous is the displacement of their primary tasks by means of an insidious falsification of their motives and goals.

Deeply concerned because of this inner decay, we feel called upon to make the following declaration.

We address ourselves to all Christians who know themselves through the belief in salvation through Jesus Christ to be responsible for the continuation of his saving work among non-Christian people. We address ourselves further to the leaders of churches and congregations, to whom the worldwide perspective of their spiritual commission has been revealed. We address ourselves finally to all missionary societies and their coordinating agencies, which are especially called, according to their spiritual tradition, to oversee the true goals of missionary activity.

We urgently and sincerely request you to test the following theses on the basis of their biblical foundation, and to determine the accuracy of this description of the current situation with respect to the errors and modes of operation which are increasingly evident in churches, missions, and the ecumenical movement. In the event of your concurrence, we request that you declare this by your signature and join with us in your own sphere of influence, both repentant and resolved to insist upon these guiding principles.

SEVEN INDISPENSABLE BASIC ELEMENTS OF MISSION

1. *"Full authority in heaven and on earth has been committed to me. Go forth therefore and make all nations my disciples; baptize men everywhere in the name of the Father and the Son and the Holy Spirit, and teach them to observe all that I have commanded you. And be assured, I am with you always, to the end of time"* (Matt. 28:18–20, NEB).

We recognize and declare:

Christian mission discovers its foundation, goals, tasks, and the content of its proclamation solely in the commission of the resurrected Lord Jesus Christ and His saving acts as they are reported by the witness of the apostles and early Christianity in the New Testament. Mission is grounded in the nature of the gospel.

We therefore oppose the current tendency to determine the nature and task of mission by socio-political analyses of our time and from the demands of the non-Christian world. We deny that what the gospel has to say to people today at the deepest level is not evident before its encounter with them. Rather, according to the apostolic witness, the gospel is normative and given once for all. The situation of encounter contributes only new aspects in the application of the gospel. The surrender of the Bible as our primary frame of reference leads to the shapelessness of mission and a confusion of the task of mission with a general idea of responsibility for the world.

TEXT OF THE DECLARATION—*Frankfurt Convention*

2. *Thus will I prove myself great and holy and make myself known to many nations; they shall know that I am the Lord* (*Ezek. 38:23,* NEB).

Therefore, Lord, I will praise thee among the nations and sing psalms to thy name (*Ps. 18:49,* NEB, *quoted in Rom. 15:9*).

We recognize and declare:

The first and supreme goal of mission is the *glorification* of the name of the one *God* throughout the entire world and the proclamation of the Lordship of Jesus Christ, His Son.

We therefore oppose the assertion that mission today is no longer so concerned with the disclosure of God as with the manifestation of a new man and the extension of a new humanity into all social realms. *Humanization* is not the primary goal of mission. It is rather a product of our new birth through God's saving activity in Christ within us, or an indirect result of the Christian proclamation in its power to perform a leavening activity in the course of world history.

A one-sided outreach of missionary interest toward man and his society leads to atheism.

3. *There is no salvation in anyone else at all, for there is no other name under heaven granted to men, by which we may receive salvation* (*Acts 4:12,* NEB).

We recognize and declare:

Jesus Christ our Savior, true God and true man, as the Bible proclaims him in His personal mystery and his saving work, is the basis, content, and authority of our mission. It is the goal of this mission to make known to all people in all walks of life the Gift of His salvation.

We therefore challenge all non-Christians, who belong to God on the basis of creation, to believe in Him and to be baptized in His name, for in Him alone is eternal salvation promised to them.

We therefore oppose the false teaching (which is circulated in the ecumenical movement since the Third General Assembly of the World Council of Churches in New Delhi) that Christ himself is anonymously so evident in world religions, historical changes, and revolutions that man can encounter Him and find salvation in Him without the direct news of the gospel.

We likewise reject the unbiblical limitation of the person and work of Jesus to His humanity and ethical example. In such an idea the uniqueness of Christ and the gospel is abandoned in favor of a humanitarian principle which others might also find in other religions and ideologies.

4. *"God loved the world so much that he gave his only Son, that everyone who has faith in him may not die but have eternal life"* (*John 3:16*, NEB).

In Christ's name, we implore you, be reconciled to God (2 Cor. 5:20, NEB).

We recognize and declare:
Mission is the witness and presentation of eternal salvation performed in the name of Jesus Christ by His Church and fully authorized messengers by means of preaching, the sacraments, and service. This salvation is due to the sacrificial crucifixion of Jesus Christ, which occurred once for all and for all mankind.

The appropriation of this salvation to individuals takes place first, however, through proclamation, which calls for decision, and through baptism, which places the believer in the service of love. Just as belief leads through repentance and baptism to eternal life, so unbelief leads through its rejection of the offer of salvation to damnation.

We therefore oppose the universalistic idea that in the Crucifixion and Resurrection of Jesus Christ all men of all times are already born again and already have peace with Him, irrespective of their knowledge of the historical saving activity of God or belief in it. Through such a misconception the evangelizing commission loses both its full, authoritative power and its urgency. Unconverted men are thereby lulled into a fateful sense of security about their eternal destiny.

5. *But you are a chosen race, a royal priesthood, a dedicated nation, and a people claimed by God for his own, to proclaim the triumphs of him who has called you out of darkness into his marvellous light* (*1 Pet. 2:9*, NEB).

Adapt yourselves no longer to the pattern of this present world (*Rom. 12:2*, NEB).

We recognize and declare:
The primary visible task of mission is *to call out the messianic, saved community* from among all people.

Missionary proclamation should lead everywhere to the establishment of the Church of Jesus Christ, which exhibits a new, defined reality as salt and light in its social environment.

Through the gospel and the sacraments, the Holy Spirit gives the members of the congregation a new life and an eternal, spiritual fellowship with each other and with God, who is real and present with them. It is the task of the congregation through its witness to move the lost—especially those who live outside its community—to a saving membership in the Body of Christ. Only by being this new kind of fellowship does the Church present the gospel convincingly.

We therefore oppose the view that the Church, as the fellowship of Jesus, is simply a part of the world. The contrast between the Church and the world is not merely a distinction in function and in knowledge of salvation; rather, it is an essential difference in nature. We deny that the Church has no advantage over the world except the knowledge of the alleged future salvation of all men.

We further oppose the one-sided emphasis on salvation which stresses only this world, according to which the Church and the world together share in a future, purely social reconciliation of all mankind. That would lead to the self-dissolution of the Church.

6. *Remember then your former condition: . . . you were at that time separate from Christ, strangers to the community of Israel, outside God's covenants and the promise that goes with them. Your world was a world without hope and without God* (Eph. 2:11, 12, NEB).

We recognize and declare:

The offer of salvation in Christ is directed without exception to all men who are not yet bound to him in conscious faith. The adherents to the non-Christian religions and world views can receive this salvation only through participation in faith. They must let themselves be freed from their former ties and false hopes in order to be admitted by belief and baptism into the Body of Christ. Israel, too, will find salvation in turning to Jesus Christ.

We therefore reject the false teaching that the non-Christian religions and world views are also ways of salvation similar to belief in Christ.

We refute the idea that "Christian presence" among the adherents to the world religions and a give-and-take dialogue with them are substitutes for a proclamation of the gospel which aims at conversion. Such dialogues simply establish good points of contact for missionary communication.

We also refute the claim that the borrowing of Christian ideas, hopes, and social procedures—even if they are separated from their exclusive relationship to the person of Jesus—can make the world religions and ideologies substitutes for the Church of Jesus Christ. In reality they give them a syncretistic and therefore anti-Christian direction.

7. *And this gospel of the kingdom will be proclaimed throughout the earth as a testimony to all nations; and then the end will come (Matt. 24:14, NEB).*

We recognize and declare:
The Christian world mission is the decisive, continuous saving activity of God among men between the time of the Resurrection and the Second Coming of Jesus Christ. Through the proclamation of the gospel, new nations and people will progressively be called to decision for or against Christ.

When all people have heard the witness about Him and have given their answer to it, the conflict between the Church of Jesus and the world, led by the Antichrist, will reach its climax. Then Christ himself will return and break into time, disarming the demonic power of Satan and establishing His own visible, boundless messianic kingdom.

We refute the unfounded idea that the eschatological expectation of the New Testament has been falsified by Christ's delay in returning and is therefore to be given up.

We refute at the same time the enthusiastic and utopian ideology that, either under the influence of the gospel or by the anonymous working of Christ in history, all of mankind is already moving toward a position of general peace and justice and will finally—before the return of Christ—be united under Him in a great world fellowship.

We refute the identification of Messianic salvation with progress, development, and social change. The fatal consequence of this is that efforts to aid development and revolutionary involvement in the places of tension in society are seen as the contemporary forms of Christian mission. But such an identification would be a self-deliverance to the utopian movements of our time in the direction of their ultimate destination.

We do, however, affirm the determined advocacy of justice and peace by all churches, and we affirm that "assistance in development" is a timely realization of the divine demand for mercy and justice as well as of the command of Jesus: "Love thy neighbor."

We see therein an important accompaniment and verification

of mission. We also affirm the humanizing results of conversion as signs of the coming Messianic peace.

We stress, however, that unlike the eternally valid reconciliation with God through faith in the gospel, all of our social achievements and partial successes in politics are bound by the eschatological "not yet" of the coming kingdom and the not yet annihilated power of sin, death, and the devil, who still is the "prince of the world."

This establishes the priorities of our missionary service and causes us to extend ourselves in the expectation of Him who promises, "Behold, I make all things new" (Rev. 21:5, RSV).

PART VII

1972
Bangkok, Salvation Today: What Is It?

BANGKOK: AN EVANGELICAL EVALUATION

Arthur F. Glasser

Because this is my personal evaluation of what transpired at the Bangkok conference of the CWME, I had better begin by identifying myself. I belong to that segment of the Christian movement which limits the ground of religious authority to the Bible. I am deeply persuaded that all that Jesus said is normative for His Church. Hence, I accept without hesitation a central dimension of His witness — the Scriptures are the Word of God written and have "the force of law" (Carnell). I am impatient with the sort of destructive criticism that does not view Scripture from His perspective. I cannot bow at the shrine of the sort of scholarship that neglects His clear witness to the issue of religious Authority. I am neither a biblicist nor a bibliolator. Rather, I seek to follow the apostolic pattern of "living according to Scripture" (I Cor. 4:6).

As an evangelical I am also committed to certain apostolic emphases recovered for the Church in the 18th century Evangelical Awakening: the essentiality of personal conversion and the "new birth," the call to holiness of life, and the mandate of *world mission and evangelism*.

So then, I regard myself in the main stream of Christianity as biblically understood, an unworthy Christian in the tradition of Augustine, Luther, Calvin and Wesley.

Enough of this. What about BANGKOK?

PRE-BANGKOK HOPES

I came to Bangkok with feelings of ambivalence. Who could not but be excited over the privilege of attending and participating in such an important gathering. What theme could be more appropriate than *Salvation Today:* it was taken from the very words of Jesus Christ (Luke 19:9). And yet, the more I read and pondered the pre-Bangkok CWME literature the more concerned I became.

Indeed, the perusal of this material made me wonder whether the Evangelical option would ever again become a live issue in the conciliar movement. The booklet: SALVATION TODAY AND CONTEMPORARY EXPERIENCE almost convinced me that Bangkok would be a rerun of

Uppsala 1968. How could it bring renewal to the worldwide Church in her task of *world mission and evangelism* if its official literature was unable to get beyond the unwarranted inference that being "saved by Mao" is somehow comparable to being "saved by Jesus?"

Nevertheless, I went to Bangkok in a hopeful frame of mind. After all, I would be meeting with many friends, old and new. We would represent a wide variety of cultures and church traditions. This would be enriching in itself. But more, we would gather around the Bible, God's self-authenticating disclosure to His will for His people and listen to its witness to Jesus Christ. We would learn in new ways that the theme of "salvation" is central to all Scripture. In the old Testament we would find that it embraces God's acts of deliverance, preservation, and the healing of His people Israel. In the New Testament we would reaffirm that it is the all-inclusive word of the gospel, gathering into itself God's decisive and final redemptive act on behalf of all men through Jesus Christ. It is the Gospel of the Kingdom: good news for the world today and for the world tomorrow. It embraces the totality of the life and duty of the Church — the people of God — in the midst of the nations.

I dreamed! Perhaps our conference would reduce the polarization between various segments of the worldwide Church. A theme like *Salvation Today* might rally conservatives and liberals to break out of their forty year "cold war" and become less suspicious of one another and more willing to accept one another. Perhaps at Bangkok we would come to see the impoverishment all have experienced through living at a distance from one another. Hopefully, all would become more willing to take seriously the witness of any man whose commitment is to "the Lord Jesus Christ as God and Saviour according to the Scriptures" (WCC basis).

I had other reasons for being hopeful. *World mission and evangelism* — these words loomed large in the name of the sponsoring organization (CWME). This meant that we would be discussing matters of great moment to the Church in our day. The "two billion" that Vatican II reminded us were still without the knowledge of Christ; the Great Commission that was tragically omitted from Uppsala's document on mission; the issue of the non-Christian religions in the light of an enlarged understanding of *Salvation Today*, and the possibility of "liberation" in the full biblical sense becoming the comprehensive motif of the Gospel for the 70's.

Finally, I looked forward to meeting the considerable number of Roman Catholic observers expected at Bangkok. Evangelicals tend to look hopefully at new stirrings and alignments within this ancient Church. They have increasingly been finding Catholic brethren of like faith and similar evangelistic commitment within its charismatic movement and also within not a few interdenominational movements, particularly on university campuses. So then, I sought to go to Bangkok with an open heart, albeit with a measure of concern.

OFF TO A POOR START

Evangelicals were not very effective in making an "Evangelical" contribution to Bangkok. They appeared to lack the sort of reflexes that make for instant, thoughtful and gracious responses to the issues being presented in the formal addresses. When Dr. Wieser opened the conference with a report of the previous four years of study on *Salvation Today* he said many interesting and helpful things. But Evangelical sinews stiffened and guards went up when he directed us to open our discussion on *Salvation Today* by "starting from our situation and experience." I inwardly grumbled: doesn't he realize that human experience cannot compare with the Bible when it comes to setting norms for the Christian experience of *Salvation Today?* And, I was particularly nettled by his comment: "We should at least be freed from the pietistic concept of salvation as primarily a private affair between an individual and God." The New Testament speaks otherwise. Of course, salvation is not solely a private affair, for it includes participation in the life of the Church, our Lord's Body. But it begins with the removal of the alienation of the sinner from his God! And that is an intensely personal matter.

Dr. Wieser made several statements but no opportunity was afforded to challenge their validity. We sat and listened. They were similar to his pre-conference statement: "Biblical scholarship is almost unanimous in asserting the multiplicity of traditions expressed in the biblical writings of both the Old and the New Testament . . ." I took exception to his phrase "almost unanimous." Either Dr. Wieser is unaware of or indifferent to the extensive Evangelical literature that challenges the view that the Bible is a discordant conglomerate of conflicting traditions. Furthermore, what does he do with the witness of Jesus and the Apostles to the unity and inner coherence of its unfolding Revelation? Were the delegates at Bangkok expected to adopt this highly debatable hermeneutic?

Of course, one appreciates in part the problem involved in organizing a conference of this sort. There must be heavy input in the first days to generate momentum for the discussion sessions to follow. And yet, those first addresses introduced great issues one after another in quick succession. No opportunity was given to react. We were carried along in a stream of thought over which we had no control. I sincerely tried to make sense out of a multi-media presentation of the theme that involved slides flashing in rapid succession on six widely separated parts of the surrounding walls. All this while the background was filled with discordant music! I got a stiff neck twisting and turning to look at this and that (we were seated on the floor) and ended up utterly frustrated by the diversity and complexity of it all. What were they trying to do to me?

But it was Dr. Potter's address that caused me the most inner turmoil, and appeared to contribute most to Evangelical distress over Bangkok.

Unfortunately, we did not see his text beforehand. Suddenly, he was speaking, telling us that any debate over "proclaiming the gospel to the two billion or more who have never heard it . . . is totally futile." And his definition of the gospel was so incomplete: (It) "proclaims man's liberation from the forces of nature and from the fear of each other." He defended Uppsala: "Despite the controversy which it provoked, the section on *Renewal in Mission* was right in delineating the Church as a priority situation for mission today." Dr. Potter's address rolled on and on.

Immediately thereafter the floor was opened for public debate. But what to say? Evangelical strength was to endorse this stirring call to social action and the struggle for justice but affirm as well the Great Commission and its abiding validity for all who acknowledge Christ's Lordship. Dr. Potter had omitted this latter point. If we believed in *world mission and evangelism*, the focus of Bangkok must be on the two billion who have yet to hear, so that all men, whether Buddhists, Hindus, Muslims, Jews, animists or nominal Christians might have the opportunity to hear what Jesus Christ did by His death and resurrection to make them fit for God's Presence and friendship.

Unfortunately, the discussion that followed dwindled into a slashing anti-Western attack and a personality clash between Beyerhaus and Potter. Perhaps I was at fault for going to Beyerhaus' defense rather than stressing the appalling spiritual need and peril of the unevangelized.

You can be sure that I groaned over this. Evangelicals like to make speeches but are not very effective in the give and take of theological encounter. At any event, after this first encounter I abruptly concluded that if I was to participate helpfully in Bangkok I would have to enter fully into the day-to-day sequence of Bible studies, discussion groups and panel inter-actions. By listening and learning along with the rest, it might be conceivably possible for me to contribute.

WAS BANGKOK ENCOURAGING?

It is easy to pick flaws with the Bangkok conference. Among the delegates were those who frankly stated that they were indifferent to the issue of whether or not people should be given a chance to hear the gospel. I had a hard time establishing any common ground with them. They tended to argue that the issue was either irrelevant or that the infinite and divine mercy would ultimately triumph in all God's creatures. Obviously, Evangelicals can't build their missiology on such premises; they are utterly devoid of Scriptural foundation. It was interesting to note that those who were universalists doubted that any essential difference exists between Christian and non-Christians.

Others confined salvation solely to secular dimensions; a man was "saved" from his selfishness as he participated in the struggle for social justice. Bangkok confirmed to me the fact that the radical movements of the

'60's had been blunted. We saw little of the confident secularism that a few years earlier had heralded the God-is-dead movement as the wave of the future. And the theologians of revolution — though they were present — did not command the center of the stage.

I was somewhat surprised at the vehemence with which some Asian and African delegates denounced the Western missionary movement. Admittedly, missionaries had their flaws and often acted unwisely. But was this outrage justified? I wondered as to their hidden agendas. Were they aiming at wresting more concessions from Western leaders in the form of property, funds and authority? Not trusting my own judgment I sought an evaluation from a Mexican bishop, Manuel J. Gaxiola. His comments follow:

> Latin Americans being neither white nor black nor yellow, but perhaps a pleasant chocolate-brown, look amazed at the "pummeling" the white Western brethren are taking from those who come in a different hue and who at every opportunity take the time (it is our time also) to tell us they are tired of Western teachings and customs that were imposed upon them, and to remind us how much they have suffered the consequences from the misguided missionary methods used in the past by whites, whose intentions, values and methods are now resented and rejected by those who, in spite of all past mistakes, are now Christians. Someone has called this a "sado-masochist duel" with one side hurling these recriminations and the other accepting them IN TOTO either by their silence on the floor or by a grudging acceptance when talking in private or in small groups. Although we do not condone the mistakes and even abuses committed by missionaries in the name of Jesus, we do think it is about time someone stood up, be he white, black, or yellow, and say something nice about out Western brethren. They need a pat on the back (1973:67, 68).

In a very real sense, Dr. Potter was the central symbol of Bangkok. He shared with a small group his personal experience, as a youth, of Christ's converting grace and the supportive role of the Church in the years of doubt that followed. During this period he saw so much economic exploitation intermingled with "cheap grace" in the Caribbean that he considered suicide. Under the influence of a Christian friend, however, he received Christ, overcame his despair and dedicated himself to the liberation of mankind. At present this vision dominates his mind. He isn't hostile to evangelism, provided it is intimately related to bringing men into vital relationship with their neighbors as well as with God.

At Bangkok I felt I had to come to terms, not with heretical universalism or a secularized, humanistic Gospel, but with the Christian whose priorities were different from my own. In part, the resolution of this problem came as a result of our Bible studies.

As earlier intimated, not a little time at Bangkok was spent in Bible study. So many delegates wanted to participate in these studies that the program had to be rearranged at the last minute to accommodate them. For three successive days we spent the mornings in small groups examining primarily a number of Old Testament passages. This was a very exhilarating experience. No holds were barred; differences were real, passions were aroused and on occasion arguments were bluntly presented. But we listened to the Bible. And I believe God spoke to us.

True, we were not directed to study those great New Testament passages on salvation that climax the unfolding of redemptive history and expound the significance of Christ's death, burial and resurrection. Actually, a Roman Catholic faulted Bangkok for this. Fr. Jerome Haber, the representative of the *Congregation for the Evangelization of Peoples,* whose office is in the Vatican, expressed his concern that our pre-occupation with the Old Testament would result in a distorted understanding of what the Bible taught about salvation.

> I am appalled that you can discuss *Salvation Today* and all its ramifications, day after day, but not listen to what the Apostle Paul said about it. I haven't heard anyone speak on justification by faith. No one has spoken of everlasting life. And what about God's righteous wrath against sin?

Inevitably, this preoccupation with the Old Testament focussed attention, not on the Evangelistic Mandate of the New Testament, but on the Cultural Mandate with its call to all men to accept responsibility for this world. We reviewed God's concern for the poor, the exploited, the enslaved. We saw that the life of God in a man cannot but find expression in outgoing service on behalf of one's neighbor. We groaned together over the anguish of the war in Vietnam, over racism in the West, over oppressive political and economic structures in Latin America, over the powerlessness of the people of God.

We saw that the Church may be growing in numbers and in doctrinal understanding but lack an awareness of the call of Christ to participate with Him in the amelioration of the raw nerves of society. And yet, as an Evangelical, I must add that the Church may be sacrificially involved in social service and still lack an awareness of the call of Christ to participate with Him in beseeching those who do not know Him to be reconciled to God.

There are those who would say that Bangkok reflected an obsession with political realities. Compelling voices called for the transformation of oppressive social structures and for renewed efforts in the worldwide struggle for social justice. All this was regarded as the central task for the Church in today's world. But Evangelicals had to give a resounding NO! as Gaxiola observed:

> We want to go to the heart of the matter and declare that the approach of the CWME is wrong because it forgets two things: 1) It will do man no good if after he is liberated from those oppressing structures he remains internally and spiritually the same unregenerate man; 2) This was not the approach by either Christ or the apostles (1973:74).

In many ways Bangkok confirmed to me the conviction that Christians need one another. Only by meeting together and sharing in love their understanding of Scripture will they attain the unity of the faith and of the knowledge of the Son of God. Bangkok's delegates represented considerable diversity in their understanding and performance of the task of Christian mission. If one accepts this diversity and seeks to express his identity with others who profess Christ's Lordship, the gospel of reconciliation will be proclaimed to this generation and social justice will be furthered in the earth.

WAS BANGKOK DISCOURAGING?

I am afraid it was. As Gaxiola noted:

> The gatherings were permeated by pessimism, the feeling that we are at the end of the missionary task as formerly conceived. The idea that the Church itself needs to be saved, which sounds so strange to those who believe that Christians are the salt of the earth . . . The CWME ignores the great opportunities that we now have in regard to the gospel, the widespread hunger in many for salvation in specific spiritual terms, in relation to sinning men and a saving God (1973:76).

One evening was devoted to a demonstration of *Dialogue With People of Living Faiths*. This fell flat. And I was not unhappy. The issue was not Jesus Christ and the gospel. It seemed such an affront to our Church of Thailand hosts, because they had earlier told us quite buoyantly of the numbers of Buddhists in their land who were turning to Christ. And yet, when a statement was finally drafted on the subject of *Dialogue With People of Living Faiths,* not a few Evangelicals were pleasantly surprised. Not altogether, however, since it contained nothing that even approximated what the Apostle Paul described as the missionary task — "God making His appeal through us . . . We beseech you on behalf of Christ. Be reconciled to God" (II Cor. 5:20).

The sub-section to which I was assigned: *Growing Churches and Renewal* brought me unalloyed delight. For five successive days we listened to reports of the receptivity of peoples and the growth of the Church in many parts of the world. At the end we drafted a statement that contained the Evangelical priority:

> Each generation must evangelize its own generation. The concerns of Church Growth ånd Renewal are the chief, abiding and irreplaceable tasks of Christian mission.

But when this comprehensive imperative was debated by the plenary session it only barely passed. When its concluding statement was presented, speaking of "imploring" men to accept God's salvation in Jesus Christ, a motion was quickly made to strike it out as irrelevant. It was a noble moment when Pastor Seth Nomenyo of Togo spoke out and said, "Brethren, that's what this conference is all about!" The motion was defeated.

In my judgment, the discouraging element at Bangkok was the distribution of the delegates. If one is to judge by their organizational connections, only 8% were directly involved in extending the gospel among the two billion who at present do not know enough of Jesus Christ to make a meaningful commitment to Him. My problem is this: How could this 8% possibly represent the thousands of missionaries (and that includes more than 3500 currently serving in societies based within the Third World) as well as the thousands of national evangelists who are engaged in *world mission and evangelism* as these terms have been traditionally understood? At Bangkok, the majority of delegates spoke with considerable dogmatism about matters that were not within the circle of their responsibility within the Church. Their concerns were largely those of the established Churches. It was altogether natural for them to be devoted to the Cultural Mandate. They want Christians to live more authentically and manifest the sort of "works" without which "faith" is dead.

It seems to me the CWME has little future if it regards its task as somehow identical with that of the Churches. And I almost despair of its returning to the vision of the old IMC with its concern that Christ be preached to the peoples of every tribe, and kindred, and tongue and nation. Whether or not it does, depends on the determination of the new director, Dr. Emilio Castro, to pour the sort of meaning into the words *world mission and evangelism* that will enable the CWME to press ever deeper into the task of reaching the many nominal Christians within our congregations *and* the two billion beyond the frontiers of the Church.

Just prior to Dr. Castro's taking office he commented on the few delegates to Bangkok from Latin America. Only thirteen were present. He said, "The CWME must secure the participation of our Pentecostal friends. They have much to give us. But, we must not bring them in, one by one. A sizeable group should be encouraged to come in at the same time. Then they will sense their solidarity and feel encouraged to take an active part in the CWME." I rejoiced at his openness to this possibility. Would winds of change start blowing through the CWME?

In his opening address to the CWME Assembly following his induction, Dr. Castro said: "We are at the end of a missionary era. We are at the very beginning of world mission." As was to be expected, this statement was widely publicized. I've tried to figure out what he meant. With other Evangelicals, I have been tempted to come up with a dark interpretation! But, I must be positive. I want to believe that when Dr. Castro defined the missionary task as relating "all human life to the living purpose of God," we were both thinking of the same biblical categories.

On this heartening note I draw this testimony to a close. I feel that as an Evangelical I should not speak darkly of ecumenical plots, of conspiracies to sow seeds of doubt, stab at true faith, and sabotage all those who accept the Bible as the Word of God. I should be willing to initiate efforts to bridge those gulfs that separate Evangelicals from the conciliar movement. I should seek to listen and learn as well as bear witness and serve. For, in many ways, what I do with my brethren in the CWME is not unrelated to making my contribution to the task of reaching the two billion that have yet to hear of Jesus Christ.

Gaxiola, Manual J., "Salvation Today: A Critical Report", article in *The Evangelical Response to Bangkok,* Editor, R.D. Winter (1973) South Pasadena, Calif. William Carey Library

"Bangkok: An Evangelical Evaluation" was first presented as an address to the annual meeting of the American Society of Missiology, June 1973.

PART VIII

1975
Nairobi—Liberation and Justice (and a Little Evangelism?)

A. LOOKING TOWARD THE FIFTH ASSEMBLY
1. Will Nairobi Champion the Whole Man?

Donald McGavran, Peter Wagner,
Editors of CGB, July 1975

An Open Letter to the General Secretary
of the World Council of Churches

Dear Mr. Potter:

With the Fifth Assembly of the World Council convening at Nairobi in November, career missionaries and leaders of Third World Churches at the School of Missions at Fuller Theological Seminary have been studying contemporary theologies of mission today, and reading many of the documents of the World Council of Churches, Vatican II, and the Evangelical movement. We have been identifying the two main strands of theological declarations and wish respectfully to address ourselves to the leadership of the World Council.

One of the documents we have considered is your report of August, 1974 to the Central Committee meeting in Berlin, printed in the October, 1974, issue of the *Ecumenical Review*. It so well sums up the position of the World Council of Churches, that *Church Growth Bulletin* is using it as a basis for this open letter to the World Council. Our purpose is to increase understanding of what the Council is doing and to urge that, out of respect for the Word, the Fifth Assembly incorporate into its program substantial emphasis on calling men from death to life. Now, five months before Nairobi, the WCC can take action which much more truly represents the biblical revelation *and* the thinking of its constituent Churches. In our view, Nairobi must address itself boldly to the needs of the "whole man" or "whole person". We beg you to initiate such action.

As we study the theology of missions emanating from Geneva, review your report of August 1974, and inspect the documents issued to the Churches to help them prepare for the Fifth Assembly, we discern a tremendous concern with "the cries of the dispossessed, the powerless, the silent, the unrepresented, the struggle for social justice, changing the structures of society toward more justice and more community." As we read in your report (564 f) of the "wide range of studies and programmes", we come again and again to some fresh facet of this over-arching social concern. The Commission on Inter-Church Aid, you write, has been "unflinchingly active in meeting human need and seeing this need in terms of the struggle for social and racial justice." It has also "energetically carried out the Uppsala mandate to 'give the needs of development a high priority in the total programme' ."

The whole Assembly has also "agonized" over two new programmes — to Combat Racism and to encourage Participation in Development. The Unit on Education and Renewal has convened "consultations and conferences on . . . liberation, sexism, the family . . . and youth as agents for social change" . . . The Office on Education has been awakening participants to their duty "to master their environment and social structures toward fuller life in justice and community" . . .

On page 568 you point out that the World Council has taken this direction because of the "acute consciousness of a world in which the inequities of the rich and the poor, the injustices meted out to people because of their race, sex or class, the confrontation of nations in wars which threatened the whole human race has become intolerable." You hear God say: "I go before you. Now that Christ carries away your sinful past, the Spirit frees you to live for others." Bearing down heavily on the World Council, you write, is a world situation (569) which "threatens the future of international society . . . Through indifference, greed, envy, fear, love of power, and short sighted stupidity, people have created or allowed to develop a demonstrably unjust economic order."

You argue that, toward this dangerous situation, three reactions are possible. There are actually four; but you mention three — a), b), and c) as follows:
a) evade the issues by retreating into . . . mystical and religious escape.
b) exorcise the dangers by forcing them into the rigidities of a reassuring ideological or religious system which explains everything — and explains it away.
c) face the dangers head on, see them clearly, and discover new ways of overcoming them.

You maintain that the World Council's programmes are all grouped under c) and pour scorn on a) and b), which you "have tried to avoid." (570). You declare that "there is no way back for us into escapism either of disengagement or of setting up ideological or dogmatic walls of defense."

Member Churches (572) ought to back up what their representatives sitting on the Central Committee of the World Council have devised as the world programme, but you feel they are not doing so.

"The impression I have is that many of our congregations are engaged in styles of worship, Christian nurture, and programme activities which are so geared to maintaining a certain 'spiritual-security-at-all-costs' that they come perilously near to the first two reactions to the threats and challenges of our time." (573)

You write that Member Churches have not found it easy to translate insights hammered out in ecumenical debate and frontier action into the life and thinking of the congregations. This involvement gap is widening, and the Geneva Staff is "easily tempted to suffer from impatience and proud annoyance with our churches for not seeing what we see and not doing what we are endeavoring to do." (575)

At the grave risk of oversimplification, let me say that after some years of study of the Conciliar position, we think you have stated the case substantially as it appears to us in the Evangelical Camp.

Let me set forth six corresponding aspects of the Evangelical position. These constitute a sixfold appeal which *Church Growth Bulletin* is making to the Fifth Assembly of the World Council of Churches.

First, Evangelicals also live in the last quarter of the Twentieth Century and are parts of the distressed global village, whose this-worldly sufferings you describe so vividly. We have always been deeply concerned about physical suffering and oppression. Many of us have put in years of our lives with the down-trodden. Evangelicals are glad the WCC is concerned about the unjust social order and the grievous inequity in distribution of wealth. We are concerned, too. What the Lausanne Congress said about socio-political involvement being a part of our Christian duty is for most of us elementary Christian truth. On this score we are at one with you.

Second, we are amazed that Conciliar Christians achieve emphasis on this-worldly improvements by neglecting and scorning eternal salvation. The Bible speaks clearly about eternal salvation, forgiveness of sin, being saved through faith in Christ alone, and passing from death to life. The Bible says "There is now no condemnation to those who are in Christ Jesus." We simply cannot understand how the Geneva staff so cheerfully consigns eternal salvation to a footnote, or allows only that to be authentic eternal salvation which issues in the kind of social action you feel is urgent. The need of eternal salvation is part of the heart cry of the "whole man".

Indeed, we are gravely concerned lest, in your scornful dismissal of reactions a) and b), you are categorizing eternal salvation as 'pie in the sky' no longer credible to persons come of age. If this is your position, if you believe that conversion is really an "escape" unless it leads people to your kind of social action, then your tremendous swing away from evangelism becomes understandable. The finality with which Geneva refuses to give sinner-converting, church-mutiplying evangelism any significant place in its programmes makes sense only if you have previously concluded that such evangelism is a retreat into a "private world of mystical and religious escape". It would be helpful if you would tell the world how these "escape systems" which you denigrate differ from historic Christian beliefs about eternal salvation.

As we read the preparatory documents put out for the Fifth Assembly, your historic 1974 address to the Berlin meeting of the Central Committee, and dozens of other important conciliar papers, we search for and do *not* find any WCC department which has been "unflinchingly active in meeting the human need" of salvation from eternal condemnation. We would like to see the Assembly "agonizing" over new programmes to bring a hundred million nominal Christians into living relationship to the Lord Jesus, or to bring the secular masses in Sao Paulo into joyous dependence on the Holy Spirit, or to lead twenty thousand Chokosis in eastern Ghana into baptized Bible-obeying discipleship to Christ, and on and on. We look in vain for some "new and imaginative programmes" having to do with multiplying churches among the 80 million landless Harijans in India of whom at least three million, searching for life, have renounced Hinduism and converted to Buddhism in the last few years.

Third, you pen a few words about the reality of eternal salvation. For example, "God's justice manifests itself both in the justification of the sinner and in social and political justice" (565). But that is the last we hear about the justification of the sinner! The World Council seemingly plans to spend no blood, sweat, toil and tears to help sinners realize their need for justification . . . On page 577 you write, "We must seek, under God's grace . . . to undertake the differentiated mission of God . . . in the power of our risen Lord." Good words!! But that part of the differentiated mission which has to do with the spread of the Christian Faith, the multiplication of Christian churches, the baptism of millions of penitent believers, is never mentioned.

Many of our number roundly declare that the Conciliar position is rational only on the grounds of a frank disbelief in the whole biblical affirmation of eternal salvation, a change of status achieved in the twinkling of an eye, through belief in Jesus Christ, and resulting in a gloriously more human life and an enormously tougher concern for our suffering brethren. We do not want to share this opinion, so we plead from you a new and unequivocal declaration of concern for the eternal salvation of the 2.7 billion unreached people of the world.

Many of our number point out that you fail to mention the fourth reaction — that of historic Christianity — to the world situation, though it shines forth from the entire Bible and from 19 centuries of dedicated Christian life. The fourth reaction to the evil world which lies all around us is this: Recognize that fallen man's basic need is reconciliation with God through faith in Jesus Christ according to the Scriptures. And that consequently a major task of the World Council of Churches and of all Christians is to proclaim the Gospel and encourage men and women to accept the Saviour in the fellowship of the

Church, knowing certainly that power to change evil conditions will flow abundantly from the indwelling Holy Spirit to heal the sick, feed the hungry, lift up the fallen, change unjust structures, work for peace, and spread the light of learning.

Fourth, we are grieved that as between Christian brethren there should be this deep gulf. We propose a way of living in harmony. The Evangelicals at Lausanne have already said that both evangelism and social action are parts of our Christian duty. Evangelicals are already spending large parts of their mission budgets for bringing about this-worldly improvements in the populations where they serve. The salaries of advocates of social justice among Evangelicals are paid by Evangelical *missionary societies*. Indeed, we believe that if you "relentlessly expose yourselves as a Council and as Churches to the purifying Word of the Cross" you will devote at least a half of your mighty resources to Gospel-proclaiming, sinner-baptizing, church-multiplying evangelism. The alienation from your member denominations and congregations which you mention in your Berlin address would disappear if you would allocate 50 percent of your income to programmes dedicated to serving God's justice which "manifests itself in the justification of the sinner" and 50 percent to programmes dedicated to serving God's justice which "manifests itself in social and political justice."

You write, "member churches have not found it easy to translate insights hammered out in ecumenical debate . . . into the life and thinking of the congregation". (574) We suggest the Geneva Staff realize that God speaks equally truly to millions of intelligent Christians who live away from Geneva. The "insights hammered out in the ecumenical debate" are not all there is to contemporary Christian truth. Indeed, they may be somewhat warped by the vested interests which speak at Geneva. Truth may lie equally with the common person in all six continents who accepts the plain meaning of the Bible as God's Word and therefore believes implicitly that the *first* task of the Christian is to beseech men to be reconciled *to God*.

Fifth, as we have studied the two theologies of mission today, we have come to the conclusion that two radically different systems of doctrine are battling for acceptance. The one believes that the Bible is the inspired, authoritative, infallible Word. The other believes that the Bible is the words of men through which God speaks on occasion. The one believes in eternal salvation as well as temporal improvements. The other believes that temporal improvements are certain, but beyond them we are in the realm of speculative opinions. The one believes that the Church is the Bride of Christ. The other, that the Church is one of God's many instrumentalities to bring about a juster human social order. The one believes that no man comes to the Father but by Jesus Christ, as revealed in the Bible and consequently proclaims Him as divine and only Saviour. The other, that the Cosmic Christ has spoken and is speaking in all religions and consequently dialogue with other religions is the correct way of mission. The one believes that the Kingdom of God will come only as God Himself destroys the enemies of mankind at the last day, and that until then only limited justice and righteousness are possible. The one believes that a new, just world order can be brought about by the cooperation of men of good will in all religions. The list of contrasts is much longer. A division as deep and lasting as that which took place in Europe in the sixteenth century may be imminent, but we hope it can be avoided.

The fact that some Conciliars imagine themselves to have the only position possible to intelligent man today, and are tempted to "proud annoyance" with naive Christians who "retreat into religious escapism", confirms many Evangelicals in their opinion that the rift is dangerously near.

Sixth, the Nairobi Assembly may be the last opportunity for the World Council to take a truly ecumenical position, to declare fearlessly that the Bible speaks with final authority and utter clarity about eternal salvation, and reveals that it comes only through faith in Jesus Christ. It also speaks about letting "justice roll down as waters and righteousness as a mighty stream". Let the Assembly reverse the Uppsala-Bangkok trend, which is tearing the Church apart. What is needed is a world program equally devoted a) to church growth, that is, to calling men, women, tribes, clans, and nations from death to life, through faith in Jesus Christ alone; and b) to calling Christians to practice social welfare, extend brotherhood and become active in the causes designed to promote justice and liberate the oppressed. Let the Fifth Assembly propose great evangelistic programs for the extension of the Church and great social programs for the extension of humanization. Then, finally, let the Fifth Assembly encourage all its constituent Churches to allocate funds and personnel to each of the two main thrusts in accordance with their consciences.

The time is past when any bureaucracy, even that at Geneva, can dictate to Member Churches that all their giving must go to evangelism or to social action. Let the Member Churches decide for themselves. In the ultimate analysis, *the congregations will decide*. No group, however wise and good, has enough wisdom and an exclusive enough access to God's presence to tell the whole Church what to do. The day of Constantinism is over. This issue our forefathers determined when they rejected papal authority. Let the World Council put before Member Churches the main biblical options as it sees them, and then listen carefully to what the Spirit is saying to and through the Churches.

Church Growth Bulletin will be pleased to give equal space to the World Council of Churches to reply to this letter.

NOTE

Mr. Potter and the WCC Secretariat at Geneva did not deign to reply to this letter. The Editor, January 1977.

A. LOOKING TOWARD THE FIFTH ASSEMBLY

2. *The Nature of Salvation*

Stephen Neill

(Reprinted by kind permission from *The Churchman*, Vol. 87, No. 4; Winter 1973, pp. 263-274.)

Another Assembly of the World Council of Churches is almost upon us. When the Council was in process of formation, its architects were warned that the Christian world could not possibly stand more than once in ten years an Assembly of the kind that was being planned. No attention was paid to the warning. Fortunately the original purpose of having an Assembly once every five years has never been carried into effect. I was myself successful in starting the movement which led to the postponement of the third Assembly from 1960 to 1961. The pattern of one Assembly every seven years seems to have established itself. But even this is far too short an interval. It takes at least five years to prepare an Assembly that is to be really useful, and at least five years for the churches to absorb the results of an effective Assembly.

Nearly four years were allowed for the preparation of the Second Vatican Council. The Council held four long sessions. But it has become even clearer than it was at the time that the period allowed was wholly inadequate. Some of the documents presented to the Council were found to be so imperfect that they had to be almost wholly rewritten. Of the many documents finally accepted only three, or at the most four, are of the kind that really make church history.

A glance backwards into the past shows how far we have fallen back, instead of going forward, in the art of preparing ecumenical meetings. The best ecumenical assembly ever held was the Oxford Conference of 1937 on Church, Community and State. That Conference had the wisdom to concentrate on one main theme. Stalin and Hitler had risen above the horizon. Totalitarianism was the main preoccupation of civilized states and churches alike, and it was to this theme that the Conference devoted the greater part of its attention. Preparations had been going on for a long time. Under the guidance of J.H. Oldham, who had a unique flair for seeing who were, and still more of seeing who were going to be, important in the affairs of the church, no less than two hundred and fifty papers were written and widely discussed. Of these only about seventy were found worthy of inclusion in the six volumes which were published. Unfortunately these volumes are now something of a museum piece, the entire stock having been destroyed during the bombing of London. Anyone who has access to them will have the opportunity of a unique conspectus of serious Christian thinking as it was in the year of grace 1937. It was of this Conference that an unprejudiced observer, Professor J.H. Nichols wrote: "The authority of the Oxford Reports was unprecedented, at least in Protestant social ethics, and their competence enabled them to rank with the best of secular thought, a phenomenon scarcely seen since the seventeenth century."

Preparations for Nairobi 1975 have been going on for some time in somewhat haphazard fashion. But it is only recently, that is less than a year before the date fixed for the convening of the Assembly, that I have been able to see the six small folders on which the Christian world as a whole is invited to base its preparation for a world Assembly.

A first glance at the material is not encouraging. The World Council has disregarded the advice to concentrate on one major theological theme, and to attempt to produce a report which could bear comparison with the principal documents of Vatican II. We are presented with documents relating to six different themes, each of considerable importance. Twelve teams of experts in different parts of the world ought to have been engaged in study of each of these themes over the last five years, in order to digest the immense amount of material which is already available or could have been made available on each of the themes, and to make their results accessible to the world in good time for careful consideration by those who will be present at the Assembly, and by others who are qualified to form opinions on the kind of subjects to be dealt with. As it is, it is to be feared that the pattern of former Assemblies will be repeated. Pre-packaged reports will be presented, with no adequate time for discussion by the Assembly as a whole; amendments will be hastily put forward and remitted to a drafting committee; minority opinions will not be recorded; and the reports accepted by the Assembly may be altered by editorial committee in such a way as to make them mean something rather different from what was intended by the Assembly.

The quality of the material submitted is very uneven. Few of the documents qualify as serious statements based on careful theological consideration of the issues at stake. Some are of an unbelievable triviality. This is just the kind of material that we used to send out in preparation for a students' conference. We shall have to wait and see whether it justifies itself as adequate to serve as preparation for an Assembly of presumably adult church leaders.

First impressions are of a certain theological naivete in the material submitted. What is the authority on which these various statements, and especially the situation papers in which the organisers of the Assembly express their understanding of the situation are based? It was always taken for granted in ecumenical circles that Jesus Christ is our sole authority, that, as was solemnly stated by the Barmen declaration of 1934, he is that Word of God to which alone we have to hearken, whether in life or in death. It was further agreed that this Word is set forth in decisive form in the pages of the New Testament. Has this principle of authority been faithfully followed in these papers?

Jesus Christ is of course referred to. We are told in the paper for Section III, SEEKING COMMUNITY that "we believe that, in the search for wider and deeper community, it is Jesus Christ who unites, and that this quest for community, for a world community of communities, has started in Him, and will be completed in Him". This may be interpreted in a fully orthodox sense; but it would have been well, if it had been completed by the Lord's own words: "You will be hated by all nations for my name's sake" (Matt. 24:9), and "the hour is coming when whoever kills you will think he is offering service to God" (John 16:2). The offense of the Cross is not conspicuously present in these documents.

At other points there seems to be present a euphoria strangely out of touch with the tragic world in which we live. One of the headings in the same document reads: "Our neighbours everywhere are seeking community". One almost has the feeling of reading a document written in the period of liberal optimism in the nineteenth century. Surely this statement is exactly contradicted by the realities of our situation. It is the fact that large sections of the human race have passionately repudiated community. Anyone who has lived in East Africa in recent years and shared the agonies of the Asian population is hardly likely to question this statement. The intensity of feeling which helps to promote the formation of a narrow community seems to combine itself all too naturally with hatred of those who are outside that community; old dreams have died; the majority of the inhabitants of the African continent seem to have repudiated the ideal of a multi-racial society.

The same statement tells us that Christians' desire for security and identity in existing power structures and in ghetto communities continues and this may be true, though it's hard to attach any precise meaning to an affirmation so vaguely and allusively phrased. It would have been, perhaps, better if it had been plainly stated that over about two-thirds of the land surface of the world Christians are an underprivileged community. For purely pragmatic reasons the Marxist in some countries has given up the direct persecution of Christians. But he has never made any secret of his determination to eliminate every form of religion, as an undesirable survival from the past and as a hindrance to the progress of the revolution. The Muslim feels himself no less threatened than the Christian. In some non-Marxist countries, even those which have accepted the Universal Declaration of Human Rights, the Christian is not allowed to feel himself a first-class citizen. Even in what is meant as a conciliatory document, there are advantages in sometimes calling a spade a spade.

Much attention will no doubt be paid by the Assembly to the question of salvation, and, following on the lines of the Bangkok Report, there may be an inclination to interpret the term 'salvation' almost exclusively in terms of political emancipation from alien rule, or from rule which is judged not to be in the best interests of the subject population.

Almost everyone will agree that liberation from alien and oppressive rule is a good thing. Not everyone remembers that the western powers are under solemn obligation to restore the liberty of Latvia, Lithuania and Esthonia, three small countries absorbed in the course of the second world war into the Union of Soviet Socialist Republics, without even the pretence that this was carried out in accordance with the wishes of the inhabitants. Most Christians would agree in regarding as a matter of urgency the restoration to liberty of Hungary, Czechoslovakia, Poland and Eastern Germany, with the provision of such compensation as is possible for the outrages committed against the liberty both of individuals and nations. It is hard to see how in present circumstances such liberation is possible. But on a subject of such urgency it is hardly possible for a Christian Assembly to keep silence.

It may be taken as certain that much attention will be devoted to Latin America, an area in which hope and despair seems to march hand in hand.

Philip Agee's CIA DIARY (1975) is a book which is certain to be widely discussed and refuted at every point at which refutation is possible. But, even though only ten percent of what is stated in the book proves in the end to be reliable, that in itself is quite enough to show up the astonishing folly and ineptitude of American interference in the internal affairs of Latin American States, allegedly in the interest of orderly government and of fending off the communist menace. Over vast areas the gap between haves and the have-nots is as wide as it is anywhere in the world, not excluding India; but at every point the interests of the poor seem to have been sacrificed to the interests of the rich, and the nations which profess to be concerned for justice and liberty appear to have identified themselves with oppression and the defence of wrong.

It is not surprising that what is called the theology of liberation has in the main taken its origins from the Latin American situation. Many of the earlier utterances on this theme have been so confused and so lacking in theological substance as to have afforded little hold for serious consideration. At last we have a book, the THEOLOGY OF LIBERATION by Fr. Gutierrez (Eng. trans. 1973) which, whether one agrees with it or not, does deserve serious and careful study. Fr. Gutierrez accepts the general pattern of this school of thinkers — the Exodus of Israel from Egypt is taken as a paradigm of liberation, the oppressors being identified with the Egyptians and the oppressed with Israel. Some doubt exists as to the identity of the one who is to play the part of Moses. But Fr. Gutierrez goes far beyond the limits of this narrow thesis in trying to understand theologically the political realities in the midst of which he has to live.

One thing which his book makes very clear is that the themes of violence and non-violence must be given far fuller and deeper consideration than has yet been devoted to them by ecumenical assemblies. Four main views are held in the Christian world:

1. There are those who regard violence as a natural and normal Christian activity in any situation of oppression.
2. At the opposite extreme are the peace-churches, which condemn violence in every form, and regard it as irreconcilable with any serious attempt to understand the Gospel of Christ.
3. There are those who, like the Central Committee of the World Council of Churches, are prepared to condone violence, provided that it does not call itself violence, and affirms that its aims are essentially peaceful.
4. There are those who hold that violence is always evil, but that in certain circumstances it may be the lesser of two evils. I suppose I am only one of millions of Christians who, when Hitler marched into Prague in March 1939, decided that this man had to be stopped, whatever (and we really meant whatever) the cost.

It is unlikely that an ecumenical assembly will succeed in resolving all the doubts of Christians on this subject; the debate will continue. Even the position of members of the peace-churches does not seem to be perfectly logical, since the majority of them are not anarchists, do support the existence of police forces, and admit the right of states to counter lawless violence with violence, if such a situation should occur. But the problem is one of such urgency, and has been rendered so much more acute by recent events and policies within the Christian world, that it must be regarded as almost the top priority for thorough exploration and definition at such an Assembly as Nairobi 1975.

We are all more influenced by mythology than we often dare to recognize. The Marxists have shown themselves past masters in the art of the dissemination of mythology under the guise of truth. One of the myths that has proved most widely acceptable is that of the sinless victim, the proletariat. All wickedness is on the side of the strong; the weak are blameless, endowed with all virtues, and waiting only for an opportunity to exercise them in freedom.

This would be very nice if it were true. The history of political liberation does not bear out the myth. If the tables are turned and the weak obtain political power, they tend to show themselves just as full of wickedness as the former oppressors. Political independence was forced on the Sudan by a collusion of Russia and the United States at the United Nations, with little regard for the wishes of the people concerned. The result was a civil war which lasted for sixteen years and reduced vast areas of the Southern Sudan to desolation. All credit to the World Council for such share as it had in the termination of the war.

Independence in Rwanda and Burundi led to the flaring up of the age-long ill-will between the Hutu and the Tutsi, and to the resulting massacres in which it has been reckoned that a quarter of a million victims have died. The Republic of Chad has been almost ruined by a civil war, lasting over a number of years, in which the government of the partially Christianised south, aided by French troops, has been trying to reduce to subservience the mainly Muslim north. In Nigeria after independence, the savage massacres of Ibos in the northern section of the country provoked a violent outburst of Ibo tribalism, with the resulting demand for an independent Biafra and the horrors of civil war.

It would be possible to extend the list almost indefinitely. Even more serious perhaps is the deep-rooted bitterness among young people in Africa over the failure of liberation to produce the justice and equality which had been promised and expected. This bitterness is directed not at the white man, who is today only a memory, but against the new rulers. Everyone who has worked among African students knows the intensity of their feelings towards the new rich; they are likely to say "We did not get rid of the white millionaire in order to put power into the hands of the black millionaire who may be even worse than his predecessor".

To recognize this is simply realism. We all need liberation, but what we need is liberation from sin. Such doctrine is of course highly unpopular, especially among those who have accepted a good dose of the Marxist mythology. The sins of the rich are not the same as the sins of the poor; the sins of the Christian may be different from those of the Hindu or the Buddhist. But the needs are essentially the same; and, unless we say so plainly, we are simply betraying the truth of the Gospel.

This leads us a further step in the analysis of the concept of liberation. We hear rather often the saying that humanisation must precede evangelisation, sometimes indeed that in the present day world humanisation is evangelisation. To this we may agree — on one condition. The primary factor in humanisation is the knowledge of God revealed in Jesus Christ. No man is fully human unless he has come to know God and himself in the searchlight of Jesus Christ. If we suppose otherwise, we have not begun to understand what humanisation is. This is not theory. We have abundant evidence from eighty years of missionary work among the oppressed and downtrodden 'outcastes' in India. That fact that I now have to put that word in inverted commas shows that we were right. The man whom God has accepted cannot be declared outcaste by man. It was when the Christian came and sat down with the one whom society had rejected, and told him that in Christ he had been accepted by God with an acceptance that no human decree or tradition could annul, that he began to become aware of his human dignity. In a most remarkable way the believer became an individual. Previously he might seem to have been so shaped and patterned by the conditions in which he was compelled to dwell as to be almost exchangeable with his brother; for he belonged all too closely to the type. Once incorporated into Christ, he became in a new way a human being, with individuality and a sense of dignity, and a capacity to learn and understand with which he had never been credited before. And of course in the process he became discontented, and rightly, with the status which society had assigned to him and from which society offered him no escape.

The other horrible barbarism which liberation theology has inflicted upon us in 'conscientisation'. This is, in any case, intolerable in English, since the English for the French *conscience* is in many cases not *conscience* but *consciousness*. But one of hardship we have to endure is putting up with ecumenical English, and nothing is to be gained by arguing over words. What is meant by this strange word can perhaps best be simply stated as an awareness that things can be other than they are. It is true that with a certain level of human distress, of malnutrition, unemployment or under-employment, deprivation of the very elements of decent orderly living, hope, the last gift of the gods to men, flies away and escapes. There can grow up a patient, almost animal, endurance of the intolerable, a sense that as things have been, so they must always remain. Things will not change until men begin to believe that they can change. The outcaste Christian saw them change before his very eyes, as he and his friends ceased to drink, began to work, cared more for their wives and children, realised that within the limits of an unjust system great changes could be brought about. Hope had returned. If similar changes did occur apart from the preaching and acceptance of the Christian Gospel they were far less noticeable.

All this is history and not mythology. Of course, too much must not be claimed for the Christian mission. There were other notable helpers of the depressed classes, best known among them Mahatma Gandhi, who claimed that these folk must be called Harijans, the children of God, and not known by the opprobrious terms that had previously been used of them; and Dr. Ambedkar, himself drawn from one of the excluded communities. Both these men thought in more political terms than would have been suitable for the foreign missionary. But I think it is true that they both climbed up on the backs of the missionaries and profited by what they had done. It was a great day when the Parliament of independent India formally declared untouchability to be for the future illegal. It may be said, and not without reason, that acts of Parliament do not of themselves change situations, and that little in the villages has really changed. The Indian press provides evidence every day that this is so, and that an unjust system cannot be uprooted overnight. Yet progress has been considerable and the movement of the times is all in the right direction.

All that I have been trying to point out in this section is that the order of happenings in one situation which I know well was:

direct evangelism with a view to conversion
a notable recovery of human dignity
social and economic improvement
an awareness of possible change
actual political achievement.

I am not prepared to say that equally good results could not have been attained by an alteration or inversion of the order of procedure. I am saying, and emphatically, that this is something which remains to be proved; and that direct preaching of the Gospel at every stage is something that the responsible Christian cannot neglect, or will neglect at his peril. The Nairobi Assembly will render a great service to the Christian world, if it will draw the whole liberation theology out of the cloudy phraseology and mythical trappings in which it is so often obscured, bring it clearly into the light of day, and document its achievements by carefully observed and recorded examples.

I conclude this brief study with a plea that the great phrase "the whole Church bringing the whole Gospel to the whole world" should be restored to its proper place of honour in the thinking and in the expressions of the Assembly.

It has marked an improvement in our theology that we have come to see that the evangelistic entity must be the whole Church and not any special section of it. The existence of missionary societies is in itself a confession of failure on the part of the Church to be itself the Church. Further, the recognition by thoughtful "Evangelicals" that the social and international dimensions belong to the Gospel as of right, and are not alien excrescences brought in by irresponsible 'liberals', builds bridges over what appeared to be chasms, and has made conversation possible in a degree that would have been thought impossible even a few years ago. We all agree today that 'the world' is not a purely geographical expression. There is no autonomous realism in which the writ of Christ does not run. There are worlds such as those of economics and politics, which have tried to declare their own independence and to claim that Christ has no word to say to them. This is a blasphemy which the Church cannot tolerate. How the law of Christ is to be made effective in these realms is a question for the expert. But the prophetic voice of the Church must not be stilled.

But, when we have registered all these agreements, and expressed our gratitude to God for them, we have to add that the geographical is a factor that will not permit itself to be excluded. It is still the fact that one-third of the world's population has never so much as heard the name of Christ. It is true that many of these millions are in lands which today are inaccessible to any kind of Christian witness from outside. But this is not true of all.

It may be appropriate to draw attention to one or two elements in the situation which a Christian Assembly should not overlook: For the first time in history an accurate Christian survey of Africa has been drawn up, tribe by tribe. There is no reason why similar surveys should not be drawn up for other areas of the world. Why not discover where we really are in this epoch of the Church's history?

It is plain, and the Roman Catholic expert Fr. Adrian Hastings has often drawn our attention to the fact, that the success of the Church in Africa is its greatest danger. We continue to baptize thousands of Africans into the

Church every week, and we are in danger of reproducing the Latin American situation, since the provision for the teaching and training of new converts, and the development of an indigenous ministry, lag far behind the minimum demands of the situation.

It is clear that there are many areas as yet unreached by even the first pioneer preaching of the Gospel. Some of these are, no doubt, for political reasons inaccessible, even to Africans of other nations. To others the doors seem open. Shall we postpone the attempt to reach them to some mythological and at present unimaginable future? Or shall we agree that, in this area, the King's business requires haste, and repeat the words spoken by the Lord of Hosts Himself to the prophet Isaiah, "Whom shall we send and who will go for us?"

I have drawn my illustrations from Africa, since that is the continent in which I have lived for the greater part of the past six years, and in which I am actually writing these words. Much could be added by those who have had more recent experience than I of other parts of the world. This aspect of the work and witness of the Church does not seem to have received, in the preparatory documents of the Assembly, the attention which its importance demands.

Nairobi 1975 will be the fifth Assembly of the World Council of Churches. Will it also be the last? It is often light-heartedly assumed that, because an ecumenical organ exists, it will go on existing for ever. But this is not the case. At one time the lead in ecumenical enterprise was taken by the World Alliance for Promoting International Friendship through the Churches. Many of my readers may never even have heard of that body, which came to an inglorious end in June 1948, just before the holding of the first Assembly of the World Council of Churches. That which has happened once could happen again.

Assemblies of the World Council have been marked by the law of diminishing returns. Amsterdam 1948 was exciting just because it was the first, and it did manage to produce a message to the Churches which was and still is memorable. Evanston 1954 was a kind of vocal pause. New Delhi 1961 was marked by the integration of World Council and International Missionary Council, and by the admission of Russia and other Orthodox Churches to membership. Uppsala 1968 did nothing significant except to produce a number of hastily compiled reports, which no one will ever read except church historians. All advice to hold assemblies less frequently and with far better preparation, all proposals radically to change the character of assemblies to make them more effective as expressions of the mind of the Church, have been disregarded. What will Nairobi 1975 do? The prospects cannot be viewed without a measure of foreboding. Unless the Holy Spirit is very notably at work during the period which remains for preparation, and in the proceedings of the Assembly itself, Nairobi 1975 might well be the last as well as the fifth Assembly of the World Council of Churches.

B. REPORTS OF THE NAIROBI ASSEMBLY
1. The Fifth Assembly and Evangelization

Harvey Hoekstra

INTRODUCTION

The Rev. Harvey Hoekstra went to Nairobi as the Press Representative of Church Growth Bulletin. His denomination is the Reformed Church of America and his land of labor is Ethiopia. His moving letter which follows this introductory statement places readers of Church Growth Bulletin in ringside seats at the Great Assembly. They see the action occur.

Despite the fact that Mr. Hoekstra's report covers the first week only, Church Growth Bulletin is pleased to print it because it portrays brilliantly the forces which in the last week brought the Assembly back — in statement at least — closer to a full orbed Christian position. One senses the tensions, the agonizing doubts as to whether the Assembly (whose preparatory documents and planned program so carefully neglected evangelism) *could* from the floor and the committees reverse the intrenched anti-evangelism and the anti-mission position of the leaders.

The final reports indicate that the Assembly did change what its leaders had planned and did state a commitment to evangelism. We rejoice in this. Constituent Churches can now engage in evangelism, confident that they are doing what the Fifth Assembly declared ought to be done. We congratulate the World Council of Churches. Section I of the program was devoted to *Confessing Christ Today*. This did *not* mean Non-Christians Confessing Christ. In plain English this meant: "How Ought Christians to Act in Today's World" — a very big subject. In previous statements, the WCC has said very little about evangelism; but included in 12 pages of the approved report of Section I, "Confessing Christ Today", were the following explicit statements about evangelism. Readers will note that most of them hurry on to say "and social action". The World Council was terribly afraid that Christians might evangelize without changing the evil structures of society — a needless fear, but one which seems to have gripped the Council. Granting this, the strong clear statements about evangelism are good. We reproduce the following paragraphs of the approved report with joy.

"As our High Priest, Christ mediates God's new covenant through both salvation and service. Through the power of the cross, Christ promises God's righteousness and commands human justice. As the royal priesthood, Christians are therefore called to engage in both evangelism and social action. We are commissioned to proclaim the gospel of Christ to the ends of the earth. Simultaneously, we are commanded to struggle to realize God's will for peace, justice and freedom throughout society." . . .

"The Gospel always includes: the announcement of God's Kingdom and love through Jesus Christ, the offer of grace and forgiveness of sins, the invitation to repentance and faith in Him, the summons to fellowship in God's Church, the command to witness to God's saving words and deeds, the responsibility to participate in the struggle for justice and human dignity, the obligation to denounce all that hinders human wholeness, and a commitment to risk life itself." . . .

"The world is not only God's creation; it is also the arena of God's mission. Because God loved the whole world, the Church cannot neglect any part of it — neither those who have heard the saving Name nor the vast majority who have not yet heard it. Our obedience to God and our solidarity with the human family demands that we obey Christ's command to proclaim and demonstrate God's love to every person, of every class and race, on every continent, in every culture, in every setting and historical context." . . .

"We need to recover the sense of urgency. Questions about theological definitions there may be. Problems of precise implementation will arise. But neither theoretical nor practical differences must be allowed to dampen the fires of evangelism." . . .

"Confessing Christ must be done *today*. "Behold, now is the acceptable time; behold, now is the day of salvation" (II Cor. 6:2). It cannot wait for a time that is comfortable for us. We must be prepared to proclaim the Gospel when human beings need to hear it. But in our zeal to spread the Good News, we must guard against fanaticism which disrupts the hearing of the Gospel, and breaks the community of God. The world requires, and God demands, that we recognize the urgency to proclaim the saving word of God — today. God's acceptable time demands that we respond in all haste. "And how terrible it would be for me if I did not preach the Gospel!" (I Cor. 9:16)" . . .

However, Church Growth Bulletin believes that good words are not enough. Bishop Arias of Bolivia told the Assembly that:

"Evangelism has been the Cinderella of the WCC, at least to judge by the extent to which it appears in its structure, where it figures by nothing more than one office with a single occupant, in a sub-structure which is in itself merely part of a unit, and with no more than a monthly letter by which to communicate with the churches of the whole world."

Our rejoicing will be tempered until we see evangelism ceasing to be Cinderella. Compared with its allocations to the machines in New York and

Geneva, and to social action, will the WCC put as many men and women into the planning and implementing of evangelism, back them with as much money and publicity, and measure their effectiveness by the numbers who hear the Gospel and pass through the waters by baptism, into responsible membership in Christ's Church? John Stott's final words, quoted by Mr. Hoekstra, are well said. Evangelicals of all Churches (and the angels in heaven, too) will be asking themselves the key question: WILL ALL THE GOOD WORDS ABOUT EVANGELISM LEAD TO TREMENDOUS AND EFFECTIVE DISCIPLING OF THE NATIONS?

Christians will hope and pray for this outcome. The WCC has repeatedly said that to be credible evangelism must be done by people engaged in social action. Is it fair for Evangelicals now to say that Nairobi's words about evangelism will become credible only when the Council and its affiliated Churches launch and maintain vigorous programs intended to disciple *to ethne?*

Continuous passionate evangelization arises from conviction that belief in Jesus Christ — and belief alone, not works — saves a man. Conviction does not arise in hearts which have lost their faith in an authoritative inspired Bible. The studied neglect of evangelism has, to be sure, several causes; but one of the most potent is loss of Bible-based certainty. When men with a low view of the Bible control a congregation, denomination, council or missionary society, ethical concerns are all their consciences demand. Evangelization inevitably is relegated to a minor position. How far this factor will affect what the World Council does, once its Evangelical voices have returned from Nairobi, remains to be seen.

Let us nevertheless rejoice. Let us pray that God will rule and over-rule the decisions of all His servants, both Conciliars and Evangelicals, so they do much better than they intend. For, after all, His Power does work in us to achieve much more than we can ask or think.

More than anything else, let us work (in our own Congregations, Denominations, Councils, and Missionary Societies) to implement the good words which the Fifth Assembly has voiced. Insofar as it depends on us, let us multiply effective evangelism everywhere.

A word must be said about the social action-evangelism tension, which Mr. Hoekstra mentions again and again, and which formed such a very large part of the Assembly's agenda. Social action of many sorts is obviously a part of Christian life and work — and always has been. So is gospel-proclaiming, sinner-converting, church-multiplying evangelism. Church Growth Bulletin rejects out of hand the silly charge that the Evangelicals have been short on social action and long on evangelism. Just look at the budgets of EFMA and IFMA missions throughout the world. It is a rare mission budget in which more than two-thirds does not go to good works, education, uplift, medicine, and social action of many sorts. We refuse to be distracted by the baseless charge that Evangelicals have neglected humanitarian service, a charge drawn like a red herring across the trail.

The real cause of the tension is that since about 1960 the most vocal leaders in many mainline missionary societies, conciliar Churches and Councils have talked as if *the only* thing worth doing was smashing unjust structures. We say "have *talked* as if". What some mainline churches *did* was something else.

In some conciliar Churches — especially in Latfricasia — considerable soul-saving evangelism has been done, new churches have been multiplied, and people movements to Christ have been nurtured. Not nearly as much as could be, as the times call for, as God apparently desires; but still 'considerable'.

Church Growth Bulletin doubts whether the proportion (two-thirds to one-third common in vigorously Evangelical missions) is God's will today. Of course, the correct proportion changes from situation to situation and from year to year. Yet in *these* days, when fifteen decades of missions have prepared multitudes of non-Christians to accept the Saviour and be formed into Christian congregations, it is urgent that eternal salvation be not sacrificed to improvements in the temporal conditions of men. Both must, of course, be done, both are being done; but baptizing believers and multiplying churches must be emphasized. Harvest when ripe must be reaped. The single most effective step toward justice, peace and development is the formation of multitudes of new local churches. Those shouting for social justice at Nairobi were frequently sons and grandsons of converts. They would neither have been there nor have had any social concern, if their parents or grandparents had not been evangelized and incorporated into local churches. Multitudes of new churches are essential. Once established firmly on a biblical base, these can then be irradiated with economic, educational, and political measures toward temporal uplift of all sorts.

Church Growth Bulletin stands *with* the advocates of social justice. We cordially accept that the Christian elite and wealthy of all nations have a duty to help usher in God's juster more equitable social order. What we do *not* accept is that evangelism (proclaiming Christ and persuading men to become His disciples and responsible members of His Church) is of no avail and must not be done unless it is linked with programs to change the social structure. As Latfricasians throw themselves into the evangelization of Asia, Africa and Latin America, it is not necessary, we hold, for them to smash all iniquitous social structures in their communities *first*. They (and all other Christians in all other continents) proclaim, not themselves, but Christ. He has ample power, which He constantly exercises through multiplied millions of His confessed disciples, to rectify wrong conditions.

Against this background, we commend to our readers Mr. Hoekstra's fine report on the Fifth Assembly. Good reading lies ahead.

As we read Mr. Hoekstra's significant account, let us follow the struggle with close attention. As we await the final outcome, let us rejoice that evangelism was, in statement at least, given a somewhat more biblical position. Let us rejoice that, though the very important phrase "the 2.7 billion who have yet to believe" (carefully inserted by Bishop Arias and his consultants) was edited out of the final revision accepted by the Council, nevertheless the text approved calls on Christians to "obey Christ's command to proclaim and demonstrate God's love to every person, of every class and race, on every continent, in every culture, in every setting and historical context." Donald McGavran

EYE WITNESS REPORT FROM NAIROBI

Dr. Donald McGavran, Editor
Church Growth Bulletin
Pasadena, California 91101
USA

The Rev. Harvey Hoekstra
Kenyata Conference Center,
Fifth General Assembly,
World Council of Churches
Nairobi, Kenya

December 1, 1975

Dear Dr. McGavran:

I am writing at the end of the first full week of the Fifth General Assembly of the World Council of Churches here in Nairobi. More than 2,000 Christian leaders and visitors from all parts of the world, with guests from other faiths are here. African dress, crimson, purple, black and white ecclesiastical garb and western business and casual attire blend together making for a colorful assembly. 747 delegates are spending three weeks considering what they consider to be the implications for action by God's people arising out of the main theme: "Jesus Christ Frees and Unites." In contrast to the Uppsala Assembly where women and youth were relatively few, this Assembly has 20 percent women and some 75 youth members who are under 30 years of age. 300 delegates are laypersons. About 80 percent of the delegates are attending their first assembly meeting. The 120 advisors include 10 Roman Catholics and 10 "Conservative" Evangelicals. The 250 WCC staff members insure the smooth functioning of the Assembly and that the primary goals of the pre-assembly planning be realized.

It is a moving experience to be here. I have been inspired and blessed by the testimony of many from different cultures as to what Christ means to them. I shall always remember a plain African woman, speaking in very good English, standing and passionately wagging her finger at the delegates in the section considering what it means to confess Christ today. She said, "Let us never forget that Christ came to save sinners. Let no one think that because he is in prison or exploited that God will excuse him for not believing in Jesus. Let us not forget that there will be a judgment and we must prepare now to meet our God." When she sat down, I thought, she may not know all the implications of the Gospel, but in her simple and marvelous experience and knowledge of Christ, she knew what real liberation meant. It was people of her kind that had turned the world upside down. Oh, for the recovery of that compelling conviction that Christ can truly set men free to be what God intends for them to be.

The large and easily distinguished delegations from the ancient Orthodox Churches with their long beards and flowing robes witness to God's faithfulness in preserving His people and the Gospel across the centuries. The large number of delegates from the newer churches of the Third World give eloquent testimony to the power of the Gospel among all who hear. They are signs of God's blessing upon the great missionary movement of the last century without which there would be no World Council of Churches today.

It is, of course, much too early to predict what will come out of this assembly. My own reading is that the major concern that has so far surfaced in this Assembly is Evangelism and what the WCC intends to do about it. This is reflected in the response of delegates to the major speeches, the discussion in the various study groups, and in that an overwhelming majority of the delegates registered to participate in the Unit dealing with the topic, "Confessing Christ Today." Many will judge this Assembly by how it responds to the call from many for the WCC to again place Evangelism at the center of its life.

M.M. Thomas, moderator of the Central Committee of the WCC spoke clearly of the need for the Church to concern itself with Evangelism. His several references to positions taken by the International Conference on Evangelism at Lausanne indicates that WCC leaders are being influenced by this call to Evangelism. Bishop Arias, speaking on the subject, "That The World May Believe" referred to the Lausanne conference, the meeting of Roman Catholics, and meetings of the Orthodox in recent years dealing with the subject of Evangelism as evidence that the Spirit seems to be calling the churches of the whole world "to take up once again their essential and primary responsibility of evangelism."

Continuing, the Bishop said, "The moment has come to acclaim the missionary and evangelistic potential of all that the WCC has been doing through us and in our name." With sadness he noted that in fact Evangelism is of diminishing importance in the WCC structure and programs. He said:

> "And above all we must admit with shame that evangelism has been the Cinderella of the WCC, at least to judge by the extent to more than one office with a single occupant, in a sub-structure which is itself merely part of a unit, with no more than a monthly letter by which to communicate with the churches of the whole world."

The small importance attached to Evangelism in the WCC is clearly apparent in relation to this Fifth General Assembly, Pre-assembly study materials to help churches and their delegates prepare for this important gathering, the persons selected to deliver the major addresses, the actual addresses themselves, the Bible Societies' presentation based on the story of the Prodigal son, the theme of the play, "MUNTU", the use of media and art, the daily press releases all point to a firm determination of the WCC leadership to intensify the Church's commitment to the struggle for social justice and liberation to the neglect of evangelism. The legitimate concern for horizontal socio-political concerns has overshadowed and dwarfed any real concern for the vertical and personal. In the passion to help persons be liberated from oppressive structures, they pay inadequate attention to the truth that all men are enslaved by the power of personal sin and need to be set free by the forgiving grace of God as heard in the Gospel of our Lord Jesus Christ. Undervaluing the power of the Gospel of Jesus Christ to bring about true humanization, they make the mistake of seeking to bring into being a new society with persons who themselves have not yet been liberated from sin and made new by being joined with Christ in newness of life by His resurrection power.

The dominant message hurled at the delegates in the keynote address of Dr. Robert McAfee Brown and in the address by Jamaica Prime Minister Michael N. Manley has been the attack on the capitalistic system and the call for a new social order along Marxist lines. While it is true that speakers have recognized evils in the socialist societies, they have heaped most of their criticism upon America and the industrialized countries of the West. Sometimes in listening to the speeches and the press conferences that follow, I have to pinch myself that this is in fact a meeting of the Church of Jesus Christ and not a meeting of the United Nations. How right Bishop Arias, who speaks from within the WCC and the CWME, is when he says that "in fact Evangelism is of diminishing importance in the WCC structure and programs."

These major addresses in the plenary sessions of this first week have produced mixed reactions from the delegates. On the one hand the delegates appear committed to continue and intensify the struggle for social justice and liberation. The response to Dr. Brown's address and the standing ovation given to the Prime Minister of Jamaica confirm this observation. The youth delegates are here fresh from their preassembly conferences in Arusha. No one reading their declaration would doubt their commitment to the struggle for liberation and their passion to bring in a new social and economic order.

But, paradoxically, along with this continuing commitment to the struggle and the programs of the WCC that have come out of positions taken at Uppsala when humanization was lifted up as the goal of mission for our time, many delegates are voicing a deep seated misgiving about the direction the WCC is going. They do not want this preoccupation to the exclusion of evangelism. There is a widespread concern that this Assembly does not express itself decisively on this issue of Evangelism, it will be disastrous for the WCC. Failure to take positive steps confirming its commitment to Evangelism will cause a reaction in many Churches and will mean a loss of confidence and support for all WCC programs. A delegate from Australia said, "Lausanne has spoken clearly of its commitment to social action as well as the verbal proclamation. We must be equally ready to declare our commitment to evangelism."

The Norwegian delegation has been very active and vocal in this Assembly. They have shared with us how during the year representatives from member churches in Finland, Sweden and Norway had met to discuss the pre-assembly study materials to prepare for this Assembly. Thus they speak out of careful preparation and out of a deep concern as to where the WCC is going. This concern is felt so deeply that the Church in Norway has appointed a commission to reexamine its membership in the WCC and this issue will be before the Norwegian bishops' conference in the Autumn of 1976. This fact was spoken by a Norwegian delegate in the plenary for all 747 delegates and the leaders of this Assembly to note. This is all the more significant when we recall that the Church of Norway was a charter member of the WCC and has engaged itself positively in the Program to Combat Racism and has not infrequently expressed its gratitude for the leadership provided by the WCC in the struggle of the churches for social and economic justice.

Speaking on the floor of the Assembly, Mrs. Olga Dysthe, on behalf of the entire Norwegian delegation responded to Dr. Philip Potter's address with words of appreciation, acknowledging he had expressed the historic Christian understanding of the significance of "the Crucified and Risen Lord as alone the hope of the world." However, she continued:

> "This was said 50 years ago, but it is to be regretted that this dimension has not been clearly spelled out in the Assembly so far. It is not enough just to speak of the Cross of Jesus Christ and His resurrection as models for our struggle against evil and our overcoming of human obstacles. When we speak about freedom in Christ, the dimension of repentance, conversion and personal faith has hardly had the emphasis it deserves in this assembly."

The most comprehensive statement expressing the evangelical concern was made by Dr. John R. Stott who was on the program as one of three to make responses to Bishop Arias's address.

John R. Stott expressed warm appreciation for Bishop Arias's call to the WCC to put Evangelism back at the center of its life and programs. He inferred that the Bishop's address was not typical of recent ecumenical utterances. Yet the modern ecumenical movement was born of missionary passion, and an assurance had been given at New Dehli that the work of the International Council would henceforth become *central* to the concerns of the WCC. He spoke for many delegates and the churches they represent when he said, "It seems to many of us that evangelism has now become largely eclipsed by the quest for social and political liberation."

Dr. Stott then went on to list five essentials that the WCC needs to recover if it is to fulfill its true nature: 1) A recognition of the lostness of men. 2) Confidence in the Gospel of God. 3) Conviction about the uniqueness of Jesus Christ. 4) A sense of urgency about evangelism. 5) A personal experience of Jesus Christ. Continuing, he said, "The greatest of all hindrances to evangelism today is the poverty of our own spiritual experience. True evangelism is the spontaneous overflow of a heart full of Christ. Only the forgiven sinner can invite another to come with him to the cross of Christ to experience forgiveness and liberation from the sinless Redeemer."

Then, adding to his prepared text, he concluded with this strong appeal to the Assembly:

> "We are all aware of the wide gap of confidence and credibility that exists today between many ecumenical leaders and Evangelicals — if you like, between Geneva and Lausanne. What can be done about this gap? Ecumenical leaders genuinely question whether Evangelicals have a heart-felt commitment for social action. We Evangelicals say we have. But, I personally recognize that we've got to supply more evidence that we have.
>
> On the other hand, Evangelicals genuinely question whether the World Council of Churches has any longer a heartfelt commitment to world wide evangelization. They say they have, but I beg this Assembly to supply more evidence that this is so."

Already the drafters are working preparing the documents this Assembly will debate, perhaps amend and alter, and then adopt. Will the final drafts respond to the uneasiness of many in our churches about what sort of commitment the WCC has to Evangelism?

Failure by this Assembly to affirm unequivocally its commitment to evangelism will raise the question for Evangelicals in WCC member Churches as to where they can express their commitment to evangelism in programs in which both social concern and the call for repentance, conversion and faith in the Lord Jesus for personal salvation are inextricably linked. It will not do to suggest that we express our social concerns through the WCC and our evangelistic concerns through whatever may evolve from the work of the Continuation Committee following Lausanne. Such an approach will only make it more difficult on both counts for people to realize that the Gospel is the good news of what God does for one in his total being through Jesus Christ. Either in isolation from the other will make it more difficult for persons to hear the Gospel and believe it. On the one hand, social involvement with insufficient verbal witness to Christ's place in God's plans for His world will contribute to persons failing to understand the true nature of man, his dilemma and his destiny and God's marvelous provision for his total salvation from sin and its terrible consequences for time and eternity.

And on the other, the verbal proclamation of the Gospel apart from social involvement will make it more difficult for persons to believe that God really cares for them in their total persons, body and soul.

This is why I see this anticipated response of this Assembly to the call for a new commitment to Evangelism as so terribly important. The present imbalance needs to be corrected. Many persons committed to the ecumenical movement hope this Assembly will not make it more difficult for them to encourage that support in their churches for continued participation in the WCC or its programs. Many here feel deeply that the WCC needs to come back to positions more nearly reflecting the total Biblical perspective.

So far, I have heard virtually nothing to suggest that this Assembly will take seriously the now more than 3 billion who live and die without knowledge of Christ. I have not once heard the term, "Cross cultural evangelism." If this Assembly states more forthrightly its commitment to evangelism, will this lead to programs of action challenging the whole world church to harness its resources and mobilize its people *with the one supreme purpose to let all men everywhere hear the Gospel of the grace of God in Jesus Christ and be persuaded to believe in Him and become His disciples and members of His Church?* Will the WCC's call to "do theology" include the whole church's taking the whole Gospel to the whole world? Will the call to "do theology" spring from a realization that men cannot call upon whom they have not heard, and that men cannot preach unless they are sent? Three billion people wait for the Assembly to say, "Yes."

Cordially,
Harvey T. Hoekstra

B. REPORTS OF THE NAIROBI ASSEMBLY
2. Nairobi '75: A Crisis of Faith

Bruce J. Nicholls

This is one man's report of a *very complex* happening and by one who was a first-timer at such an ecumenical gathering — a fact he shared with 70% of those attending Nairobi. The *sheer pluralism* of the W.C.C. and its attempt to address itself to a wide range of global problems, political, economic, social and religious, in the space of *eighteen crowded days,* makes a balanced and fair report exceedingly difficult. Time for re-study of all the documents and reflection is needed.

Nairobi was an attempt at a consensus of traditions in which a place was found for everybody's views, including those of the observer. With the growing influence of the Eastern European Churches and the diversity of Third World Churches, including those of doubtful Christian orthodoxy, this search for consensus is breaking down. Outwardly it might appear that the goal of the ecumenical movement for the visible and sacramental unity of the Churches is being slowly achieved, but in reality a true unity of faith is being lost. The dangers of apostasy and syncretistic theology remain as acute as ever. On the surface Nairobi was an improvement on Uppsala, but the very noticeable ignoring of biblical authority and of any serious theological discussion, causes me to doubt whether the gain was substantial. The very structure of such a mammoth Assembly makes genuine democratic proceedings almost impossible. The gap between the obvious goals that the Secretariat had set for the Assembly and the concerns of the participants was noticeable. The reasonably strong evangelical participation received little visibility either in the plenary sessions or in the leadership of the sectional groups. John Stott's eight-minute reply on evangelism was the one clear exception! The fundamental unity and clear but limited goals of the equally large Lausanne Congress stood out in sharp contrast to Nairobi.

The diversity of people attending Nairobi was impressive — 664 delegates from 286 churches, together with advisers, delegated observers, observers from international organizations, press, staff and visitors together totalled more than 2,300. Almost half the delegates were from the Third World. Ninety-six came from the Eastern European Churches. Twenty percent were women and 10% were youth — a higher percentage than in the previous Assemblies.

The W.C.C. faces an identity crisis. The Assembly was ambivalent in its attitude as to how far the W.C.C. exists to reflect the concern of the member Churches and how far it exists in its own right as a prophetic voice leading the Churches to a fresh understanding of their mission. The trend to theological radicalism and left wing politics of the Secretariat was evident in the choice of plenary speakers, but among the participants particularly those from Europe, there was a decided conservative reaction and a desire to give a much stronger emphasis to evangelism than the organisers of the Assembly had originally planned. Only the future will tell how responsive the Secretariat is to this concern of the member Churches.

All such international conferences raise the fundamental issue as to whether the expenditure of time, energy and finance justifies such a large gathering, especially when the consensus approach offers so little clarity in its message to the Churches. Perhaps the future lies in smaller gatherings organized on a national or regional scale with defined and limited goals and a stronger measure of fundamental agreement among the participants.

THE AUTHORITY AND USE OF SCRIPTURE

The Assembly was projected as a celebration, a participation in the praxis of Jesus Christ freeing and uniting. The experience-centred approach of Bangkok was taken as a model for Nairobi. The small group Bible studies, the experimentation in worship of many traditions and the brilliant use of drama, dance, films and the daily wall newspaper all contributed to make Nairobi an experience in unity and liberation. The one page message of the Assembly to the world "An Invitation to Prayer" was a summary of what the Assembly had experienced together. It called for prayer to the Creator to help to conserve the earth's resources for future generations, to the God of love to help sustain world community, and to the God of hope to struggle against injustice. But there was no reference to the authority of Scripture or of the proclamation of the Gospel to the lost.

The Assembly was also an attempt to find authority in the consensus of Christian traditions. The assumption was made that the New Testament is the record of the traditions of the early Church and that these have been supplemented and enriched by the traditions of succeeding generations of Christians. The Moderator, M.M. Thomas, offered a synthesis of ecumenical, Orthodox, Catholic and evangelical traditions, especially in the area of evangelism and mission. Yet the Orthodox delegations were intransigent in their insistence on the primacy of the traditions of the first six centuries as the only basic for eucharistic unity. In a somewhat triumphal spirit Dr. Philip Potter spoke of the ecumenical tradition as embracing the whole oikoumene with only the Roman Catholic Church to be gathered in. He made no reference to the vast numbers of conservative evangelicals who stand outside the ecumenical movement, or to those regions of the world, such as Latin America, where membership in the W.C.C. is still a very small minority of the Churches of the region.

One of the most disturbing aspects of the Assembly was the minimal emphasis given in the papers and reports to the Scriptures as the authoritative Word of God. The crisis of faith in the W.C.C. is clearly one of authority. The history of the ecumenical movement reveals a clear shift in its attitude to and use of the Bible. The founders of the W.C.C. believed the Bible was normative for their message to the world and the unity of the Bible was assumed. The biblical theology school dominated by Barth, which deeply influenced early ecumenical thinking, reached a high water-mark at the New Delhi Assembly, 1961, where the phrase "according to the scriptures" was added to the simple doctrinal statement of the W.C.C. The givenness of the Bible as a testimony to salvation-history and its uniqueness were stressed. Bible study had a central place in the New Delhi Assembly's programme.

The fourth conference of the Faith and Order Commission at Montreal, 1963, proved a watershed in W.C.C. thinking about Scripture. Kasemann denied the unity of New Testament ecclesiology and raised the hermeneutical problem of the relevance of the biblical message to the modern world. The Dristol meeting of the Faith and Order Commission 1967, further questioned the unity of Scripture and interpreted the Bible as a variety of traditions and insights which must be examined, each in their own cultural setting. There was no agreement as to whether the Bible was normative of truth or a product of the traditions of the early Church, or only one element in the complexity of Christian truth. The Uppsala Assembly reflected the same uncertainty. A study report was presented to the Faith and Order Commission at Louvain 1971, in which the content of the Faith was further questioned. The inspiration of the Bible was held to be its inspiring character. The report asks, "Why should not Basil, Augustine, Thomas, Luther, or some modern author be inspired, too? Surely it was their work of interpretation that led to the Bible speaking again with fresh authority?" This loss of the authority of Scripture as normative produced a hermeneutical crisis. The New Delhi approach to hermeneutics as "map reading", by which the acts of God in biblical history provide a clue to understanding the present world, was gradually replaced by a situation hermeneutic in which the cultural content was the controlling factor. The cultural life situation determines the use made of the Bible and imposes its own unity on it. At Nairobi the new hermeneutic was evident in numerous ways. The passages selected for the small group Bible studies under the theme "Jesus Christ Frees and Unites" were chosen to illustrate the theme of human liberation and the perspectives of the biblical writers adapted to this "relational centre". It was a reversal of historic evangelical hermeneutics.

The new hermeneutic was applied in an imaginative way in the parable of the two lost sons presented by the United Bible Societies. The dynamic equivalent principle of translation was applied not only to specific cultural metaphors such as "he fell on his neck", but also to the basic goal of the parable. The presentation suggested that the younger son was right to break with his father in the interests of self-determination and the elder son was right to stand up to his father and that the parable is an open-ended story to show how the father can keep both sons. While these insights reflect accurately the tensions in modern family life, it can be seriously questioned whether any valid exegesis of the passage can support them.

The cultural context rather than the biblical message dominated the addresses of all the plenary sessions with the limited exception of Bishop Arias' paper on Evangelism. In the opening position paper by M.M. Thomas, the Moderator of the Assembly and Chairman of the Central Committee of the W.C.C., I noted only one reference to the text of Scripture, in what was a theological and well-documented review of the issues before the Assembly. Again the report of Philip Potter, the General Secretary, and Robert McAfee Brown's address, "Who is this Jesus Christ who Frees and Unites?", began with scriptural exposition but soon left it to deal with issues of social, economic and political oppression. None of the women speakers in "Women in a Changing World", or Prime Minister Manley's address "From the Shackles of Domination and Oppression", or Professor Charles Birch's address, "Creation, Technology and Human Survival" made more than a passing reference to the text of Scripture. Many of these authors quoted profusely from human authors and U.N. documents, but remained silent on the Word of God. The use of Scripture in the sectional reports varied considerably. Section I "Confessing Christ Today", gave serious attention to Scripture while others, particularly Section IV, "Education for Liberation and Community", and Section V, "Structures of Injustice and Struggles for Liberations", had no reference to Scripture whatever. Similarly, it was disturbing that no attempt was made to deal with biblical principles or passages of Scripture that had given rise to conflicting interpretations in any of the social issues debated, such as sexism, racism or the widening gap between rich and poor. It was evident that some speakers owed more to the theories of Karl Marx than to the biblical interpreters. I enjoyed the eight Bible study group sessions as times of sharing inter-personal experiences, but there was virtually no attempt at exegesis of the passage, in our case Romans 8. No reports of these groups were asked for in the plenary sessions.

Thus it was clear that the "crisis of faith" in the W.C.C. is a crisis of authority. Any attempt to find a consensus of Scripture, tradition and experience will end in confusion. The subjectivism of the current approach to hermeneutics only deepens the crisis. The failure to relate Bible study to the discussion of political and social issues only accentuated the impression that Nairobi was a shadow United Nations, and as someone rather unkindly added, a "third-rate one with few political experts".

THE UNITY OF THE CHURCH AND THE UNITY OF MANKIND

A passionate call for visible unity has always been central to the ecumenical movement. Since Uppsala a new dimension has been added. The unity of the Church is a sign of the unity of mankind. This expanded concern was given considerable attention at Nairobi.

New Delhi described God's will for unity in terms of one fully committed fellowship of all God's people in each place, in all places and in all ages. Uppsala emphasized that the search for unity is a quest for diversity in unity and continuity. The idea of conciliar fellowship was added by the Faith and Order Commission at Lauvain.

In Spain 1973, it was stated "The one Church is to be envisaged as a conciliar fellowship of local Churches which are themselves truly united. In this conciliar fellowship each local Church possesses in communion with others the fulness of catholicity, witnesses to the same apostolic faith and therefore recognizes the others as belonging to the same Church of Christ and guided by the same Spirit". At Nairobi the section report "What Unity Requires" expanded the theme of conciliar fellowship as an aspect of life of the one undivided Church functioning at different levels. It is "an interior unity" of Churches separated by space, culture or time.

The Orthodox emphasis on a Christ-centred dimension to the Church is welcomed as an alternative to a secularized Christianity which reduces the doctrine of the Church to that of a unified classless society with humanistic goals. On the other hand, the Orthodox intransigence on the eucharist makes unity impossible. Although the Orthodox Churches participated more fully in Nairobi than in Uppsala and with the election of Russian Orthodox Metropolitan Nikodim of Leningrad as one of the six Vice-Presidents of the W.C.C. the general disenchantment of the Orthodox churches with the prevailing secular mood of the W.C.C. may mean that the Orthodox Churches will find a new affinity with the Church of Rome. It was significant that the protests against the secularized policies of the W.C.C. whether in plenary or in sectional sessions, came either from Evangelicals or from Orthodox participants. With the continuing confusion among ecumenical Protestants, we may yet see Evangelicals, biblical Catholics and Orthodox standing together in defense of the Biblical Faith. The future of Roman Catholic relationships with the W.C.C. remains uncertain. In his greetings to the Assembly, Pope Paul wrote "May the assurance of our fraternal solidarity be a support to you in the coming years", but he gave no indication that the Catholic Church would join the W.C.C. in the foreseeable future. Many observers doubt that Rome will ever do so. At Nairobi eucharistic services were celebrated separately by the Orthodox and by the Protestant Churches. At the one attempt at a united eucharistic celebration the Orthodox were present but did not receive the elements.

The Uppsala concept that the unity of the Church as a sign of the unity of mankind was endorsed by Philip Potter when he said, "I want to keep always before our minds the fact that the ecumenical movement is concerned with the oikoumene the whole human race as it struggles to discover what it means to be human in the purpose of God. In his address, "Visible Unity as Conciliar Fellowship", Dr. John Deschner argued that visible unity has to do with classism, racism, sexism and the segregation of the handicapped as much as it has to do with denominationalism. He and other speakers argued that this unity in the Church is only the forerunner of the unity of mankind. Dr. Robert McAfee Brown of California noted that Jesus Christ divides as well as unites, but even here he was thinking more of the division between the oppressed and the oppressor. Brown asserted that Jesus is only provisionally the divider, for in the end he will unite the whole human family. This universalistic hope had an eschatological content. There was no distinction between the Kingdom *of God now* and the *Kingdom of God to come* when the King returns. The Assembly was sadly silent on the theme on the wrath of God and the final judgment of heaven and hell.

This emphasis on a secular eschetology means that the leadership of the Assembly, impatient with any concept of gradual reform, were open to the idea of violence in order to bring about radical change in society. On the models of the Church — State alliances as in Eastern Europe and in Zaire, it was evident that many Third World leaders and Africans in particular, were looking to governments to support their programmes for the unification of the Church and for the achievement of social goals. I fear we are seeing the beginning of a return to a Constantinian era in which the Church is in danger of losing its prophetic role against corruption in national politics and of becoming a partner in the restriction of religious liberty and freedom to propagate the Christian faith. We may see increasing persecution against religious ministries. The vigorous defence by the Russian delegates of their own government's and Church's concept of human freedom and their total rejection of a letter to the Assembly by two dissident Orthodox members appealing against the ill-treatment of religious prisoners in psychiatric clinics and nursing homes, was a warning to all at Nairobi. In the post-Nairobi era powerful church groups may seek political support for the enforcement of policies of moratorium and the restriction of evangelism by evangelical groups. At the same time political rulers will use the Churches as tools in the interests of national unity.

The New Testament teaches that unity is always unity in truth and faithfulness to the apostolic witness. It warns against the spirit of anti-Christ and denounces false doctrines. As Dr. Klaus Runia has noted, when we speak of "true Church", we must also speak of the "false Church". This the

W.C.C. refuses to do. Their over-stress on "the sin of division" makes it difficult for them to speak against heresy. Fifteen new Churches were admitted to either full or associate membership of the W.C.C. during the Assembly. All but one of these belonged to the Third World. In accepting them there was little emphasis given to orthodoxy in belief as a necessary factor in membership. African independent and splinter Churches are applying for membership. Will the W.C.C. be able to reject those with syncretistic and heretical beliefs and practices?

THE PRIORITY OF EVANGELISM

Since the merger of the International Missionary Council with the W.C.C. at New Delhi, evangelism has received less and less attention. "Uppsala", wrote Dr. McGavran, "has betrayed the two billion who do not yet know the Gospel". At Bangkok, programmes for dialogue with other religious faiths and politically-motivated projects replaced the historic understanding of evangelism as the mission of the Church. In the original planning for Nairobi, no provision was made for a section on world mission and evangelization; however, the impact of the Lausanne Congress on the W.C.C. member Churches meant that this traditional concern could not be ignored.

Despite the fact that Philip Potter had told the synod of Catholic Bishops in Rome 1974, "The conviction of the World Council of Churches has been that evangelization is the ecumenical theme *par excellence*", he made no reference to evangelism in his general report to the Nairobi Assembly. He did speak of repentance and renewal of faith but this was in the context of the struggle for a shared life in community and for a just society. However, the plenary session on Evangelism was one of the highlights of the Assembly. Bishop Mortimer Arias of the Methodist Church in Bolivia in the keynote address on "That the World May Believe", reminded the Assembly that "the intention to 'stay together', which was the basis of the World Council, is necessary to the indispensable task of the Church of Christ: the evangelization of the world". He referred to the 2,700 million who do not know Christ and live under global ideological or religious systems. He rightly stressed that the one medium for the communication of the gospel was the Christian and the Christian community. Dr. John Stott's long-awaited reply was received with considerable enthusiasm by the Assembly. But it was disappointing that the planned plenary debate on the theme had to be cancelled as the allotted time for the session had expired. There was widespread reaction against an emotive and vindictive reporting of Stott's address in the Assembly newspaper Target. After acknowledging the positive contribution of Arias' address and a sympathetic reference to the twenty-seven theses of the document "Evangelism in Latin America Today", Stott questioned whether the Bishop's address was typical of recent ecumenital utterances. He noted "It seems to many of us that evangelism has now been largely eclipsed by the quest for social and political liberation". Stott made five affirmations of what the World Council needed to recover. He called for a recognition of the lostness of men and the judgment of God, the need for confidence in the one revealed Gospel, conviction concerning our stewardship to proclaim the uniqueness of Christ, a sense of urgency about the priority of evangelism, and the need for a personal experience of Jesus Christ. In a final word that applied to all of us he said, "I sometimes wonder if the greatest of all hindrances to evangelism today is not the poverty of our own spiritual experience. True evangelism is the spontaneous overflow of a heart full of Christ".

The report of the section "Confessing Christ Today" was undoubtedly the best statement of the Assembly. It affirmed the Church's evangelistic responsibility and called upon the Churches to confess Christ alone as Saviour and Lord. It stressed the costliness of conversion and discipleship and deplored cheap conversions without ethical consequences. It declared, "We regret that some reduce liberation from sin and evil to social and political dimensions, just as we regret that others limit liberation to the private and eternal dimension". The report spoke with sensitivity on the many economic, political and ecclesiastical structures that obscure the confession of Christ and which themselves are oppressive and dehumanising. It emphasized both personal and communal confession of Christ, the importance of worship and a Christ centred life-style. At least a third of the participants in the Assembly asked to be assigned to this section, indicating a widespread desire for a spiritual emphasis in the Assembly. It is hoped this report will have an effective influence on the member churches and we hope the W.C.C. Secretariat will press the many practical recommendations of the report upon the Churches. With an over-committed programme and shrinking income the W.C.C. faces a crisis in the priorities of its programme.

On the negative side some of the theological assumptions embedded in the presentation and discussion on evangelism were disturbing. At times Bishop Arias slipped into an incipient universalism. He described his experience of an integrated evangelistic programme of proclamation and action among atheistic Bolivian tin-miners struggling to rise above their oppressive working conditions. "All that was missing was the naming of the Name and we had to recognize that perhaps these people had more of Christ in them than we who spoke in His name", he said. He echoed the idea of anonymous Christianity when he said, "To evangelise is to help men to discover the Christ hidden in them and revealed in the gospel. All men and all human values are destined to be recapitulated in Christ". "Universalism" replied John Stott, "fashionable as it is today, is incompatible with the teaching of Christ and his apostles, and is a deadly enemy of evangelism".

In line with current ecumenical language, the Bishop also argued for a holistic and integral approach to evangelism. He endorsed Emilio Castro's statement that "Social justice, personal salvation, cultural affirmation, church growth, are all seen as integral parts of God's saving act".

In a significant document entitled "Jesus Christ Frees and Unites" prepared by the elders and deacons of the Nairobi Batpist Church as an evangelical response to the pre-Assembly documents the authors made the important distinction between the soteriological purpose of evangelism and the ethical concerns of social justice. While evangelism and social action are not exclusive of each other, they must not be confused. Nairobi did little to clear this confusion, so evident at Bangkok. The present ecumenical trend of including all of God's mission in the world as salvation is but another form of the liberal social Gospel and parallels the controversy in the medieval church on the holistic nature of faith and works. The Chicago Declaration 1973 is a significant evangelical contribution on salvation and ethics, and deserves careful study.

Another disturbing factor in the discussion on evangelism was the attempt by M.M. Thomas to synthesize the findings of recent consultations on evangelism, namely Bangkok 1973, Lausanne 1974, the Bishop Synod in Rome 1974, and the Orthodox Consultation at Bucharest 1974. Although he noted that Lausanne clearly distinguished between evangelism and social action, Thomas argued for the consensus of these consultations in their affirmation of the comprehensive nature of salvation. To my mind the theological assumptions and defined goals of Bangkok and Lausanne are as different as cheese is from chalk, and it is impossible to gloss these differences. It was significant that Thomas' call for "a Christ-centered syncretism" caused some embarrassment to the Assembly.

SEEKING COMMUNITY: THE COMMON SEARCH OF PEOPLE OF VARIOUS FAITHS, CULTURES AND IDEOLOGIES

The section under this heading dealt with the goal of mission and dialogue between living faiths, which is a very sensitive area in contemporary ecumenical thinking. Although Metropolitan Gregorias (Paul Verghese) of India made it clear that the purpose of this section was to seek world community and not to debate dialogue, the inter-relation between the two were such that one could not be discussed without the other. For Dr. S.J. Samartha, Director of the Programme for Dialogue with People of Living Faiths and Ideologies, the concern for the unity of mankind and world community replaces evangelism as the primary concern of the W.C.C. He claims that the impact of Eastern religions on Western culture and the decreasing influence of Christianity in many countries has intensified the desire for accepting religious plurality and the necessity for co-operation between religious communities. As evidence of this concern, a Hindu, a Buddhist, a Jew, a Muslim and a Sikh were invited as guests to participate in the reality of religious plurality. Some of their insights were incorporated in the report.

The search for a theological basis for world community proved unsatisfactory in the light of the total absence of any attempt at biblical exegesis. In the desire to minimize doctrinal differences and to maximize social involvement at the community level, the vertical and spiritual dimensions of the debate were completely over-shadowed by the horizontal ones. Some participants wanted to describe the concern for global community as "wider ecumenism"; others felt that the term "ecumenical" should be referred to as an inter-religious one.

The presuppositional thinking of the leaders of this section were never openly acknowledged. It is, however, clear that a very significant change has taken place in ecumenical thinking. The Hendrik Kreemer stress on the "dis-continuity" between the religions of man and the revelation of God which dominated the W.C.C. since the Tambaram Conference, has given way to a sympathetic understanding of universality of God's revelation. The emergence of a theology of "a cosmic Christ" at the New Delhi Assembly and the popularizing of anonymous Christianity by Karl Rahner and others, are factors that have prepared the way for a wider acceptance of a relativistic theology. In this climate there is little sympathy for a unique and final revelation in Christ made known through the written Word of God as the only basis for the salvation of men. The assumption that special revelation is only a particular case of general revelation has always been in the discussion on common spirituality which some implied as "seeking to understand with empathy the dimensions of worship, devotion and meditation in the religious tradition and practice of the partners". Others rejected the term empathy on the grounds that spirituality is not a neutral factor. Christian prayer, for example, cannot be assimilated into other forms of spirituality. The final draft warned against the demonic in any religious or spiritual tradition and expressed a pastoral concern for those who feel threatened by the hazards of sharing spirituality.

A last minute addendum to the report presented to the plenary session was a preamble to the introduction which gave a welcomed emphasis on the need to proclaim the great commission, to recognize the skandalon of the Gospel and to oppose any form of syncretism "incipient, nascent or developed". Strong opposition to this warning came from a number of Asian theologians, some of whom argued that Christianity itself was essentially syncretistic.

In the discussion in this section there was sharp debate on the nature and use of dialogue. Raymond Panikker's statement in the preparatory document that the Christian "puts his trust in truth. He goes unarmed and ready to be himself converted. He may lose his life; he may also be born again", was parallelled by Dr. Samartha's statements in a press conference.

In the areas of culture and ideologies the sectional report reflected many valuable insights shared by participants in the discussions. It stressed the diversity of culture, the secularity of technological culture, the continuity between village and city cultures. The belief that Jesus Christ both affirms and judges culture, that the Church is embodied in culture but not incarnate in it, are some of the contributions that evangelical participants were able to make to the report. It was rightly noted that the present disunity of Christians makes a mockery of the new community in Christ as a model for world community. The discussion on ideologies and the search for community was dominated by participants from Eastern Europe and Cuba. The challenge of Marxist socialism enabling the Church to see its own oppressive structures was discussed. Many questions were raised but few answers given. Unfortunately there was virtually no discussion on biblical eschatology, without which any seeking of the world community can only lead to a false utopia.

CHRISTIANITY AND CULTURAL IDENTITY

The relationship of Christianity to national culture was a recurring theme that pervaded many aspects of the work of the Assembly. The section on Education for Liberation and Community spoke of alienation from culture and national history, and warned that educational systems and institutions are often mirror-images of society reinforcing their practices and values. The increased Third World participation in the Nairobi Assembly brought into sharp focus the tension between Westernized Christianity and national aspirations for self-identity and unity. The urge to harmonize the plurality and cultures in the interests of Christian unity and world community surfaced again and again in group and plenary discussions and in experimentation in forms of worship. It appeared to many observers that the passion for cultural identity eclipsed the concern for faithfulness to biblical truth.

The assembly was made a platform to vent feelings of resentment against the missionary movement as being western, triumphalistic and neo-colonialistic and the fore-runner of new patterns of oppression and of sterile forms of theologican understanding. While it is true that the missionary movement has sometimes been an unwitting tool of Western colonialism and has been insufficiently sensitive to cultural values that are consistent with the biblical revelation, the contribution of the missionary movement to sacrificial service and compassion for suffering and oppressed peoples was unfortunately not heard at Nairobi. Ecumenical preoccupation with the plurality of gospels and with cultural theologies was very evident at Nairobi. Black theology of North America and South Africa emphasizing black consciousness and the recovery of the dignity and power of the black man in self-knowledge was given a sympathetic hearing. Similarly with the Liberation Theologies of Latin America and Asia. African theology emphasizing the dignity of the African through the re-discovery of African culture and practices in African traditional religions naturally received the greatest attention at Nairobi. Professor John Mbiti, a leading exponent of African theology, advocates transposing the immensely religious traditional life of African people into a Christian life style in order to fill the vacuum created by modern technological society. At Nairobi the late Dr. Byang Kato, General Secretary of the Association of Evangelicals of Africa and Madagascar, expressed his concern that the sources for African theology are increasingly becoming African traditional religions rather than the Bible. In their attempt to interpret the pre-Christian and pre-Muslim African experience of their gods, Kato saw African theology heading for syncretism and universalism. He declared that it is not black theology we need, but the application of Christian theology to the African situation. "It is not a black Jesus or a black god we want, but obedience to the omnipotent God of the Bible".

Two events that took place during the Assembly illustrate this tension. The All-Africa Conference of Christian Churches, the co-ordinating structure for ecumenical activities in Africa, took time out of the Assembly for an elaborate and well-prepared ceremony of laying the foundation stone for their proposed 12 million shillings continental headquarters located on the outskirts of Nairobi. The colorful ceremony involving several professional dance groups, centred around the chief guest, President Kenyatta. The proceedings had the aura of a political event rather than one called to give glory to God. The rough-hewn foundation stone dug from Lake Turkana on the Kenya-Ethiopia border where archaeologists have found the oldest human fossils, symbolized that Christianity was being built on the prehistoric civilizations of Africa. The President spoke of the impact of pre-Christian knowledge of our fathers, which influenced and shaped early Christianity in North Africa. He called for the Africanization of the Church and appealed for a return to the genius of authentic cultural traditions. As an observer I felt that Christianity in Africa was in danger of becoming a tool for the furtherance of national aspirations and the uniformity of culture and religion.

The second event was the play Muntu presented on the second day of the Assembly. The AACC had commissioned a Ghanian playwright, now working with the University of Nairobi, to present his interpretation of what Africa's past had to say to Africa's present. Muntu, the word for men in several African languages, and his sons and daughters are in search for community identity and for the essence of BEING free. The play opens with scenes in the pre-Christian era symbolizing men's harmony with nature and the rhythm of the seasons. Comparative peace and happiness reign in the tribal society. The modern tragedy began with the arrival of the Christian missionary holding the cross in one hand and a gun in the other, followed by traders offering bargains in silks, cottons, and with guns and liquor, and by a mining engineer grasping for gold and diamonds, alongside merciless Arab slave traders. The missionary, eager for mass conversions, limits his interests to the spiritual while the colonists defraud the Africans of their land and turn them into slaves. This, in turn, leads to a second cycle of oppression in which Muntu's second son becomes a ruthless military dictator oppressing his own people. In their increasing alienation the people long for the days of their ancestors. At last Muntu himself returns to revive the old religious patters. A powerless messiah, Nana, synthesising Christian and pagan traditions, hovered in the background. The play ends abruptly with despair. Nothing which Africa has learnt or suffered has brought back harmony. The future is dark and unknown. The play raised many important issues but gave a one-sided interpretation of Christianity in Africa. The implicit call to return to pre-Christian culture is no answer to the complexity of the modern world.

The call for moratorium, which has become a major issue in ecumenical thinking since Bangkok, received surprisingly little direct attention during the Assembly, though the AACC had asked for it to be put on the Agenda. Evangelicals are not opposed to moratorium rightly understood, if in particular situations it leads to the strengthening of national leadership, a new thrust in evangelism and church growth and the release of resources for unevangelized areas. The Lausanne Covenant drew attention to this point. The Theological Commission of the AEAN meeting in Nairobi prior to the MCC Assembly, published a statement asking for a theological clarification of the call for moratorium. Unfortunately the statement was given little publicity during the Assembly and provoked little discussion.

THE STRUGGLE FOR LIBERATION
AND THE QUEST FOR HUMAN DEVELOPMENT

Undoubtedly the main focus in the planning of the Nairobi Assembly was the theme of liberation from political, economic, social and personal oppression. This holistic interpretation of liberation articulated at Bangkok pervaded every session of the Assembly. We were faced with the enormity of institutional evils confronted with the specifics of oppression. As Evangelicals we were convicted of our generalizations which often do little more than maintain the status quo. At the same time we were appalled by the lack of awareness in the discussions of God's sovereignty in the world and that He alone can save individuals and nations from destruction. It was a heyday for Pelagianism.

The issues raised were selective. Racism continued to be the number one item on the Agenda. Professor Brown pre-empted the issue with a self-condemnation of himself as one who was white, a male, a member of the affluent class and a citizen of the U.S.A., all of which he called "a litany of shame". The programme to Combat Racism, which was instituted since the Uppsala Assembly, was endorsed and criticism of the misuse of its funds for violent programmes of liberation largely muted. Racism in South Africa was once again singled out for attack and various embargoes proposed. Several multi-national companies were named and condemned for their technical and financial involvement in nuclear collaboration with South Africa. It appears that any hope of change through peaceful reform has been abandoned.

Resolutions calling for the observance of fundamental human rights in several parts of the world were adopted. In Latin America, details of oppression were listed and the governments of Argentina and Chile were singled out for special mention. World powers were asked to respect the autonomy and territorial integrity of Angola. The three liberation movements were only mildly criticized for their failure to establish a unified government along peaceful lines. The rights of the Palestinian people to self-determination were recognized but there was no condemnation of oppressive Arab economic policies nor of the PLC's goal to eliminate Israel as a nation. A plea for the respecting of the holy places in Jerusalem and freedom for each community to worship was accepted. The Assembly appealed for the implementation of the Helsinki agreement: an amendment expressing concern about the restriction of religious liberty in the USSR was carried by an overwhelming majority, but, following strong protests from the Russian delegation, revoked and after much behind-the-scenes debate and a special evening session, a new motion was passed deleting the name of USSR and asking for a report at the first meeting of the Central Committee. In this failure of nerve, many delegates felt the W.C.C. had lost its credibility and forsaken its prophetic function by its selective indignation.

Sexism was singled out as a major social evil. It was argued that as long as women were excluded from decision-making processes, they would be unable to realize their full partnership with man, both in the Church and in society. A change was needed in the theological understanding of equal participation in society, and in relationships, particularly in the family. There was a strong voice in favour of full ordination of women to the ministry. The Assembly set a commendable example in responding to this concern. Thirty percent of the delegates were women, two of the six new Vice-Presidents are women and women shared equally with men in chairing the sessions. However, in all the presentations on sexism, no attempt was made to give a biblical basis to the new stance and only one speaker recognized the existence of deliberate sin in sexism.

The growing gap between the rich and poor nations was rightly recognized as a major issue of our time. The only solution offered to this evil was that of radical, socialistic democracy. This was particularly true of the brilliant address by the Hon. Michael Manley, Prime Minister of Jamaica. Some of the suggestions for public participation and peoples tribunals had a familiar Marxist ring about them.

A plenary address on "Creation, Technology and Human Survival" by Professor Charles Birch, a biologist from Sydney, was by far the most significant paper in the area of human justice. He saw the world as on a titanic collision course. Only a change in direction could avert total disaster. In a well-documented address he outlined five threats to survival, namely, population explosion, which will add a billion people in the next 15 years; food scarcity, in which the present 300 million people now living at starvation level will increase to a billion within 35 years; the rapid depletion of non-renewable resources such as fossil fuels; global pollution which is doubling every 14 years; and the threat of war with stock-piling of atomic bombs. He argued that technology is an uncertain blessing and he appealed for a sustainable global society with zero population growth, zero growth in consumable goods, and zero growth in pollution. He failed to deal adequately with the problem of war.

Birch is an admirer of process theology. Arguing that ecology is an essential element in salvation and evangelism he put his hope in man recognizing the intrinsic value of nature in which God is present. His appeal for a change of heart towards nature fails to grapple with the problem of sin against God and ignores the ultimate hope of the second coming of Christ and the new heaven and new earth.

In a personal discussion with Dr. Birch, he admitted that his position was basically one of pan-entheism which sees God in everything and everything in God, an interlocking relationship between the Personal and the All. Pan-entheism closes the gap between the Creator and the creature, blurs the nature of sin, and has no place for a biblical eschatology. It undergirded the neo-platonism of the medieval mystics and is central to the theologies of Teilhard de Chardin and J.A.T. Robinson. It is at the heart of the movement towards universalism and syncretism and it constitutes the most fundamental theological crisis facing the W.C.C. today.

A CONCLUSION

The W.C.C. faces an acute crisis of faith and ethics. David Edward commented on Uppsala "For the sake of the world, the next Assembly should be more theological". This did not happen at Nairobi. Unless there is a return to truly biblical theology before the next Assembly the W.C.C. ship is on a perilous course. As evangelical theologians we must act responsibly and by God's grace address ourselves to the issues of our contemporary world with a prophetic voice. But we must do more. Our doctrinal understanding must begin with the Word of God and not with the cultural context. We will recognize the priority of a fully-orbed theology of world evangelization which takes seriously the lostness of man. We need a fresh understanding of the Church and its discipling of the nations in relation to the Kingdom of God. We need to recover the First Article clarifying the relationship of God the Creator to God as Saviour, and a renewed emphasis on the cross, the resurrection and salvation by grace alone through faith. In the power of the Holy Spirit we need a new, confident but humble trust in the Lordship of Jesus Christ enabling us to stand against temptation, persecution and death itself. We are called to be faithful interpreters and communicators of the one Gospel. This will inevitably involve costly self-sacrifice.

It is of supreme importance that we Evangelicals who acknowledge the full authority of Scripture stay together as a worldwide community, recognizing the diversity of gifts and ministries that God has given to each of us. We must support those Evangelicals, who, in good conscience and as belonging to member Churches of the W.C.C., accept responsibility to maintain an evangelical witness within the ecumenical structures. We must equally support those Evangelicals, who in good conscience, will continue to remain totally apart from the W.C.C. and who through strictly evangelical structures proclaim the whole counsel of God. May Jesus Christ free and unite us to be His ambassadors of judgment and hope to a dying world.

NOTE

The Rev. Bruce Nicholls' "Nairobi '75: A Crisis of Faith" is specially valuable as an *immediate* reaction of thoughtful Evangelicals who took Nairobi seriously, attended all sessions as observers, and wrote reasoned balanced responses. Were they to write today or tomorrow, they might change a word here or a sentence there; but this is what they did write. It goes into the record just as all the other articles do. This is how the debate sounded as it took place. — The Editor

C. THEOLOGICAL ASSESSMENTS OF THE ECUMENICAL/EVANGELICAL SCHISM
1. Pre-Suppositions in Contemporary Theological Debate

Klaus Bockmuhl

(The Report of the 1975 Consultation
of the Theological Commission of the
World Evangelical Fellowship,
New Delhi, India and Guernsey,
Channel Islands, U.K., pp. 36-43.
Used by kind permission.)

Recent years have seen within Protestant Christianity a growing polarisation between some ecumenical and evangelical thinking.

In speaking of ecumenical theology we positively have to bear in mind that as much as the term "evangelical" covers a number of different theological convictions, so the ecumenical movement continues to comprise a diversity of opinions.

There are more or less independent opinion units within the World Council of Churches, like the confessional Churches. Today theologians of the Eastern Orthodox Churches are increasingly taking on a position of importance where they reserve to themselves the right to openly disagree with certain phenomena and theologoumena of official ecumenism. This was first felt at Uppsala, showed again in Orthodox criticism of the Bangkok mission conference, and can now be seen in Orthodox statements regarding the forthcoming WCC Assembly in Nairobi. Next to the Orthodox Churches there are the Anglican and Lutheran communions which do, though not always, exert theological influence as to co-determine the course of the WCC to a degree in keeping with the weight they carry.

Furthermore, there is often a notable divergence of opinion between church leaders all over the world on one hand, and WCC staff spokesmen on the other. Therefore "ecumenical theology" here is meant to signify the theology of individual theologians or of groups of theologians who have been allowed prominence in the ecumenical movement, especially in the pronouncements made by some of its more prominent officers and in its Geneva staff publications.

It would be false and fatal indeed if we were to identify the Churches with the ecumenical theology described in this paper. Rather has it become necessary again to speak distinctly of the ecumenical movement instead of wrongly thinking of the Churches as mere members of a World Church directed from Geneva.

I. Pre-Suppositions of Some Ecumenical Theology

Thesis: The fundamental pre-supposition of some ecumenical theology in recent years has been the "conversion to the World" (H.J. Schultz), the this-worldly, immanent interpretation of Christianity, and the reduction of theology to anthropology. Although the concerns of man, "the world" and immanence all have a legitimate place within Christian theology, the shifting of interest and expression in some ecumenical theology has been so indiscriminate and onesided that the Christian message has begun to lose its identity. The claims of the world have become more important than the claims of the Gospel.

Man-centredness of theology — this steadily maintained guiding principle is the consequence of the departure point originally chosen. Already in 1950, when J.C. Hoekendijk was in charge of the WCC's study department on mission and evangelization, he sounded the call. Mission has to begin with the study of its vis-a-vis. The addressee became more important than the message. This led to a first wave of influence of sociological, including neo-marxist, theories upon ecumenical theology.

This departure point was later confirmed in W. Hollenweger's statement, "The world sets the agenda". This catchword might (as much as "world" is a term with different meanings in the New Testament) have a good sense, saying that the Church must take care of the actual needs of men like the Good Samaritan. The same phrase, though, in its limitless ambiguity has since been taken to legitimate and demand the acceptance of the values, aims, and intentions of secular modern man.

It has generally been characteristic of the method of approach of some ecumenical theology to "begin with the situation", not with the Gospel. Consequently, the pre-supposition ("the world") has, as is always the case, determined the result. Whoever begins with secular man, ends up with a secularized gospel.

This can be shown from a number of theological concepts.

1. "Salvation" as a central Biblical theme has been re-interpreted as humanisation of man and his world and thus been reduced to this-worldly significance. Hoekendijk began to interpret "salvation" by the O.T. idea of *shalom* instead of the N.T. equivalent *apolutrosis*. He meant to introduce a

total conception of salvation, soul and body, but — as *shalom* describes a state of existence of man, whereas *apolutrosis* described an act of *God* — he also effected a silent change of subject in the concept of salvation from God to man. Salvation takes on earthly colours, and its significance in the perspective of God and eternity falls into disregard.

Immanentism in soteriology in consequence means the reduction of sin to social sin, and of conversion to God to conversion to social action (E. Castro 1966).

2. The same reduction of biblical concepts to this-worldly contents is to be observed in the now dominant ecumenical concepts of liberation and unity as extensions of "salvation". Both are understood in terms of social ethics, both reduced to anthropological categories. Ecumenical documents interpret the phrase "Christ liberates and unites" so that the subject is interpreted by its predicates, but not the predicates by the subject which should determine the contents of the predicates, i.e. liberation and unity.

3. This is proof, too, for the tendency to reduce *Christology* to a standard anthropology. The full and the specific contents of Christology wanes. Christ becomes a code-word for certain this-worldly developments.

4. *Ecclesiology*. In a this-worldly, humanistic theology the Church necessarily takes second place to humanity. Hoekendijk in 1965 (in "The Church for Others" — still the manual for understanding ecumenical theology!) explained the Church as "paroikia" of the world, because the Church has its true oikos or centre not in God but in the world. Thus the Church is reduced to a satellite of the world, revolving around the world as its true centre. The Church becomes a fading phenomenon or perhaps remains as the world's master of ceremonies responsible for arranging its celebrations.

If one can believe reports, J. Moltmann said in Utrecht that any political, economic and religious institution could be allowed to exist only insofar as they made future world peace and world government their purpose. The Church therefore is no longer to have a specific purpose of its own, or a centre beyond the world. Consequently several ecumenical leaders recently stated that the WCC must no longer aim only at the oikumene of Christian Churches, but take on the oikumene of mankind.

5. The same reduction to this worldliness is expressed in the ecumenical notion of *eschatology* which now is an immanent conception of the future, an eschatology of development (M.M. Thomas at Bangkok), with no Return of Christ or Last Judgment as separate entities. Where there (though rare nowadays) is a mention of the Kingdom of God, it means "the accomplishment of the Kingdom of God in history, where the poor will live in affluence and the suppressed will be liberated" — an immanent goal to be attained by men. It is a do-it-yourself eschatology, the Last Things in the hands of man.

6. The guiding principle of immanentism proves itself true even in the

ecumenical concept of *religion*. Today the new emphasis on religious experience is being taken account of and catered for. But it is religious man who generates and dominates that mystique of immanence and the universe which the Dossier I for Nairobi presents and which is well known from the later writings of J.A.T. Robinson. Christ here becomes a mere symbol for many religious productions.

7. Proof of this process of anthropologisation of theology are the remaining terms of contract. There are no more religious, only social antitheses; not God and man, time and eternity, heaven and earth, church and world, immanence and transcendence but suppressors and suppressed — if there is any contrast left at all. God is in fact out as a subject in ecumenical theology. The Great Commandment has been reduced to its second half: love thy neighbour as thyself — the definition of love has been reversed.

8. Behind these examples of a conversion to the world stands as their would-be legitimation the fundamental idea of an ontological concept of salvation of the world. This basic belief in the redemption of the whole world as already fulfilled and effective, appears in form of two theses which seem to be the governing principles of ecumenical theology. One is, as put in the words of C.O. Arevalo, S.J.: "All history is sacred history", and the Church must recognize God's Voice in the demands of men in its time.

The prophetic ministry of the Church is here understood not in the sense of the preaching of repentance, but as the task of the theologically identifying secular forces as God's tools, in analogy to Isaiah's calling (45.1) Kyros God's Messiah. History as revelation, not revelation as history, — this principle is of paramount importance in the pronouncements of Hoekendijk, M.M. Thomas and others, and has served to argue for Christian support of powerful movements of the day.

The other principle is mainly employed to motivate the programme of "dialogue" with other religions and ideologies. God is at work in them, too (Devanandan in N. Delhi 1961, Khodre in Addis Ababa 1971). This means the relativity of truth in all religions.

If the idea of an effective, "cosmic" redemption of all the world is true and if God, as it were, acts predominantly outside the Church, then mission, proclamation of the Gospel, and conversion must be superflous, even highly inappropriate. Where the First General Assembly of the WCC in Amsterdam 1948 still prayed for mission, understood as growth of the Church, as ecumenical concern, today mission is re-interpreted under the direction of tolerance on principle, as reciprocity of witness in dialogue, i.e. the common discovery or the mere search of the truth together.

Wherever we look we see the reduction of the reality and authority of God and His word. This-worldly concern has its degree of truth, but not if it means the change of subject in theology from God to man, as is observed in some ecumenical theology. Here theology has been given its field in inter-human relationships. "Humanisation" as a programme for action has secretly been matched by anthropologisation as the principle of theory. It is man's sovereignty instead of God's. The WCC is made to look like a Human Rights Movement with mystical overtones.

If predominant ecumenical theology today is characterized by "conversion to the world" and by the tendency to thoroughly elevate men to be the subject of theology and the measure of all things to whom the message has to be adjusted and accommodated, then this theology is essentially another version of well-known earlier *theological liberation*.

Theological liberation puts man into the centre of theology. "To speak about God is to speak about man" (Bultmann). It is a liberal theological stance to neglect the gulf between God and man, the sinner and convert, the Christian message on reconciliation of God and man into a programme of Social Gospel. Liberalism makes Christ nothing but the great example of humanity, minimizes the role of the Church, and in all its different fashions consequently alters biblical eschatology in order to make it fit into immanence.

Liberalism makes possible the idea of history as revelation (Gogarten), thinks a mystique of the immanent a splendid solution of the problem of religion (Schleiermacher) and has pioneered the revelation of truth in all religions. Wrote E. Troeltsch: "Missions in the traditional sense has to be replaced by the mutual recognition and common development of those basic religious truths which all these systems contain", and the notorious document "Re-Thinking Missions" (U.S. 1932) described the relationship between the different religions as a common search for truth. "The Christian will look forward, not to the destruction of these religions, but to their continued co-existence with Christianity, each stimulating the other in growth toward the ultimate goal, unity in the completest religious truth."

Theological liberalism has always been the programme of *mediation* between Christianity and secular culture, even (and mostly) at the price of reducing God to a peculiar Christian interpretation symbol of immanent world phenomena and events that are happening anyway. If theological liberalism was the accommodation of Christianity to the supremacy of the Enlightenment, some of today's ecumenical theology may be seen as the adaptation programme of Christianity for what is called today's "second enlightenment". It is the genuflection of theology before secularism and — if such a thing were possible — the adjustment of Christianity to the modern Kingdom of Man.

Not its rationalism (it may perhaps soon become irrationalist), not its internationalism (it may perhaps soon become nationalist or even racist — if the proposed "search for self-identity" and "God at work in the longings of people" are valid), — not its contents, but its method and principle, the acceptance of secular man as its departure point is the characteristic pre-supposition of much of contemporary ecumenical theology.

II. Pre-Suppositions of Contemporary Evangelical Theology

When it comes to the subject of evangelical theology we encounter greater difficulties in laying hands on the hare. One can easily sense the difference between, say, German pietism, and Anglican evangelicalism with its strong reformational scripture orthodoxy.

Another difficulty arises in that we cannot base our consideration on documents uttered by some central authority or bureau when it comes to determining the common characteristic of Evangelicals. Moreover, there is the deeper problem that Evangelicals have not always been particularly passionate and explicit in matters of doctrine and definition! An attempt at describing must be made though, even if it should be coloured by the continental European outlook of the present writer.

A good concise description of the fundamentals of evangelical theology is given by Bishop Lilje when in his autobiography he says about Evangelicals: "Their essential common characteristic is their determination to stick to the witness of the biblical Christ." This covers a good bit of ground.

1. Evangelicals believe that God revealed Himself in Jesus Christ, and not all over the place. Christ is at the centre and His work of redemption holds the highest place. This means that the Gospel is primarily the message of reconciliation of man with God as taught by Jesus (in the Parable of the Prodigal Son) and St. Paul (II Cor. 5). This reconciliation is effected in Christ's innocent suffering and death at the Cross. i.e. His vicarious suffering for us.

2. Evangelicals believe in the necessity of a man's *personal relationship* to the redeeming work of Christ, "personal" meaning an individual acceptance of God's grace in Christ by faith, not just through membership of an institution, and b) reconciliation with God as a conscious existential experience of life, i.e. conversion, and not just as a matter of intellectual cognisance.

Christ's redemptive work has to be accepted, and John 3:15 and II Cor. 5:19f are taught without the curtailments known from the ecumenical concept of "cosmic redemption". Evangelical theology basically thinks in terms of sin and grace, lostness and conversion. Its eschatology of catastrophe, visible return of Christ, final judgment and eternal life becomes the framework, even the motivation of its preaching of redemption.

Not only is there to be a personal relationship to Christ's saving work of Golgotha, but also an individual and existential relationship to the living Christ which is manifested in a life of prayer and sanctification.

3. Bishop Lilje is also right in stressing the "biblical Christ". Evangelicals do not eclectically take Christ as a symbol of better humanity, or revolution, or as a code-word for our various religious experiences. Christ as He is fully described in the *Bible* is the standard. "The biblical Christ means Christology

according to the Scriptures. The authority validity and sufficiency of the Scriptures is therefore a fundamental pre-supposition of all evangelical thinking.

4. Also *"witness"* is a specific and essential evangelical concept. Christ's sufferings for us are not to be kept in the storage of theology; they need to be proclaimed to every human being. Evangelicals underline the importance of the Great Commandment of Christ (Matt. 28) and stress the need for mission and evangelization (in the sense of proclamation of the Word, to be sure). This again presupposes that the dualism of church and world is not to be resolved before Christ's second coming; the two are thoroughly distinct bodies.

It would be an over-simplification to say that today's Evangelicalism is a straight successor to that Biblicism which opposed and proved an alternative to theological liberalism at the beginning of this century. It is too little conscious of the task of theology for that. Moreover evangelicalism proper with its slightly exclusive concentration on soteriology and eschatology lacks a theology of the First Article, of creation and providence. What would be the religious value of other religions in evangelical theology, what its stance on dialogue and indigenisation? What is the meaning of nationhood, what the legitimate place of "finding one's self-identity and expressing it"? And what would now be the place of the prophetic ministry of the Church in society and of social ethics — even if they are *not* the same as salvation in the biblical sense, but belong to creation ethics?

Also, evangelicalism partly lacks a theology of the Third Article. It has little to say about the person and work of the Holy Spirit (but seems to participate in the "honourable shyness", if not nervousness of the Churches of the Reformation when it comes to pneumatology) and not much more as to the doctrines of the Church and the sacraments.

Even in its very central field, the authority of Scripture, one finds few reasoned and universal theological presentations.

This is due to the fact that evangelicalism always being more bent to the practical tasks of Christian living, its theological thinking — if there is any at all — often is more a kind of sentiment and conviction, less a developed, thought-through, and ready representation of the teachings of the Bible.

This is a sore point. Great changes happen first in books, then in seminaries and lastly in the broad reality of denominational life. The same is also true for the strengthening and quickening of a Church. Evangelicalism, as one can see in the history of many formerly evangelical seminaries, organizations, or periodicals, has paid and is still paying a high price for its negligence of the task of theology. It has experienced the sad moments of mourning: "Those that I have swaddled and brought up hath mine enemy consumed" (Lam. 2:23). And also in the future, as Gottfried Osei-Mensah said at Lausanne, the existence or non-existence of vital evangelical theology may be decisive for the turn Christianity takes, e.g. in Africa.

Pre-suppositions of evangelical theology surely exist but they need to be spelled out in disciplined, sustained, and patient theological effort.

III. Appendix: Analogies of Polarization With Roman Catholic Theology

Contradictions similar to those between ecumenical and evangelical theology which are no longer merely the contrasting extremes of the same comprehensive biblical truth, seem to be existing within Roman Catholic theology.

Roman Catholicism today may be characterized by theoretically three different positions. *One* is the theology of the Second Vatican Council which stressed the need of renewal of Catholic theology through a new encounter with the Bible, thus relieving theology from the overall dominance of tradition. But this position which might conceivably be a partner of evangelicalism in several aspects of theology, today seems to exist only theoretically. There are strong centrifugal forces at work in the Roman Catholic Church. A polarization is under way, and the theology of the Second Vatican Council could easily become an uninhabited middle between two strong wings that grow more and more apart.

The second stream of thought is theological liberalism which characterizes much of today's prominent Roman Catholic theological publications. The *aggiornamento* slogan of Pope John XXIII has sent the younger elite of Catholic theologians not only to the Bible, but beyond to Bible criticism and the whole liberal reign of reason. (This could easily be shown from the development of Catholic moral theology since 1905). There is a kind of Bible criticism, individual liberty of thinking and teaching, a contestation of the central church authority, and also an embrace of the "Social Gospel" which thoroughly resembles the mind of modern Protestantism. There is the idea of "latent Christendom" outside the Church to match the ecumenical notion of "cosmic redemption", and also the pronouncement that salvation in its full sense may be found in other religions, too.

Hans Kung's devout and mild rationalism is based on a critical meditation of the Scriptures, a meditation for which the miracle of the feeding of the 5000 and many other Gospel relations are legendary. His factual disregard of the binding power of tradition as shown in his latest book ("On Being Christian", 1974), proves that Kung is a Protestant, and in many ways a liberal one.

Others describe Catholicism as "the best Protestantism that ever was", and Schleiermacher, the chief witness of liberal theology and its mediation of Christianity and culture, looms behind ever so many definitions of Catholic theologians who seems to have decided for a kind of "modern churchmanship".

It is this spirit that dominates the books and the faculties of Roman Catholic theology. Bishops take a more moderate position, and the Pope has more than once expressed apprehension and anxiety over the developments. "The Church and its theologians" is as much of a problem in Rome today as it was and still is in Protestant denominations. It remains a deep question whether it will be possible for the authorities to stop this torrent of theological modernism and recover the ancient doctrinal unity, with measures like censorship or a global anti-modernist legislation as in 1910.

There are also, thirdly, some ultra-conservative groupings in the Roman Church for whom even the present authorities in Rome are too liberal and in whose eyes the Pope is in the hands of evil counsellors. But they exercise little influence due to the fact that all major means of communication seem to be in the hands of the liberal party.

IV. Conclusion

The decline of some ecumenical theology began with the justified request "The whole Gospel for the whole man!", but with a onesided interest and expression of the "whole man". Today we need to again stress not only the whole man, body *and* soul, individual *and* community, but "the whole Gospel", this and the other world, man and God, life on earth, and the life of resurrection. It is no good, in reaction to some otherworldly phase in the history of Christendom, to reduce Christianity to thisworldliness. Our task is to live *here for there,* but not to replace the former by the latter or vice-versa. When it comes to the will, it is God's will only, and not God's will and man's will.

In short, we need to make God again the subject and object of theology. A conversion of theology is certainly needed, but not its conversion to the world, rather a simple conversion to God. Theology's true themes are God's sovereignty. His great deeds and His commandments, His heaven and His earth — *His* earth. Theology needs to be turned Godwards again. It should, true to its definition and destiny, teach again the knowledge and the love of God. We need to help theology back to its proper sources and purpose; to the Scriptures and to prayer, and to the upbuilding of Christians and the Church.

For Evangelicals it means to take up the task of theology altogether and to provide Christendom with a public theological alternative to the secularism, both sacred and secular, that now prevails.

NOTES

1. See "Confessing Christ — In Orthodox Theology", Background Material for 5th General Assembly of the WCC, Nairobi 1975, Dossier for Section 1.
2. Study based on findings of my book, *Was heisst heute Mission? Entscheidungsfragen der neuren Missionstheologie,* Giessen and Basel 1974.
3. See Background Materials for Nairobi.
4. Dossier for Section 1 at Nairobi, German edit. p. 64.
5. Ibid, p. 55.
6. As quoted by N.H. Soe in his *Christliche Ethic.* *62.2nd Germ. edit., Munich 1957, p. 400.

7. In his thought-provoking recent essay, "Lausanne between Geneva and Berlin", Peter Beyerhaus has suggested that there are at least six different groups or attitudes of "Evangelicalism". He discerns the "New Evangelicals" around Billy Graham, as opposed by, secondly, the Fundamentalists of the ICCC. A third group (for which I presume Peter Beyerhaus would stand himself) are the "Confessing Evangelicals" who take a more confessional stand in matters of church and doctrine. Then there are the Pentecostalists, the "Radical Evangelicals" stressing socio-political commitment, and finally some "Ecumenical Evangelicals" who are not on principle at variance with the present outlook and course of the WCC. See W. Kunneth/P. Beyerhaus (ed.)l *Reich Gottes oder Weltgemeinschaft*, 1975, pp. 294-313).

8. "Memorabilia", 1973, p. 241.

C. THEOLOGICAL ASSESSMENTS OF THE ECUMENICAL/EVANGELICAL SCHISM
2. *Two Theologies of Mission Battle for Control*

Donald McGavran

("The Christian Herald"
Grand Rapids, November 75, p. 10)

Responsiveness to the Gospel in Africa, Asia, Latin America was never greater. David Livingstone and William Carey would rejoice at its magnitude. Substantial expansion of the Christian faith has been going on for more than twenty years in Sub-Saharan Africa, Korea, Brazil and other regions. Much more could occur. The potential is tremendous.

At just this time, however, two sharply contrasting theologies of mission are battling for control of the mission apparatus. The outcome will determine whether, in the century which lies ahead, great non-Christian populations in all continents are won to Christ, or whether the Christian faith is sealed off to those peoples who now confess it. Yet most Christians are blissfully unaware of the potential struggle.

Most Christians support missions more strongly than any other cause. That about three billion of the earth's four billion are living (and dying) without confessing Christ is for Christians reason enough to pray for missions, give to missions, and encourage their sons and daughters to become missionaries. Most Christians imagine that missions consist very largely of proclaiming the Gospel, leading people of other lands to believe on Christ, and become reliable members of his Church. Christians are aware, of course, that mission work is varied — medical, educational, agricultural and evangelistic — but are confident that the purpose of all forms is that men and women become disciples of Christ and heirs of abundant and eternal life. The net outcome of Christian missions is, they think, that churches of Jesus Christ multiply to the great benefit of the human race. American churches think that the typical missionary puts most of his time and money into propagating the Gospel. That he does not do so would surprise them. That a theology of missions has been developed which affirms on theological grounds that he *ought not to* would dismay them. To observe *"missions"* in which not five dollars in a hundred sent to the missionary society goes (through missionaries or younger Churches) into gospel-proclaiming, church-multiplying missions would greatly distress them.

Particularly would most Christians be offended by the fact that this theology (which diverts attention from evangelism and focusses it on social action, de-emphasizes conversion and baptism, and plays down the multiplication of churches throughout the non-Christian world) has gained control of many missionary societies precisely at a time when, in many populations and many cultures, multitudes are in the valley of decision and can be won to Christ.

The new theology in effect snatches defeat out of the jaws of victory. Missions today face many exterior obstacles — collapse of Western empires, the rise of nationalism, inflation, the spread of Marxism, and the like. But the obstacle most likely to arrest the vivifying spread of the Good News is one inside the Church — a new theology of missions which affirms that evangelism and the multiplication of cells of believers are not nearly as important as it is for Christians everywhere to practice brotherhood, fight for peace, share the wealth, smash iniquitous social structures, and bring in the Kingdom of God. Let me now describe the new theology of mission and contrast it with the classic.

The new theology, with roots going back some decades, formed a coherent whole and was espoused by many leaders and their societies during the years 1955-1965. It surfaced as the only right "mission policy" at the Fourth Assembly of the World Council of Churches at Uppsala in 1968. It has been in the saddle of the conciliar wing of the Church ever since. It carried the day at the Fifth Assembly of the World Council of Churches at Nairobi, Kenya, November 20 to December 10, 1975.

First to recognize the new theology and to draw up a declaration on world mission on the (contrasting) biblical base was the great Wheaton Congress in April 1966. Its proceedings are published in a volume entitled THE CHURCH'S WORLDWIDE MISSION.

I myself, who in 1965 had spent forty-two years in a conciliar mission, only in 1967 saw clearly that a whole new theology of mission had been formed and become official! I had considered the deviations which kept appearing in the late fifties and early sixties to be abberations of certain leaders. I expected that when these errors were pointed out they would be renounced. But in the spring of 1968 the mass of evidence finally convinced me that a well-constructed erroneous theology of mission had seized control of much of the mission apparatus and would dismantle the missionary movement and halt the spread of the Gospel.

As editor of the CHURCH GROWTH BULLETIN, I took the bold step of devoting the whole May 1968 issue to the subject. I addressed an Open Letter to the World Council of Churches in a symposium of articles authored by Drs. Winter, Tippett and myself. Mine was entitled, "Will Uppsala Betray the Two Billion?" Readers of the *Church Herald* can watch the two theologies join battle by reading THE EYE OF THE STORM (Word Books). It prints without comment fourteen articles written by advocates of the classical theology of missions and fourteen by advocates of the new. It is vigorous debate. Opinions clash and blood is drawn.

Since that time, scores of articles voicing one position or another, have appeared in journals read by leaders of missions, missiologists and theologians. The practicing Christians who contribute more than 300 million dollars a year in North America alone for missions have, however, remained largely unaware of the struggle. They find it difficult to believe that such a large shift of theology could take place. It is time that those who carry on mission by their sacrificial giving got thoroughly well-acquainted with the new theology of mission. It determines the policies, budget distributions, missionary sendings, kinds of work, goals sought, and a thousand other activities paid for by them.

To be sure, there are not two clear-cut theologies. Rather, there are two groups of theologies, each composed of many different schools and shades of opinion. Mission, in the midst of the vast mosaic of mankind, is a coat of many colors. Multitudinous tasks make up "missions". Nevertheless, it is essential today to identify two basic theological positions, recognizing that different schools of thought will be found within each and that in some cases it may be difficult to assign a specific school of thought to one or the other of the major positions described.

These two positions are complicated. It takes me twenty hours of lecture time to describe them. In compressing description to the small compass of one article, I can scarcely hope to avoid over-simplification.

One hallmark of the new theology of missions is the substitution of humanization for Christianization. Oh, to be sure, the "new" missiologists still talk about God, but without taking His commands and promises as revealed in the whole Bible seriously. Thus the great Bangkok meeting which affirmed that "Salvation Today" means very largely this-worldly improvements, based its argument exclusively on Old Testament texts, which do say that God "saved" his people by giving them quails, water, victory over enemies, and the like. Bangkok, neglecting Acts 4:12 and similar passages, concluded that "salvation" meant temporal improvements.

In 1968 the World Council of Churches in its Commentary to the Geneva Draft for Section 2 wrote:

> We have lifted up humanization as the goal of mission because we believe that more than other (positions) it communicates in our period of history the meaning of the messianic goal. In another time, the goal of God's

redemptive work might best have been described in terms of men turning toward God . . . The fundamental question was that of the true God, and the Church responded to that question by pointing to him. It was assuming that the purpose of mission was Christianization, bringing man to God through Christ and his Church. Today the fundamental question is much more that of TRUE man and the dominant concern of the missionary congregation must therefore be to point to the humanity in Christ as the goal of mission (page 34).

Peter Beyerhaus in MISSIONS WHICH WAY says,

This radical displacement of the center from God to man and the replacement of theology by anthropology is not a painful slip by some extremists of the theology of secularization. Rather, it has become the declared program according to such key figures in the World Council of Churches as M.M. Thomas, the chairman of the Central Committee . . . This "focus on the human and the human situation" appears to me to be the crucial — in fact the disastrous — turning point in the present course of the ecumenical movement (pages 86-87).

Incidentally, no one has written more cogently or more fairly to the critical situation in the theology of missions today (which affects not merely the World Council of Churches, but the mission apparatus of most mainline denominations) than Professor Beyerhaus of Tubingen University, a Lutheran and a well-known missionary leader. His MISSIONS WHICH WAY and SHAKEN FOUNDATIONS are fascinating and essential reading.

Sharply contrasting with the new theology, is the classical theology of mission, which believes that the central question in all classes and conditions of man is how man may be justified before God and may have communion with him. This question, classical theology believes, is neither outmoded nor old fashioned, and is the key to effective humanization.

This central question rests on what men believe about the Bible. In 1968, I wrote in the INTERNATIONAL REVIEW OF MISSIONS,

The central thrust of the New Testament wells up in passages like Matthew 28:19; Romans 1:5; John 14:6; I John 5:12; Romans 10:11-15; and II Corinthians 5:18ff. HOW AUTHORITATIVE ARE THEY? *(Eye of the Storm,* 181).

Christians who believe that these are ultimate truth and utterly dependable, who believe the Bible is the only sufficient rule of faith and practice, inevitably agree that Christians should work and pray that all men may have the opportunity to accept Jesus Christ as Lord and Saviour and become his disciples and responsible members of his Church.

The new theology does not take these and other similar passages seriously and in consequence does not believe that it makes an eternal difference whether men accept the Lord Jesus and are baptized in the triune name. Thus it finds fault with evangelism and church growth as simplistic, unaware of modern scholarship, behind the times, out of touch with reality, and wrong on a thousand counts. Thus the highway is made ready for mission to become NOT Christianization but humanization. With humanization as the goal, we can welcome as comrades all those (of whatever religious faith or lack of faith) who are working against oppression and for brotherhood.

Classical mission has, to be sure, always worked for the liberation of men and the spread of justice and brotherhood. No force in India has struck more powerful blows for the eradication of untouchability than Christian missions. The disappearance of slavery from Africa would have been impossible without classical mission with its deeply biblical theology. Where Christ is enthroned in the heart, social amelioration follows. Never as much as it might, never as much as God wants, but in beginning and in promise LIBERATION OCCURS.

It will occur much more as Christ's Church, conscious of its divine mandate, disciples larger and larger segments of mankind. Once they are enrolled, they will be instructed and will be indwelt by the Holy Spirit. Never as much as they might be, never as much as God wants, but still in substantial measure. Classical theology of mission has always stressed Christian nurture and the practice of a Christian way of life; but classical theology of mission has always insisted that before you can have many college graduates, you must enroll large numbers of children in the first grade. Before you can build skyscrapers, you must have reinforced concrete. Mud bricks won't do. The essential thing is that persons become committed to Jesus Christ, baptized and conscious members of his Church. AFTER THAT the indwelling Holy Spirit, the magnificent teachings of the Scriptures, the insights and proddings of the world Church, and the providential guidance of God the Father Almighty, will bring in (and ARE bringing in) many temporal improvements, much growth in grace, many beneficial structures of society and much more of God's rule on earth.

To summarize, I quote what I wrote in the CHURCH GROWTH BULLETIN:

> Two radically different systems of doctrine are battling for acceptance. The one believes that the Bible is the inspired, authoritative, infallible Word. The other believes that the Bible is the words of men through which God speaks on occasion. The one believes in eternal salvation as well as temporal improvements. The other believes that temporal improvements are certain, but beyond them we are in the realm of speculative opinions. The one believes that the Church is the Bride of Christ. The other, that the Church is one of God's many instrumentalities to bring about a juster social order. The one believes that no man comes to the Father but by Jesus Christ as revealed in the Bible, and consequently proclaims him as divine and only Saviour. The other, that the Cosmic Christ has spoken and is

speaking in all religions and consequently dialogue with other religions is the correct way of mission. The one believes that the Kingdom of God will come only as God himself destroys the enemies of mankind at the last day, and that until then only limited justice and righteousness are possible. The other believes that a new, just world order can be brought about by the cooperation of men of good will in all religions. The list of contrasts is much longer. A division as deep and lasting as that which took place in Europe in the sixteenth century may be imminent, but we hope it can be avoided.

Laymen and ministers should determine what kind of mission they intend to carry on. Blind support of any kind of "mission" is foolish. Find out what theology underlies the missions you support. What views of God, the Bible, the cross, justice, salvation, eternal life, the Kingdom of God, the Church, and justification underlie the missions you pray for and give to? They make a tremendous difference in the outcome you can expect. "Are grapes gathered from thorns or figs from thistles?"

C. THEOLOGICAL ASSESSMENTS OF THE ECUMENICAL/EVANGELICAL SCHISM

3. Berlin Versus Geneva: Our Relationship with the "Evangelicals"*

Hendrikus Berkhof

The people we now refer to as "evangelicals", and who used to be simply orthodox evangelicals of a confessional or pietistic type, have always played their part in the ecumenical movement and in the World Council of Churches. In the course of the Fifties, however, if I am not mistaken, they became a problem which has found a permanent place on the agendas of various WCC commissions ever since. Up to the time of Uppsala the problem still lay dormant and attracted little attention. But from at least 1970 onwards it became a burning issue, and today it is not just a problem we have on our hands but a war. On both sides people have come to the conclusion that one is *either* an evangelical *or* a friend of the World Council of Churches.

The leading part in this concentration of the forces of evangelicalism has been played by German theologians. The underlying basis appears to me to be a combination of confessional Lutherans and pietism. Both these have deep roots in German history past and present. But the contemporary movement takes its bearings mainly from The Barmen Declaration of 1934 rather than from the classic confessional documents. This could be significant. In the Thirties, the attitude of these circles to the Barmen confession of faith was often lukewarm and even one of suspicion. Today it is quite different. The Barmen Declaration has clearly provided the model for both the Frankfurt and Berlin Declarations. This does not mean that the classic confessions have been superseded. The object now is exactly the same as that of the fathers in Barmen, namely, to restate the substance of

---

*Comments on the book Reich Gottes Oder Weltgemeinschaft (Kingdom of God or World Community): The Berlin Ecumenical Manifesto on the Utopian Vision of the World Council of Churches. Dr. Berkhof is the Professor of Dogmatic Theology at Leiden University and President of the Netherlands National Council of Churches.

these classical confessions in the form of a positive affirmation of faith accompanied by a polemical repudiation of false teaching. Such a clear trumpet call, it was hoped, would rally true confessors all over the world, whatever their individual confessional background and prepare them for the struggle.

This objective was obviously not sufficiently realized. Peter Beyerhaus' article on "Lausanne between Berlin and Geneva" — to my mind the most important in the book — helps to explain why not. All who wish to be ecumenically informed today should read it. It contains an absorbing passage in which Beyerhaus divides the evangelicals into six groups or tendencies (pp. 307 ff). He labels the group to which he himself belongs "the confessing evangelicals". "They take a more confessional view of the Church than the neo-evangelicals and lay great emphasis in particular on the contemporary confession of the faith in the form of a repudiation of the heresies of our time" (p. 308). He frankly acknowledges that most Anglo-Saxon and third world evangelicals found this aspect of repudiation, this insistence on a firm decision to oppose the heresies of the WCC, too much for them. Hence the appearance of this full-length Berlin book, intended as an amplifier for the Berlin Declaration.

THE NATURE OF THE BOOK

Despite the title, the attack is not directed solely against the World Council of Churches but also against the Lutheran World Federation, the World Student Christian Federation, certain Catholic groups, the German Evangelical KIRCHENTAG, Taize, and to some extent even Lausanne. But the main focus is on the WCC. To obviate the danger of debiting all statements indiscriminately to the WCC's account, the second half of the book (pp. 373-513) consists of many quotations, frequently lengthy, and many others occur in the body of the text. These quotations are in many cases sprinkled with asterisks. Five asterisks signify fully official statements; one asterisk indicates that the quotation is a personal statement by an individual theologian. The use of this system is an attempt on the part of the editors to play fair with the people they criticize, a sincerity not always in evidence in the attacks of some others. Yet the application of the system is often questionable. Why, for example, assign three asterisks to statements made by the Lutheran World Federation, which takes full responsibility for its own pronouncements, and in this way equate them with statements made by "officers of the WCC"? (This serves to conceal the fact that Werner Schilling is unable to cite any WCC statements in support of his thesis of an "ecumenical enthusiasm for Mao".) Again, why are two asterisks (signifying "personal statements by ecumenical delegates") assigned to a Muslim speaker in Ajaltoun (p. 456) and on another page even four asterisks (p. 225)?

In the first half of the book we have, firstly, the full version of the Berlin Declaration and related documents (pp. 16-73), and then twenty articles, most of which expand some section of the Berlin Declaration but others of which have previously been published in a different context (among the latter, Soloviev's short story of the Antichrist). In style and value there is a great unevenness between the articles. Bishop Graber's essay on "Ecumenism and Secret Societies" does not really belong here at all. Jean G.H. Hoffmann's two articles are more demagogic in character. The articles on Marxism in M.M. Thomas and on the Maoism of the WCC provide no proof whatever of what their titles insinuate. But other articles, especially those of Wisloff, Grunzweig, Rugg, F.W. Künneth and Byang Kato, present severe but substantial attacks which must be taken seriously.

The common bond between all the articles is the desire to demonstrate that the WCC no longer seeks the proclamation of the Gospel throughout the world, but strives rather for a purely horizontal social and political humanization and unification of mankind by means of religious pluralism and syncretism. Unwearyingly, the authors point out again and again that with such a programme the WCC is on the way to Antichrist. They believe that the last days are just around the corner (the word "apocalyptic" frequently appears) and that in the decisive hour the World Council will stand on the side of the enemies of Christ. We need only look at the picture on the dust-jacket and read the well-known essay by Soloviev!

DIALOGUE THE BEST WAY

What should our reply be to these very serious accusations? The easiest solution would be to pinpoint and demolish the (very numerous) weaknesses in the argument. All this would achieve, however, would be to reinforce the convictions of the already convinced and to harden positions still further. Even if our opponents were no longer to regard us as Christians in any real sense, it would be quite impossible for us to return the compliment. This means we are obliged to continue the discussion and to do so indeed more seriously and humbly than before. We are fond of talking of dialogue in the WCC. Here is an excellent and urgent opportunity to show how far we are ready for the demands and the risk of such a dialogue.

It will lighten our task if we keep the following points in mind:

1. Our opponents here are not fundamentalists of the International Council of Christian Churches. They try to be fair and honest. They follow the work of the WCC with the closest attention. Some of them have previously cooperated in the World Council or one of its agencies.

2. They are also aware of good points. In particular they take a favourable view of "Faith and Order". Earlier (under Visser't Hooft), it is said, things were in general much better. (But the good that still exists in the WCC today cannot mitigate the severity of the verdict; it is precisely the amalgam of good

and evil, of faith and apostasy, which constitutes the demonic character of the World Council!)

3. The controversy which appears here is not new but coeval with the ecumenical movement itself. Consider the opposition between Anglo-Saxon and European or German ways of thinking in Stockholm 1925. (Hoffmann's contrast on p. 88 between "the original inspiration" of Stockholm and the later politicization is therefore completely false; today's tensions were present from the very outset, as a task to be tackled.)

4. Nor can the controversy be dismissed as a purely domestic German affair. In its theological form it is typically German but in doctrinal content it is ecumenical. Not only in Europe and North America but equally even in Eastern Europe, Asia, Africa and Latin America we find countless Christians with the same strongly held suspicions of the World Council of Churches or at any rate the same type of evangelical faith. We in the WCC must resist the temptation to allow strategic differences (Lausanne) to induce us to underestimate the real spiritual bond between these evangelicals.

5. The German language is entirely different from the English language. The former could be described as "categorical", the latter as "pragmatic". Kraemer once told me how difficult it was to explain to an Anglo-Saxon audience the controversy between Barth and Brunner about the ANKNUPFUNGSPUNKT because the English equivalent "point of contact" is a common expression without any theological stress. In this book I sense the existence of the same problem at every step. In the German language, words like "neue Menschheit, Dialog, Ideologie, Revolution, Utopia, Gruppendynamik", and so on, have a deep, almost metaphysical undertone which is not present in their English equivalents. It must always be remembered that the vocabulary of the WCC has been derived from the English "language game".

6. At the same time it is equally important to remember that there has been in many respects a substantial shift in the WCC since, say, 1965. The chief cause of this shift has not lain in the WCC itself but in the rapid growth of tension between the First and Third Worlds. The Council has taken this to be a central challenge to which it has responded by increasing its statements and activities in the field of social and political ethics. New concepts like "development", "revolution", "racism", "liberation" advance to the centre of the stage. The press and other public media take a much closer interest in, and in a few years convey to the public a quite new "image" of, the WCC. Does this mean that there has been a fundamental change in the Council? The Berlin people think it does. Or does all this simply add up to a provisional response to a "command of the hour"? A response in which the basic conceptions which sustain the WCC (basis, doctrinal discussion, mission, help to the distressed, and so on) are still pre-supposed and continue always to survive the adaptations and developments which are provisionally called for on this side or that? Here it seems to me is one major question for

the dialogue between the World Council and the evangelicals. In this dialogue both groups can only deepen their understanding.

SHIFT IN WCC EMPHASIS

I deliberately said "one" major question. If the World Council takes its opponent seriously, it finds THE major question elsewhere. A Dutch theologian of the last century, caught up in the struggle between different church parties, once wrote: "Appropriate the truth contained in an error and you appropriate for yourself its strength!" That should really be the golden rule for all church controversy and apologetics. But for the most part these consist in efforts of self-justification which are bound to remain unfruitful. Only the self-criticism which lets itself be corrected and enriched by the other party can be fruitful. For me, therefore, the main question presented to us by the Berlin "Black Book", is this: What truth do we have to learn from it?

The origin and the history of the World Council of Churches have been shaped by many forces but by none so deeply as by Anglo-Saxon Protestantism, with its amalgam of Calvinist theocracy, British pragmatism and the optimistic American belief in progress. European theology has certainly exercised its influence but more as a corrective than as an inspiration. And German Lutheran theology has undoubtedly been the one to feel its critical remoteness most deeply. It senses here that "fanaticism" which for Lutherans is the greatest of errors because it confuses the Word and the Spirit, the Kingdom of God and the kingdom of this world, emphasizes sanctification at the expense of justification and regards the future more as a human task than as the gift of God. From Stockholm to Uppsala and since, European theology and especially that of German Lutheranism has raised here a warning finger, without, however, being able to offer any alternative to the existing plan.

From 1965 onwards, the Anglo-Saxon forces acquired, as I have already indicated, fresh momentum because, much more than other constituents of the WCC, they have the possibility of a positive and creative response to the growing challenge of the Third World.

But there is a negative side to this development and a price to be paid I fear that we in the World Council of Churches are still far from being sufficiently concerned about this. Berlin accuses Geneva of "ideologizing" and I believe they are right. But we need to make a distinction here. An ideology is not in itself a bad thing. It is in fact the choice of perspectives, goals and rules which enables us to tackle a situation actively and formatively. An ideology in the sense of a conscious choice of principles from the Gospel is simply essential for programmes of a social and ethical kind. In this sense even Barmen was an ideology. But there is always the danger that such a choice is no longer regarded as a temporary selection from the richness of God's Word, a selection which must constantly be understood in terms of the Word of God, inspired, criticized and relativized by the richness of that Word. Otherwise the ideology becomes an idol. Many evangelical terms such as justice, renewal, reconciliation, fellowship, liberation, etc., have acquired an ideological function in the World Council of Churches. With a view to their social and ethical utility they take on a much more restricted meaning than is proper to them in biblical usage; "righteousness" then becomes not so much the righteousness which is given as the righteousness which is demanded; "liberation" not so much deliverance from our own sins but rather from the social and political sins of others, and so on.

Not that the biblical plus-value is ever denied in this ideological restriction. But in the long run it cannot be merely presupposed without the loss of its critical and de-ideologizing force. I see here a great danger for the WCC which we can only escape if we first become fully aware of its existence. The conclusion I would draw from this is that we must have done with our "genitive theologies" (theology of development, of liberation, or revolution, etc.) because not only do they contain no prophylactics against ideologization but they actually serve to rationalize the ideals we have acquired from outside the Word of God.

The same point can be made in another way. It is possible to draw up a list of concepts which are, so to speak, writ large in the WCC and another list of those which are writ small, as for example:

FRUITS OF FAITH	root of faith
RANGE OF SALVATION	centre of salvation
OUR RESPONSIBILITY	God's action
SPIRIT	Word
CONVERGENCE WITH THE WORLD	opposition to the world
PENULTIMATE HOPES	the ultimate hope
DEVELOPMENT	conversion
FINAL GOAL	the way of the cross
and so on.	

For a time this relationship of large and small may be ideologically justified but, as I see it, it has no adequate basis in Scripture and is therefore in the long run not justified.

NO ALTERNATIVES OFFERED

The next question would concern the consequences of this necessary shift and extension of emphasis for the WCC's action in the field of social ethics. I do not believe that it would point us in a fundamentally different direction. The Berlin book strengthens me in this conviction. It offers no alternatives for practical action. The possibility of an alternative way is touched on twice: once in connection with the theme of "dialogue" (p. 228), and once in connection with the "moratorium" (p. 298 f.). In both instances I had the impression that our standpoints were not so very far apart and would even approximate very closely in discussion and in practice. Rolf Sauerzapf's article unfortunately constitutes a sombre exception. He writes about the Programme to Combat Racism and gives the impression that real Christian action can be seen in Vorster, Smith and in Portuguese colonialism of the past. That would represent an alternative, of course, one very similar to that championed by the ICCC. If Berlin were to give it official backing, there would be in fact a profound gulf between us which would certainly extend to the very heart of our opposing views of the Gospel. But the other articles remain silent on this point. It is stressed over and again that the Gospel "naturally" has political and social consequences. But this conviction remains in small print. The inevitable result of this, as I see it, is that what is writ large is threatened with ideologization.

I continue to believe, therefore, that the World Council of Churches provides provisionally correct guidelines for worldwide Christian action. If, however, the apparently necessary extension and deepening were to take place, this would involve, as I see it, the following changes in what we say and do:

1. We would not be in a hurry to prepare a suitable theology but examine far more thoroughly the biblical arguments and limits, instead of taking for granted the desired result.

2. We would proceed much more carefully — with fear and trembling — being always ready to listen carefully to Christians whose opinion differs from our own, always ready to relativize our convictions and to change our course.

3. We would be more critical towards the claims and demands of the world and give priority to trying to serve the world by those insights from God's Word which the world itself does not yet perceive, and is (as yet) unwilling to acknowledge.

The Berlin book with its tedious repetitions also offer an ideology, namely, an apocalyptic ideology. This ideology is bound to remain fruitless for ethical action because the last days only leave room for witness and suffering. But it would be a mistake not to sense behind this ideology the genuine spiritual concerns by which these people too are moved. Berlin wants to build a wall against us. But under the guidance of the Holy Spirit, it could, contrary to its intentions, open up for us instead a way into new territory.

(Reprinted by kind permission of the Publications Office of the World Council of Churches from the January 1976 issue of the Ecumenical Review, pages 80-86.)

C. THEOLOGICAL ASSESSMENTS OF THE ECUMENICAL/EVANGELICAL SCHISM

4. Nairobi – No Turning Point

(The March 29th, 1976 issue of the Information Service
of the German Evangelical Alliance)

Through various reports on the Fifth General Assembly of the World Council of Churches, the impression has been created that in Nairobi, the WCC readjusted its course significantly. Accordingly, the balance of concerns which had been upset by one-sided concentration on socio-political themes was restored by a deepened interest in the Bible and by the desire for a new spirituality. The danger of the Christian faith being mixed with other religions in the wake of Geneva's dialogue programme was banished. In Nairobi, it is claimed, Evangelicals and Ecumenicals laid the foundations essential for future cooperation and fellowship.

The European Confession Congress, the Conference of Confessing Fellowships and the Association of Evangelical Missions were represented by observers at the Fifth General Assembly of the World Council of Churches in Nairobi from 23rd November — 10th December, 1975. They have studied the procedures and results of the Assembly and have arrived at the following conclusions:

I. Nairobi did not change the course of the WCC in a biblical direction.

1. This judgment refers not so much to the member Churches affiliated to the WCC, but rather to the Ecumenical Centre at Geneva with its worldwide network of co-workers and advisors. For it was the Geneva staff that prepared and conducted the Fifth General Assembly, and it is this staff that will mainly implement the reports and resolutions.

2. 'Jesus Christ frees and unites' was the theme of the General Assembly. We agree to this, as long as it is developed on biblical lines. *Jesus Christ* is confessed rightly only by the faith of His Church, on the unchangeable

foundation of the apostles and prophets (Matt. 11,16ff; Eph. 2,20). He alone *frees* through the Word of His truth (John 8,31-36) and through His atoning death, from sin, the devil and eternal lostness under the wrath of God (Rom. 6,18; Gal. 5,1) to righteousness and the blessed assurance that we are God's children (I John 3,1-3), and *unites* us with all those who have been born again by water and Spirit in His body (I Cor. 10,16) without regard of any social differences; He unites us into a fellowship in confessing His name (Matt. 10,32) and in His loving service (Gal. 5,13); in suffering under anti-Christian powers (Phil. 1,29; Rev. 7,14) and in the hope of His victorious return (I Thes. 2,19; I Cor. 15, 23-26).

3. But in this biblical sense there was hardly any testimony to the crucified and risen Jesus Christ at Nairobi. For Holy Scripture was not the only source and guideline of all the ecumenical deliberations and resolutions at the Fifth General Assembly. The Bible served only as *one* point of reference alongside the 'challenges of our modern world' and the ideological propositions of our time.

II. In Nairobi, the numerous protests confirmed the reservations about the unbiblical course of the WCC which had been pointed out especially by the Berlin Declaration on Ecumenism 1974.

1. Evangelical, Lutheran, Orthodox and other voices protested against a watering-down of the Gospel to a programme of socio-political liberation. They warned against the danger of a disintegration of the Church of Jesus Christ into a world community of all religions and ideologies. They refused to let themselves be manipulated during the consultations into an engineering of the results.

2. These delegates were able to force through a partial inclusion of their convictions in the reports passed by the General Assembly:
In the report on Section I, the Christ presented to us in the New Testament was not replaced by a multiplicity of christological images. The report on Section II confirmed the unity of the Church as having its origin in the Triune God.
In a preamble attached to the original report on Section III, the majority of the delegates dissociated themselves from syncretism. But these same reports contain many doubtful statements. They are, as the Information Department announced, not binding for the Geneva staff, but are merely recommendations to the Churches.

III. The impulse from Lausanne 74 had its impact on Nairobi – many delegates re-emphasized the urgency of mission and evangelism.

1. Section I 'Confessing Christ Today' quite spontaneously formed a fifth

sub-group; this group occupied itself with the urgency of evangelisation. Under pressure from the delegates, and against the draft drawn up by the Geneva staff, mission and evangelism were included in the new WCC Constitution as tasks of particular importance. The previous one-sidedness in the WCC's concept of mission, with its emphasis on socio-political activity, was rejected. The talk was then of a 'holistic' approach to non-believing persons: In each respective situation, proclamation and socio-political action should go hand-in-hand.

2. And yet the shadows cast on this pleasing awakening cannot be mistaken. Precisely in this connection, many exhibited an obvious tendency towards universalism in their thinking. For example, in the report from Section I, all mention of the fact that Man without faith in Jesus Christ is lost, was deleted. For many — especially African and Asian — delegates and advisors, the issue of evangelisation as a call to believe was not the focal point of attention. Some were more concerned with socio-political actions, others with dialogue. So in the end, the Assembly did not pass any practical decisions for the renewal and strengthening of the Geneva Department for World Mission and Evangelism. Thus it becomes altogether questionable whether there will be any new evangelistic efforts within the WCC.

IV. In their handling of human rights in the Soviet Union, the Programme to Combat Racism, and the Palestine problem, the assembled delegates loaded guilt upon themselves over against persecuted Christians, innocent persons, and the People of Israel.

During the debates on political world problems, the General Assembly *behaved more like a second UNO than an Assembly of Churches.* The tug-of-war-like voting reflected the crass differences of opinion between the power blocs and revolutionary groups. By giving way to massive pressure and ideological prejudice, the Assembly allowed itself to be prevented from commenting on politically explosive themes in the spirit of truth and love.

1. The attempt to break through *the WCC's one-sided silence on the oppression of Christians in communist-ruled countries* was frustrated by the protest of the Russian Orthodox delegation.

2. The Assembly did not comply with the explicit and emphatic appeal that within the framework of the controversial Programme to Combat Racism, no organisations that use violence should receive support. *In spite of the massacres carried out by various liberation movements,* reports of which have become known to the public, *the majority of the delegates decided in favour of continuing support,* also for such groups as have proclaimed that they will use violence even up to the point of destroying human life.

3. The delegates resolved that Israel should be called upon to withdraw to the borders of 1967. A motion to the effect that the WCC should dissociate

itself from the UNO's condemnation of Zionism as a form of racism was rejected. Thus it became evident that *the WCC does not think in terms of biblical salvation history.*

V. *The leaders of the WCC have not given any signs of changing direction in spite of the Assembly's opposition to their present course. The self-contradictory decisions of the General Assembly enable them to continue their present course unchanged.*

1. The preparatory material for the Fifth General Assembly, compiled by the Geneva staff, showed a blurred, unbiblical Christology, and a concept of salvation couched in neo-marxist language. They shifted the goal of ecumenical unity from fellowship in the Body of Jesus Christ to a world community of all religions and ideologies. The ecumenical advisors also tried to influence the work of the various sections in Nairobi in this direction. The lectures and dramatic presentations, ordered by Geneva, pointed in the same direction.

2. By the slogan 'spirituality for combat' a new and questionable element was introduced into the ecumenical movement. In it, traditional piety, charismatic extremes and eastern mysticism are combined with revolutionary theology. This reveals a new form of justification by works, which is to speed up the Churches' political activities and lay the foundation for a future inter-religious world community. This was already partly realized during the conference devotions in songs, prayers and confessions.

3. In spite of clearly expressed criticism in Nairobi, the Geneva centre was not motivated to abandon even one of its programmes nor to reorientate them biblically.

4. Compared with the last seven years, the radical slogans of false ecumenism came through somewhat subdued in the Nairobi reports. They are largely surrounded by statements which sound biblically correct or half-correct. This combination of truth and heresy increases the danger of spiritual confusion after Nairobi.

5. The elections to the WCC offices — the six presidents, the Central Committee and the Executive Committee — were prepared beforehand by a nomination committee and confirmed en bloc by the delegates. It is to be feared that the new occupants of the various posts will enable the Geneva staff to follow unpeturbedly their course adopted since Uppsala 1968 until the next General Assembly.

VI. *Even after Nairobi, Bible-believing Christians have no other choice but in critical dissociation from the WCC to go their way as disciples of Jesus Christ.*

1. In recognition of the fact that the earlier complaints against the WCC

have not been settled in Nairobi, they must now, just as before, remain watchful and test the spirits carefully.

2. They should call upon the leaders of their Churches to insist that the WCC change its course in accordance with the biblically grounded protests in Nairobi. If this has no effect, they should call upon their Churches to *end their cooperation in the WCC*, and, where this lies within their legal possibilities, to *withdraw from the WCC altogether.*

3. At least as individuals, they should by word and deed (e.g. public protests, cancelling of donations) *refuse to accept any responsibility for unbiblical decisions and actions on the part of the WCC.*

4. They will put all their strength into the spiritual struggle for those brothers and sisters who occupy responsible positions within ecumenical structures.

5. They will *implement major biblical injunctions such as missions, evangelisation and loving care by their own evangelical organisations,* independent from ecumenical structures.

6. They know that the true unity of the Church of Jesus Christ cannot be identified with the structures of the WCC. Therefore they foster relations with all those Christians in the world who eagerly expect the return of their Lord.

Signatories

For the European Confession Congress:
   Bishop Oskar Sakrausky, Vienna
   Bishop Erling Utnem, Kristiansand
   Professor Dr. Peter Beyerhaus, Tübingen
   Professor Dr. Walter Künneth, Erlangen
For the Conference of Confessing Fellowships:
   Superintendent Reinhold George, Berlin
   Rev. Rudolf Bäumer, Espelkamp

EPILOGUE

EPILOGUE

Donald McGavran

The reader has studied sixteen essays setting forth the new Conciliar concept of Mission and twenty-four setting forth the Evangelical. He has seen what leaders of both sides have written. The main positions held and many arguments for each have become clear.

Conciliar-Evangelical Debate has not been an exhaustive survey; but enough has been presented for readers to understand the two Schools of Thought. "Classical Mission" and "New Mission" have in turn taken the platform and aired their views. Mission as "world evangelization and discipling *ta éthne*" has been set forth attacked and defended. Mission as "humanization, liberation from poverty, oppression and exploitation," has been set forth attacked and defended.

The picture of "New Mission" is complex. Yet it is fair to say that at its heart lies a view of mission as humanization — a humanization toward which men of good will in every religion and every ideology are pressing. In consequence, "conversion" from this religion to that, from Marxism to Christianity or from Shinto to Presbyterian Faith is de-emphasized. Just as among Christians, it is deemed unnecessary for salvation to renounce Baptist faith, it may be, or Lutheran or Roman Catholic and turn to Methodism, similarly, it is not required for men of other religions (Judaism, Islam, Buddhism, Hinduism or Animism) to leave their ancestral faith and become Christians. Evangelism (seeking for the lost and persuading men to become disciples of Jesus Christ and responsible members of His Church) is considered of minor importance. "Mission as humanization" and "evangelism as unnecessary" are basic elements of New Mission.

That this is fair judgment is amply substantiated by Geneva's ten year record of denigrating evangelism and church growth. The following paragraph also, quoted from *Drafts for Sections: Uppsala '68*, gives clear evidence of the main thrust of the New Mission.

"We have lifted up humanization as the goal of mission because we believe that more than others it communicates in our period of history the meaning of the messianic goal. In another time the goal of God's redemptive work might best have been described in terms of man turning towards God rather than in terms of God turning towards men . . . The fundamental question was that of the true God, and the church responded to that question by pointing to Him. It was assuming that the purpose of mission was Christianization, bringing man to God through Christ and his church. Today the fundamental question is much more that of *true* man, and the dominant concern of the missionary congregation must therefore be to point to the humanity of Christ as the goal of mission."

There it stands, clearly stated for all to read. In times past, turning to "the true God" used to be what men need. Today, however, they need something else. Today the great question is "that of *true* man and the dominant concern of the missionary congregation must be to point to the humanity in Christ" as what mission intends to achieve on a worldwide front.

FIFTEEN DECISIVE YEARS
IN THE HISTORY OF CHRISTIAN MISSION

Conciliar-Evangelical Debate covers a crucial fifteen year period in the history of mission. In 1960 the classical biblical concept of mission was firmly in control in Geneva, New York, Berlin, London and practically all the missionary societies in the world. By 1975 the concept of New Mission was firmly in the saddle. During those fateful fifteen years a radically different concept of mission was conceived, born, grew to manhood, seized control of the leaders of the ecumenical movement, and captured the mainline Protestant missionary societies around the world. Only the Evangelicals remained free — and theirs was a hesitant freedom. Many of their leaders made tentative moves toward changing *their* goals to something more modern, more relevant, and more in line with the battle for justice, brotherhood and plenty.

One must not suppose that a few men conspired to form and promote the new concept of mission. The process was much more open than that. The end was not clearly seen. It was generally agreed that with the collapse of European empires and the rise of hundreds of younger denominations, major changes were demanded in the form of historic missions. Since most men writing or speaking on these subjects saw their own particular part of the world field, they had differing opinions as to what was required. Many changes were advocated as "the contemporary trend in missions." These were voiced by leaders of missionary societies from both the right and the left. The movement by which the New Mission pictured in this volume finally emerged in 1967 was much more a groping than a confident pressing forward.

A summary statement such as this Epilogue cannot attempt an exhaustive history of the formation of the concept of New Mission, complete with its theological justification. That history ought to be written soon. Here,

EPILOGUE–*McGavran*

however, all that I shall attempt is to sketch four factors which played a prominent part in the movement of thought and led Conciliar denominations and missionary societies off in one direction and Evangelical off in another. They gave opportunity to men with certain theological perspectives to fashion the New Mission which this volume has been describing as it developed through the fifteen decisive years.

First was the collapse of European Empires. Christian missions have never been a function of empire. It is a gross overstatement to portray them as the religions side of an expanding imperialism. Nevertheless, more with Roman Catholic Missions before 1800 A.D. and less with Protestant Missions, dedicated Christians did evangelize countries into which they could get. These often were those conquered and ruled by European nations. While in the minds of ardent Christians, missions had little to do with white rule, in the popular mind the connection was by no means small. Consequently when European rule collapsed, and missionaries were expelled from all of China in 1948, from North Korea and North Vietnam shortly thereafter, it was easy for Europeans to think that missions, as we have carried them out, are definitely at an end. The multifarious bearings of this fact on the long range policies of missionary societies are evident.

An overwhelming tendency followed, some twenty years after independence of the new nations, for them to believe that their poverty had nothing to do with over-population, lack of technology, lack of Christian Faith, low state of literacy, and other similar internal deficiencies. Their poverty was caused solely — they felt — by the oppression of the developed countries which were ruthlessly exploiting the rest of the world. This simplistic view, aided by the guilt complex of European leaders and their readiness to perform astonishing acts of public penitence, has made it easy to project Christian mission as restitution. All those sections of the Church which have a low view of the Scripture now regularly maintain that proclaiming eternal salvation through faith in Jesus Christ is a hypocritical performance unless it is made credible by massive acts of restitution. One wonders whether they hold it possible for a poor nation to evangelize a rich nation. How do they understand the evangelization of Athens and Rome by the common people of Jerusalem? Whatever the answer, this contemporary trend played a significant part in the formation of New Mission.

Second was the rise of Younger Churches. Many of these had existed prior to World War II and indeed to World War I, but their importance in self-ruled nations was vastly more than in those ruled by Europe. After 1947 it was clear to all missionary societies that great power must be given at once to the Younger Churches. They must in no way be ruled by the West. They must not even seem to be ruled by the West. Yet the missionary task was by no means done — in fact, in vast reaches of the world 'The Younger Churches' formed a minute one or two percent only of the total population. In some places they formed one-tenth of one percent. The task was to make the Younger Church really self governing and at the same time to continue as much mission as possible. In some cases leaders of the Younger Churches, men of great sagacity and spiritual power, were most helpful in solving the problem. In other cases the tide of nationalism overwhelmed them and they began to think "We have chased the white men out of governmental positions. Now we must chase them out of church positions, too." Years of great tension followed and are still with us. No path is more thorny and more beset with half-truths and half-solutions. And none more significantly affects the essential question of what contemporary mission really *is*.

Various formulae were devised and explained. Partnership in Obedience . . . No More Foreign Missions . . . No More Missionaries at All . . . Only Fraternal Delegates . . . Fusion, Dichotomy, Modified Dichotomy . . . these and many more were manufactured, tried, adjusted, and on occasion discarded. Mission is no longer missionaries from the West going to the East. Now it is missionaries from East and West speaking to people West and East . . . Mission is a two-way street. Every Church should be carrying on the mission of God in the place where it lives . . . Winning the world for Christ is not the goal. That is triumphalism. The Church is not going to include everyone. All it can hope to be is a small minority of the population, a sign of God's presence in the midst of an evil world . . . The list of ideas launched and discussed is very long. All affected the form of the Christian Mission to the world.

Third was the massive erosion of belief in the inspiration and authority of the Bible. Literary, historical, and form criticism left many educated Christians with the conviction that the Bible was not in any sense an authoritative Book. It was one voice among many. Far from being the unified revelation of the True God, the Bible was a composite, each part of which recorded what men in different situations had thought. Pluralism held the field. Dr. Peter Beyerhaus has written cogently to this root of the Mission as Humanization school of thought.

Other religions were also ways to God who had spoken through them to a greater or less degree. This point of view had been expounded on a world platform by the Laymen's Enquiry of 1930. William Hocking had taught that the age of church planting was over. Each religion should reconceive itself in the light of other religions. Out of the process, something rather like Christianity would emerge. His view was totally rejected in 1930, but by 1960 something very like it was coming back into prominence and its advocates held many of the high positions in the missionary world. Dr. Visser t'Hooft has written cogently to this in Chapter 3 of his *The Ecumenical Movement and Future.*

Fourth was the spread of the Marxist world view reinforced by the increasing number of countries in which Marxist minorities seized control of the army and the government and subjected everything to their will. Since they claimed to be the party of the common man and were working toward a classless society, they pictured themselves as leading a war against exploitation, imperialism, injustice, poverty, the oppression of both the masses and the Third World nations. Marxists picture religion as an opiate deliberately administered by the ruling classes to fix men's attention on heaven and keep them from demanding justice on earth.

Where this Marxist view saturated men's thinking, it was natural and easy for Christians to reason that the Christian Faith can make a better case for justice, mercy, brotherhood, and plenty than any atheistic ideology. Can make . . . should make . . . can launch world mission as a mighty campaign against every form of exploitation of the masses . . . as in fact humanization and horizontal reconciliation of man with man.

These four roots contributed in varying degrees to the formation of the New Mission. Taken together, they formed a potent package. An erosion of faith in eternal salvation, a growing conviction that all that really mattered was an ethical relationship of man to man, a guilty conscience over past imperialisms, a prudent policy de-emphasizing conversion in nations which hate Christianity, a resolve to build up young weak denominations by inner renewal, education, medicine, and development rather than encourage further accessions of raw new converts — these and other roots united to form a consistent doctrine of a New Mission which "lifted up humanization" as its goal. In times past, mission had been profitably described "in terms of men turning to God". Now mission must be described in terms of liberating man from all that exploits and oppresses him. "Mission is concerned with the message of the New Humanity in Christ and with shalom (peace, mutual well-being). This means the achievement of a truly human existence in a just society . . . and involves participation in the struggle for a just society. But such a struggle may necessitate radical changes in the structures of society . . . The more the established order resists the changes needed, the more violent becomes the struggle" (Drafts: p. 43).

Such New Mission was not necessary in order to achieve a just society. Classical Mission which believed in the inspiration of the Bible, a personal God, the Father Almighty, eternal salvation and heaven was still quite possible. Furthermore, the biblical view of God and man, sin and salvation, was a much more powerful stimulus to just and brotherly action than the truncated view which rested on a low view of the Bible, was skeptical about eternal salvation, and believed that God was at work as much out of as in the Church.

Nevertheless, to Europeans suffering traumatic shock from loss of empire, indulging in an emotional orgy of guilt and self-abasement vis a vis the Young Churches, flooded by scientific secularism, believing that the biblical view was nothing more than a pre-scientific way of thinking, subjected to Marxist world views, and facing the huge inequities of the developed and the developing nations, *mission as humanization was an appealing view.*

Furthermore, if one chose his texts carefully, the view could be given a thoroughly biblical color. "Salvation" in the Old Testament was truly deliverance from enemies, hunger, thirst, disease, and various other temporal perils. "Conversion", through a skillful use of the Greek and Hebrew words, could be made to appear not turning from the world to Jesus Christ, but any kind of turning away from oppression, ignorance, hunger, want, and evil conditions, to any kind of abundance, learning, freedom and pleasant living. By carefully choosing the verses quoted, "the Kingdom of God" could be described as composed of men anywhere (of any belief or unbelief concerning God or gods) who strove for a just social order.

By 1960 the early forms of the new concept were being expressed in many phrasings. They were still clothed in traditional language: gospel proclamation, the mission of God, the ends of the earth, the grace of God, the leading of the Holy Spirit, the whole man — these and similar phrases were freely used. The new concepts took many shapes and were in fact amalgams of classical mission and the shape of things to come. Each was the thought of some one groping forward to what missions ought to be in this changed world. These many attempts to describe New Mission surfaced in hundreds of articles and thousands of speeches by mission leaders and churchmen on both sides of the Atlantic and around the world. Most of them did not see the goal toward which their efforts to restate mission were trending. Most of them would have denied that humanization was their goal, or that they intended to de-emphasize evangelism. Nevertheless, the seeds of the New Mission which *Conciliar Evangelical Debate* has set forth were by 1960 clearly visible.

In late 1965 or early 1966, the gropings toward a New Mission which fitted the new age ended and a clear consistent and radically new concept emerged and took command. When the history of the world mission between 1960 and 1968 is written, we shall know who were the architects of this view and be able to trace exactly how it wove together the various strands I have described and others into one consistent whole. The movement of ideas was no doubt powerfully reinforced by political moves at Geneva which vaulted into positions of power men who held these opinions rather than others.

This Epilogue must not venture into that fascinating field. But the story must be told. The radical turn (by which world missions, which had built up a mighty apparatus and an annual income of hundreds of millions of dollars directed toward world evangelization, was in a few years turned around and headed in a totally new direction) is too epochal an event to remain hidden from view. Contributors to mission need to know how it happens that the plane of missions headed for Jerusalem was hijacked and taken to Philadelphia.

THE JULY 1968 ISSUE OF THE INTERNATIONAL REVIEW OF MISSIONS

This volume contents itself with letting protagonists of both sides describe and defend their positions. However one small vignette of history casts such an interesting and revealing ray of light on the process that, in addition to printing the documents concerned in Part III (the years 1965-1968), I am going to explain their significance. They indicate very clearly what the New Mission was *against*. Not only was New Mission determined to emphasize humanization; it was simultaneously determined to de-emphasize evangelism. The July 1968 issue of the International Review of Mission presents a small but crucial bit of evidence. The story is as follows.

In October 1965, the International Review of Missions printed an article by me, entitled "Wrong Strategy: The Real Crisis in Missions" which is reproduced on pages 97-107 of this volume. On the second page of that article appears a paragraph typical of what many missionary leaders were saying in the early sixties. I took it almost word for word from an article by a well known mission executive. It was the kind of thing which was passing as correct mission thinking. It stresses *other things* than conversion, evangelism and church growth; *other things* than discipling the nations and eternal salvation. It might almost be said that the common factor underlying all the forms was this: Mission is not discipling, not evangelism, and not church planting. It is other good things.

When in the spring of 1965 I submitted that article to the Editor of the IRM, the leaders of the WCC had not yet finally defined New Mission. Geneva did not see humanization as replacing reconciling sinners with God. The Editor of the IRM still gladly printed an article (in October 1965) maintaining that mission ought:

to tailor strategy "to fit each of the thousands of separate communities so that in it the Church may grow" (p. 103);
to take church growth with life and death seriousness;
to use "anthropological and sociological factors to promote church growth";
to divise "a right theology of church growth"; and
to put into operation hard bold plans for proclaiming Christ and persuading men to become His disciples and responsible members of His Church.

The article must have caused considerable unease among the leaders who were fashioning the concepts which were to undergird mission as humanization. It advocated exactly what they were coming to feel was wrong strategy, out-worn imperialistic mission, and triumphalism. I have wondered whether they did not take the editor to task for accepting the article.

At any rate, the Geneva Secretariat spent the years from 1966 to 1968 preparing for Uppsala — the Fourth Assembly of the World Council of Churches. The International Missionary Council had become the Commission on World Mission and Evangelism of the Council and the crucial question before it was just this : What is World Mission today? What is its bold new mandate? The general thought could be phrased as follows:

This Commission must not thrash old straw. It must face forward. It must address itself to the new world and speak to the needs of men tomorrow. Mission must cease to be winning men to Christ, promising them eternal life and eternal salvation, and multiplying churches. This comes close to being an opiate. It must become fighting the battles of mankind, combatting injustice in every form, liberating men into the freedom of Christ, and uniting them in one global Church. Action unites. Doctrine divides. Let us work at humanization together. That is modern mission.

As the preparatory documents (which were published in early 1968 under the title *Drafts For Sections, Uppsala '69)* were being written, it seemed likely that the huge shift to humanization (from vertical to horizontal reconciliation, from eternal salvation to salvation today) would encounter major opposition.

So the Editor of IRM was instructed to demolish that article of October 1965 — which claimed that right strategy in mission was church growth. An impressive galaxy of writers from all over the world was recruited. J.G. Davies from England, Walter J. Hollenweger from Germany and Geneva, Matthew P. John from India, Jordan Bishop a Roman Catholic from Bolivia, Marie Louise Martin from Africa and France, Mme Gouzee from Belgium, and Herbert Neve from North America.

The format was to be that of open discussion. The opposing articles were to be submitted to Donald McGavran and his reply was to be printed with theirs. A couple of his friends, J.B.A. Kessler and Melvin Hodges, were asked to write on kindred topics — but were not told of the seven carefully aimed articles demolishing church growth which was considered an erroneous strategy of missions.

The seven authors were carefully chosen. Matthew P. John belonged to the South India Jacobite Syrian Church which has never evangelized in 1700 years of its history, and which has lost large numbers of its members to Roman Catholics, Anglicans, Mar Thoma Syrians, Pentecostals and others. For Mr. John, Church Growth meant "preying upon other denominations". As soon ask Ben Gurian if he favored Arab union! Mr. John's opposition could be counted on.

Similarly Father Bishop of Bolivia — a country where almost every baby is baptized in the Roman Catholic Church — saw the task of missions precisely *not* as extending the Church but as improving it, perfecting it, winning justice for oppressed Christians, and developing it.

Mme. Gouzee — a charming member of "a minority church" in Belgium belonged "by family, profession, friends, political concerns and cultural interest to that world which Dr. McGavran sees as having rejected Christ and therefore as lost." She said she often "felt nearer to the evangelized than to the evangelizers." Hers was a remarkably perspicuous and fair rejoinder. She recognized (p. 160) that the authors of *Drafts For Sections* were advocating the diametric opposite of church growth. She was (p. 162) well aware of the reasoned position of Hollenweger, Casalis, Keller and Hoekendijk. She granted that *overseas* the strategy of church growth might be rather good — but that *worldwide* the emphasis should be on quality and effectiveness of Christian life. It would not be unfair to sum up her article as saying that in Europe we need "not church growth but renewal."

The other four were chosen because they had already espoused the "New Mission" position and were ready to defend it.

All told, a remarkable concentration of fire was directed at the 1965 article which advocated church growth as the correct strategy of missions. The bombardment was timed to come out in the July 1968 issue of the International Review of Mission just before the Fourth Assembly and to warn any who might be tempted at Uppsala to plead for the Great Commission, eternal salvation, and reconciling men to God or classical missions. They, too, would be demolished. What Geneva advocated was the new shape of mission. Discipling the nations was anachronistic, triumphalistic, and unsuited to the modern world. Evangelistic missionaries would no longer be sent. Humanization was the goal.

The plan of action was clear. The World Council of Churches would use its great influence to change mission from conversion to social action, from discipling the nations to championing the oppressed, from persuading men to believe on Christ to persuading them to be more brotherly, whatever they believed.

The radical nature of the shift was skillfully disguised. The old words were deliberately used. Mission, evangelism, conversion, salvation were all notable by their presence; but they all had new meanings (See page 237). A further example is found in the use of the phrase "the Kingdom of God." Those promoting the new concept often spoke of the Kingdom of God. "The Gospel of the Kingdom will be preached throughout the whole world as a testimony to the nations" (Mt. 24:14) was a favorite passage. It was interpreted to mean that the Gospel of "a Fair Deal for the Underprivileged Nations no matter what they believe" *displaced* the Gospel of God's Kingdom consisting of those who believed on His Son, were baptized in the Triune Name, obeyed Christ as King and displayed His Rule in their hearts. The average reader would suppose that champions of New Mission were advocating classical biblical mission; instead of which these words of the Bible were intended to portray an interest in justice, equality, a division of the wealth and brotherhood *which displaced any interest* in conversion, in a turning through faith in Jesus Christ from death to life, in a new status granted by God on the basis of a man's faith in Christ, entirely independent of any righteous works which man might do. Classical mission was to be replaced by social action, disguised as the New Mission. The whole apparatus of Mission — its good will, missionary societies, headquarters, income of hundreds of millions, missionary staff, international headquarters, and linkages with younger Churches, was not only to be devoted to humanization, but was to be separated from world evangelization, church growth, the multiplication of baptized believers and congregations of the redeemed.

THE CONTINUING BATTLE 1968 to 1976

The July 1968 International Review of Missions was merely the opening gun. At the Fourth General Assembly of the World Council of Churches, the Geneva staff fought vigorously to prevent the inclusion of any reference to the two billion who have yet to believe. Only very strong pressure by the whole Norwegian delegation and some other Evangelicals at several successive plenary sessions finally over-ruled the staff and forced the following sentence in. It stands out like a sore thumb. Nothing in the context fits. It is an import from classical mission starkly planted in the midst of an exposition of new mission.

"It (the Church) has an unchanging responsibility to make known the Gospel of the forgiveness of God in Christ to the hundreds of millions who have not heard it." *(Eye of the Storm:* 251-252)

At Bangkok, December 1972, as Arthur Glasser reports in his essay in this volume, Philip Potter announced, "Any debate over proclaiming the Gospel to the two billion or more who have never heard it . . . is totally futile." Convictions and affirmations to that end were not allowed to be voiced. In effect, proclaiming the eternal Gospel was ruled no part of salvation today.

By 1975, when the Fifth Assembly met at Nairobi, the issue had become sufficiently clear and the magnitude of the shift away from classical biblical mission to mission conceived as humanization was widely enough recognized and criticized, that a small grudging concession was made to the biblical position. Mortimer Arias of Bolivia was asked to prepare a major address to the plenary session in which he advocated *evangelism and social action together*. The Council then framed and passed the five brief paragraphs reported in the Church Growth Bulletin for January 1976 reproduced in Harvey Hoekstra's article in this volume. In the reams of material framed and passed by the Council these five must occupy a minute proportion of the total linage — perhaps one percent.

There is no reason to believe that the World Council of Churches will devote any sizeable part of its budget or its time to promoting great commission missions. What Mortimer Arias described as past policy appears likely to remain the fixed policy of the Council —

"Evangelism has been the Cinderella of the WCC . . . where it figures by nothing more than one office with a single occupant in a substructure which is in itself merely part of a unit and with no more than a monthly letter by which to communicate with the churches of the world."

Mr. Arias might have added that the monthly letter describes all kinds of fringe activities which pass as evangelism and seldom if ever tells of open efforts to win unbelievers to faith in Christ and membership in His Church.

This plan to de-emphasize evangelism and church growth seems likely to continue. The policy described in *Conciliar-Evangelical Debate* was framed about 1965 and has been followed consistently ever since. The Geneva leaders believed (correctly) that it would be opposed. They dug in for a long fight. There are no indications of a change of mind. Indeed, as long as the present leaders remain in the saddle they may be expected to carry out what is clearly their conviction. They may very well be saying, "Here we stand. God help us, we can do no other." If the Council wants to emphasize classical mission together with social action, it must choose another team. The present team is committed to social action *without evangelism*.

WHAT CAN BIBLE BELIEVING CHRISTIANS NOW DO?

Standing squarely in the middle of the Storm, with the cyclone whirling all round them, several courses of action are open to Bible believing Christians.

They form a substantial block in every country. By their convictions they are limited to those actions which the Bible clearly sanctions and requires. They intend to do what the Bible says. They believe that the Bible is God breathed and God inspired, and is not merely what men in different times and circumstances have thought. They hold that the Bible comprises a unity arising from its divine Author. It is the words of men, to be sure, but at the same time it is the written Word of God. It had meaning for the men by whom and to whom it was written, but at the same time it has meaning for all men of all time. It is infallible, the only rule of faith and practice. What can Bible believing Christians do? First, *they can do what the Bible, seen in its totality and heard reverently, tells them to do.*

Second, *they can recognize the storm.* The days when Christian mission meant one generally agreed on course of action are over. Now 'Christian mission' and all the significant words associated with it are being used in radically opposed meanings. Bible believing Christians will sacrificially support some Christian missions; some they will resolutely oppose. Gone are the days when it was safe to pray for and give to anything which went under the name "Christian mission" — any missionary society, any commission on mission and evangelism, any missionary. Today one must ask: Is the mission advocating "works righteousness" or "justification by faith"? Does it believe in eternal life granted by God's grace through faith in Jesus Christ, or does it preach the gospel of the full dinner pail?

Since, for prudential reasons most programs of mission include many different kinds of action, the question really becomes one not merely of what is claimed but what is done. Of key importance in any estimate of the Christian character of the program is the proportion of resources spent for sinner-converting, church-multiplying evangelism. Many other good things ought to be done, are being done, and will be done. That may be taken for granted; but the key question must be asked, "To what degree is this program calling men from death to life?" We live in the center of a tremendous debate over the essential nature of Christian Mission and must recognize the storm.

Third, *Bible believing Christians can champion the masses and the developing nations.* In *Understanding Church Growth* I have written

> Christian mission stands at one of the turning points in history. A new order is being born. Its exact form is hidden from us; the forces which combine to make the new world are far too complex to allow anyone a clear view of the outcome. Yet it seems reasonably certain that whatever else happens, the common man is going to have a great deal more to say in the future than he has in the past . . . (p. 259).

This is no new role for biblical Christians. The awakened masses of Asia and Africa and Latin America are awake in large part because of the missionary movement of the past hundred and seventy-five years. Only after millions of the Depressed Classes had become Christians, multitudes of them had been transformed, and it appeared likely that all seventy million of them would become Christian, did Hindu India begin to treat these victims of the Hindu social order justly. The emancipation of the slaves in North America came only after a tremendous campaign had been carried on by the Church. Biblical Christians repudiate the cannard that they have been lax and negligent in championing the masses. No one has championed them more than Christians. This is not to say, of course, that more cannot be done today, and that more could not have been done in the past. There is always room for improvement. Be that as it may, now in the last years of the Twentieth Century, when the masses have awakened and the Marxists are claiming to be their best friends, Bible believing Christians should redouble their efforts to champion the masses.

The basic reason for this, of course, is the biblical mandate. This is what the Bible is all about. The exodus from Egypt was of slaves. God led them out to the Promised Land. The Lord Jesus came to preach the Gospel to the poor, proclaim release to the captives . . . and to set free those who are downtrodden. Not many wise, not many powerful, not many of noble birth

... but the foolish, the weak, what is low and despised — these are called and transformed into a chosen race, a royal priesthood, God's own people. The Bible calls men to faith in Jesus Christ and membership in His Church precisely to liberate them and to set them to work proclaiming to others the excellence of Him who has called them out of darkness into His marvellous light.

Fourth, *biblical Christians can multiply evangelism.* They will multiply evangelism among the masses and bring multitudes of common people to transforming faith in Jesus Christ. They will feed them the Bread of Heaven till their souls are satisfied. They will be confident that there is no more effective way to alleviate this world's poverty and loose this world's chains. Those who know themselves to be citizens of heaven, make better citizens of earth. Those who know they will eat pie in the sky by and by, have a keener conscience on distributing apple pie to their comrades here on earth. Biblical Christians evangelize with a clear conscience. They know the surpassing worth of the Treasure they are offering. They will not be deterred by the jibes and jeers of unbelievers. They will proclaim Jesus Christ, the power of God and the wisdom of God. And they will bring multitudes out of Egypt and guide them carefully through the desert to the Promised Land flowing with milk and honey.

Biblical Christians will continue to pour mighty resources into the evangelization of the developing nations. Nothing could give Brazil, it may be, or India more power to change the social structures now hampering advance, to discover resources for the good life, and to achieve greater degrees of health, learning, production, and equitable distribution of opportunity and income than for many millions of Brazilian and Indian citizens to become ardent, Bible-obeying Spirit-filled Christians. Churches of Jesus Christ, feeding on His Word and seeking His will, are the most potent factor in that transformation of men and nations which will happen as God's Kingdom spreads on earth. Indeed, essential to the spread of the Kingdom of God, as defined and described by the Lord Jesus, is a belief in Himself, confessed before men. Churches in all continents should increase the number of missionaries. Missionaries — be they Koreans, Norwegians, Canadians, Americans, Peruvians, or Nigerians — are part of God's Task Force at work bringing in His Kingdom. The Kingdom in all its fullness, of course, will not come till the Lord returns. Till then, it is a limited goodness set about with much evil, beyond the power of men to change.

Fifth, *Bible believing Christians will participate in the struggle for justice and human dignity,* will work against all that hinders human wholeness and press forward relieving suffering, feeding the hungry, healing the sick, lifting the fallen and changing evil structures in those parts of the human fabric where they have power. Humanity owes a debt of gratitude to Christians who have seen remediable evil structures and demanded that they be remedied.

What ought to be done depends as a rule on what can be done. For ages slavery seemed a fixed part of the human scene, so Christians said little about it. But when in the eighteenth and nineteenth centuries it became possible to outlaw slavery, Christians demanded action. At first only a few far sighted Christians spoke; but God backed their vision and more and more Christians (and some others) enlisted in the fierce battle against slavery . . . Similarly warfare against that most terrible of all evil structures — the business of making and selling alcoholic beverages — was begun, waged, won, lost and now has to be waged again. Today, racism, unequal distribution of resources and income, mechanization and industrialization, modernization and urbanization, all pose ethical problems of a complex and challenging nature. Again Christians are deeply concerned and are in the forefront of the battle. Again just what can and ought to be done must be discovered. Much of what is being advocated is romantic and impractical. It cannot be done. It must be shelved for the present. The good that can be done always outweighs the good that cannot be. This truth must not, of course, become an excuse for doing nothing. Great service of mankind is urgently needed.

Sixth, Bible believing Christians must avoid three errors and launch two actions. The first error is the simplistic notion that the poor are poor simply because they have been exploited or abused and the sole enemy of advance is the entrenched privilege of the West. This is so obviously a partial analysis, animated by emotion rather than by reason, that it would be laughed out of court but for the guilt complex of the West. Thoughtful leaders of the developing nations must not be misled by the litany of penitence which it has become de rigeur for Westerners to repeat, into thinking the notion well based.

The second error is to form a theology of social action which carefully excludes the absolutes of eternal life and eternal salvation and focusses entirely on temporal improvements. We must not imitate the cheap skepticism of Marx and Mao. They do not believe in the soul, God the Father Almighty, salvation by faith in Jesus Christ, eternal life, heaven and hell, but this is no reason for Christians to abandon these eminently reasonable tenets of faith which so mightily undergird social action.

As I wrote in *Understanding Church Growth*

> God the Father Almighty is just and . . . will give those who love and obey Him power to treat other men justly . . . just men can build a just society. This just society must be clearly differentiated from the ultimate Kingdom of God — that reign of perfect goodness when death itself shall have been abolished . . . Man can do nothing to bring that in. The just society of which I speak is the kindlier, more humane order which by God's grace arises within family, neighborhood, city or state as the number of Christians mutliply. Since a just society must be built not by, but *out of* men who are profoundly interested in the welfare of others and are determined to devise structures which provide justice for them, as such men and their churches multiply, the structures of society will become more and more righteous (p. 253-254).

EPILOGUE–*McGavran* 395

The third error is "me-too-ism". When the headlines scream of race, some Christians scream of race. When they scream of over-population, some Christians scream about that. And when they are silent on drink, weak Christians never mention the subject. When the world sets the agenda, Christians would do well to beware of it. Our measures are something else. Our standards are set for us. We march to a different drummer. When we are most faithful to our Lord and His revelation in the Bible, we are much more likely to speak to the deepest needs of men, and much less likely to be turned off when the current fad is replaced by something else.

Two urgent actions must be launched. First, the irradiation of all denominations and congregations, all Bible Schools and theological training schools with humane moves immediately practical for Christians in those conditions. For some, social action will mean simply sending their daughters to school. For others, it will mean withdrawing their deposits from banks in caste ridden Calcutta or picketting nearby liquor shops which are debauching whole populations. The campaign for social action is suffering today because it appears to be so entirely an anti-Western, pro-Marxist, anti-capitalistic campaign. In reality the social structures and economic, political and social bondages of men are enormously varied and suitable Christian responses are multitudinous *and indigenous*.

Second, whole congregations and fellowships of Christians must agree on a quantified Christian standard of life. What is needed is a 'rule of life' which (1) spells out what 'the simple life' means in each country in terms of dollars and cents, and (2) specifies what portion of income should be ploughed back into good deeds and evangelism, and (3) enlists members who pledge to live on that basis. The individual is almost helpless against the pagan pressures of modern life. But communities of the concerned, all living according to one rule, could function. Monastic orders which withdraw from the world? No. Monastic orders made up of whole families in gear with the world but pledged to a clearly defined simple life? Yes. With what we now know about health and nutrition, it is quite possible for congregations employed in the secular world and its organizations to live on fifty cents a day per person (or equivalent) and stay in abounding health. Other expenditures could be defined in a similar fashion and life would be improved. The balance of income could be devoted to specific enterprises which were effectively changing men and societies in particular populations. Great advances in social action wait on the development in all countries of such congregations and associations — particularly among middle and upper class Christians.

The seventh course of action open to Bible believing Christians is a limited withdrawal from all Christian organizations which advocate semi-biblical or unbiblical courses of action. The word limited is important. As long as the organization persists in a sub-biblical (a largely humanistic or secular) direction, support, prayer, and enrollment will be withheld. When it swings into paths which Christians recognize as pleasing to God, support will be resumed.

The six point plan of action outlined by the German Evangelical Alliance in its March 29th, 1976 issue (see immediately preceding article) describes a realistic relationship to the World Council of Churches. The evidence available today indicates quite clearly that the Council intends to continue its one sided stress on social action to the substantial eclipse of great commission mission at home and abroad. As long as this policy is maintained, Bible believing Christians have no other recourse than withdrawal. This is true for those in conciliar denominations and those in non-conciliar.

The time may come — and sooner than many of us imagine possible — when the conciliar denominations missionary societies and the World Council of Churches will recognize the amazing responsiveness of the contemporary world, its openness to Christian belief, the winnability of many of its multitudinous populations, the ripeness of many pieces of the rich mosaic of mankind, and will institute honest programs of evangelism and church growth on a world scale. When that time comes, Bible believing Christians will rejoice and will support these denominations, missionary societies and councils. Till then, limited withdrawal would seem to be the correct course of action.

Ships which have been caught in a great cyclone — if they survive — tell of passing out of the storm back into fair breezes and sunny skies. God grant that the Storm in Christian Missions, which has wrought such devastation and sent so many good ships to the bottom, may pass. God return the Church to fair breezes and sunny skies of plain biblical mission. There is much work to do. Three billion have yet to hear the Gospel. Multitudinous kingdom structures wait construction. Limitless good deeds remain to be done. Millions of new congregations have yet to be established. God speed the day when the good ship mission under billowing sails again speeds to its destination.

ABOUT THE EDITOR

Donald McGavran was born in India, and served as a missionary in India for thirty-four years under the United Christian Missionary Society. He has taught missions in this country for the last eighteen years and is the dean emeritus of the School of World Mission and Institute of Church Growth of Fuller Theological Seminary in Pasadena, California. Dr. McGavran has a B.D. from Yale Divinity School and a Ph.D. in education from Teachers College, Columbia University. He is well known for his church growth theory and research, and has written many books, including *The Bridges of God* and *Understanding Church Growth*.

BOOKS BY THE WILLIAM CAREY LIBRARY

GENERAL
The Birth of Missions in America by Charles L. Chaney, $7.95 paper, 352 pp.
Education of Missionaries' Children: The Neglected Dimension of World Mission by D. Bruce Lockerbie, $1.95 paper, 76 pp.
The Holdeman People: The Church in Christ, Mennonite, 1859-1969 by Clarence Hiebert, $7.95 cloth, 688 pp.

STRATEGY OF MISSION
Church Growth and Christian Mission by Donald A. McGavran, $4.95x paper, 256 pp.
Church Growth and Group Conversion by Donald A. McGavran et al., $2.45 paper, 128 pp.
Crucial Dimensions in World Evangelization edited by Arthur F. Glasser et al., $6.95x paper, 480 pp.
Everything You Need to Grow a Messianic Synagogue by Phillip E. Goble, $2.45 paper, 176 pp.
Growth and Life in the Local Church by H. Boone Porter, $2.95 paper, 124 pp.
Here's How: Health Education by Extension by Ronald and Edith Seaton, $3.45 paper, 144 pp.
A Manual for Church Growth Surveys by Ebbie C. Smith, $3.95 paper, 144 pp.
Reaching the Unreached by Edward C. Pentecost, $5.95 paper, 245 pp.
Readings in Third World Missions: A Collection of Essential Documents edited by Marlin L. Nelson, $6.95x paper, 304 pp.

AREA AND CASE STUDIES
Aspects of Pacific Ethnohistory by Alan R. Tippett, $3.95 paper, 216 pp.
The Baha'i Faith: Its History and Teachings by William M. Miller, $8.95 paper, 450 pp.
A Century of Growth: The Kachin Baptist Church of Burma by Herman Tegenfeldt, $9.95 cloth, 540 pp.
Christ Confronts India by B.V. Subbamma, $4.95 paper, 238 pp.
Church Growth in Japan by Tetsunao Yamamori, $4.95 paper, 184 pp.
Church Planting in Uganda: A Comparative Study by Gailyn Van Rheenen, $4.95 paper, 192 pp.
Circle of Harmony: A Case Study in Popular Japanese Buddhism by Kenneth J. Dale, $4.95 paper, 238 pp.
Crucial Issues in Bangladesh by Peter McNee, $6.95 paper, 304 pp.
The Emergence of a Mexican Church by James E. Mitchell, $2.95 paper, 184 pp.
The How and Why of Third World Missions: An Asian Case Study by Marlin L. Nelson, $6.95 paper, 256 pp.

La Serpiente y la Paloma (La Iglesia Apostolica de la Fe en Jesucristo de Mexico) by Manual J. Gaxiola, $2.95 paper, 194 pp.
People Movements in the Punjab by Margaret and Frederick Stock, $8.95 paper, 388 pp.
Profile for Victory: New Proposals for Missions in Zambia by $3.95 cloth, 224 pp.
The Protestant Movement in Bolivia by C. Peter Wagner, $3.95 paper, 264 pp.
The Protestant Movement in Italy: Its Progress, Problems, and Prospects by Roger E. Hedlund, $3.95 paper, 266 pp.
Protestants in Modern Spain: The Struggle for Religious Pluralism by Dale G. Vought, $3.45 paper, 168 pp.
The Religious Dimension in Hispanic Los Angeles by Clifton L. Holland, $9.95 paper, 550 pp.
The Role of the Faith Mission: A Brazilian Case Study by Fred Edwards, $3.45 paper, 176 pp.
Solomon Islands Christianity: A Study in Growth and Obstruction by Alan R. Tippett, $5.95x paper, 432 pp.
Taiwan: Mainline Versus Independent Church Growth by Allen J. Swanson, $3.95 paper, 300 pp.
Tonga Christianity by Stanford Shewmaker, $3.45 paper, 164 pp.
Understanding Latin Americans by Eugene A. Nida, $3.95 paper, 176 pp.
A Yankee Reformer in Chile: The Life and Works of David Trumbull by Irven Paul, $3.95 paper, 172 pp.

THEOLOGICAL EDUCATION BY EXTENSION

Principios del Crecimiento de la Iglesia by Wayne C. Weld and Donald A. McGavran, $3.95 paper, 448 pp.
Principles of Church Growth by Wayne C. Weld and Donald A. McGavran, $4.95x paper, 400 pp.
Theological Education by Extension (revised edition) edited by Ralph D. Winter, $9.95 paper, 656 pp.
The World Directory of Theological Education by Extension by Wayne C. Weld, $5.95x paper, 416 pp. *1976 Supplement only*, $1.95x, 64 pp.
Writing for Theological Education by Extension by Lois McKinney, $1.45x, 64 pp.

APPLIED ANTHROPOLOGY

Becoming Bilingual: A Guide to Language Learning by Donald Larson and William A. Smalley, $5.95x paper, 426 pp.
Christopaganism or Indigenous Christianity? edited by Tetsunao Yamamori and Charles R. Taber, $5.95 paper, 242 pp.
The Church and Cultures: Applied Anthropology for the Religious Worker by Louis J. Luzbetak, $5.95x paper, 448 pp.
Culture and Human Values: Christian Intervention in Anthropological Perspective (writings of Jacob Loewen) edited by William A. Smalley, $5.95 paper, 466 pp.
Customs and Cultures: Anthropology for Christian Missions by Eugene A. Nida, $3.95x paper, 322 pp.
Manual of Articulatory Phonetics by William A. Smalley, $4.95x paper, 522 pp.

Message and Mission: The Communication of the Christian Faith by Eugene A. Nida, $3.95x, 254 pp.
Readings in Missionary Anthropology edited by William A. Smalley, $5.95x paper, 384 pp.

POPULARIZING MISSION

Defeat of the Bird God by C. Peter Wagner, $4.95 paper, 256 pp.
God's Word in Man's Language by Eugene A. Nida, $2.95 paper, 192 pp.
The Task Before Us (audiovisual) by the Navigators, $29.95, 137 slides
The 25 Unbelievable Years: 1945-1969 by Ralph D. Winter, $2.95 paper, 128 pp.
World Handbook for the World Christian by Patrick St. J. St. G. Johnstone, $4.95 paper, 224 pp.

REFERENCE

An American Directory of Schools and Colleges Offering Missionary Courses edited by Glenn Schwartz, $5.95x paper, 266 pp.
Bibliography for Cross-Cultural Workers edited by Alan R. Tippett, $4.95 paper, 256 pp.
Evangelical Missions Quarterly Vols. 7-9, $8.95 cloth, 330 pp.
The Means of World Evangelization: Missiological Education at the Fuller School of World Mission edited by Alvin Martin, $9.95 paper, 544 pp.
Protestantism in Latin America: A Bibliographical Guide edited by John H. Sinclair, $8.95x paper, 448 pp.
The World Directory of Mission-Related Educational Institutions edited by Ted Ward and Raymond Buker, Sr., $19.95x cloth, 906 pp.